Cover Art
Carlo Marochetti
*Richard Coeur de Lion*,
1856 Bronze
Old Palace Yard,
Palace of Westminster, London

The

# Tribe of Sylvan

*Threshold of*
*European Man's Ascendance*

by

PHILLIP HATHAWAY

Hardcastle Publishing
New York

WARNING: Both professionals and amateurs are herein warned that the performance of THE TRIBE OF SYLVAN, THRESHOLD OF EUROPEAN MAN'S ASCENDANCE, or any portion of its contents, is subject to payment of a royalty.
THE TRIBE OF SYLVAN, THRESHOLD OF EUROPEAN MAN'S ASCENDANCE, has full protection rights under the copyright laws of the United States of America, all countries protected by the International Copyright Union, including the British Commonwealth and the dominion of Canada, and all countries protected by the Berne Convention, the Universal Copyright Convention, Pan-American Copyright Convention, and all countries with which the United States of America has a reciprocal copyright relation. All rights, including professional and amateur stage rights, motion picture, lecturing, public reading, recital, radio broadcast, television, sound recording, video recording, filming, all other forms of mechanical or electronic reproduction, such as DVD, CD-I, CD, CD-ROM, information storage and retrieval systems and photocopying, and the rights of translation into foreign languages, are fully and strictly reserved. Special emphasis is placed upon readings, the permission for which must be obtained from the Author or his agent in writing.
Any resemblance to persons, living or dead, with the characters in this book, is purely an unintended coincidence.

# Table of Contents

## PART II
### CIVIC VIRTUES

## PART III
### THE SYLVAN LIFESTYLE OF HEALTH

# *Author's Foreword*

" AND he loved her, as he loved the light of Heaven.
And as the light of Heaven varies, now
At sunrise, now at sunset, now by night
With moon and trembling stars, so loved Geraint
To make her beauty vary day by day,
In crimsons and in purples and in gems."

Lord Tennyson's words from *Idylls of the King* express something akin to my love for our tribe incomparable, together unconquerable, and here, the flower of which is christened *Sylvan*. Sylvan means "of, relating to, or inhabiting the woods, consisting of or abounding in woods or trees." That is an appropriate name for our tribe since we dwelt in the European woods for 40,000 years, give or take a day or two, apparently in harmony with this vast, pristine forest. Paleontologists tell us our brains were decidedly larger then, and this cerebral advantage provided enough common sense for our ancestors to revere the great woods, especially the oak. Thus, it is tempting to speculate that a connection to them is why we now tend to cherish the old-growth forests more than others, even with our smaller craniums.

Sylvanism is a pragmatist's philosophy. For, nothing is

more pragmatic than nurturing our health, which is a central premise of Sylvanistic thought. Indeed, our nurtured health is the gateway to our future and sublime society. That is why Plato said, "Utopia must begin in the body of man." So generous consideration is given to the Sylvan lifestyle of physical well-being. And what could be more pragmatical than securing the future for our children's children? For their sake, I have humbly endeavored to "rightly divide the word of truth" regarding Jeffersonian ideals that have been purposefully perverted, particularly those that affect the rights of man and, ultimately, our progeny. In so doing, I have sought to create a philosophy for the family. The father will find a guiding star, the mother will learn of ways to strengthen her children's minds and spirits, and all will meet the express personification of Sylvanism, one of the mightiest heroes of all time. Most truly, he is a hero for our time, as well, for he saved his people from a juggernaut of unearthly wickedness, much as we face today. He did so with a powerful secret, one which we will behold by the Sun's light upon our Sylvan journey.

This writing, I suppose, had some beginnings when I was a young boy. At the age of ten, my fifth-grade teacher introduced me to an exquisite piano rendition of "Claire de Lune." A work so delicately tender, with unhurried, flowing irresistibility, that all the priests and prophets of this realm could not do what Claude Debussy did with that simple melody—prove the divine. I was awestruck by Bach's inventiveness, Beethoven's overwhelming grandeur, and Mozart's lively vitality. Offenbach, Liszt, and Borodin were also favorites.

The Dutch masters of the 1600s piqued my wonderment when seeing one of their original pastel portraits, which, phenomenally, captured more detail than the most sensitive camera lens. What extraordinary dynamism is portrayed by

Rembrandt, the master of light and dark, in *The Night Watch*. I first beheld his work printed on the top of a cigar box at a local drug store while waiting to be picked up from school. The cigar's brand name was Dutch Masters, so I referred to his *Syndics of the Drapers Guild* by that name until I saw the original in Amsterdam. I learned that Italians, the most prolific artists of all, comprised two-thirds of the art in the world's museums. Michaelangelo, perhaps, was foremost of these.

When twelve years old and devoted to developing my skill as a sketch artist, it was only natural that I became fascinated by a black-and-white photograph of the breathtaking intricacies, sculptures, and architecture of Notre-Dame Cathedral. The flying buttresses' architectural design, allowing more space for the gem-like stained glass windows and the sheer immensity of that stunning microcosm of our artistry, fascinated me. Delighted satisfaction swelled in my chest with the thought that such a superlative creation was the masterwork of my people.

Their vision of excellence also pervades medicine, with virtually every advancement in that field. From Hippocrates, the father of all medicine, and Galen, the most accomplished physician of ancient Greece, to sixteenth-century William Harvey, the first to correctly describe the circulatory system, and Sir Alexander Fleming, who discovered penicillin in 1928. These medical modernizations are shared freely with the world, especially with the people of poorer nations. Yet, this should come as little surprise because we give by far more money, goods, and services to charitable causes than any other people. So, it is of little wonder that Dickens deftly touched our hearts with those generous, dear ole souls, Mr. Fezziwig and Mr. Pickwick, characters considered fools by many of those from outside our tribe. Yet, the magnanimity of our tribe members, who inspired the creation of those dear ole fictitious souls, is the bedrock of the most advanced societies in history.

A sizable library could barely contain the long cavalcade of contributions, stretching endlessly over the plains of history, of our true Prometheans, for their inventions are the substratum of most human advancements. Eratosthenes, a Greek mathematician born c. 276 BC, measured the circumference of Earth without leaving his home in Cyrene. Euclid, another mathematician of ancient Greece, was the author of *Elements*, which served as the primary mathematics textbook for twenty-one centuries. The Polish polyglot and polymath Nicolaus Copernicus (1473-1543) established the celestial mechanics of the planets. And Sir Isaac Newton, the English luminary of the Scientific Revolution, developed early physics, the theory of universal gravitation, and calculus. His impact upon modern physics is virtually impossible to overstate. Therefore, some people feel he is the most influential secular person in history. Finally, Nicola Tesla's polyphase alternating currents are the template for electricity that lights our cities and, except lesser-used direct currents, drives all electrical devices. Tesla also invented remote control and, rather than Marconi, radio waves of all kinds. We typically use these two inventions seamlessly throughout our lives. What is more, the X-ray, crucial to every medical facility throughout the world, is also his invention.

This litany of unparalleled accomplishments is not meant in a braggadocio way or as an opportunity to gloat. Those are not Sylvan traits. Instead, it is an expression of *work and love*, which, incidentally, is our motto. It is also a mild and reasonable response to baseless rhetoric used to attack people of European descent, which has been generously bandied about by the media for the past century, especially the systemic racism of *critical race theory*. Of course, we want all people of every hue and color to truly prosper, free to enjoy their cultures without the slightest trace of tyranny or oppression of any kind. We want this for our tribe, as well. For we, as a race, stand before an existential threat that, day by day, looms ever nearer. So, let the fool return to his folly. But let the savant draw near and be the wiser.

Now, let us choose the ablest guide for this journey, one who embodies all the most exemplary traits of Sylvanism. Is there such a one among us? Let us find him in a way recommended by that sage philosopher, Seneca.

"From him, you'll take whatever you wish . . . What happiness, what a fine old age lies in store for the man who's put himself under the patronage of such a person! He'll have a friend whose advice he can seek on the greatest or least important matters, whom he can consult daily about himself, from whom he can hear the truth without insult and receive praise without fawning, and who will provide a model after which to fashion himself.

"There is a common saying that it was not in our power to choose the parents we were allotted, and that they were given to us by chance; yet we can be born to whomever we wish. There are households of the most distinguished intellects: choose the one into which you'd like to be adopted, and you'll inherit not just the name but also the actual property, which is not to be hoarded in a miserly or mean spirit: the more people you share it with, the greater it will become."

In that sense, our guide and godfather is the man who inspired my founding of this tribe, my penning of this book. For, among the parade of millennia, made bright with the kings and commodores of heroism, one is monarch to them all—Alfred the Great, King of the English. For who has stood alone with perfect valor before such hordes of otherworldly terror and yet won? Who has been more generous to his conquered foe who committed unspeakable outrage to his people? And who has dreamt of and implemented a wide array of futuristic advances within Western Civilization?

Although Alfred was indisputably great, we must never give way to hero-worship of him or any other personage, for this would be an abdication of our sacred responsibility to overcome towering challenges, excel to the fullness of our abilities, to achieve greatness itself. So, rather than worshiping Alfred as our hero, let us instead admire and deeply respect his heroic deeds as standards of Sylvanism.

After all, four of his life-giving ideas are integral to our twelve tenets: friendship, a good deed every day, good works cannot fail, and leaving good works behind us. Before reading his incomparably heroic life story, let us hold our venerated subject before the unclouded brilliance of critique, considering what other men have said about him.

"A man beyond the hopes of emulation . . ." Sir John Spelman, seventeenth-century aristocrat.

"I know not whether there has ever been a man on earth worthier of posterity's respect." Voltaire, renowned French author and philosopher.

"The most perfect character in history." Edward A. Freeman, author and historian, best known for his monumental *History of the Norman Conquest.*

"Amidst the deepest darkest depths of barbarism, the virtues of an Antoninus [Marcus Aurelius], the learning and valor of a Caesar, and the legislative spirit of Lycurgus, were manifested in this patriotic king." Edward Gibbon, author of *The History of the Decline and Fall of the Roman Empire.*

"This is the story of the only English king to be known as 'the Great.' He was a seasoned warrior, a scholar, a poet, a law-giver, an architect of towns and ships . . . he launched the greatest literary renaissance that Anglo-Saxon England ever knew." Benjamin Merkle, author of *The White Horse King; the Life of Alfred the Great.*

One of the foremost things I should mention regarding Sylvanism is that it is not a religion but a way of living. Likewise, neither did Prince Siddhartha Gautama, the first Buddha, seek to begin a religion, and it would have most grievously saddened him to know that his Aryan Path, as he called it, has been all but lost, replaced with a religion utterly unrecognizable to him. In *The Outline of History*, masterfully researched and written by H. G. Wells, we see that "Under the overpowering influence of these sickly imaginations the moral teaching of Gautama have been almost hid from view. The theories grew and flourished; each new step, each new hypothesis demanded another until the whole sky was filled with forgeries of the brain, and the nobler and simpler lessons were smothered under the glittering mass of metaphysical subtleties." Such is empty religiosity. Whether Oriental or Occidental, its adherents differ little, the heights of their ecstasies often equaling their inward irresolution. Sylvanist philosophy, by contrast, is attuned to practicality. And submission to nature, which is one of our foremost tenets, is supremely practical, for here we find our appropriate position and posture. Every virtue of man follows.

And now, dear friends,

> If there be one worthy Light of my life,
> One True Light, made thus so by Beauty,
> Great Lady, I bow, I give thee it all,
> Light jets beaming from pen, to page, to thee.

P.H.

*Somewhere in the New World*
*June 6ᵗʰ, 2017*

# PART I

# THE PHILOSOPHY OF SYLVANISM

Chapter One

# The Paragon of Sylvanism

NOW, cast your mind back, long, long, and long ago . . . perhaps two thousand years ago and many more, when some of our forefathers lived in what is now Denmark. They were of those mighty Germanic tribes, the Angles, Saxons, and Jutes—indomitable in battle, lusty with beautiful life, bright of countenance, and tall.

When the ice giants blasted across the North Sea on relentless glacial nights, touching every heart with their icy fingers, our ancestors would huddle by the fireside. Here, tales were sometimes told of wayfaring seamen who journeyed to an emerald island across the wine-dark waters. These tales inspired wonder for our forefathers' families had increased in numbers and needed more land fertile for farming. To them, this land was so strange, so far away.

Yet, it beckoned.

Finally, over one thousand six hundred years ago, around AD 410, the vision of this luscious isle of green began to draw them across the frigid, rolling North Sea. There, some found friendship with Prince Vortigern of Britain, who eventually made a treaty with the Saxon chiefs, Hengist and Horsa, both names in the old Saxon language meaning horse. The Saxons were fond of giving men the names Horse, Wolf, Hound, Bear, and the like since they lived amongst these creatures. On behalf of Prince Vortigern, according to their agreement, Hengist and Horsa drove the Picts and Scots from Britain and thus were given welcome to settle there with their families. So, they came.

When the sea breezes blew gently from west to the north, the clouds were thin as a silk lattice, and the water spangling blue, they knew the conditions were right for setting to the waves in small wicker baskets made water-resistant with animal skins and tar. In these, they paddled cross the dark and heaving English Channel.

For the next hundred years, family after family left their native land, braving the North Sea in their little, sea-worthy crafts, pioneering to their new home called Britain. Over the coming years, the Angles and Saxons settled the whole country south of the Thames, except for Cornwall, part of Hampshire, the Isle of Wight, and Kent, which were settled by Jutes. The Angles, Saxons, and Jutes later joined as one tribe, becoming known as the Anglo-Saxons or simply Saxons. They were quite barbaric, sacrificing both animals and, possibly, humans to their god Woden, and with equal barbarity, they took over the land and rule from the native Britains.

Then something happened suddenly. In AD 597, as a giant strides forth in one mighty step, the Saxons and their society progressed with astonishing speed, for, as we compare this event to the arch of mankind's ascent over millennia, it was, indeed, meteoric. The profundity of this event stopped their merciless sacrifices, much of their brutality toward fellow men, and crossed the threshold of what would become an urbane, well-mannered society: Augustine of Canterbury began converting them. This exchange of one religion for another was, overall, a societal advancement. Yet, at the same time, some people justifiably wonder if the Saxon primal spirit was weakened rather than enriched by it; perhaps, the individual became more subdued to the benefit of the group.

Nevertheless, with Christianity came writing and knowledge, the extent and variety of which were previously undreamt of by these, our forefathers and cousins. This, mixed with their rich Germanic culture, became the foundation of a social florescence of peace and rich prosperity that steadily spiraled upward. This is why Thomas Jefferson said, "Has not every restitution of the ancient Saxon laws had happy effects? Is it not better now that we not return at once into that happy system of our ancestors, the wisest and most perfect ever yet devised by the wit of man, as it stood before the 8th century?" The Saxon laws worked particularly well in the little villages and hamlets of Britain where everyone was kith and kin, too well known to one another to behave as badly as our contemporary leaders, whom precious few of us have ever met. The most common social disruptions were arguments between families, which were settled by common law.

Halcyon days were these of blessed peace,
Love's infinite 'neath emerald canopies,
Joy-filled rhapsody of birds in chorus,
All living hues of field and the forest,

Wild with the charging buck the springing doe,
Greenwood temple where man was loath to go,
Young loves escaped where others ne'er saw,
Those Sun diamond streams of Shangri-la,

Blossoms of a thousand, thousand loves sweet,
Thus, in turn christened innocent heartbeat,
To till with kindness and in hardihood,
With oxen and plow and carving dark wood,

Kettle and distaff roof of flaxen thatch,
Throughout all the world what culture can match,
Men all and one abandoned to freedom,
Unshackled living none can exceed him,

For Blood and Earthiness 'tis axiom,
Of fair-eyed gleam called Anglo-Saxon,
This the secret, this the quintessence,
Of his full unpretending presence.[1]

But in AD 793, the Vikings raided the remote monastery in Lindisfarne, luxurious with gold and treasures, savagely killing all the monks and priests. In a letter written to the King of Northumbria, Alcuim of York said of this raid, "For nearly 350 years we and our fathers have dwelt in this most beautiful land, and never before has such terror appeared in Britain, such as the one that we are suffering from this pagan nation. Nor was it thought that a ship would at-

---

[1] "Fair-Eyed Gleam Called Anglo-Saxon" was written while eating lunch on the banks of a brook surrounded by a little forest, where I would relax in nature for a while at noon when writing this book.

tempt such a thing. Behold the church of Saint Cuthbert, splattered with the blood of the priest of God, plundered of all its treasures, a place more venerable than anywhere in Britain is given over to pagan nations for pillaging . . ."

Successive raids increased in frequency and size over the decades. Thus, the naïve Saxons, made gullible and kindly from centuries of peace, often paid tribute to the invaders in vast fortunes of gold, called *Danegeld*, with the understanding that they would leave peacefully and never return to Britain. This wishful appeasement, however, was useless for the Vikings virtually always made a mockery of their word, a spiritual weakness, causing the vulnerability that would ultimately lead to their collapse, a critical dynamic that we shall visit again with vivid clarity. Alas, finding an unguarded victim in the gentle-minded Saxons, the Vikings came with their Great Heathen Army to take everything.

In the many horrific battles that followed, the two sides would face one another, forming a "shield wall," their shields forming a wall of defense. They would then engage in what was similar to a scrum in a rugby match in that they would both push forward, but using spears, hammers, and swords and with calculated tactics yet little strategy. It was, to be certain, bloody hell. The Vikings had an advantage because they commanded a standing army, whereas the Saxons were primarily farmers from villages across the countryside, whose families depended upon them for protection and to produce food at home. Over the years of waning battle, the Vikings were poised to crush the life out of the Saxon people.

Under this gloom of oppression, in the year AD 849, a sparkling little light came to Earth and was personified.

The little light arrived as all of us do; however, over 1,000 years later, we are beneficiaries of his gifts. He was the fifth son born unto King Ethelwulf and Queen Osburh of Wessex, whom they christened Alfred, meaning *elf wisdom*. He arrived unexpectedly, for the queen was well into her forties when he was born, which was quite a phenomenon, for, during this time, most people only lived into their mid-thirties.

Alfred's teacher, friend, and biographer, a Welch monk named Asser, wrote that he was his parents' favorite and loved learning from an early age. "He was extraordinarily beloved by both his father and mother, and indeed by all the people, beyond all his brothers; in inseparable companionship with them he was reared at the royal court. As he advanced through the years of infancy and youth, he appeared comelier in person than his brothers, as in countenance, speech, and manners he was more pleasing than they. His noble birth and noble nature implanted in him from his cradle a love of wisdom above all things, even amid all the occupations of this present life; but—with shame be it spoken!—by the unworthy neglect of his parents and governors he remained illiterate till he was twelve years old or more, though by day and night he was an attentive listener to the Saxon poems which he often heard recited, and, being apt at learning, kept them in his memory."

We may assume that because her other sons were much older, the eldest being twenty-five years Alfred's senior, his parents delighted in their miracle baby who precociously developed a natural affinity for poetry, the Queen's beloved art. When Alfred was yet a little boy, his mother offered a small book of Saxon poetry to the first of her five sons who could memorize all the poems. The exquisitely bright and beautiful little book was handwritten with richly ornate lettering and illustrated flamboyantly with red, green, and blue on yellow vellum. Alfred immediately prized it. Yet, being unable to read, his mother's challenge seemed rather impossible. However, as we shall see, clever versatility was one of his strong points, so he memorized all the poems with the help of a reader. Alfred won the book against the competition of his much older brothers and treasured poetry all his life.

Being fifth in line for the kingship, it seemed unlikely that he should ever ascend the throne. So, this was far from his mind while a little boy as he traveled with his father along the network of old Roman roads through the Wessex countryside, visiting his father's subjects. On these trips, Alfred watched his father deal with the common folk, ensuring that they were well treated, experiences that became indelible lessons of virtue writ upon his heart.

In the evenings, they were right royally entertained by burly men, unafraid of blood, bruised ribs, or a broken nose during rugged wrestling matches and fights with the quarterstaff. There were competitions of swordsmen, spearmen, and archers who could send the grey goose feathers of an arrow whistling to the center of a target's bull's eye at a hundred paces. There were tricks on horseback, horse races, foot races, and falcons trained to hunt and fight from the heavens for their masters in battle.

Later in the evening, all would feast and quaff mead, wine made sweet and thick with honey, from gold- gilded bull horns as they sat round a roaring fire in the mead hall. These, albeit, were not mindless drinking parties, as Alfred found drunkenness deplorable. For, Alfred was in awe of his father's subjects, these mighty men of valor, so able-bodied and fearless, and would have been sharply disappointed to see them lose their deportment and dignity from too much wine. By contrast, because he possessed a superior intellect, Alfred was fascinated when the poet struck the harp, singing tales of courage, especially those tales of brave men who sacrificed their lives for their fatherland. Those, I feel, are the times he became a true nobleman.

Here, it is appropriate to say a word about nobility: those who are the truly brave, are those who are most tender-hearted. Commoners, particularly those who possess a common spirit, assume that tenderheartedness or kindness is a weakness. Often, they will make this foolish assessment of a lady or gentleman who exhibits well-bred manners. Yet, *tender are the brave*. For, they possess enough strength to be tenderhearted and, at the correct times, stern as tempered steel. By comparative antithesis, the cowardly are cruel, lacking the willingness to live above the tendencies of a bully, giving full vent to the lower human nature that imagines itself extolled by mistreating those lives, human and nonhuman, who are weaker than themselves. So, we are fortunate that *noblesse obliges*—the moral obligation of those of high birth or powerful social position to act with honor, kindliness, and generosity—was background to virtually all of Alfred's thoughts and actions. Had this not been so, he would have never reached the very pinnacle of kingliness that he attained.

These aristocratic ideas were further galvanized when, in AD 853, he was sent as an emissary to Pope Leo IV, which, it appears, was a bit of a publicity stunt designed to endear the hearts of Rome and Europe to the people of Wessex since Prince Alfred was only four years old. Indeed, we know he was a beautiful little boy who could capture the adoration of all who met him with his involuntary, innocent charm. Moreover, it bespeaks of the prince's unique precocity, for he must have also been exceptionally well mannered, articulate, and confident for his father to place him on display in this fashion—the very pride of Wessex and the budding flower of the Saxon race.

Embarking from Wessex on over a thousand-mile journey to Rome, Alfred's party traveled through Canterbury then across the English Channel to Calais, France, where they followed the *via Francigena*, a pilgrim's pathway of connecting roads with a series of eighty hostels, inns, and monasteries stationed every fifteen miles or so. Yet, they dared not tarry, for highwaymen lurked in the darkened way, and, worse, marauding Danes were known to sweep down upon unprotected pilgrims from their longboats in the Frankish rivers. And of late, Saracens had besieged the gates of Rome and, although they had been driven away, still posed the threat of kidnapping pilgrims, who would be mercilessly sold as so many cattle in the slave markets of Arabia. Yet, Alfred was jealously protected by a sizable bodyguard of mighty men of war. Thus, he handily survived these dangers, and, after a few months into their journey, they crossed the Alps of Switzerland. In a few more months, they descended into Italy, eventually beholding the breathtaking splendors of opulent Rome—the Pantheon, the Coliseum, and St. Peter's Basilica, where Charlemagne was crowned a little more than fifty years before. And now it was the little prince who would be crowned.

Pope Leo declared him his spiritual son and "gird him with the honor and outward trappings. . . of the counsel of Rome," giving him a sword, robes of white and purple woven with gold and silver threads, then placing a crown upon his fair locks. Representing Wessex to the pope must have profoundly edified the little prince's self-confidence, allowing his charisma to flourish even at this tender age. And we may be certain that the wonders of the grand architecture, the sophistication of the manners, customs, the expensive clothing, and delicacies of the palate, altogether was a healthy expiation of the little boy's mind. For this Roman kaleidoscope of the senses fell on good, fertile soil within his royal heart, these worldly experiences not whetting an appetite in him for worldliness. Indeed, the future king was impervious to the love of riches and, during his reign, used them purely as a utility to command his kingdom.

And so, the finest prince who ever set foot in Rome made his debut in the Eternal City.

How the stratosphere of Roman society must have been set abuzz, enamored by his effortless charm. Even then, albeit, he must have sensed the invisible intentions of thunderous applause, the false praise of men, the flourish and fanfare of trumpets, all of which he never favored above the divine mandate to serve his subjects.

Upon Alfred's return to Wessex in AD 854, his older brother, Ethelstan, died. This was a shocking and sad loss, but not a particularly stinging one since Ethelstan was more than twenty years his senior and had been away almost all of Alfred's life ruling in Essex, Kent, Surrey, and Sussex on behalf of their father, the king. Yet, about this time, his little heart was bitterly broken for his beloved mother, who loved him as the darling of her heart, left him, never to return this side of heaven. 'Twas an unwilling departure irresistibly beckoned by death, for only this could have separated these two souls so spiritually intertwined. I imagine young Alfred may have held the books of poetry that she had given him close to his chest in proxy of her precious touch.

Smitten by death's icy fist, Alfred's father, King Ethelwulf, began to consider the finitude of his Earthly life. "During an Easter feast at the royal estate in Wilton, in AD 854," says Benjamin Merkle, "Ethelwulf announced a significant gift—an unprecedented royal tithe. In front of his four surviving sons, a handful of bishops and other churchmen, and a collection of his noblemen, the King of Wessex declared that he would give one-tenth of all his properties to the church 'for the praise of God and his own eternal salvation.'"

Following this declaration, the king further announced that he and Alfred would make a pilgrimage to Rome; at age six, this would be Alfred's second trip to the City on Seven Hills. Upon their glorious reception, a spectacle later commemorated by Raphael in fresco, they bestowed priceless gifts upon the new pope, Benedict III. Among these were a crown of gold weighing four pounds, a Saxon sword with zig-zag inlays of gold, ornate gold candelabras to light the pope's sanctuaries, and several other gifts of inestimable value, all of which must have inspired breathtaking wonder in the papal court. So great was Ethelwulf's munificence that it overflowed into the streets as the common folk scrambled for the gold and silver coins stamped with his likeness that he threw to them. If the commoners had snickered at Ethelwulf's retinue of "cross-gartered" Saxons late from the Wessex boondocks, wide-eyed at civilization, their laughter was now that of joyous praise! This set a precedent for kingly behavior that Alfred assumed throughout his life, becoming like the generous monarchs of old known as "ring-givers" by their adoring subjects.

At home once again, he reveled in the company of his father's war chiefs at the mead hall, and we may be certain he was enthralled by the ever-popular tale of his day in epic verse that may have been often recited there— *Beowulf.* The namesake and hero of the tale had the strength of thirty men.

> ". . . he thirty men's grapple,
> Has in his hand, the hero-in-battle."

The young boy and future king was transfixed with keen imaginings as the poet sang of the Saxon sense of fairness within Beowulf's heart and his confidence unshaken, even brazen, when faced with seemingly outrageous impossibilities. For, since the huge and hideous monster Grendel fought with no weapon, Beowulf chose to fight him bear-handed, as well. And I am certain Alfred was keenly attentive while listening to the poet waxing on about Beowulf's chivalry and greatness of heart that drew Unferth, his cowardly, chastising competitor, into his sphere of friendship, treating him with every courtesy.

Neither was the finer gist of the tale lost upon the prince. 'Twas akin to a message Lord Tennyson presented many centuries later in his poem "Sir Galahad" in which the protagonist declares,

> "My strength is as the strength of ten,
> Because my heart is pure."

Thus, within his mind and, more importantly, within his transparent heart, Alfred assumed the spiritual persona of Beowulf, who never turned away from a confrontation that threatened his people, no matter how overwhelming the enemy. Perhaps, it was from this tale that he embraced the idea of the hero who fights long, fights hard, fights until he wins, and never, never surrenders. Here, he heard of Beowulf, who greatheartedly forgave a taunting rival, and, perhaps, this is why Alfred would later forgive and befriend his former foe, the mighty Viking chieftain, Guthrum.

Moreover, all the enemies that Alfred might face would pale in comparison to Grendel, who, like Polyphemus, tore his victims to pieces and ate them alive. Maybe Alfred felt that any lesser foe would be a relief.

Facing the Vikings *en masse* may not have been much

of a reprieve, however. For the last eighty-five years, they had been invading in one swift, brutal attack after the other. At first, their invasion consisted of marauding the small villages during the summer then retreating home for the wintertime. Yet soon they secured a permanent beachhead that grew into a colony and, over the years, became a military occupation of central Britain. This they called the Danelaw.

Thus, the British heptarchy of seven kingdoms ruled by seven kings faced the Great Heathen Army that had morphed into the Danelaw nation on their northern border. And, battle after bloody battle, six of the seven kings of Britain were overthrown by the Vikings, most of whom died heroically in combat, others in the most horrific torture for the entertainment of those berserk invaders, other kings fleeing in bitter humiliation. So, by the gray wintertime of AD 878, none dared stand against the army of wild men who sought to please Odin with a multitude of human sacrifices. None except young Prince Alfred and his brother Ethelred, King of Wessex.

Then came the Battle of Ashdown. Ethelred spent time in prayer before the clash and, so, arrived late with his men. For Alfred had held the line against the Danes, who were shocked by that surge of fresh men led by Ethelred and soon broke and retreated. Although an accident, that surprise attack strategy gave Alfred and Ethelred a stunning victory.

However, Ethelred died later from wounds received on the battlefield at Ashdown, and Alfred was "crowned or consecrated as king at either Winchester or Kingston Upon Thames, where the ancient coronation stone of the West Saxon kings, which gave the town its name, still stands."

Thus, Alfred began his rule with a great victory. Yet his was, nevertheless, a monarch of a kingdom occupied by overwhelming enemy forces. Gathering his few men about him, he prepared to make an announcement. They probably thought he planned to flee to Rome, where he would be safe and richly honored. There, the erudite king could luxuriate in the presence of the world's most learned men, comprehensive libraries, and exquisite poetry of unparalleled beauty. He knew well the limitless opportunities to be savored while living upon the City of Seven Hills.

So, they must have been somewhat dumbfounded when he stated that he would remain in hiding, assemble an army of farmers about him, seek the enemy's weakest points, attack them without ceasing, and retake his kingdom. If ever Beowulf was personified in a man, 'twas Alfred, for he understood the mindset that eminent French philosopher Jean-Paul Sartre would crystalize many years later with these words, "Freedom is what you do with what's been done to you."

By his twenty-ninth year, he was a combat-tested veteran who rushed wide battling into enemy lines "like a wild boar," shocked to great power by the love of his people, his land, and his faith.

That is a critical point, which we must understand with perfect clarity, so please kindly allow me to restate it: he was elevated to great power by the love of his people, his land, and his faith. His power did not come from hatred. It came from love. But woe unto him who met Alfred in battle, for that opponent was crushed with utter brutality.

Although driven from his throne and hunted everywhere both night and day by the Norse invaders with demonic intensity, he vowed to never give up. His four elder brothers had died, leaving him as the sole heir to the throne, and, perhaps, his zest for life was his way of compensating for these wretched losses.

Thus, Alfred would have victory, albeit ever so small. So, with a face like flint against defeat, he led his war-weary band of loyal men to the Isle of Athelney, a hidden lagoon surrounded by swamps, and there prepared to meet his enemy again and again with hammer, axe, and sword.

And so, it was that, although vastly outnumbered, Alfred struck fear in the hearts of the Vikings. One after another, Alfred led lightning quick assaults against the invaders, often catching them by surprise, leaving no prisoners. Thus, he proclaimed his unconquered spirit to them, and, equally important, he sent a message to his Saxon people to take heart and never surrender. Many legends surround Alfred during these, his times as a homeless king, living by stealth and cunning. While they are almost assuredly fanciful folktale and fable, they do, however, portray his true character. One tale is of his compassion for the poor and downtrodden, although he, himself, was none the better.

One day, while his men were away fishing for dinner, Alfred and his wife stayed behind with a servant on the little Isle of Athelney. It was then that a beggar seeking bread came to them. Alfred sent the servant to find what food he could, and when the servant returned with only a little wine and a crusty loaf of bread, Alfred gave the beggar half of all they had. Later that day, the fishing party returned with a bounty's catch, and, behold, the wine and loaf of bread shared with the beggar were increased to their original portions. For, the beggar was none other than St. Cuthbert, whom Alfred had entertained unaware and who, because of Alfred's kindness, would become the king's sword and shield in battle.

In another folktale, William of Malmesbury tells of Alfred wearing the garb of a juggler and wandering into the Danish camp, where he was obliged to perform for the crude hordes. His theatrical charm and jaunty hilarity were magnetic, compelling them to demand that he remain with them for several days. Roaming freely throughout the camp, he spied their readiness, their numbers and planned his next thunderbolt raid, all the while being unwittingly paid quite handsomely by the enemy for his espionage.

Yet, the most famous tale is of Alfred being separated from his men, alone and woebegone, coming upon a cottage where a peasant swineherd lived with his wife. He did not reveal to these, his lowly subjects, his regal identity but allowed them to assume he was merely a wandering commoner. One day, while the swineherd was away in the pasture, his wife set cakes to baking and, sternly charging Alfred to watch the cakes lest they burn, busied herself with other chores.

However, Alfred was fraught with ambiguity about his own conundrums and, although he was seated directly in front of the oven, failed to notice the smoke bellowing as the cakes began to char. The wife gave Alfred a thorough berating as though he were the village idiot, shouting, "You're perfectly willing to eat the cakes but unwilling to turn them when they're burning!" Alfred could have taken some royal prerogatives at this point, but was humble, like a good English schoolboy 'neath the scolding.

As we have observed, although these stories are fictional, they yet portray a true image of Alfred and something more—a measure of love from the faithful followers who spun them.

Now, the historical facts. The villages of Britain were being stormed by Vikings who butchered the young and old alike, raping, and murdering women without the slightest trace of mercy. Each time another village fell, Alfred must have felt like a drowning man who gasped air for a split-second only to be crushed by yet another crashing wave that dragged him to the depths, holding him there in a death-like grip.

Nonetheless, he was able to maintain communications with the farming yeomanry, who were eager to fight these maniacal invaders. And he knew the redemption of his people lay in his ability to instill within these warriors a singular idea:

A sense of purest nobility. For, he knew the *noblesse oblige* would honor his commitment even though doing so might mean facing a terrible death.

Alfred kept this high, noble flame burning in the people's hearts and thus was able to muster an army of farmers throughout the countryside. Alfred had won several small skirmishes yet was victorious in only one full battle—the Battle of Ashdown. Suddenly, he faced the biggest battle of all. In May of AD 878, the mighty Viking chieftain, Guthrum, led the Great Heathen Army across the land like a black flood. Alfred rushed to marshal his forces, who followed him in quick march to meet Guthrum at the Battle of Edington.

As Alfred and his men drew near, they heard the ferocious Norsemen beating spears against their shields with deafening tumult from a mile away, and, as they came nearer still, the lowbrows shouted ribald insults about the last Saxon women they had ravaged.

The Saxons quietly formed their shield wall and marched toward their ghastly foe, painted as grotesque demons for this final battle. The "berserkers," naked except for their freakish paint and weapons, were shock troops who had hysterically whipped themselves up into a frenzy with drugs, chanting and dancing in circles with the hopes of gaining supernatural powers from Odin.

Now, with the specter of bright megadeath in their distorted faces and with ear-splitting banshee cries, the berserkers suddenly flew at Alfred's shield wall as human missiles. Yet, they were easily dispatched by the wall of noble Saxon yeomen.

Then began the battle of shield wall against shield wall, waging onward from morning till mid-afternoon. Sweat and blood flowed freely hour after hellishly long hour as the momentum swayed from one side, then to the other. Any Saxon who became discouraged or cowardly, who forgot his high and noble calling, would cause weakness in the wall, and, as a mighty dam gives way to one tiny leak, the shield wall would collapse letting in a raging tide of the enemy and an ensuing massacre.

The men on both sides grew weak. Sweaty hands that gripped the spear bled and blistered and began to falter. Yet, against soul-crushing pain, bloody wounds, and death, the heart of nobility remained true within the breasts of the Saxon men. At last, a small breach was forged into the Danish line. The Saxons poured through like a flood as the enemy shield wall crashed and fell. Alfred weighed into the fray, wide battling with axe and hammer, as the Vikings panicked before this inexorable juggernaut of death.

Alfred took no prisoners on the battlefield, and mighty Guthrum, and a few of his men surrendered. Yet, rather than torturing him for sadistic entertainment as Guthrum would have done to Alfred, the young king of Wessex honored him with a feast in the mead hall, arrayed him in dazzling white, gave him costly gifts, baptized him, even adopted him, and in a Christian church christened him with the name Ethelstan. Alfred's stunning magnanimity had a lasting effect, for Ethelstan served him faithfully for the rest of his life.

This was a glorious triumph. Be that as it may, the Viking hordes still controlled approximately half of Britain, and many battles were waged until the Vikings were defeated. Appropriately, it was Alfred's grandson who finally defeated them at the Battle of Brunanburh in AD 937.

Now, it would have been easy for Alfred to rest on his laurels after his victory at Edington, for this victory assured that Wessex was safe and secure. Yet, he immediately began working on logistic strategies that allowed the Saxons to make a quick offensive response and assume battlefield supremacy over the Vikings. Then he organized what some scholars believe to be England's first navy. Upon completing these plans, which were uniquely innovative at his time, rather than focusing upon war, his industriousness became galvanized upon what might be called nation building, which would become the foundation of our modern society and inspiration to Thomas Jefferson.

Alfred learned to read, write, and translate Latin, and having done so, realized the fantastic treasure trove of knowledge in the many books that lay in their churches collecting dust. So, he did something that catapulted his people hundreds of years ahead of similar societies: he established schools for every freeborn child in Britain in which they learned to read and write the Saxon language, a privilege formerly reserved exclusively to only a few highborn aristocrats.

Asser said that King Alfred, "showed himself a minute investigator of the truth in all his judgments, and this especially for the sake of the poor, to whose interest, day and night, among other duties of this life, he was ever wonderfully attentive. For in the whole kingdom the poor, besides him, had few or no helpers; for almost all the powerful and noble of that country had turned their thoughts rather to secular than to divine things: each was more bent on worldly business, to his own profit, than on the common weal.

"He would avail himself of every opportunity to procure assistants in his good designs, to aid him in his strivings after wisdom, that he might attain to what he aimed at; and, like a prudent bee, which, rising in summer at early morning from her beloved cells, steers her course with rapid flight along the uncertain paths of the air, and descends on the manifold and varied flowers of grasses, herbs, and shrubs, essaying that which most pleases her, and bearing it home, he directed the eyes of his mind afar, and sought that without which he had not within, that is, in his own kingdom."

Philosophy, mathematics, architecture, literature, and especially poetry, were now taught to commoners. He restructured the road network across the country, improving communications, safety, commerce, and defense against invasion.

He established a systemic legal code, providing consistency of law from village to town to city that afforded justice for all. These, and many more modernizations, unified and strengthened the individual, and, moreover, they emphasized the transcendental importance of the individual member of society, introducing individuated freedoms previously inconceivable to the medieval common man. And so, for the last eleven hundred years and more, the Renaissance of Alfred stands unequaled in England.

Now, let us never forget one of the simple secrets of Alfred's greatness: his word and obligation to his people were inviolable.

In turn, his people were great because he instilled this oath keeping idea within them so that the vilest crime in his kingdom was to break one's word. "Alfred insisted that every Anglo-Saxon man keep his oaths and pledges," says Benjamin Merkle. "Instead of a prohibition of murder, treason or some other heinous crime, the king saw oath breaking as the greatest threat to the endurance of his kingdom. Although this prioritization of the keeping of oaths may seem strange to the modern mind, to the Anglo-Saxon it was clear that keeping one's word stood at the foundation of civilized society."

Paramount was that the *noblesse obliges*—those of high birth and powerful social position—always behave with honor, kindliness, and generosity, their word stronger than oak. These were the true aristocrats and exemplars of individual and social integrity who mirrored Alfred's many chivalrous deeds. The resulting incorruptibility ensured a peaceful society in which lock and key were obsolete, relics of a lesser age. And, most importantly, Alfred knew that a nation of men such as these would be a shining shield wall, spiritually blinding and unyielding to every enemy. For, above all the persuasions and entreaties, beyond all the stratagems and tactics of war, this state of wholeness among men broke asunder the ironclad will of the Great Pagan Horde. Thus, was one of King Alfred's secrets.

Yet his overarching secret that secured his every success and victory was the love of his people. That love drove him to conquer the Vikings, a feat so fantastic that it was thought by almost all others to be an utter impossibility and unworthy of intelligent consideration. Indeed, his love for his people overcame this and vaulted him to the high court, granted to no other English king. Let us follow his example, then, and with great love, cherish our people; for this will ensure their freedom and our posterity's freedom for generations to come. This is how we shall win.

Now, having given thought to but a few of King Alfred's accomplishments, for here we have only  considered
his  grander deeds in those brief and passing reflections, it is
little wonder that Charles Dickens said this of the monarch of England's monarchs.

". . . under the Great Alfred, all the best points of the
English-Saxon character were first encouraged, and in him
first  shown. It has been the greatest character among the
nations of the Earth.

"I pause to think with admiration, of the noble king
who, in his single person, possessed all the Saxon virtues.
Whom misfortune could not subdue, whom prosperity
could not spoil, whose perseverance nothing could shake.
Who was hopeful in defeat, and generous in success? Who
loved justice, freedom, truth, and knowledge? Who, in his
care to instruct his people, probably did more to preserve the
beautiful  old Saxon language, than I can imagine? Without
whom, the English tongue in which I tell this story might
have wanted  half its meaning.

"As it is said that his spirit still inspires some of our
best English laws, so, let you and I pray that it may animate
our English hearts, at least to this —to resolve, when we see
any of our fellow-creatures left in ignorance, that we will do
our best, while life is in us, to have them taught; and to tell
those rulers whose duty it is to teach them, and who neglect
their duty, that they have profited very little by all the years
that have rolled away since the year nine hundred and one,
and that they are far behind the bright example of King
Alfred the Great."

Chapter Two

# Sylvanist Thought

A LIENATION from nature is mankind's most conspicuous problem, the solution of which is its most urgent need. To be certain, every problem we face, ecologically, societally, and individually, is a derivative of this unnatural estrangement.

Cosmopolitan machinations have, as many of us know, destroyed much of Earth's flora and fauna. Yet, these intrigues have also led to our self-alienation, which is just as surely destroying us individually and socially. All the while, some of us neurotically command ourselves to save the ecosystem from our crimes against nature without the willingness for our own natural reconciliation and redemption.

For the unredeemed individual cannot redeem society. And, the unredeemed society shall ever suicidally crush the flora, the fauna—and itself.

Thus, as a species, we have become quite lost.

This is a way home.

Sylvans are united together in goodwill beneath an un-furled banner emblazoned with our maxim, *work and love*. We are one, international tribe comprised principally of the ancient Brits, the Celts, the Danes, the indigenous French, the Germanic people, the Saxons, the Scandinavians, and the Slavs. These are the descendants of the ancient Indo-European race known as Aryans, which is largely accepted as the ancient word meaning *noble*. Interestingly, the name Ireland is a derivative of the word Aryan. Notwithstanding our internationalism, Sylvanists are also romantic national-ists, dearly loving our respective fatherlands.

Yet, we preeminently cherish our one and great tribe, its people resplendent with beauty and gentility, its rich, pleas-ing culture, its art, and science. This, our genetic lineage, extends back in time over forty millenniums 'gainst a background of striving unto sweating blood, mass starva-tion, bitter weeping, the black death, and pitched battles wherein dire victories were narrowly won with uncommon valor, requiring the gift most noble. "Greater love hath no man than this, that a man lay down his life for his friends."

Innumerable sacrifices, indeed, were made by our tribal members for the higher good. Perhaps the zenith of this fan-tastic human ascent culminated in the city-state of Athens about three thousand years ago. It appears this Athenian Miracle may have been performed by the ancestors of our contemporary Slavic cousins; in *Everyday Life in Ancient Greece*, C. E. Robinson said, "Sometime in the thirteenth century before Christ, a tribe of Greek-speaking folk who called themselves Achaeans came down from Eastern Eu-rope into the peninsula we now call Greece." Martin P. Nilsson states in *The Minoan-Mycenaean Religion* that "the aristocracy consisted of fair-haired invaders from the North."

Our forefathers founded high civilizations such as

this, resting upon six pillars: government, trade, architecture, art, religion, and writing, as all evolved cultures are today. The understructure of their civilizational eminence, however, seems to have been the written word. Unrivaled in beauty and wisdom, the ancient Greeks' literature was built upon a great language, at once so versatile and melodic that it could emulate every delicate tone and tint of the heart, all the colors of the most vivid imaginings. As an artist with a limitless palate, they composed masterstrokes of poetry, drama, philosophy, rhetoric, history, mathematics, and science. Awestruck are those who are blest to read the original texts, undiluted by translation. Their literary triumphs were matched by the architecture of their temples— religious experiences merely to behold, the sublime realism of their statues poised with perfected grace, their exquisitely painted pottery, mosaics, and murals.

Yet, this miraculous culmination of art and science happened not easily. The Athenians had a far-flung foundation, ancient and wild. As Pushkin said, "Upon the brink of the wild stream, he stood and dreamt a mighty dream"— ten thousand times ten thousand—until its final materialization. For, as when a pebble is cast into a pond, the first ripples being turbulent, becoming less so and less frequent until the pond is tranquil once again, so did turmoil erupt many times over during thousands of years before Athens became great. Over these millennia, the waves of chaos became less and less troubling, reoccurring less until the refinement of the little city-state ever so slowly blossomed. Forty thousand years was this, built by the tribe of which we are members, all a catalyst for us, their posterity. And as a vast, deep, and spreading forest lies within the tiny oak seed, so the Athenian Miracle lies within one ruby drop of our blood.

This gift most precious, bequeathed in loving kindness from our fathers to mothers to children to our tribe—our great and mighty tribe.

The Marvel of Athens was hastened when those blood ancestors of ours invented vowels; a fact that may seem trite unless we consider that words are labels for an infinity of thoughts, the thoughts immeasurably exceeding the labels. Therefore, with this hitherto unknown ability to label thoughts of greater intricacy, they communicated with advanced nuances and subtleties, thus capturing significantly more thoughts with their language, unmatched in its sophistication. This, too, required untold years of upward refinement that eventually became the bedrock of their unrivaled society.

Let there be no mistake, dear cousins, this unrivaled miracle that occurred in Athens so long ago is our fate to rival and exceed. May this vision be our Joyous Gard.[2]

Now, let us focus our attention further upon the contemporary benefactors of these romantic, sweeping events of history—our Sylvanistic tribe. Its members live a lifestyle of robust mental and physical strength in which women are women (XX) and, indeed, men are men (XY), which are chromosomally immutable.[3]

---

[2] Joyous Gard is an allusion to the castle of Sir Lancelot after his conquest of the forces of evil who unlawfully occupied it.

[3] The sex chromosomes form one of the twenty-three pairs of chromosomes in each human cell. Females possess two X-chromosomes, whereas males comprise one X-chromosome and one Y-chromosome. The X-chromosome spans about 155 million DNA building blocks, representing approximately five percent of the total DNA in human cells. Of course, that extraordinarily elaborate

Some may fall short of the following standard traits, which we seek to emulate. Nonetheless, they are the classic qualities we strive toward:

Our men often tend to be alpha males who attract the best women, their paramours naturally following them, not because it is demanded, but simply because women follow strength, which many of our men exude involuntarily. Our women, and others follow us for we are following something preeminent to ourselves—something exceeding narrowminded egocentricities. We needn't, therefore, regard ourselves as being overly important. To be sure, our inner toughness allows an easy, courteous, well-mannered behavior, for gentlemanliness is an unmistakable hallmark of manliness. We can endure pain, priding ourselves in how much we can take. And so, we shrug off minor "slings and arrows." At the same time, our high self-esteem demands respect and disallows abuse, for nature requires that we never become anyone's doormat.

Pericles (c. 495-425 BC), whom many consider the greatest leader of Athens, said, "We are lovers of beauty without extravagance, lovers of wisdom without loss of manliness. Our citizens attend both to public and private duties, allowing no absorption in their own affairs to interfere with their knowledge of the city's. The man who holds aloof from public life, we regard as useless. We are noted for being at once the most adventurous in action and the most reflective in preparation thereof. We yield to none, man to man, for independence of spirit, many sidedness of attainment, and complete self-reliance of limbs and brain."

Our background thoughts, being congruent to a superi-

---

composition is unalterable by changing one's physical appearance.

or intellectual language, afford a soft-spoken demeanor, one that is rarely loud. Our men are incomparably gentler and more respectful of our women than any other tribe throughout all the world. Of this, there can be no doubt, whatsoever. We treat women with deference, yet not with prudishness but manly virility. At the same time, we know the betrayal of a woman's physical and emotional boundaries is a brutish cruelty that more easily wounds the fairer sex. So, we revere the sanctity of this living temple.

> "Beauty crowns them with wholesome pride.
> Virtue makes them most admired.
> Modesty makes them seem divine."[4]

These, our women, are physically and intellectually vigorous. With a smile brightened by vivacious life, without spending hours every day gazing at themselves in a mirror while hiding their face with too much makeup, they attract an alpha male, whom they eagerly follow by desire. By contrast, they are repelled by a beta male, although he may be extraordinarily wealthy; indeed, many of the world's wealthiest "males" are nothing more than unscrupulous, finagling betas since they can never compete honestly with an alpha. While our women are not attracted to a man who cannot pay his bills, which is appropriate, wealth is not her measurement of a man. For she knows that happiness can never be bought. Neither can all the world's money provide one night of blissful sleep, nor can it restore the health of a baby after the doctor says, "I've done all I can," and walks away.

As golden apples complement a silver bowl, our wom-

---

[4] From an unknown author.

en's intuitive wisdom is the matching counterpart to that of
their men, and, thus, it is dearly treasured by their manly
partner. For, this virtue and many others, their men praise
them, placing high value upon their advice. Not ensnared by
the curse of looking backward, wherein others reject their
own descendants, they welcome that shimmering light, esoteric before science, infinitely captivating upon its arrival,
the joyous mirror of the mystical union we call a family.
This, another source—a deeper source, of their wholesome
pride. All the family comes to them for their healing aura of
femininity, a life-giving elixir aglow upon their unmasked
countenances. Together, with the man's council of hardihood, 'tis a light unseen, yet seen, shining from two
unclouded souls. These fleeting little vignettes of glimmer-
ing life, these unforgettable cameos of living kindnesses, are
so often the sustenance that, together, helps us face down
many trials and heartaches. As brave Odysseus said,

"And as for yourself, may the gods grant all the desires,
Of your heart, a husband, a home and a wonderful oneness,
Between you, for nothing is better or greater than a home,
Where man and wife are living harmoniously together,
The envy of evil minds, but a very great joy,
To men of goodwill, and greatest of all to themselves."[5]

Therefore, our men and women, through smart, hard
work, together accomplish more than any other tribe,
somehow rising above the terrestrial fray, and will ever do so
as long as we protect our souls. For, Sylvanity is a lifestyle
wherein virtue is highly esteemed and recognized as the fount

[5] Translation of *The Odyssey* from the original Greek by Ennis Rees.

of all our happiness. That is why sagacious Aristotle so aptly said in his work *Politics*, ". . . happiness is the realization and perfect exercise of virtue, and this not conditional, but absolute."

We strive, therefore, to be good stewards of the Earth and all life upon it, partaking of life-giving food. Therefore, Sylvans love to be in nature, dining *al fresco* as often as the weather permits, giving fancy to our sense of humor with games, sports, singing, and lighthearted, good-natured tricks here and there. Indeed, we make an art of creating healthy picnics with family, friends, and neighbors while possessing an equal affinity for vigorous exercise and breathing an abundance of fresh, clean air.

As mentioned earlier, we do not presume to be overly important and consequently do not take ourselves too seriously. And so, here, it may be good to mention a story by philosopher William James, who tells us of a man who began experimenting with laughing gas. During such ventures, he would understand, with perfected clarity, the mysteries of the Universe. Upon his recovery, however, the revelation would vanish. Thus, although it would require considerable effort, he decided to write the answer while engaged in one of his explorations to be analyzed later with sobriety. This he did. Grasping the paper with trembling excitation, in anticipation that he would behold the Sphinx of life's equation he found he had written, "A smell of petroleum prevails throughout."

Three good lessons come from this story: First, we believe in developing a good sense of humor with which we can laugh at ourselves when wrong. Secondly, like this man, Sylvanists are not always right about everything. The third lesson being that we do not feel the need to be right about everything, a relief valve of sorts that also frees us from the hypocrisy under which religionists are heavily burdened. For, as mentioned in the foreword, Sylvanism is not a religion.

At the same time, we, the finite, can possess an inexplicable knowing but never an academic understanding of the Infinite; anemic attempts to do so by religious philosophers and scholars are "much ado about nothing," being little more than mental cartwheels, a search for the Grail. Instead, let's assume a Socratic path to understand what little we may about the Everlasting: What causes the human heart to beat rhythmically while, yet, in the womb and continue to do so with almost perfect tempo for possibly a century? It is electrical impulses, of course. What causes these electrical pulsations in us and, simultaneously, in trillions of other living beings? No one knows.

And, what causes Earth to travel around the Sun, its gravitational pull counterbalancing Earth's centrifugal force so that it travels in predictable orbit? This is virtually identical, say physicists, to a central nucleus having several electrons revolving around it in mutual electric attractions, all within a given atomic boundary. This seems more analogous since both electric and gravitational forces vary in inverse proportion to the squared distance from each other, resulting in the *same* type of elliptic orbit as Sun and Earth. In other words, nucleoli and electrons are subatomic replicates of our solar system, or *vice versa*. Aren't these examples of the handiwork of God?

In an echo of Pythagoras' geometrical theology, Immanuel Kant might say this wonderworking of the Universe is merely evidence of an architect rather than a creator, or perhaps, just as easily the creation of the whole by the parts themselves. For, within the factual parameters of dispassionate logic, design does not necessarily imply Designer, since we might project our notion of design into the Universe attempting to attribute our mundane version of commonsense to it and to further project an image of its Poet who, low and behold, looks much like us. And so, countless philosophies do little more than repetitiously redress the argument of, design therefore Designer and whether the design be explained cosmically, mathematically, ethically, or religiously, none can prove the existence of God.

Yet, there remains a supersensual knowing, one that transcends terrestrial logic. For the Subject upon which all else is predicated is infinitesimal, whereas we are finite and limited by mortal thoughts. Therefore, the sub-atomic replication of Earth's orbit 'round the Sun and incalculable phenomena like this are not logical evidence of God's hand, but spiritual messages transcending sensual knowledge, penetrating our poor, darkened hearts with light unseen. Thus it is, perhaps, an appropriate spiritual boundary to view nature as our only divine window and thereby, without further theological explanation, *to know*.

For, rather than believing that God exists, which implies a certain lack of knowing, we know quite calmly, and this without effort of chanting or ceremony. Being close to nature is enough for us. Yet, we are neither deists who worship nature nor are we a cult. We are not pagans. We have no vestures, relics, or any other religious paraphernalia. We have neither initiation nor secrets. We have no sacraments nor rituals.

All about Sylvanism is done in the broad light of the noonday Sun without shadow of turning away. And, Sylvanity has no sainted individuals or anyone like them. We, of course, greatly admire some individuals with the clear knowledge that they have faults and weaknesses very much like our own. Therefore, we recognize King Alfred's greatness principally because of his work, which was prolific, extraordinary, and unexampled throughout history; indeed, he is the Sylvan measurement of all that a man could hope to be; yet, at the same time, we recognize his common humanity. And, as he was preordained to ransom his people, thus we have been ordained to be here at this very point—at this precise time.

For, dear friends, we are not merely a curious little baga-telle of stardust twixt two ice ages spiraling meaninglessly through the eternal vastness of the ether.

We are here for a reason and purpose demanded of red-blooded men and women: to work and to love as we care for our families, our people, and the flora and fauna.

Yes, Sylvanity is something one does. Consequently, we do not rely upon sacraments or rituals, holy men, or priests, which are religious substitutes for our own legiti-mate work and love. Neither have we anything, whatsoever, to do with magic nor the occult, for these, too, are always substitutes for honest, wholesome, hard work and love; iron-ically, religiosity and magic are shockingly similar.

It is unfortunate, indeed, that some organizations are ostensibly lovers of nature and overtly promote healthy life-styles, but their covert core values are occultism. Moreover, it is also not uncommon to encounter Trotskyism or Marx-ism at the center of organizations that present an environmental and peaceable veneer, the shadow objective of which is the demoralization of a society's individual members spreading to national insurrection. This is not the case with Sylvanism. A Sylvanist may not, even in the slightest way, practice or be involved in such things.

We are only plain, hardworking, everyday folk with many flaws. We do not float about on a mystic cloud in which we are so heavenly minded that we are of no Earthly good. Nor are we condescending or better than others.

We agree with one mind, one heart, one view,
We wish blessed peace, rich prosperity,
Full freedom for every race, creed, and hue,
These rejoicing in their posterity.
Culture, custom from high hill to steeple,
Liberated from tyranny's ill hand,
We too vouchsafe freedom for our people,
Resplendent with beauty this Tribe of Sylvan.

At the same time, we do not feel obligated to love those who, overtly or covertly, seek our harm. Neither do we feel obligated to indefinitely feed, clothe, house, provide unlimited medical attention for them, or endlessly educate them. These rights are not universally deserved. They must be earned. We work to earn them. We do not demand that other people give them to us. So, it is absurd that others demand that we give them what we have worked to earn, yet what they are unwilling to earn through their own work. Sylvanists, for example, would never enter a country without a passport or visa, demanding upon arrival that the citizens of that country give them a permanent monthly allowance for their every need and want, defiantly, even militantly, claiming these privileges as free rights. They are neither free nor a right. Sovereign citizens must pay for them through forced taxation.

Such rights can only be taken upon the doom of that ironhanded night when the citizenry become bonded slaves of foreign invaders. As we shall see quite clearly in our further discussion, claiming that everyone, except us, has a right to everything and that we must finance their right to enjoy it is nothing more than a strategy devised by pseudointellectual Karl Marx. Indeed, Marxism is merely economic revolution followed by the pervasive theft of a nation by international bankers.

Nonetheless, we listen quite keenly to such people as these Marxists since they may be more brutally honest than our friends who wish to nurture our friendship with kindness. For we can learn much from our enemies, especially in ways which we can improve ourselves. To be certain, we may hear the unvarnished truth from them, which we must accept with an appropriate degree of humility. Yet, we often hear them spin carefully crafted lies, for as Michaelangelo was to the Sistine Chapel, so are some tribalists to mendacities; they are manifold, meticulous, huge, and seemingly unending.

So, their remarks should be considered judiciously, measured by the ice-cold facts, by wisdom, and by asking these two questions: Will it harm the family? Will it harm the flora or fauna? For anything which harms the family harms each of us and, in turn, harms Sylvanity, our societal tribe. Likewise, anything that harms the flora and fauna, of which we are but members, also hurts us since moment by moment we depend upon them for our next breath, our next drop of water, our next meal.

When our enemies muster the courage to confront us face-to-face with negative criticism meant to harm us, often the wisest response is to simply say, "Thank you," and nothing more. This response may surprise them, leaving them with little more to say. For, as Mark Twain suggested, "Never argue with stupid people, they will drag you down to their level and then beat you with experience." Indeed, a simpleton despises the truth. What is the truth?

"Beauty is truth, truth beauty," said John Keats. Yes, the truthful is beautiful; the untruthful is ugly. This, incidentally, is our evaluation of art: it should be an expression of beauty and truth. Now, a beautiful man or woman can be a pathological liar, of course; their beautiful body, an expression of the idea human form, which is recognized subliminally, but housing a mendacious mind and spirit.

Once again, we are not obligated to love our enemies. Neither do we particularly hate them. For although our motto is work and love, we are not necessarily great lovers. Therefore, we are not great haters. Not wishing to be on either end of this spectrum, we find reality and peace of mind somewhere in the middle. Indeed, should we try to be too good, we quickly outstrip our abilities to do so, becoming hypocritical, our very words becoming fictitious, just as the religious zealot rarely matches his pontificating with deeds. The fable of Icarus brilliantly teaches us this lesson.

Long ago, Icarus and his father, Daedalus, were imprisoned in an inescapable tower stronghold. Yet the ingenious Daedalus devised a plan of escape through the air. Using the feathers of birds that alighted atop their prison, which were fashioned together by candle wax, he made two sets of wings, one for himself and the other for his son. As they readied for their flight to freedom, Daedalus sternly warned Icarus not to fly too high, for such nearness to the Sun would melt the wax that held the wing's feathers in place.

Leaping from the tower, they began to sail through the air and over the sea. Yes! They could fly! Exaltation, however, overcame Icarus, who, against his father's warning, flew higher and higher, soaring in ecstasies. Daedalus cried out, "No! You're flying too high! Too close to the Sun!" But Icarus heeded not his father's pleas, and soon, the wax binding the feathers of his wings began to melt, and suddenly he fell to the sea and drowned.

The ancient fable of Phaeton teaches us the same lesson. This contemporary rendition in whimsical rhyme of a father gently admonishing his son is titled "Phaeton" and was written by Morris Bishop.

> Apollo through the heavens rode
> In glittering gold attire;
> His car was bright with chrysolite,
> His horses snorted fire.
>
> "The chargers are ambrosia-fed,
> They barely brook control;
> On high beware the Crab, the Bear,
> The Serpent round the Pole;
> Against the Archer and the Bull
> Thy form is all unsteeled!"
> But Phaeton could lay it on;
> Apollo had to yield.
>
> Out of the purple doors of dawn
> Phaeton drove the horses;
> They felt his hand could not command,
> They left their wonted courses.
> And from the chariot Phaeton
> Plunged like a falling star —
> And so, my boy, no, no, my boy,
> You cannot take the car.

Both fables from ancient Greece are good reminders that should we try to be too good—to be the shining example—we eventually make fools of ourselves and far worse. By contrast, if we become a light to others, it is probably unintentional, although we hope to be inspirational in some ways; yet, should we do so, such a light shines far less by words and much more by smart, hard work, and clean living. For, we do not feel an obligation to be the light of the

world, although this would not be harmful should it happen
involuntarily. This is quite fortunate because Sylvans and
Sylvanity are imperfect, as the Universe in which we live is
imperfect; yet the Universe's imperfection allows our relaxed comfort for humans are, quite possibly, its most
imperfect inhabitants. Sylvanists realize this. We know
the Earth and all Earthly life are harmonized to a key vibrating with nature, whereas humans are, in many ways,
nature's aberration, a mistuned key without agreement of
pitch, if you will. Because of this alienation from nature,
Sylvans humbly seek a reformation. This reform we humbly seek by turning away from both synthetic and spiritual
vulgarisms, which destroy the Earth, its atmosphere, its
flora, its fauna, our bodies, and, to be certain, our very
souls.

This reformation seems impossible to many. For, we
were born without fur, feather, fang, or claw, and so have
endlessly improvised for our naked vulnerabilities, often
in ways that have been destructive to all of life around us
and to ourselves; for we cannot transcend the *human condition*; and this *human predicament* is untamed by society
and its laws, which we must embrace or live without the
commonwealth of social order and therein yield to animal
instincts. And so, we suppress our savageness and mimic
civility until it becomes second nature. Yet, our lower nature is our first nature, and it often overrides urbaneness
since it is attuned to the unconscious mind, which is unquestionably supreme to the conscious. Indeed, the
unconscious is the realm of aboriginal urges, and, at times,
these overwhelm the conscious repository of mores, norms,
and laws. The severity and frequency of these transgres-
sions depend upon a complexity of factors, such as the
absence of nurturing or chemical imbalances, which, over

the centuries, seem elusive to the hand of science yet always culminate in social deviancies. Therefore, we cannot and do not expect utopia. Notwithstanding, Sylvans know this: We can do what appears to be impossible; to stand foursquare in the face of ethnocide and yet triumph. Moreover, only approximately three percent of a nation's population is needed to implement lawful, revolutionary change. And this is the key to our victorious, non-violent insurrection: submission to nature. The height and depth of the socio-political implications of this simple change are extraordinary. For, by contrast, we have been tainted with a barrage of unnatural sights, sounds, and thoughts, which have compromised the very essence of our people, so that for many years we have tolerated these poison darts. We can tolerate them no more. And so, we envision nature as our beckoning lodestar on this, our starward journey. Although submitted to nature, we simultaneously acquiesce to societal pathos, and we readily reconcile this dichotomy of the wild with the civilized lest we assume the heart and mind of the jungle beast or worse. This is why *work and love* is our maxim and rallying cry, for it is the hallmark of normality, paving the path to all human refinement, which in turn leads to every bonafide advancement, each one of which comes at a dear and precious price.

Yes, to be sure, the well-adjusted person works and loves, and that normality is the bedrock of the highway leading diametrically away from the primordial swamp. *For, honest work is our only problem solver.* It is the cure-all of our spirit, the healer of our soul, cleansing us of ill thoughts, invigorating the body, crowning us with the calm confidence to look another in the eye without blinking nor turning away shamefacedly.

As Carl Jung said, "All neurosis is a substitute for legitimate suffering." In other words, we behave neurotically because we resist the countenance of our flaws rather than striving with appropriate measures to correct them. This is the simplest, most transparent form of work, which makes us good men and women. From that point, discovering our self-suited profession is more straightforward, for our idiosyncratic talent is not hidden beneath a clutter of unresolved issues.[6] For most of us, this is a long, challenging road. Although once ventured upon, our daily toil may cease to be laborious and instead therapeutic joy wherein work is a light burden or perhaps not a burden at all. In this sense, work is the gateway to love. And, dear friends, *love is the recognition of value.*

Now, how do we think of something or someone whom we value? How do we treat a thing or person for whom we possess high regard? Do we not conserve and nurture the object of our esteem? If we disvalue something, isn't it unlikely that we will love it? Therefore, isn't it true that the more genuine value we recognize, the greater is our capacity to love? So, let us seek and, when appropriate, praise the virtues of others. Yet, let them be truly worthy of our appreciation rather than saccharine falsehoods, by which we hysterically attribute goodness where none exists, leading to imagined realities and further afield from nature. That is akin to the Marxist ploy of political correctness, is it not? With bright contrast, let us embrace the uncompromising facts as subjects of nature. For, this is the time, dear friends, to work and love true heartedly with all the fullness and fearlessness that nature demands.

---

[6] I expound on this subject in *The Psychological Elegance of Talent.*

Chapter Three

# The Tenets

"WHICH is more useful, the Sun or the Moon?" The great philosopher Kuzma Prutkov posed the question aloud to himself and, after pondering it for some time, being assured that he had arrived at the appropriate answer, said, "The Moon is the more useful, since it gives us its light during the night, when it is dark, whereas the Sun shines only in the daytime, when it is light anyway." Professor Prutkov was not consulted about our tenets; for, after all, he comes to us from the fanciful musings of poets Count Alexi Tolstoy and the brothers Gemchushnikov.

We hardly need consultation, of course, for many of us may quite easily find these tenets to be self-evident common sense. Wherefore, then, the need? It is simply for two reasons.

First, because we are incessantly receiving, whether we want them or not, contradictious messages that, ever so gradually, begin to meld with our opinions and, in this way, slowly change them. I would dare say that many of us, who are old enough to make an observation over the last twenty-five years, might find that we were more conservative at the beginning of that time. And this matters not whether we are Tory or labor, republican or democrat, religious or unreligious. Should we be one of those who withstood the mind bender's disinformation in stalwart fashion, aboard the social ship of state, we have all the same, been swept down the coursing turbulence with our fellow passengers. We may, at times, and more often than we like, find ourselves agreeing with them to avoid rocking the boat by broaching a debate with one who is (let us be kind) less than philosophical. Indeed, political correctness is intolerant since it is comprised of readymade opinions, which non-thinkers adore. For there are few things more passionately distasteful to a political "correctee" than fair-minded thought. So, it is easy to lose one's point of reference in such a society, in which it seems insurrection is all about us. The tenets serve as an anchor.

Secondly, we need the tenets and their expositions because the media purposefully omits crucial facts contained within the tenets that are, to put it mildly, newsworthy; so much so that ignorance of them threatens our very existence. For these reasons, we launch our ship of state, sovereign and free, sailing t'ward a more virtuous society based upon nature, in order that we may agree upon common ideas about ourselves and society.

These tenets embolden us. They give us a voice, free and strong, whereas our freedom of speech has been brutally silenced by craven social engineers. These, our tenets, our worldview, our *weltanschauung*, are faithful reminders in a world that beguiles and beckons us away from wit and wisdom. And so, they define us as one great and, let there be no mistaking it, one mighty tribe with one mighty voice. Though it is mighty, let our voice be not rebel-rousing rancor. Let there be ten thoughts contemplated for every word spoken. Yet, let us speak them boldly.

I. The highest law is the Law of Survival. All laws are parenthetical to this one law, overlording all else.

*The US Army Survival Manual* begins, "Many survival case histories show that stubborn, strong willpower can conquer enormous obstacles. One case history tells of a man stranded in the desert for eight days without food and water; he had no survival training, and he did nothing right. But he wanted to survive, and through sheer willpower, he did survive.

"With training, equipment, and the will to survive, you will find you can overcome any obstacle you may face. You will survive." Likewise, we are designed to fight and triumph over any challenge. Mindful of this thought, let us consider the three most fundamental existential threats that beset us ever more menacingly.

Before doing so, it is fair to mention that many people enthusiastically argue that artificial intelligence (AI) should be one of these three threats. To pose a threat to us, however, AI must acquire cognitive abilities on par with humans, which its masters have not granted. Innovative hurdles block this path that have not been overcome, such as the powerfulness and size of the microchip. To reach the next era of processing power, the transistor must become so small that, at the molecular level, the silicon chip will melt, destabilize, and, perhaps, leak. So, for AI to threaten us, the silicone must be replaced and then massed produced, a process that may require many years; even then, many more years will be required for AI to think like humans, and this assumes that technology does not experience an innovation impediment caused by external factors such as economic collapse.

Nevertheless, AI's menace is easily stopped by a kill switch program disallowing harm to any human, a treaty that must be universally agreed upon by the tech giants. One may argue that, in such a case, our enemies or a rogue technocrat would simply omit such a command from his robotic army; we would throw down the gauntlet by programming our AI to seek and destroy such robots. Public transparency among both commercial and military technocracies is the linchpin to these caveats; *blockchain technology,* which we will discuss later, may achieve this transparency. So, while AI may be a threat to monitor, it does not appear to be a present menace.

Others argue that nuclear war should be one of the three threats; this, however, is a tool wielded to a large degree by popular opinion, which is overwhelmingly against it, and, let us pray, to a lesser degree by those unstable personages who attain high office by pretense. For even they know nuclear war means Mutual Assured Destruction (MAD) and their own suicide, an act well within the scope of the mentally deranged. Yet, we may be somewhat consoled by the fact that others also oversee the keys to Armageddon; for, a critical path of secure codes must be authorized before the launch of intercontinental ballistic missiles, and we trust that within this path are those who, by passing top-secret crypto clearances are among the mentally grounded. Of course, nuclear weapons were *not* built to be used. They are principally strategic deterrents.

Nonetheless, they are unacceptable and can only become obsolete by popular opinion as we gain control of the media. Presently, however, no other existential threat is more demanding and foreboding than ecological collapse. Therefore, it is foremost of the three dangers that now bear down upon us.

1. Ecological collapse

Since we depend singularly upon our planet's bounty for our next breath of air, our next sip of water, and our next morsel to eat, the ecosystem is essential for our survival. Yet, ecological degradation is sweeping the globe because of the population explosion. At the same time, many treat the Earth rapaciously. The wealthiest man in the world was introduced recently to a large audience, and before he walked onstage, the host cursed the Earth using the vilest language, which is so wicked it was hitherto unimaginable. But it should be no surprise since that richest of men is rampaging nature while being hailed as a hero. So, due to the geometrizing surge of humans, many of whom disregard our life-giving Earth, we have much work ahead of us.

The only path to redemption of our flora and fauna is self-redemption. In other words, we must save the inner ecosystem, our bodies, before we can restore the outer ecosystem, simply because those who are poor stewards of their bodies will typically mistreat our flora and fauna. And so, I devote approximately one hundred pages of this book to physical health since it is the undivided gateway to reversing ecological collapse. Should you wish to investigate this existential threat further, I encourage you to read my book *The Hathaway Equation: The Plan to Halt and Reverse Ecological Collapse*. The equation renders climate change a moot point and dramatically improves our lives physically, socially, economically, and, most vitally, ecologically. In addition to the ecological implications of robust health, is the improved ability to lead our tribe with strength and confidence as we advance to heights undreamt. Furthermore, full appreciation for *The Tribe of Sylvan* might not be possible without reading *The Hathaway Equation*.

## 2. Loving our enemies

Loving one's enemies is a foundational, Christological notion that has permeated much of European thinking over the centuries, influencing even secular decisions and life-styles of our people. There can be little doubt that our enemies are pleased with its prevalence. Indeed, it seems very likely that they have propagated it amongst us, defending it in the face of reason to their strategic advantage, which is a particularly insidious form of psychological warfare. For, if I may be forgiven for being so blunt, many of our people are used, in our enemy's words, as "stooges" in these clandestine chess moves within cold wars. The openly Marxist communist Dean of Canterbury Cathedral, Hewlett Johnson, was a stunning example.[7] In flowing robes and decorous rapacity, Johnson made a facade hero of Stalin in concert with the dictator's mass rape, horrific torture, and murder of tens of millions of Christians. The "red dean," as he was called, could not hear their weeping cries for mercy within the Elizabethan stateliness of his sprawling palatial manor amongst wealth and servants. Nor was he troubled by the hypocrisy of acquiring riches by pretending to champion the plight of the poor while crushing them 'neath his heel. Stalin's gifts and promotion of Johnson's books mollified such triflings that may have arisen within the dean's conscience, which appears to have been numbed as though

---

[7] I do not imply that all the deans are like Johnson. The Very Reverend John Arthur Simpson, OBE, for instance, who was the Dean of Canterbury Cathedral from 1986 to 2000, was a conservative, fundamentalist Christian. I was a guest in his home, and we discussed these matters in some detail over lunch.

"seared with a hot iron." And so, Johnson's writings, though plagiarized from Soviet propaganda, were widely influential. Indeed, the First Secretary of the Communist Party of Cuba, Raul Castro, told Johnson that people believed his pro-communist ideas because he was a priest. Alas, many of Johnson's ilk are with us today, well-paid and industrious, because of the irrational tolerance that the concept of loving our enemies has wrought.

Of course, Sylvanists are respectful friends to Christians, whose faith implies universal love. And so, it is essential to stress before discussing the notion of loving one's enemies that we will always defend Christians should they be assailed by extra-tribal groups or anyone else. Moreover, though we may respectfully critique biblical interpretation, as we do here, we do not dissuade the practice of Christianity or suggest Christians abandon their faith. We merely present ideas with dispassionate reason, allowing them to lead wheresoever they will, seeking balance with this gyroscope of common sense: *we exalt our creator above empty religiosity.*

To be sure, many of our tribe are devout Christians, others cultural Christians who wish passersby Merry Christmas and, perhaps, read *A Christmas Carol* by Dickens at that charitable season when our people express so much goodwill to one another. Indeed, we thoroughly agree with Christian ideas of traditional family values and other virtuous teachings, which in many ways have been an antidote to communism and a world of other evils. We agree it is often a good practice—a mentally healthy practice—to follow the admonition of Luke 6:28, "Bless those who curse you, pray for those who despitefully use you." That is usually best done from a particularly safe and faraway distance, however. And, of course, King Alfred might have been one of the most central figures in all of Christendom.

So, it is with kind respect when we say that this favorable gestalt, nonetheless, upon deeper inquiry, dissipates to a degree as the idea of loving one's enemies, historically, becomes but a faint reflex to Christian teaching, the schism of some of its foundational parts, therefore, glaring forth. By contrast, the fountainhead of Sylvanism is submission to nature, and nature fundamentally forbids loving those who seek our destruction since such a notion suggests morbidity and lifelessness, which our bodies recognize *epigenetically*. In other words, though our DNA is naturally unchanged, our genetic information is slightly modified by loving an enemy in a series of numbing molecular death wishes.

Nevertheless, Christ admonishes his disciples to love their enemies at least twenty-seven times in scripture, whereas we feel this might be unwise and dangerous. However, the polarity of Sylvanist and Christian philosophies is not pervasive. They align in many ways. Perhaps the injunction of loving one's enemies is merely a point of interpretative perception.

But irony upon irony, although taught to be the ultimate pacifists by Christ, it seems evangelicals are often the first to rush to war, the faint reflex to the master's teaching vanishing altogether, replaced with dogmatic ideas and actions that are anathema to the Prince of Peace. Albeit the wise are loath to declare war without justification supported by quite a number of well-researched and compelling facts. Zealous religionism, on the other hand, sometimes inflames our egocentricities, providing the pseudo-rationale and, in turn, the incandescent rage for war; Christ's teaching of turning the other cheek in these circles, becoming mystically invisible; for religious mania always leads to sectarian doctrine, a saintly cloak often hiding many a blackened vice. Such contradictions of belief and behavior are what psychiatrists might refer to as "sharply split." It must be. For the notion of loving our enemies has never been practiced by any nation when confronted with war, although their leaders and citizens claimed to be followers of Christ's teachings.

This is also a war 'twixt nonsense and common sense. For a nation collectively loving one's war-waging enemies would result in "sociocide." And so, the leaders of Christendom neurotically command themselves to return warmongering for warmongering as if it were not diametrically opposed to, perhaps, Christ's foremost precept. To then counterbalance their inability to love their enemies, they hate them all the more vehemently rather than dealing with them as rational-minded men who would otherwise be unaffected by a religious hysteria that interferes with judicious thinking. That is a classic example of Jung's concept of the shadow personality becoming more strident when denied and suppressed. Yet without this combustible and religious ardor that compromises logical thought, often thoroughly negating it, our tribe can fight smarter, harder, longer, until victory with superior efficiency to any other tribe throughout the world. Yet, let us fight with the visors of our helms wide open to behold the battlefield in the full light of the noonday Sun, unafraid to countenance our foe eye-to-eye, assessing his true identity as fighting men must.

But mightn't they, under normal circumstances, be a dinner guest in our home with whom we could share the art of conversation and a laugh or two? If we are honest, isn't it possible that we could become good friends? And with equal integrity, let us be plainspoken about precisely whose banner we are marching beneath; does this banner herald the best interests of our people? Or is it an extra-tribal ploy to create fratricidal strife amongst us? For these reasons and many more, we greatly prefer precious peace over the unspeakable miseries of war.

We always prefer love over hate. Hate always loses. Yet, as we mentioned earlier, Sylvans are not great lovers in the whimsical, religious sense; therefore, we are not great haters. Thus, we have no obligations to love our enemies; at the same time, we do not particularly hate them. We neither love nor hate them. Rather than having extroverted or introverted feelings about them, Sylvans are rather ambiverts regarding our enemies. Therefore, we merely treat them as a danger, as enemies. We will even listen to them with keen interest and become the wiser for having done so.

Our first allegiance, however, is to our survival. For only slaves and servants are forced to provide for the safety of others, particularly those who hate them. Yet, the communist mind benders expect us to welcome those into our fatherlands who wish us harm, providing not only for their safety but every other need and luxury. Indeed, the ideologies of these "emigrants" encourage violence against us—stealing from us, lying to us, even rape, and pedophilia—all emboldened by the followers of Marx who flood our countries with these fanatical devotees who are of military age, our once quiet neighborhoods blaring with their rancor of war. And our considerable fighting acumen is for naught should we become subservient to these hellions by applying Christ's teachings to the conundrum of turning back tidal wave upon ever mounting tidal wave of hatemongering hordes. Should we not resist them as they rape and torture our women before our very eyes, and not resist them still as they do the same to our little children and esteemed fathers and mothers? Aleksandr Solzhenitsyn categorically described those same horrific acts upon his people by the invading Marxists in *The Gulag Archipelago*.

By contrast, King Alfred the Great loved his enemies *after* he defeated them, and this observation is not a negative criticism of the king but a conclusion of sane behavior in which nature overrode nonsensical ideology. Perhaps, that aligns with Christ driving the money changers out of the temple with a whip. For, should Christ's admonition to love our enemies be taken literally, then he must have understood with divine clarity that this would imply slavery and death by fire and sword. In such a case, neither Christians nor Christ's teachings would have endured past AD 100 or so, and our people would have never heard of them.

Or, if this admonition was simply metaphorical, are we to assume we needn't love our enemies completely but only theoretically, in pretentious overtures of friendship during peace when not threatened by them? This, it seems, cannot be the case since Christ allowed himself to be shamefully mistreated, mocked, savagely beaten, and crucified by his enemies without resistance. Let us, then, consider those whom Christ, *literally or figuratively*, depending upon one's scriptural interpretation, admonishes us to love, carry military gear the extra mile, not resist, freely give anything asked of us, forgive indefinitely, and turn our cheeks for them to strike a second time.[8]

---

[8] Matthew 5:18-22 and 5:39-44.

3. Communism

The hellish power presiding over Washington, D.C. and the European Union is Marxist communism. Its grip and grasp of every form of the media, the global economic hegemony, the very structure of our societies and neighborhoods, and even the advancing armies of our enemies cannot be overstated. It faces not the sunlight but hides amongst shadows. It wears raiment of holy white, holding a dove in one hand while grasping the pommel of a poison dagger hidden 'neath its cloak with the other. It commits crimes so heinous to stagger belief, then orders newscasters whom we implicitly trust to blame the most innocent, often branding them as "racists."[9] It grins, not smiles, walking within the halls of congress and parliament. Its quest for war is forever insatiable while proclaiming its harmless love of peace throughout the world. Yet over one hundred million souls savagely murdered by this thing cry out for justice, saying, *"How long, O Lord?"* The deafening voices of another two hundred seventy million spirits, whose precious bodies were massacred by its accomplice, roar with one thunderous word, *"Judgment!"*

'Tis time for this ideological Grendel to die the death. First, we must know more of the beast. Karl Marx, best known for his social theories, which became known as Communist Marxism, was born in 1818 in the German Rhineland, yet he was not a German national in

---

[9] Marxist communist Magnus Hirschfeld coined the word "racist," almost exclusively to persecute those of European descent. Read the chapter *Essential Sylvanism* on page 443 for ideas to respond to such baseless allegations.

spirit but an internationalist, or what is commonly referred to as a "globalist." Although his father apparently converted to Christianity for business reasons, both his paternal and maternal grandfathers were rabbis with strong Talmudic backgrounds. "Virtually all of his work, indeed, has the hallmark of Talmudic study," says Paul Johnson in his book, *Intellectuals.* It seems Karl never outgrew his terrible twos. As a boy, he began writing poetry about his two consuming obsessions: the girl next door named Jenny, whom he later married, and, of course, world destruction. Karl would sometimes enter episodes of paroxysms lasting days on end, and these, perhaps, combined with his socially destructive ideas, earned him the distinction of being deported from Belgium, France, and Germany, living most of his life in London as a stateless person. According to Johnson in *Intellectuals,* a comrade ideologue named Karl Heinzen described the permanently angry Marx as a "cross between a cat and an ape," with "disheveled coal-black hair and dirty yellow complexion," who was so "intolerably dirty" that it was difficult to discern if his suit was covered with a gloss of mud or just filthy and brown. An aura of stench was perpetually all about him, as a cloud that required stoic conditioning to endure. Perhaps, Karl's challenges were far worse than the infantilism of the terrible twos, for his father said that he was convinced his son was possessed of a demon.

Masquerading as an indefatigable champion of the working class, he never had a job nor a yearning to associate with the common man. Possibly the only proletariat, or working-class person, with whom Marx had any contact whatsoever was Helene "Lenchen" Demuth, the housekeeper of the two-room house where the Marxes endured life in poverty. Lenchen fathered Karl's child, but he never had a relationship with the boy, and when his wife, Jenny, discovered that Karl was the father, she left him.

Marx predicted that capitalism would become a less stable economic system as the wage-earners, or proletariat, grew in numbers, becoming more dissatisfied with their positions in life. He theorized that would, in turn, ignite class warfare with the bourgeois, or property owners, erupting in a revolution whereby the workers would take over all commerce. A new epoch of man's ascent would be ushered in by the ostensibly benevolent Marxist agitator, in which all men would enjoy life equally. Such egalitarian philosophical notions may have keen appeal to the masses who dream of bettering themselves in a single step; yet, they are comparable to a circular argument at best and a downward spiral into chaos should they be given judicious thought. For dissatisfied workers, enthralled with excitation to a fevered pitch by the vision of a utopian society from a speech by a communist rabble-rouser, will seldom ask these sophomoric questions:

How would the issue be settled as to who would lead a company "appropriated" by communist rebels? Who would occupy the corporate office as chief executive officer, and who would remain on the factory floor assembling widgets? Who would create a marketing campaign to attract customers to buy the widgets? And which members of the proletariat, a predominantly phlegmatic group by nature, would be sanguine enough to lead the sales force? Who, from the ranks of the proletariat, would solve a multitude of extremely complex accounting problems formerly assigned to a skilled team of certified public accountants who were, each and every one, trained for eight years to master their craft? Upon doing away with the legal counsel, who from amongst the workers would be able to wield the mighty sword of the law in court on behalf of these thousands of newly managed corporations? Who from the proletariat possesses the savvy to immediately, with no training or experience, make bold decisions affecting multiplied billions of dollars and the livelihood of a teeming host of workers?

Undoubtedly, a tremendous talent pool exists within the working class, yet this talent requires years to develop adequately. And what shall become of the motivation to perform exemplarily? Should all be equal, performing with equal skills, all must be paid equally; for, to recognize the superiority of only one worker would negate the very notion of a classless society; that one single worker immediately becoming a member of the middle class. To be sure, consequently, the classless society is a society bereft of motivation.

To better understand Marxian contradiction, let us suppose you are a college student and, rather than joining your friends at campus social clubs drinking beer and going to parties 'til the early hours of the morning, you rise early to study before class and, after class, you study further at the library. You have a perfect class attendance record. Your dedication is evident in your grades, for you are given the absolute highest marks and the corresponding honor of *summa cum laude*.

Now, let us imagine that the students who rarely went to class and failed every course because they watched television all day and drank beer all night were given part of your excellent grades so they could pass with average scores. In fact, your perfect grades were dispersed to all the students, no matter if they studied, attended classes, or not. Would you, nonetheless, be willing to work as diligently for your grades and attend every lecture? And how would you feel, if those excellent grades of yours were taken from you without your consent and against your will by brute force? This is a revealing anecdote of Marxist communism.

Another fallacy of his theories, which Marx describes as "the solution to the riddle of history" is the abolition of land and private property ownership with the intent to introduce a truly classless society. This will, of course, require a "dictatorship of the proletariat" during a transitional period of undetermined duration. I do not recall that he reconciled man's alienation from the land and all of his property in his work *Alienated Labor*; for are not the fruits of a man's labor indissolubly intertwined with his self-worth, and this principally with his relationship to the land, which he lovingly tends and proudly calls his own?

The ideologies of Marx are so contradictious, so poorly developed, so catastrophic in their outcomes that I can only guess that we know of them purely because a robber baron or two fancied the idea of implementing them for their own *coup d'état* and colossal theft from entire nations. Elated with the discovery of a weapon that could be wielded by only a few men against whole nations, even world regions, all robber barons of any note began extolling the false virtues of Marxist communism to the poor and downtrodden. So, it seems Marx's ideas are iconoclastic for the sake of the iconoclasts who destroy before pillaging; nothing more, nothing less is this ideology than a blunt instrument in the hands of such shadow tyrants for their mendacious tyranny against the unsuspecting people they purport to defend.

Little wonder that Karl Marx sent a laudatory letter of praise to none other than Abraham Lincoln, congratulating him for implementing Marx's morbid ideology after Lincoln's war against state sovereignty, which the double-speak mind benders labeled the "Civil War." Neither is it surprising that one of the foremost communists of the twentieth century, Fidel Castro, gingerly laid a wreath in deep respect at the Lincoln Memorial. These are telling actions of the communists, who readily adore Lincoln while always disparaging Washington and Jefferson. They are able to deceive the masses by discombobulating the history surrounding these men simply because Marxist communists utterly control Western media, their principal conduit for distributing false narratives. As communist Joseph Stalin said, "Ideas are more powerful than guns. We would not let our enemies have guns, why, therefore, should we let them have ideas?"

This is why the media is the crown jewel of our struggle. It influences and eventually forms the opinions of enough of the masses to guide the direction of society's remaining, somewhat unwilling majority. And, its power often supersedes rationality, leading the populous to make false assumptions about many things, including urgent matters that jeopardize our very survival.

For these reasons, one might debate that the media itself should be first among our existential threats. After all, isn't it true that we cannot redeem ourselves from the suicidal notion of loving our enemies and other perils without controlling our media? This is a meaningful point. Nevertheless, the media is simply a conduit of Marxism that lies firmly within their domain. And so, we will continue our discussion of communism.

The West has been plagued for many generations with subversive ideology, or weaponized ideas, purposefully distributed by the media. This is why Thomas Jefferson said, "I really look with commiseration over the great body of my fellow citizens who, reading newspapers, live and die in the belief that they have known something of what has been passing in the world in their time . . ." Since

Jefferson's day, the media has continued to produce an avalanche of armed thoughts designed to change the perception of reality; this occurs very slowly, very subtly until a popular opinion unthinkable two decades previously becomes today's norm in a false evolution of society. True social development, by contrast, occurs organically without forsaking reality, firmly based upon nature. Yet, morals and all social tabu in the West have been manipulated by ideological insurrectionists, including whether a mother stops the beating heart of her child within her womb, as well as in which direction the armies of the world shall march. The point of penetration is demoralization, the place at which members of society begin to negotiate their morals unconsciously. Once this prolific degradation of morality has been instilled, it is so ingrained as to be irrevocable. Exposure to facts becomes inconsequential, for facts have become immaterial to those compromised by subversive ideology. And once morals have been compromised, destabilization of other societal pillars is possible such as economic structure, foreign relations, and education, the fall of which is often beyond full recovery.

Much of the molding of today's public opinion derives from television, which should come as no surprise since, as we shall discuss in greater detail later, Americans watch 360 trillion hours of television every ten years. They, of course, are not alone. The global hourly intake of televised messaging must range in quadrillions through the course of a decade. And so, the multimillion-member army of automatons parades in measured tread with catatonic stare—all in near perfected agreement, ever loyal to their programming, defiant to any ideas beyond their own, tolerant only of the narrow vision to which they have been institutionally bonded. This is a pitiful tragedy. So much so that it threatens our existence, for this mentally mechanized army has not been infused with benevolent ideas. By the time children complete elementary school, they have watched 8,000 murders, and by age eighteen, they've watched 200,000 acts of violence. Yet, television is only one of the many forms of media; books, magazines, theater, cinema, news, and the internet are a few of its other venues. With this prolific deluge of brutality, and even the heroization of it, the media entices the members of its audience with a steady drip, drip, drip of poison to negotiate its morality, even to entertain the notion of killing their fellow man.

And so, malignant ideas arise in the otherwise peaceful mind protected by virtuous industry rather than the mental numbness from decades of endless programming. Unconsciously, they easily give ambivalent assent to simply doing away with those who live far away and speak another tongue, particularly when lies have been presented about these other people by those who masquerade with a plain face as rational, trustworthy leaders and as though their lies were facts. Thus, by controlling the media, the international communists maintain their global monopoly on violence.

This is the goal of the mind benders, about whom we have much to say in our journey, for they pose an ominous threat since they control the media, and he who controls the media controls, or at least affects, everything. As a carnival showman diverts one's attention while quickly maneuvering three walnut shells to hide the location of the single green pea, so does the media create shell games to hide timely matters that urgently require our attention, especially the machinations of international bankers. The media will never shine its light upon these darkest of deeds, for would the glove contend with the hand that animates it, the very thing giving it form and strength?

Albeit some economists believe we may stand upon the threshold of an era of economic liberty unexperienced by mankind since societies began to form many thousands of years ago and thus be emancipated from Marxist economic slavery. We must consider this opportunity with cautious optimism, for most innovations seem to carry latent challenges along with their solutions. Time shall tell. But to understand the profundity of this advancement, let's first give thought to the problem it portends to solve— economic war, a warfare aptly described by film director Karen Shakhnazarov.

"I've started to agree with some independent American experts who say that the US is run by financial oligarchies. Basically, about ten families who own the whole banking system and the Federal Reserve. They basically run the US, it's in their hands. To the adherents of materialism, I'd say I don't see any conspiracy here because, my dear friends, it's logical. If you've created such a large-scale financial system that envelops the whole world, you're supposed to create a global political system as your next step. And national sovereignty is your first hindrance. In this sense, the election of Trump is a rebellion of some kind, an almost crushed rebellion now, but not yet quelled. Trump represents the national American state. And from the perspective of the elite that aims to create a global world, where national sovereignty becomes a formality, the world turns into a new tower of Babel which is run by the intelligent . . . They don't consider themselves villains . . . but intelligent people who understand finance. Russia may seem archaic to them. An archaic land that hinders historical progress. They believe that it's a historical process. And, we seem to be opposing this historical process. From this perspective, it's just a matter of time for them. They are dedicated not just greedy. Dedicated people are much more dangerous. So, I believe we can't negotiate with them. We can only reach a temporary compromise. I think they're afraid of our achievements in the defense field. But these achievements won't stop them. They still believe this historical process is on their side. They are one hundred percent convinced. I personally believe this is a grave mistake because I don't believe in the uniformity of the world. I don't believe a new Babel tower could be created."

Should we agree with Shakhnazarov, we observe, among other things, that this Marxist economic death star is spectacular with power, bent on crushing national sovereignty, the preface of destroying individual autonomy, and that its imperial agenda is nonnegotiable. How would King Alfred, whose life inspired this book, battle against such Marxist terrorism? I am certain the basis of his victory over this economic warfare would have been the same as his victory over the Great Heathen Army: *the love of his people*. Let this never be misconstrued as triteness. For love, never hate, is where all masterpieces are created, even masterpieces of strategy. And as all masterpieces are elegant, so might we see elegance within the slaying of this wretched economic dragon, its claws reaching to the four corners of the Earth itself. So, let the love of our people ever be the basis of our struggle.

To understand this global economic beast more clearly and how it might be slain, let us start at its beginning. Some might say it had partial beginnings around A D 600 in ancient Lydia, the land we now know as Turkey. Let us suppose a Lydian farmer went to market to buy a team of oxen to plow his field. He found a man selling two prize oxen and presented the man with a deed to the land he wished to trade for them. The farmer also brought his brother, who gave solemn oath, testifying of the land's size, fertility, and suitability for farming. But the ox seller shook his head, saying, "Your land may be as you say. Yet, how can I trust you? I have never seen you before. And, even if you show me the land, it may still belong to someone else who has gone on a long journey or is simply holding the land as you claim to be." Then the ox seller held forth a small gold disc engraved with a lion's head and said, "I'll trade my oxen for one of these. I know how much it's worth because King Alyattes decrees it so, and his word is law. And woe unto him who faces the king's terrible wrath. Thus, his majesty protects us. For, though we cannot trust one another, we can trust the king."

This is the key: we may no longer need to trust king, or government, or bank for monetary exchange, all of which are controlled by Marxists; now, we can make transactions with utter transparency through blockchain technology, which creates a permanent record that is widely verifiable. This, along with what I call sovereign currency, has the potential to make banks obsolete.

The strength of sovereign currency is that its value is based upon scarcity, precisely as gold is valuable because of its limited supply. There are several types of sovereign currency, just as there are several types of precious metals and stones, each of which is valuable because of its rarity. This is the Austrian philosophy of economics; value derives from finite availability. By contrast, the Keynesian school of economics is based upon fiat currency that is produced by a printing press with nothing of value to justify its worth, the economic theory adopted by the United States Government when it abandoned the gold standard. This accelerated the dollar's ongoing devaluation, and the Keynesian philosophy will eventually bring the dollar to zero, where, historically, all fiat currencies end. Yet, the media reports that prices are rising because of a phenomenon they label "inflation," which they claim is caused by greed when, in truth, the dollar is actually decreasing in value, and so more dollars are required to buy something of static value. When, for example, you pay $2 for an avocado when it was only $1 last year, and there have been no strikes, crop failures, or other interventions that could have caused the avocado's scarcity, the value of the avocado did not suddenly increase, but the value of the dollar most definitely *decreased*. So, rather than goods and services generally rising in value, what is really occurring is the dollar's devaluation until one day it will be worthless. This is one of the many economic crimes of Keynesianism since most people are unable to react to such a monetary collapse, losing everything when it inevitably occurs on the rue morning when they awaken to raging social chaos. This is Marxism.

Communist economic warfare is further waged on an inconceivable scale by Keynesian governments as they steal from us through deficit spending compensated by taxing us and our children's, children. For example, upon birth, each American baby is presented with a tax bill of approximately $42,000 from which he or she will never receive a benefit. Neither have the parents received a benefit from this taxation, nor have they been told how the money was spent, or to whom it was given. The United States Federal Reserve, a private bank, which is categorically unconstitutional, simply prints literally trillions of dollars and presents Americans with the bill. However, we know in general that this stolen money is used to finance multitrillion-dollar wars while over 327 million American taxpayers languish in economic slavery and face the threat of monetary collapse.

As Tennyson said,

"Theirs not to make reply,
Theirs not to reason why,
Theirs but to do and die."

Yet now, for the first time in human history, we may
be able to emancipate ourselves from the glaring eye, sinister with greed, of an invasive government that takes
what is rightfully ours. Now our children may never, in
all their lives, need set foot inside a bank, which might soon
become a relic of a bygone age. And so, it may be possible
that more autonomy and wealth will be enjoyed by Everyman, for the global economic hegemony may soon loosen
its grip upon mankind. Blockchain technology and Austrian economics provided by sovereign currencies, both of
which we control rather than governments and banks, may
be two redeeming factors in our liberation from communism. How poetic that this death-dealing economic
Grendel, as big as the globe, should be slain by two inventions created in a spirit of transparency.

We will now consider another vital Marxist tool: the
heterogeneous society. Humanity, as a whole, is collapsing
the ecosystem, yet we, as a race, are participating in our
biological demise explicitly because we are behaving in
ways that are against nature, or, in other words, in ways that
are profoundly abnormal. This abnormality is due in no
small measure to an unconscious surrendering to a seamless
bombardment of socially inserted programming, the myriad
repetitions of which heighten one's susceptibility to suggestion. These factitious messages find particular fertility within
contemporary lifestyles that are unprecedentedly less strenu-
ous, which, in turn, afford more idle thought and, therefore,
supple pliability for the mind-bending media. These
cause an array of concocted perversions that have led to our

present and general anemic condition. By forthrightly rejecting these messages, especially political correctness, we will
begin to love ourselves, not as pitiful narcissists who are
ultimately self-loathing but as red-blooded men and wom-
en. This healthy respect for the individuated self and the
larger tribe that such individuals comprise, will manifest
itself in countlessly beneficial ways, three of which will be
a cherished genetic preservation, an involuntary love of
the rich loamy soil of our homeland, and a defense of
them both as nature herself unambiguously demands of us.
Therein, we shall have a place to live free from oppression, occupation, or invasion from alien foreigners who by
their nature seek to destroy our cultures, our nations, our
race. Thus, our prize is, in a word, *normality*.

For, isn't it only normal to love one's family, one's
homeland, one's culture, one's people, and, above all, one's
progeny? Isn't it normal to feel a certain degree of fraternity
with one's genetic cousins, or at least those who share the
same color of eyes, color and texture of hair, skin color,
facial features, social values, and ancient heritage? This
is why racially integrated societies fail miserably, a truism
patently obvious to the casual observer. Yet, the mass social destruction of heterogeneous societies has also been
proven quantitatively by exhaustive analysis—the most
comprehensive analysis of its kind ever conducted—at one
of the world's most prestigious universities, with its findings being replicated with ever-increasing accuracy in
several subsequent studies. We will discuss this study with
some detail in Tenet VI.

It seems these feelings of identity amongst our people
have intensified with the African and Middle Eastern invasion of virtually all nations and regions in which our
people live: Australia, South Africa, New Zealand, Canada,

Western Europe, and the United States. Wherefore the expediency for our countries to cease to be Caucasian, whereas it is altogether unnecessary for Nigeria, and many other African nations, to cease to be Black? Why mustn't Saudi Arabia cease to be Arab, most of whom are tribal Bedouins? Why is this politically correct while Caucasian countries remaining Caucasian is not?

Why are all churches forbidden by law in Saudi Arabia while mosques, financed by that same country, are throughout all of Christendom? And why does Saudi Arabia accept no refugees whatsoever, but all nations that are predominately of European descent must welcome massive numbers from Africa and Arabia? Even a blind man can see these striking inconsistencies. Indeed, millions of people around the globe freely enjoy racial tribalism without massive immigration of extra-cultural people to their sovereign nations. The many Native American tribes keep meticulous track of their bloodlines, honoring those with as little as one-sixty-fourth of tribal blood, giving special benefits to them, excluding all others from their tribal nations.

The Han Chinese race, comprising approximately ninety-two percent of China's population, is bound together with genetics and a history spanning more than four thousand years, deeply rooted in distinct cultural traditions and customs. Some of them are quite Sinocentric, feeling that they are the world's most advanced people. Mass immigration, albeit, is not imposed upon them, as it should never be. Indeed, many racially-oriented tribes maintain the nonnegotiable prerequisite that one is a direct member of their bloodline. This is perfectly acceptable to Sylvanist thought, for we would never object to their tribal laws, or any law particular to any other tribe. All must be free to preserve their posterity and culture. This is something the

Japanese do so well; their tribe is resplendent with beauty and a glorious history that has been racially preserved for centuries. And, the indigenous Polynesian people of New Zealand, the Maoris, are particularly tribal, which we applaud. Yet, I've never heard of anyone in the media railing against Maori racism or Native American racism, Chinese, Japanese, or Arabic racism. Neither have I heard of the media accusing these tribes of racial supremacism, nor have I heard of any of them being summoned to court for a hate crime upon the basis of exclusion of other races from their tribes. All these examples of tribalism and many more are perfectly acceptable, admired, and encourage by Sylvanism.

For all people, to the foremost corners of the Earth, must be free to celebrate the variegated nuances and subtleties of their exclusive culture and custom. They must be free to preserve their posterity, the absolute substratum of freedom and, perhaps, the foremost of bio-psychological normalities.

Normality, defined by nature, consequently, is the antidote to avaricious internationalists. For, it is their mass propaganda campaigns of lies, played out by craven marionettes tastefully dressed as politicians, that have flung wide the floodgates of primitive countries, especially their prisons and mental institutions, to invade our homelands, which our forefathers have valiantly raised from the Earth with plow and sickle and hammer. So, shall our venerable baton, symbolic of cornice and capital atop the highest pillars wrought by man, be handed to strangers from a strange and unevolved land? Shall we humbly and freely give them the very Earth beneath our feet? They fire no bullets. Shrapnel in starbursts of death explodes not in ear-piercing thunder above our heads. Battle tanks do not crush everything about us, shaking the ground we defend. We needn't fight in roaring combat for weeks in a blizzard without sleep or a morsel of food. No, the only projectiles launched by the invader's political allies are a barrage of calumnies. Shall we cower before mere words? Shall it not be justified, then, before a righteous heaven that the courageous dead who rest 'neath our battlefields shall rise to curse those weaklings who blaspheme their names with cowardliness before invaders whose only weapons are words?

At the same time, some of those who have invaded our homelands feel religiously justified in rape and murderous violence against peaceful, law-abiding citizens. And, in some of our nations, there are illegal laws—those violating national constitutions—that treasonously allow the incarceration of citizens who dare speak a single word against the invasion of their fatherland. England is especially oppressed. In Rotherham, over 1,400 children were systemically raped by the invaders while the police refused to listen to outraged parents. Men who tried to file a report with the South Yorkshire Police about the rape of their daughters by these invaders were told that if they complained again, *they* would be arrested for hate crimes.

This shall change.

In the meantime, we must withstand the invasion; for, this is not an organic migratory phenomenon set against the backdrop of history's long and wide-reaching saga, heralding a new epic of human advancement. 'Tis the precise opposite: a strategic invasion by men of military age, a harbinger of human digression, and, let there be no mistaking it within the minds of my dearest cousins, *slavery*. Even now, fraught by the weight of this tyranny, some European nations have fallen under wave after wave of the besieg-

ing onslaught purely because noxious traitors, masquerading as pious politicians, have made it unlawful to speak
against this "sociocide." And so, many bemoan in whispers
with heads hung low that our homelands are demograph-
ically, electorally irretrievable. To this, I say lift your head.
Stand and fight as one Sylvanic tribe, and we shall win them
back.

We fight lawfully, intelligently. As a boxer is confident that he will win, simply because he possesses an
unconscious, inexplicable knowing, as though he can vividly
see his victory in the future, he does not remain sitting in
his corner when the bell rings. He does not say to himself,
"I will relax and rest in this comfortable chair. I do not
want to be drenched in sweat and blood, take body punch-
es, struggling to the last ounce of my energy. After all, I am
going to win. I'll let someone else fight this battle." Never.
He stands and fights. Yet, he is patient. His strategy is intelligent and well planned, his tactics honed to a science.
He cautiously but aggressively approaches his opponent,
keeping him off balance, causing him to expend most of
the energy of the fight, mercilessly pounding his weaknesses and injuries. And in the split second when the
opportunity for the knockout blow comes, he delivers it with
the full might of his legs, chest, back, right arm, and all his
weight in an instant of explosive devastation.

Like this simile of a boxer, we shall win in courts
where we will change laws by voting in elections and winning electoral candidates—*all nonviolently*. As we do, let
us always remember that fighting for our people is the
highest and most noble calling. 'Tis a fight chivalrous. For,
we protect the weak. We defend the poor. We are lawful.
Reverent before our mighty task, we never advocate hate.
And, in the midst of the fight, we can enjoy life, enjoy our

friends and family. We can smile and laugh wholeheartedly. Such happiness may become easier with the advent of the technological transilience which, as we have mentioned, is being championed by our people. So, there are practical reasons to be optimistic about our victory. Yet, dear friends, our victory must be certain, for although this is a spiritual war, we fight for our very flesh and blood.

So, let us choose from our arsenal the weapon most vanquishing: *the love of our people.* Choosing to love over hate is not a cowardly reaction to political correctness but submission to a power that protects us, body and soul. Before love, neither material nor spiritual weapons shall prosper against us, for the love of our people is a blazing light from which our enemies must turn away in trembling. They fear us. Let there be no ambiguity about this. They know we shall win.

Yet, before our glittering constellation of almost one billion separate lights can give us this victory, its sweeping power must coalesce into one vast super engine—one great and mighty Sylvanist Tribe. For, only two or three percent of our people can influence socio-political events, whereupon the majority will, in turn, follow to their great benefit. Therefore, let nothing or anyone stop you from reading this book in its entirety. It is the most intelligent action you can take for your future and the future of our children's, children's children who are asking to be born. For, a man and woman raising children in a safe homeland within our rich culture is only normal, isn't it? Therein lies the path to our fatherland, which shall be likened to the many racial tribes across the globe. This is our prize. It is the identical prize we want for all races of men. For, we want them all to do well and to prosper, too. Yet, we've much work to do. And so, we will continue our discussion of communism by describing it in a word:

*Sabotage!*

For Marxist communism is most elegantly defined as *relentless social vandalism*. And what better way of sub-version than unlawfully opening the floodgates to foreign people who hate us and our culture. We will once again refer to the city of Rotherham, England. According to the BBC, "Children as young as 11 were raped by multiple perpetrators, abducted, trafficked to other cities in Eng-land, beaten, and intimidated . . ."

"The inquiry team noted fears among council staff of being labeled 'racist' if they focused on victims' descrip-tions of the majority of abusers as 'Asian' [Muslim] men.

"Professor Alexis Jay said: 'No one knows the true scale of child sexual exploitation in Rotherham over the years. Our conservative estimate is that approximately 1,400 children were sexually exploited over the full in-quiry period, from 1997 to 2013.'

"The inquiry team found examples of 'children who had been doused in petrol and threatened with being set alight, threatened with guns, made to witness brutally vio-lent rapes and threatened they would be next if they told anyone.'" Police believe one particularly beautiful 14-year-old girl, Charlene Downes, was "cut up and minced into kebabs by a grooming gang."

Sir Roger Scruton writes about this atrocity. "Ordi-nary people are so intimidated by this that they repeat the doctrines [political correctness], like religious mantras which they hope will keep them safe in hostile territory. Hence people in Britain have accepted without resistance the huge transformations that have been inflicted on them over the last thirty years, largely by activists [communists] working through the Labour Party. They have accepted immigration policies that have filled our cities with disaffected Muslims, many of whom have now gone to fight against us in Syria and Iraq. They have accepted the growth of Islamic schools in which children are taught to prepare themselves for jihad against the surrounding social order. They have accepted the constant denigration of their country, its institutions, and its inherited religion, for the simple reason that these things are *theirs* and therefore tainted with forbidden loyalties.

"And when the truth is expressed at last, nobody is fired, no arrests are made, and the elected Police and Communities Commissioner for Rotherham, although forced to resign from the Labour Party, refuses to resign from his job. After a few weeks all will have been swept under the carpet, and the work of destruction can resume." [10]

Similar atrocities are happening across Europe, North America, and everywhere our people dwell.

The communist saboteurs are pleased with the "leadership" of Rotherham. Yet the Marxists would have more pleasure if these madmen could behave in our fatherlands as they do at home. On April 20, 2016, *The Daily Mail* published an article titled, "ISIS execute 250 women in Mosul for refusing to become sex slaves under the group's 'sexual Jihad.'" An October 26, 2016 article by Katie Mansfield in *The Express* is titled, "Barbaric ISIS

---

[10] Sir Roger Vernon Scruton, "Why Did British Police Ignore Pakistani Gangs Abusing 1,400 Rotherham Children? Political Correctness", *Forbes,* August 30, 2014.

mangle 250 children in industrial dough kneader and cooks rest alive in oven." A July 17, 2015 report by Sarkis Zeronian published by *Breitbart* is titled, "Five children among ninety-four crucified, flogged and caged by ISIS for 'eating during Ramadan."

Ninety-four people, including children, were crucified for eating during Ramadan? It beggars belief.

But these are not long-ago bizarre crimes from a barbarous age committed by a once inhuman people who are now civilized. It is happening today. And the Trotskyite communists are arranging for these people to be your next-door neighbors.

An entire library could not contain the countless ways that Marxist communists sabotage our homelands. For, although our governments may be structured as sovereign states, Marxism permeates every tone and tint of our Western societies, creating *societal communism* and, in turn, communistic thinking and behavior. Thus, many who live among us are virtual communists and sympathizers, unaware that they support a regime of unconstrained violence.

But take heart, dear cousins, for such oppression creates the very power that crushes itself. Yet, let us hasten its implosion by studying this, the book of our people. Tell others and invite them to read it. And soon, the devilish power that presides over Washington, D.C., and the European Union shall implode. For although fraught with specters and phantasms of many terrifying shapes and colors, we will soon discover that only a craven, piteous Marxist hides behind the curtain of Oz.

Now, progressing thus far along this Sylvan path, we have learned that the law of survival is preeminent among all laws, overruling them. We have learned that our salient existential threats are three:

1. Ecological collapse, fomented by the sheer numbers of humans, which is predicted conservatively by the United Nations to exceed 11 billion thirsting, hungry consumers by 2100. However, the UN's high estimation is 16 billion by 2100, more than double our present population. As mentioned previously, *The Hathaway Equation* holds a solution to that conundrum, which is not, incidentally, eugenics, sterilization, or compulsory.

2. The religious notion of loving our enemies, especially those who are actively destroying us. We neither love nor hate them. We simply treat them as enemies.

3. Communism: The beguiling wiles of Marxist communism use mind-bending ideas designed to ensnare our people, such as "political correctness," "discrimination," "critical race theory," and a word they coined to cast false guilt upon us, "racism." Such mind-boggling softens up the weak-minded for the slaughter. Indeed, Marxist and Trotskyite communism has killed a conservative estimate of 120 million people and opens the floodgates to those whom Islamic expert Bill Warner, PhD, calculates have killed another 270 million.

No other people can overcome these threats. But we can. As you shall see, our plan to do so is simple yet challenging. Only fear not. For, dear cousins, a fearless heart is the key to every lock. So, with red-blooded courage, made so by the steadfast love of our people and disavowing hatred, let us continue our discussion of Sylvanistic thought with its second premise.

## II. Sylvans Recognize We Are Subjects of Nature

Ancients navigated Orion's star,
That swirling Axis Throne of the Night far,
Center of all heaven's glittering night,
A hunter never closing his eyes bright,

Yet his eyes shall ever and anon gaze,
A thousand thousand years beyond our days,
Planets rotating all in elegance,
Spinning without us in celestial dance.

Rather than a discourse of increasing the forest canopy of our cities, preserving old-growth woods, and returning our aquatic treasures to their pristine condition, all of which we envision, we will, instead, in this section consider the philosophy of submission to nature, our present alienation from it, and how we will once again acquiesce to this, our singular North Star. This philosophy will drive our strategies, which will stimulate a plethora of tactics that we will implement on the ground with our neighbors. Thus, shall be our recrudescence of natural human behavior.

Now, the most expeditious path to emancipating ourselves from plasticine thought and returning to the Garden is to consider facts, many of the most prominent of which have been purposefully distorted. Disambiguating some of these intentionally perverted social norms that influence much of Western thought will be our objective in this chapter, and so we will continue in this vein.

It is both laughable and lamentable that some men feel they should, or could, conquer nature. Yet, far more laughable is the notion, which is incomparably profound in its absurdity, that such a triumph can come from the pitifully small minds of these "masters of the Universe," as they call themselves. The more these concocted lies are believed, the more they beckon t'ward the rocks upon which these imbecilic sirens are perched. So perverse is this notion of nature being subjugated to man that it is dangerous, as proven in its destructive history. One of the first occasions in which we find this worldview is in Genesis 1:28. "And God blessed them, and God said unto them, Be fruitful, and multiply, and replenish the earth, and subdue it: and have dominion over the fish of the sea, and over the fowl of the air, and over every living thing that moveth upon the earth." This admonition has been the philosophical justification for rampaging through field and forest, killing defenseless, innocent animals for several thousand years. Therefore, it begs consideration. However, in doing so, we wish not to cause a quarrel with those who prescribe to biblical beliefs, to whom we extend a hand of genuine friendship. For many Sylvans are believers, while others are what might be called culturally religious.

First, it is noteworthy that the word Earth is misspelled in this verse. It is misspelled in all other translations of the Bible, too. This misspelling is almost ubiquitous in secular literature, as well, so we do not exclusively single out the biblical error. The correct spelling of the word is capitalized, as are all proper places and things. Of course, it could be argued that "earth," in this instance, refers to the soil, yet by reading the remainder of this verse, we see its implication is planetary. What could be a more proper place or thing than the very place and thing upon which we live and, second by second, utterly depend upon for our next breath, our next drink of water, our next meal? The names of the other planets are routinely capitalized, and when they are not, we consider them misspelled. Thus, why do we relegate our planet to a lesser status? It is the subliminal assumption of unmerited privilege. In other words, we take Earth for granted.

Furthermore, the philosophy of Genesis 1:28 excites the lower nature of mankind, which, when given much authority at all, especially unlimited rule, as in this divine command, appeals to its oppressive tendencies. For, it seems most humans are subject to this reactionary state that is almost involuntary in its response and might be the irreducible premise of a torturer. It reminds me of a hunter I knew, fortunately for only a short while, who said, "When I start feeling down, I go out and kill something." I assume his self-esteem was so low that it required this act of imaginary supremacy to boost his poor self-image temporarily. This illusionary state, unconscious in some but conscious in the depraved, of being better than another living being simply because one can kill it, appears to be the solitary motivation for sport hunters. For, after pondering the hunter's lust for "sport" killing, I can find no other reason for wanting to kill an innocent, defenseless animal. This psychosis is the act of transgressing healthy personal boundaries, and, should the hunter's unconscious be given its unadulterated voice through hypnotic trance, it might say: "I must invade another's body to gain *homeostasis*, emotional equilibrium, to feel that I am normal," which is similar to what the hunter said, whom I earlier quoted, but in a more truthful expression.

Sir Thomas More discussed the self-inflicted psychological injury of sport hunting in his masterwork *Utopia*. "But if the pleasure lies in seeing the hare killed and torn by the dogs, this ought rather to stir pity, that a weak, harmless, and fearful hare should be devoured by strong, fierce, and cruel dogs." The Utopians "look on the desire of the bloodshed, even of beasts, as a mark of a mind that is already

corrupted with cruelty, or that at least, by too frequent re-
turns of so brutal a pleasure, must degenerate into it."

It may help the reader's perspective to note that I was
a rifle expert in the army for three years and under solemn
oath to engage the enemy, particularly if that enemy invaded
my homeland, whether it be an equal or unequal contest,
and never surrender, fighting unto the very death. Yet, to kill
an innocent animal for "sport," who has little chance
against a heavily armed, well-equipped hunter, is neither
sport nor manly. The supposition that it could be so is an
absurdity. It is an act of *cowardliness*. That is never the
Sylvanist way. Of course, we do not begrudge a grizzly bear
for salmon fishing or a jaguar for chasing down an impala.
They do so for food, taking no more than they and their
families need. Similarly, if the unlikely event should un-
fold of our isolation in an arctic region where food was not
readily available, then trapping a rabbit and eating it to
survive would simply be obeying the law of survival, the
highest law, which, as we have seen, supersedes all others.

In contrast to Genesis 1:28, rather than subduing and
having dominion over the other animals, Sylvanists appreciate their majesty, beauty, and largely peaceful ways, for
most are herbivores, and, so, we are cognizant that they
have equal claims to the Earth and its bounty.

Let us now consider another way in which behavior
against nature has been popularized, turning literally millions
of unsuspecting people against her. The United States of
America's Declaration of Independence reads, "We hold
these truths to be self-evident, that all Men are created
equal, that they are endowed by their Creator with certain
unalienable Rights, that among these are Life, Liberty and
the Pursuit of Happiness." To appreciate the gist of Thomas
Jefferson's words, we must understand that they were di-

rected to King George III who was imposing tyrannical demands, restrictions, and martial law upon the thirteen British colonies of America and, later, military invasion. "Let Facts be submitted to a candid World," declared Jefferson as he began listing the twenty-seven offenses leveled at the British monarch. So, while the Declaration of Independence was a public announcement of the first-order, it was also clearly an indictment of King George III, which Jefferson knew would be read with the keenest of interest by the king and the peers of his realm. The divine right of kings was the claim of King George to rule over the colonists, but Jefferson was declaring that God created colonists and kings equal by stating that "all men are created equal," and that the divine right of kings is both indivisible and indistinguishable from the divine rights granted to the commoners who colonized New England.

Was Jefferson also saying that two men, one a congenital simpleton, the other a chess grandmaster, are equal? Was he saying that a man who could not budge a bale of hay with both hands and a man who could toss a bale of hay over his head with one hand are equal? Was he saying that a man found guilty of rape, murder, armed robbery, and high treason compared to a physician who saved one hundred cholera patients, sacrificing his life to do so, are equal? In the first cases of these examples, the men are woefully inferior to the later examples. Of course, Jefferson was not implying such men, or all men, were equal, except in their right to life, liberty, and pursuing happiness without the interference of a distant monarch; yet, even these rights could be revoked by law in the third example.

Marxist mind benders have, however, twisted Jefferson's words to imply that all people are equally qualified or can be endlessly educated to be so. Thus, the mentally challenged are rewarded while those possessing a superior intellect are penalized; the least gifted pushed forward, the eminently gifted held back; those with the least integrity, uplifted, those with the highest integrity, dishonored. And, the Marxist mind bender's weaponized perversion of equality exacerbates a law of nature, that is rarely given cognizance and less often spoken of in societally communistic societies such as prevail in Western Europe and North America. Yet, I have articulated it in a way that all may clearly understand: When an inferior is treated as an equal to a superior, the inferior will always try to disrupt, usurp, or even destroy the superior. As we shall see in the proceeding pages, this societal fact is played like a maestro plays his Stradivarius as Marxists instigate race riots, class warfare, and the destruction of the establishment. The Marxists, of course, have nothing with which to replace advanced society, for they are maladroit at all things save destruction, a gift that they have fine-tuned to an art exquisite.

In a sincere expression of goodwill, we want non-Sylvans to truly prosper and excel, having families and rejoicing in their unique and variegated culture; yet, while we are willing to help, we expect them to live at their expense, rather than ours. Approximately $23 trillion of US taxpayers' money has been given to "inner city families" since the 1950s. Some feel that this is reparation for slavery. Yet, let the truth be known, I am unaware of any case of our tribe venturing to Africa to enslave the natives of that continent. This was principally done by slave traders from outside our tribe, whose members were in league with the Ashanti kings of West Africa, who made extraordinary fortunes by enslaving and selling their people. As we have previously noted, it is also intriguing that while over eleven million

slaves from West Africa were sent predominantly to the
Caribbean, Brazil, and North America, over fourteen million were enslaved in East Africa and sent to Arabia.
There, the men were castrated upon arrival, bespeaking of
the heartlessly cruel way in which both men and women
were mistreated by those Saracen slave traders. We hear
nothing, however, of this Saracen enslavement simply because the media cannot cast blame upon us for this
tragedy, as they incorrectly blame us for those who were
enslaved in West Africa and brought to the British Colonies and later to the United States.

Surprisingly, less than four percent of Americans
owned slaves before the Civil War; yet twenty-six percent
of slave owners in New Orleans at that time were Black.
Thus, in New Orleans, it was six times more likely that
slave owners were, in truth, Black. We, in fact, were the
first to end slavery since Cyrus the Great did so around 600
BC. In May of 1772, the judgment of Lord Mansfield freed
a slave, beginning the anti-slavery movement in Britain. William Cowper, an English poet, wrote in 1785: "We have no
slaves at home—Then why abroad? Slaves cannot breathe
in England; if their lungs Receive our air, that moment they
are free. They touch our country, and their shackles fall.
That's noble and bespeaks a nation proud. And jealous of
the blessing. Spread it then, And, let it circulate through
every vein."

Incidentally, long after the British abolished slavery,
Abraham Lincoln's family still owned slaves. Several years
later, the Slavery Abolition Act of 1838 was passed by parliament. Yet, the South was taking steps to free all its
slaves prior to the Civil War. It is important to note that
this war was not fought to free slaves but to centralize the
government, which was the Hamiltonian philosophy,

whereas the Jeffersonian philosophy supported state sovereignty. Debates between the two camps began before the ink dried on the Declaration of Independence. The Hamiltonians could not convince Congress to change the spirit of the founding documents, so they started the Civil War, which is most accurately described as the *War Against the States*, for it usurped state sovereignty, and took more rights from United States Citizens than any other act in history. Indeed, Alexander Hamilton did great harm to the United States of America, and Abraham Lincoln willfully expended the lives of 620,000 fellow citizens, causing many catastrophic injuries and unspeakable misery for the sake of this unlawful power grab.

The Civil War Trust states that "The Civil War was America's bloodiest conflict. The unprecedented violence of battles such as Shiloh, Antietam, Stones River, and Gettysburg shocked citizens and international observers alike. Nearly as many men died in captivity during the Civil War as were killed in the whole of the Vietnam War. Hundreds of thousands died of disease. Roughly two percent of the population, an estimated 620,000 men, lost their lives in the line of duty. As a percentage of today's population, the toll would have risen as high as six million souls."

These facts are important for us to know since they have been purposefully suppressed over decades upon decades as the media and others have blamed many of us for slavery and the Civil War. When first we hear the facts after believing lies, the truth may sound quite strange. Sylvanists, of course, are exceptionally erudite, so their research is cordially invited regarding the matter. The ideological weapons of "unnaturalism" are further reinforced by the Marxist mind benders with their first line of defense, the hallucinogenic blue pill known as political correctness.

We, by bright contrast, are *naturally* correct, meaning
that our philosophy is a derivative of nature, our thinking
based upon nature's patterns. With their mind-numbing,
guilt-inducing weapon against free speech—political correctness—the Marxists have sharply curtailed rational
discussion and, in turn, our freedom. For, we have no freedom without free speech. Of course, this is why the ancient
Greek playwright, Euripides, said, "A slave is anyone who
cannot speak his mind." And so, they have enslaved many
people of the nations, depending solely upon the credulity
of the feebleminded. This is plasticine thought and abhor-
rently unnatural.

Be not deceived, dear reader, the central manufacturer
and global distributor of these synthetic cognitions is
Marxist communism, an ideology unconquered upon the
fall of the Soviet Union, as many assume. This was simply Russia's liberation from communism, along with several
other Eastern European countries. For, at this writing, the
Marxists stride forward, strength upon strength, with ever-
increasing power, enjoying hitherto unknown influence to
break the back of the middle class until there are none but
the poor and the opulently wealthy Marxists themselves.

To be sure, they are not members of the poor working-
class, nor are they their champions as they would have us believe; quite the opposite, their international, economic
hegemony controls every bank and all the economies of the
West, and this with orchestrated oppression. Thus, internationalism is their strategy, nationalism their enemy. And, let
there be no mistaking it amongst those who seek to embrace
nature, political correctness is the Marxist methodology of
suppressing the brightest and best of our societies—in
other words, the aristocracy. For when the Marxists overtly
take over a country, they persecute or kill us, along with the

Christians, and, in a topsy-turvy agenda, replace us with weak-minded people who are easy to control and master in every way. This has been vividly illustrated in Russia, where the Marxists created the Department of Atheism, the only such governmental department in the world at the time, along with special military units, the mission of which was to beat and kill Christians. *The Persecutor,* by young and handsome author Sergi Kourdakov, is his emotive autobiographical account of this iron-fisted oppression, in which he was a squad leader of "persecutors" until he, himself, was converted. Greatly revered Russian historian and author of *The Gulag Archipelago*, Aleksandr Solzhenitsyn, survived such persecutions to warn us of these Marxist anti-Christs. The following is one of the more enlightening quotations in this our tribe's book and worthy of the reader's close examination. Solzhenitsyn said:

"You must understand, the leading Bolsheviks who took over Russia were not Russian. They hated Russia. They hated Christians. Driven by ethnic hatred they tortured and slaughtered millions of Russians without a shred of human remorse. The October revolution was not what you call in America the 'Russian Revolution.' It was an invasion and conquest over the Russian people. More of my countrymen suffered horrific crimes at their bloodstained hands than any people have ever suffered in the entirety of human history. It cannot be understated that Bolshevism was the greatest human slaughter of all time. The fact that most of the world is ignorant of this reality is proof that the global media itself is in the hands of the perpetrators."

I am saddened to report that over thirty million defenseless people, almost all of whom were Russian and
Ukrainian, were murdered by the head of the Red Army,
Leon Trotsky, whose birth name was Lev Davidovich
Bronstein. Many of his victims were worked to death, others
were hideously tortured to death in unspeakable ways, but
most were shot in the back of the head and dumped in mass
graves. The tearful pleading for mercy from terrified
young ladies who were clinging to their newborn babies,
the bitter weeping from sweet little boys and girls, the fran-
tic cries from blossoming young lovers, the confused
trembling of esteemed old fathers of wisdom found no
resonance where a soul was absent within the breast of
these reprobates. All these people of ours were murdered
for two and only two reasons: because they were of European descent and because they were Christians.

There were, however, millions more victims. These
words are emblazoned on the Victims of Communism Memorial in Washington, D.C.: "To the more than one hundred
million victims of communism and to those who love liberty." Some people feel that this estimate is low, with the
high estimation being around one hundred eighty million
lost souls, most of whom were defenseless people who
only wanted to farm the land and raise their families.
We are grateful for this monument.

Yet, where is the outcry of the populace? Why is this
not mentioned in our children's textbooks? Where are the
international days of remembrance? Why is Hollywood
silent, making no movies about it? Whereas there are
countless movies, books, plays, documentaries, and numerous museums and memorials about other atrocities in
which far, far fewer people were executed? Alas, the
heartbreaking story of this unimaginable massacre of some
of the world's finest people is kept a closely held secret,

underscoring Solzhenitsyn's statement that "the global media itself is in the hands of the perpetrators."

It has been many years now since Russia has won her hard fight to free herself from communism, and, as a result, the church is flourishing. In response, former presidential candidate Pat Buchanan wrote, "In the culture war for the future of mankind, Putin is planting Russia's flag firmly on the side of traditional Christianity." And, although he is a United States Citizen, Larry Jacobs with the World Congress of Families made a telling observation: "I think Russia is the hope for the world right now." This is a remarkable statement, yet one with which I agree.

Since the Russian triumph over communism, their aristocracy is blossoming once again. There has even been talk at the highest levels of the Kremlin of reestablishing the Romanov Dynasty. This would be a day of glorious brightness for Russia and her people. Indeed, it would be a day of rejoicing for all our tribe.

Meanwhile, the Marxist mind benders have been extraordinarily successful in Western Europe and North America where they have covertly taken over these regions, the masses therein groomed to think like communists, being forced fed, from cradle to grave, with their invidious, twisted version of "equality." And so, it has become incumbent upon privately owned businesses, by law, to hire unqualified people since they are, nonsensically, according to political correctness, equal to those who are qualified. Noncompliance to these equality laws, known as *affirmative action* in the United States, is heavily penalized, which ensures their universal adherence. Sylvanists, on the other hand, believe that the most qualified person, whomsoever that may be, should be hired.

Yet, those weak-minded of society are quick to accept repetitive suggestions; and, even those of a sturdier mentality are subject to repetitive subliminal messages, neurotically commanding themselves to pretend what they've been told to believe: race does not exist, it is a social construct. These same soft targets for the mind benders would rather fit in with the latest social fashion, even to the point of racial suicide, helping the mind-twisters to ethnically cleanse their race. Their poison message is more easily accepted by those who are loath to think for themselves, preferring emotional reflexes attuned to Pavlov's dogs, rather than a logical assessment. Indeed, they have abdicated their responsibility to think, which is a flagrant crime against nature.

In an allusion to Coleridge's *Rhyme of the Ancient Mariner* in which he writes, "Water, water everywhere, nor not a drop to drink," I say, *Data, data everywhere, nor not a thought to think.* Here within the Information Age, never has factuality been so ignored while warped information, employed as poison, is ubiquitously embraced. Thus, is the Marxist war on nature.

It is immeasurably more important for the trendy set (the political correctees who vehemently deny that they are politically correct) to satisfy others who give not a whit for their welfare as, together, clinging to their cell phones, they rush headlong over the cliff. And, let there be no question about it, cell phones are programming—politically correct programming and wholly unnatural. Vegetating before a computer in a catatonic stupor is an exchange of robust life for puppetry. In a similar exchange for life, *The New York Times* recently revealed that the average American watches 5 hours and 4 minutes of television each day; that's 304 minutes a day, 110,960 hours a year, 554,800 hours every five years, 1,109,600 hours every ten years.

Now, give thought to the population of the United States:

(324,420,000 US population) x

(1,109,600 hours watching television every ten yrs.)

= 359,976,432,000,000 lost man-hours every ten years.

Rounded, that is 360 trillion man-hours lost every ten years and 720 trillion man-hours lost every twenty years. These astonishing figures represent the United States alone. This comatose stare into the bluish poison glow is mesmerizing many, many more people the world over, causing unfathomable human degradation.

In his work of wisdom *Politics*, Aristotle says such mass manipulation is the technique of tyrants. "Also, he [a tyrant] should impoverish his subjects; he thus provides against the maintenance of a guard by the citizen and the people, having to keep hard at work, are prevented from conspiring. The Pyramids of Egypt afford an example of this policy; also the offerings of the family of Cypselus, and the building of the temple of Olympian Zeus by the Peisistratidae, and of the great Polycratean monuments at Samos; all these works were alike intended to occupy the people and keep them poor."

Whereas the ancients had the pyramids, the temple of Zeus and the monuments at Samos to show for their work, we have nothing to show for watching television or a computer screen for decades except the lock-step penalization for original thinking and the implanting of synthetic thoughts. These portals to hell, which we call television and cell phones, block the path to the health and well-being of your everlasting soul, placing it in imminent jeopardy. Remove them or reduce their use, for it is how you, my dear reader, are being programmed for self-destruction.

Finally, although it is axiomatic to many of us, I suppose it can never be overstated, or stated too frequently, that we are members of nature. For many have disavowed their natural membership, not as often with words as with unnatural actions; and these actions, dear cousins, are a spiritual malignancy that metastasizes with geometric momentum across our precious Earth. This, our fall from grace, may have begun when our forefeet and legs became hands and arms, if this, in fact, happened at all. Or, perhaps, the upward gait was our creator's beckoning; either way, I assume we have not been terribly pleasing to our Lord. Yet, now that we are upright and an anomaly among other mammals, we must be reminded that we are members of a family of living wonders rather than the "crown of creation," destined to use our hands and arms to serve our fellow recipients of divine light, whether bipeds, quadrupeds, or the flora upon which we are utterly interdependent.

And so, should our souls yet possess an atom of living light, we stand hushed and bowed before the Giver of Life for these wrongdoings. Yet, because the Infinite is miraculously generous with perfect forgiveness, we are given new chances, new beginnings every morning. "Great is thy faithfulness." Amidst our errors, should we but turn away from darkness to behold the Light, we are even given the divine grace to laugh and make sanguine plans for the future; for we are divinely, genetically predisposed to a keen sense of humor, to visualizing bright plans over the horizon.

At last, and at last, the premise of our alienation from nature is simply self-alienation, the reconciliation of which is a pathway of facts, where few dare venture.

III. Love is a positive, constructive force.

We can understand certain things, such as art, by first understanding their opposites, as these tend to accent the true shape, color, and balance of the objects of our inquiry. In this way, the authentic values of hues, curves, and juxta-positions are more fully appreciated. Likewise, we can understand much about love by considering its diametric counterpart, which we will now attempt.

First, we denounce hatred, animosity, revenge, and even complaining because it literally kills us. For, hatred is the ultimate form of complaining. And complaining is, therefore, a modified form of hatred that debilitates our bodies. Yes, when we complain in an antagonistic way, our body releases cortisol, a death hormone that attacks the adrenal glands, quite literally making us sick, thus shortening our lives. Be calm.

Think of King Charles I. He was calm and profoundly dignified before the executioner's axe, though he had many justified complaints, and over time, he made these with dignity according to law. Yet, when they were unlawfully denied, having done everything that could be done, he bade farewell to his sweet wife and little children to face death with an elevation of character that none could forget. His noble decorum before the executioner caused remorse among the people and even regret amongst his enemies. Perhaps, it would be good to think of him when we are cut off in traffic, when a product we have purchased is defec-tive, or when a customer service representative is woefully incompetent. Be calm. Even before the many-headed beast that seeks our extermination, be calm amidst the perilous fight, all the while focusing on that bright and morning star, the love of our people.

Secondly, we denounce hate because it imperils our

very souls. Now, this is a great mystery that the author does not pretend to understand fully, yet it appears that events within the corporeal world are manifestations of those occurring within the world unseen. In other words, should we do harm to our bodies with hatred, correspondingly, we may, perhaps, harm our everlasting souls as well. If true, this is the foremost reason to denounce hate. However, it was explained second because it could not be appreciated without first defining the way in which hatred harms our temporal bodies.

Third, hatred harms society and its several members, whereas we want our societies and the individuals who comprise them to thrive with abundant living. What is more, our ethical scales are balanced by favor or fault toward the family; consequently, harming an individual member of society inadvertently impairs the family.

Therefore, rather than hating our enemies, which creates negativity and destruction, it is far more intelligent to focus our energies on loving our Sylvan tribe, for this begets positivity and constructiveness. Yes, though it may seem *cliché*, love is, indeed, the answer. This does not mean we are lilies of the field or delicate snowflakes offended at every turn, melting before a single molecule of opposition. Not at all, dear cousins. As King Alfred the Great was made mighty in battle by his love for his Saxon tribe, we are made mighty by our devoted love for our tribe, Sylvan. And so, like him, we love our people and this deeply. For love is bold and brave and unafraid, wherewith a man lifts his face to clean sunlight with nothing to hide from any living being in all the world.

Hate, by contrast, is, as we have seen, channeled through certain ideologies, some feigning to be religions, some of which pretentiously champion the working class. Has paranoia become an accomplice of their hatred so that they fear to show the true colors of the banner they march beneath? For, doesn't hatred perpetually cling to the shadows for fear of being found out? Since these charlatans are bereft of love, they are quite literally incapable of building anything that rivals our societies or replacing them with another social structure except one in which all the world becomes their slaves. In this way, they hope to destroy our tribe and every last vestige of it. Therefore, let them fight from below. We shall fight from on high.

## IV. Ethics

The family—a man, a woman, and their children—is the irreducible bedrock of society. Therefore, anyone harming the family, harms society, from which we derive our protection, our security, our neighborhoods, our national identity, and even our racial identity. Why, then, should we countenance, even in the slightest way, the chipping away at our social foundation, the family? To do so is ludicrous. Likewise, harming the flora and fauna is counter-logical, even suicidal, since we are simply their ecological comembers and utterly interdependent with them for air, water, and food. Thus, Sylvanists measure the question of ethics, of good and evil, and the variegated degrees within that wide spectrum by posing these questions:

Is it good for the family? Does it harm the family? How will it affect the family? Is it good for the flora and fauna? Does it harm them, and how will it affect them?

This is true north of our ethical compass. We do not claim to be right all the time, attributing this claim instead to the compass itself. Nor do we claim to be the compass. We simply measure ourselves against it. Unless we tacitly differentiate between the compass and ourselves, we shall become moral imposters. For a compass is not human. And it would be the grandiosest of frauds to feign godlike qualities, a twisted pretension that moralists and religionists often attempt.

Moreover, because of our human nature, which is endlessly counterintuitive, at times, we harm both the family and the flora and fauna. We readily admit this, though with humble remorse. Yet, while confessing this shortcoming, we do not abandon our standards or the sincere desire to align with them as much as we can. For this alignment is society. In other words, the point at which line $c$ (compass) intersects line $h$ (human nature) is point $s$ (society), with lines $c$ and $h$ being mutually unique even within their intersection, which illustrates the isolated distinction of ethics from individual.

So, while we bear the standard, we are not its epitome; we merely uphold it the best we can because therein lie the purest elements of civilized society. Neither do we uplift it because we are good but quite the opposite, and there is human comfort in this reconciliation not enjoyed in vain religiosity; remember, neither Christ nor Buddha were profoundly religious but spiritually minded.

It might be helpful to conceive of the Universe as imperfect and humans as possibly its most imperfect residents. Thus, we belong here, imperfections, as the world around us is imperfective. And this comforting acceptance is found within the folds of Sylvanistic thought, which does not require its adherents to be right all the time or to be ethical examples, although we may, at times, do so unwittingly, for, remember, it is not us but the compass itself that points the way.

Now, we will discuss the family and its present conundrum. Thus, let us begin at the beginning—parenting. Good parents are keenly aware that during infancy, the wiggling attempts of motor control, the fear of a strange new world, colossal and frightfully odd, the proper utility yet unknown of their extended tiny hands and feet, all together must be acknowledged with tender maternal and paternal gesticulations, and this without fail. The normal mother and father will do so involuntarily; indeed, these infantile gestures shall be an irresistible charm, endlessly entertaining, and many times more so than all the worldly theatrical productions might muster. Moreover, we must be mindful that this infantile body language is a veritable mime played out by our son or daughter, a heroic effort to communicate by this new little Earthling. To be sure, baby is born into a foreign clime and terrain, and whereas other animals will adapt in a few weeks unto self-sufficiency, humans require many years to build *psychocentric*[11] foundations due to our cerebral capacity, which is virtually inexhaustible in some cases.

Consequently, mother and father, please let there be no mistaking it; these wigglings are more than wiggles. They are pantomimes purposefully conducted with all the courageousness that a baby can mobilize as a fully-justified cry for your help. Should these venturesome signalings be ignored, that future man or woman shall be unable to relate to others easily and, depending upon the austerity of the neglect, might be without natural affection. So, it is unlikely that we can overemphasize the importance of your parenting and attention, for it will indelibly mold the personhood of your son or daughter.

In addition to the acknowledgment of our children's efforts to gain our attention, which we may incorrectly interrupt as mere squirming, lovingly holding them is preeminent amongst every act of parenting besides feeding. *Development and Psychology* revealed that in infants from environments where parenting and normal touching were absent, the stress hormone cortisol significantly differed from children raised by normal parents, the difference even lasting into adolescence. Cortisol is released in re-

---

[11] Psychocentric is a word I coined that means the understanding that we are individual and separate from others, which is the premise of healthy boundaries that are essential for a well-adjusted, productive life.

sponse to fear or stress by the adrenal glands, and is commonly known as the "fight-or-flight" response chemical. Elevated cortisol levels disturb learning and memory, lower immune function and even affect bone density; it may also increase the instances of high blood pressure, cholesterol, heart disease, depression, mental illness, and contribute to a lower life expectancy. Levels of cortisol remained notably higher in children who had lived in orphanages longer than eight months than in those who lived there only four months. So, we see that only four months without normal touching can have not only psychological but lasting physiological effects, a poignant illustration of the acute need for children to be lovingly touched and held by their parents—not sent to daycare or school at age two.[12]

Today, albeit, we see parents doing this very thing: sending their babies to school at two years of age and younger, a practice that has become the choice of many "sophisticated" parents who are "in the know" and, perhaps, a little too lazy to care for their babies at a time when they so dearly need them. I wonder if any of them know this method was introduced by Marxist Leonid Sabsovich. Working under the communist dictatorships of Lenin and Stalin, he argued for a separation of children from parents starting in the earliest years of childhood development in order to atomize the family and then control its separated members. Indeed, Sabsovich said, "The question of joint dwelling for children and their parents can only be answered in the

---

[12] For further insight into the brilliant opportunity of parenting, read *The Warmth of the Sun* toward the end of Part IV.

negative. Infants are best located in special buildings where the mothers can visit for feeding." He continues by saying, "Pre-school and school-age children should spend most of their time in spaces designed for their learning, productive work, and leisure. It is clearly pointless to provide space for them in the same dwelling as their parents, where they would return at night."

This is sublime madness. Yet, it is a madness not surprising to see in Western nations, most of which are societally communistic, their citizens marching in lockstep cadence to the tune of mind benders whose ultimate agenda is precisely identical to that of Sabsovich.

By sharp contrasts, good parents know that birth to five are the determining years in which children, our future men or women, are psychologically programmed, and this irreversibly. It is hoped that by good parenting, our children will progress in a timely manner through the emotional stages from infancy, to adolescence, to adulthood. Nevertheless, although their infancy or adolescence might be perpetually galvanized by irresponsible parenting, the normal life span will chronologically carry them down, down a torrid river in which they are unable to swim. Inexorably along, they are tossed upon tormenting wave, some gasping for air, others drowning, as they are helplessly swept along from minor to young adult, to adult, middle age to elderly, each stage bearing the stamp of pre-adolescence or adolescence but never emotional adulthood. Some have only a dim inkling that adulthood exists, its nebulous concept fading in and out of consciousness, now a fog, now a diffused vapor. For bad parenting is not something one outgrows. Although it can be managed, it is permanent.

Therefore, pseudo-modern ideas of leaving children at daycare at the age of two, or any time during their first five years, is woefully nonsensical and dangerous. Contrariwise, infants who are lovingly held for long periods, let's say at least fifteen to twenty minutes at a time, and gently touched and acknowledged every few minutes during their waking hours grow and gain weight more normally than babies without this contact. What is more, they tend to require less time in the hospital after birth and encounter fewer medical complications during their first year. Let there be no mistake. These are life-giving touches. For, those without them, although they receive adequate feeding, bathing, and medical attention, may die from lack of acknowledgment. This was graphically exemplified during the 1980s in Romanian orphanages wherein extremely high infanticide rates were observed, although the babies were provided with essentials, excluding routine touching due to insufficient staffing.

So, while passing on the golden baton of our genetics is the most intelligent way of leaving good works behind us and, therefore, we should do so prolifically within the bounds of marriage, we also reverently embrace the somber responsibilities of carefully parenting our children, our priceless treasures. For therein lies our future Athens.

In addition to targeting children for destruction, Marxists expend enormous time and energy sowing the seeds of strife amongst our men and women. These noxious seeds, a plethora of which are sown among us, slowly strangulate our people with animosity, even hatred, then separate us from those who would otherwise become a spouse, whose tender love and support might further draw our green and growing souls t'ward the Sun.

Therefore, let us not speak ill of our men or women, giving the beast a foothold to drag us down amongst its miserable denizens who grope in darkness. Rather than critiquing the opposite sex, let us critique ourselves. For, we must be fully attentive to our growth should we hope to respond to the divine unction, lest we vicariously seek the life force of another and so become psychologically parasitical. Instead, as men and women who are each wholly complete and thus available to unite as one, let us hand-in-hand lift our faces to Sunrise light. This act is the premise of our ethics, for, as you recall, anything that harms the family is one of those many shades of evil. This, of course, includes those who would sow salt within our garden, so green, in wicked hopes that they might kill our life-giving seeds before they germinate and bloom. Let the reader, therefore, be infused with ideas that cause Marxian ideologies to retreat and vanish as snow before the cloudless springtide:

Men will attract good women not by waiting for them to come along nor by seeking them out. Men will find good women by becoming good men. We will thus set our sights on the alpha male for our template. Though Alfred is "beyond the hopes of emulation," should measuring us against his standard make us stand a little taller, a little truer, then it will be a worthy endeavor.

Like the great king, an alpha male needn't disparage women. He hasn't the need. For, rarely does a good man belittle others, particularly those who adore him. Women come to him, follow him, admire him. They know he is in charge. He doesn't fawn over women with saccharine niceties, thereby signaling surrender before the spinning electricity begins. Of course, a woman may accept the surrender, that is, if it is permanent. The alpha knows this and chooses not to set this imbalanced precedence. He, instead, allows the woman he admires to think about him from afar, which creates the anticipation she relishes within her heart. He asks himself—"Do I want her to be the mother of my children?" Can he agree with the Athenian of long centuries ago who said this to his bride: "The pleasure to me will be this, that, if you prove yourself my superior, you will make me your servant and there will be no fear lest with advancing years your influence shall wane; nay, the better companion you are to me and the better guardian of the house to our children, the greater will be the esteem which you are held at home; and all will admire you . . . ." This is the way in which an alpha male courts a lady. He does not see how many mares he can add to his stables; virility may be male, but it is not manliness.

Such apothegms are all very well and good, but what of the fifty years that men live under the influence of that heavy drug testosterone? It is not easy.

An alpha is never haughty unless, for example, in an expression of his distaste for political correctness, which he unapologetically disdains. In contrast as brilliant as death and life itself, he is naturally correct, attuned to the honest roughness of the wild without forsaking gentlemanliness. The manly man hardens his body with weightlifting, aerobics, and meals of life-giving greens and fruits. His height matches his proper body weight. He stands like a man, with feet spread wide, head high, shoulders back; it feels normal to place his fist on his hips, not in his pockets. These mannerisms are as flashing beams of light to women, pulsating with excitations they rarely see and feel.

He makes his way in life. He eats well, lives well. This does not mean he is necessarily wealthy, for wealth is most clearly *not* the measure of a man; as we have seen, many cowardly betas weasel their way into riches, the sumptuousness of which "turns to gravel in their mouths." Simultaneously, an alpha will quickly grasp an ethical opportunity to make more money should it arise, knowing all the while that he "can meet with triumph and disaster and treat those two imposters just the same." Either way, he finds a way to win. For, he must build a nest. It needn't be palatial. But it must be safe and stable, a place of refuge as "far from the madding crowd" as possible. It is his responsibility to pay the bills and keep plenty of food on the table for himself, his wife, and children. If a man has done these deeds, he has done his duty. Yet, should a man also be a source of strength and kindness, should he be calm amidst the storm that assails his life and the several lives about him, then he has done more than many a great king.

This, however, has been made treacherously complex for our men. By law, others who are less qualified must be hired in his place and promoted, with hardly a threat of being fired. He represents the only social subset without a hiring quota of any kind, a student union or fraternity at his university, generous scholarships based upon his race and gender, lending preferences from banks, business start-up aid from the government, and many other privileges. He has a lesser legal standing in court. These disadvantages alone make building and maintaining a nest quite challenging beyond the normal trials of marriage and leading children through infancy and adolescence.

We must, and will, change these social norms and laws that are against our men.

Having a family is yet further convoluted for our men. The *Oedipal complex*, the cause of uncounted ruination of otherwise healthy families, is an often-unknown mental disease that simply must be understood before marrying and having children. Thus, we will discuss it later in this section.

Indeed, this complex and source of dysfunction is poignantly exacerbated by feminism, a gross misnomer since it is the very antithesis of femininity and, in fact, seeks to crush women. And so, we will now give attention to this bewitching Marxian strategy with the intent of carrying a torch for women because we love them for many reasons. Foremost of which is because of their very nature. Secondly, they are integral to the family nucleus. Third, because of their incomparable beauty among all women. Thus, we carry this torch to penetrate those nooks and crannies with arc lit clarity, desperately hidden by the communist social engineers whose intent is "the turning" of a warm living heart, to one of corpse-cold stone.

So, never in the least do we accuse or attack our women. For, this would be to fall prey to the very trap set for us, the gender wars. It is with this benevolence that we shall continue by considering the Marxists' orchestrated atomizing of the family.

As Marxists cajole common working men into an enticing social contract of status and economic promise, yet in which they receive less than they had before, so they beguile women into a gaily painted panacea that she often discovers all too late, is *hell*. Therein she is captured in the curse of looking backward, envisioning the missed love, the missed family, the missed fulness of life. It is true, dear friends, that some women choose not to have a family for what may be good reasons. Some of our cousins endured intense trauma as children and are unable to cope when re-experiencing these episodes vicariously through their family, a replication of events too terrifying to manage. Others simply want their freedom. These, and other reasons are perfectly acceptable.

On the other hand, there are a great multitude of our beautiful women who have been swindled into sacrificing their children and the faithful companionship of a husband through planned duplicity wherein the blessed touch of baby, the expanse of love unapprehended and, therefore, unimaginable of that innocent touch reaching to you, her worshiped goddess, is swept forever away. The life-bearing touch, channeling divine light to her, and a purer light from her unto you . . . your many pasteled paradise gone astray. The pretty dresses, the birthday cakes, and parties, hearing her cherubesque first prayer for mommy, the tearful parting for first grade, the hilarious antics and dress-ups, the prom, graduation day, college, her wedding day until your baby's baby comes to you. Then, once again, the touch of radiance is all about you. As we shall see in Part IV, William Shakespeare devotes seventeen sonnets to this beauty, this wonder, and especially this wisdom of having children.

But dearest cousins, Marxists trap their feminine victims by encouraging promiscuity while scorning those who would become mothers. In his work *Marx, Engels and the Abolition of the Family*, Richard Weikart says that Marx and Engels envisioned a society in which "People would no longer be subject to what is natural. Even if people had a natural bond to their children, no provision of this would be made in communist society. Thus, any sexual relationship between mutually consenting persons would be possible. What would not be possible would be the security of a life-long marriage." Marx and Engels would have been ebullient over the successful implementation of their ideology in American and European culture. For, the spell is cast, the web is woven with the sweet, unctuous words of the media, twisted to beckon our tribe across healthy psychological boundaries; words exampled by Orwellian doublespeak such as *women's liberation* and *feminism*, both intentional oxymorons of sorts cleverly designed to disorient both hearer and speaker. As we shall see, the women's movement is merely a glove, Marxist communism the cruel iron fist within this glove that crushes women.

Let us be quick to acknowledge, once again, we do not cast blame upon our women, for they, along with most of our men, have been beguiled in every way by our foes, the august masters of mendacity. Given the grandiose magnitude of their lying apparatus, the almost inexhaustible depths of their war chest, all driven by maniacal wantonness, it is a near wonder that any of us have been able to unravel the formulaic encryptions of their stealthy plans.

But we know.

True feminists, the most virulent of whom are from outside our tribe, are dedicated Marxists and merely a fashionable version of Rip van Winkle's termagant wife, the busy-body gossip who would rather ruin an innocent life than speak a kind word. She is the poison-tongued backbiter, pompously singing hymns of political correctness, who so richly deserves the name hypocrite. These "silly sin-laden women" merely channel their unhappiness via feminism, a pseudo-ideology as empty as the vacancy between their ears. Each one being nothing more than, in a word, a *troublemaker*. Even so, let us again underscore that these are the enemies from without our tribe who so richly merit our judgment, these extra tribal foes who "creep into houses, and lead captive silly women laden with sins, led away with divers lusts." So, it is with genuine empathy that we must ask all our tribe, "What evil spell hath bewitched thee?"

Now, there can be little doubt that some women need to be liberated from, let us say, a bad marriage. This is not a point to be debated. Doubtlessly, some men need liberation from the same. So, the argument that only women need liberation is somewhat of a moot point since men could make the identical argument with equal rationale and vigor. Thus, as we direct this inquiry appropriately toward the communist culprit, we ask, *liberate women from what, unto what?* Is it liberation to work forty hours a week in high-pressure jobs, placing women on par with men's incidence of heart attacks, hair loss, and stress-related emotional problems? Have the Marxists benevolently liberated women from a man's protection, many of these same men being perfectly agreeable and eager to pay all their wive's bills? The valiant fight for freedom portrayed in Hollywood's depiction of the oppressed woman is a small percentage of such cases. Quite the opposite, these "kindly" mind benders have liberated women from the generally stable, but certainly not perfect, environment of a home and the love of a family, and in this way, negated the lives of millions of babies who would have grown to become the future men and women of our societies. After all, 'tis easier than their mass murder programs; and in this plan, mothers stop the beating hearts of their babies—over sixty million in the United States since 1973.

If not for the Marxists' "liberation" of women from the bonds of marriage, many millions more would have been granted divine life. Thus, the Marxists' crowing altruism: they have liberated women from returning the ultimate gift that our ancestors valiantly vouchsafed, hour by hour, day by day, through 400 centuries[13] of

---

[13] The Smithsonian National Museum of Natural History estimates that the remains of Anatomically Modern Humans, referred to as Cro-Magnon, are approximately 30,000 old. "The skull of Cro-Magnon 1 does show traits that are unique to modern humans, including the tall, rounded skull with a near vertical forehead. A large brow ridge no longer tops the eye sockets, and there is no prominent prognathism of the face and jaw." However, archaeologist K. Krist Hirst says, "Neanderthals all died out between 41,000–39,000 years ago—probably at

struggling ascent—the gift of life itself. This most heinous of thefts, colossal in its scope, could singularly be
planned by the reprobated mind perfected, a trait in which
they glory. Let there be no doubt, the success of this fiend-
ish assault ignites cheers amongst the mind benders. For,
although they have used traitorous members of our tribe as a
mask to carry out their devilish desires in their appointed political cabinets, in spurious elections, and, unwittingly, on
the battlefield, the destruction of our tribe is cardinal
amongst their stratagems.

As a result, they must "liberate" women from becoming
mothers—to implement the ethnic cleansing of our people.

Yet, as the living nucleus of the family, women
have matched tone to tint of children's character, and our
resulting societies, rich with every note and coloring of
abundance, peace, and liberties unparalleled. However, in a
single generation, women were culturally chastised relent-
lessly by the media for being wives, for being mothers,
the media-mongers looking down in lofty, supercilious superiority upon anyone who dares to step beyond the poison
boundaries of political correctness. It is reminiscent of Aldous Huxley's prophetic warning of our not fully human
society in *Brave New World,* wherein the word "motherhood" is met with gasps of horror.

---

least partly a result of competition with early modern humans—but their
genes and those of the Denisovans live on within us." H.G. Wells states
in his work *The Outline of History* "But finally, between 50,000 and
25,000 years ago, as the Fourth Glacial Age softened towards more
temperate conditions, a different type came upon the European scene,
and, it would seem, exterminated Homo Neanderthals." Because of this
disparity, the representative figure of 40,000 years is used in this book.

Yet, onward, the surrealism goes as women are cor-ralled like cattle into the confines of these unnatural borders, wherein they are prodded ideologically to violate their personal and psychological boundaries. The media mantra being something akin to . . . cross these societal boundaries that have enriched the families of your ancestors for thousands of years . . . cross your personal boundaries that guard your children and family or face persecution by the "trendophiles." Although empty-headed scarecrows, the trendophiles possess genuine influence among women, and this is why Madison Avenue marketing is based upon the desire of women to please others, giving fashion gurus whimsical license to introduce "the latest must-have" every few months.

This soft point, this vulnerability of women's wishes to please, is exacerbated by the misnomer of women's lib-eration, which, in turn, exacerbates the phenomenon known as the Oedipus complex, which was mentioned earlier.

Understanding childhood emotional progression is an extremely valuable by-product of understanding this psy-chological complex, dramatically portrayed in the brilliant work *Oedipus Rex*, written by one of our Slavic cousins, an ancient Greek tragedian named Sophocles. If we hope to re-store the family, it is important to understand the Oedipus complex, for this destructive dynamic has been exacerbated to epidemic proportions by the women's movement. Of course, as we have mentioned, the women's movement is merely the glove, Marxist communism the cruel iron fist within that glove that crushes women. And so, we learn far reaching insight to save the family by understanding *Oedipus Rex:*

In Sophocles' play, a warning is given to King Laius that his son will one day kill him. He asks his wife, Queen

Jocasta, to kill the child. Yet she cannot, and so asks a servant to take the child to the wilderness, leaving him to die. But a compassionate shepherd rescues the boy and takes him to King Polybus of Corinth, who raises him as his own. The boy becomes a man, his true royal lineage unbeknownst to him. One day he is driving his chariot down a narrow pathway, wherein he meets another charioteer approaching from the opposite direction. The opposing chariot is driven by his kingly father, who claims royal prerogative and the right of way. Oedipus does not yield, for, although unaware, he too is of regal blood. Their argument leads to challenges, escalating to a fight in which King Laius, as was predicted long ago, is killed by his son. Oedipus then drives his chariot to his dead father's kingdom, informing the queen that he has killed her husband. They are rapturously attracted to one another and become lovers. He ascends to the throne, assuming his father's role. Then, as fate would have it, Oedipus discovers the horrifying truth—he has killed his father and is in the midst of a torrid love affair with no one less than his mother, the queen. With this abysmal revelation, Queen Jocasta hangs herself, and Oedipus gouges out his eyes.

Not an altogether happy-go-lucky play is this, but imperatively enlightening for our discussion. In like manner, women who are "liberated" sometimes instigate unnatural loyalties from a son, siding with him against her husband, the boy's father. This may be so very subtly tempting since a mother's son is a half physical personification of herself and, moreover, came from her womb and was nursed by her. The encouragement of the mother needn't be expressed in words, although sometimes this occurs. Without the proper boundaries and a little maternal encouragement, the boy becomes pretender to the throne rightfully occupied

by the father, and chaos ensues. This sickness is rarely con-
summated physically, yet sometimes, I regret to say, it is so.
Such madness must be reported to the proper authorities
without delay. For, even in cases of less extremism in which
the Oedipal syndrome is purely emotional, it is uniquely destructive within families—a collision of the Sun and Moon
with the Earth afire.

At the same time, an infant boy naturally has a crush on
his mother; this is perfectly normal, but this infantile infatuation  must be outgrown by five years of age with the aid of
gentle discipline. It should not really go on beyond this point,
being lovingly discouraged by mother as she teaches her
children  proper boundaries, especially that mother and father enjoy a secluded bedroom, which is off limits to
them once they reach the age of five. Of course, the
mother must possess healthy boundaries herself before she
can teach them to her children between the crucial devel-
opmental period of birth and five years.

Even after the age of five, children will need to knock
on the bedroom door when frightened by imaginary monsters
or  thunder or when needing a drink of water. Yet, there must
be exclusivity in the parental relationship, in general,
demonstrating a tender but firm off limits. In this way, the
children will learn in a kindly but gently effective way that
father and mother are too big for their competition. Parents
needn't be the slightest bit unkind in establishing this rule
of bedroom seclusion and other forms of exclusivity. Simply remember that setting boundaries will help your child
develop normally from infantilism to adolescence to
adulthood, whereas subjects of the Oedipal complex will
likely remain suspended in infancy, even through old age.

It is important to note that the Oedipal complex has a
mirror image: the Electra complex, which is "the unre-

solved, unconscious libidinous desire of a daughter for her father." We may assume, without supporting quantitative analysis, this is more prevalent in a chauvinistic society.

Overall, it is an emotional and ethical law to which we are all subject: infancy must be completed before the stage of adolescence can begin, which must be completed before the commencement of adulthood, and this sequentially, although many people attempt skipping a stage or two.

Think of an infant child: he or she is busy crossing virtually every boundary, and this is to be expected and is even endearing and endlessly entertaining while doing so. Now, think of an infant-adolescent man: he, too, is busy crossing every boundary, except that it is neither endearing nor entertaining. It matters not if he is endued with a sparkling of charismatic lure, as this will merely enable more infantile-adolescent trespassing. In the rarified instance that he may, somehow, acquire fame and fortune, he is even so forever beset with legal and relationship quandaries. Think now of an infant-adolescent woman: though she may be blest with breathtaking beauty, a magnetic, effervescent personality, and charm, she will, yet, be a continuous interloper who must, tragically, be chased away or chooses to run away herself. In both cases, the man and woman never advanced to adolescence with enough solid footing to remain there but vacillated to and fro in regressions to infancy. Throughout human history, and without exception, skipping the stages of personality development has never worked. To attempt it is a violation of a fundamental law established by nature, one that has sweeping ethical implications.

Another metaphysical poison arrow within the quiver of those who attack our ethical values is the notion that certain initiated persons have attained their sophisticated superiority in large part to their irreverence. Yet, reverence is natural. It is the norm. It seems, however, that no one is to be revered, except the media moguls, of course, and this most deeply, along with a few whom they carefully select. Included are their manufactured, propped-up demagogues who compete to see who can most loudly parrot the teachings of their patron saints: Marx, Lenin, and Trotsky. These persons and their minions shall be worshiped. The media will ensure it with false portrayals of them, even inventing quotes, that they never made and attributing these to them. It matters neither how vapid their true morals nor the true depravity to which they descend—the lower, the better. All must be irreverent.

Even the local ballet was recently touted as particularly acclaimed because of its irreverence. And, "coming of age," a euphemism for irreverently casting away one's virginity as though it were a dirty garment, is a manifestation of this supposed enlightenment, replicated endlessly in the media's every satellite. Promiscuity, however, is a hallmark of mental illness and a prescription for unhappiness. For, promiscuity, and all other variations of irreverence, always involve crossing our own, and others, personal boundaries, the respectful awareness of which is rudimentary to mental health. One need only give thought to the synonyms of irreverence to comprehend the media's intent: derision, discourtesy, impertinence, insult, mockery, profanity, ridicule, rudeness, sinfulness, blasphemy.

Young people are extremely susceptible to these ideological weapons since they are striving to overcome the gravitational pull of infancy on their quest to adolescence, then, from adolescence, attempting the giant leap to adulthood. This journey is not easy. So, it is natural for young people to want to do it themselves, rejecting parental advice and authority. And thus, they are rebelling partly for this reason. To some degree, this is healthy and normal. Yet, at the same time, Marxists seek to exacerbate this normal, innocuous rebellion by encouraging them to accept irreverence, and all its synonyms, as somehow witty and cultivated. For instance, I was invited to spend the Christmas holidays with friends, whose festivities included watching a Christmas movie. The writer, director, producer, and stars of this "Christmas" movie were, alas, all non-Christians, each of whom ironically possessed a pronounced antipathy for Christ and Christians; and irony upon irony, my hosts were, themselves, unsuspecting Christians. The movie was replete with crude language, rude behavior, and overt meanness, which the children of my host adored.

As Sylvanists, of course, we are not prudish. Be that as it may, vulgarity is neither entertaining nor clever. Such irreverence is an affront to one's soul, enabling its slow, unperceived asphyxiation, the foremost symptom of which is increasing blindness to beauty until its invisibility.

The paramount reverse of these "deaththoughts" is awe in the presence of the divine, in which one thousand, thousand beauties, invisible to others, are brilliantly luminous before us. This, dear cousins, is natural.

The reader may yet well ask: Why has irreverence, in general, and boundaries, specifically, attained such prominence in this, our book? Because reverence and boundaries are together the spiritual garden wall, unseen yet in every way vitally real, saving us and our children from a wasted life amidst crime and the sheer misery of serial dysfunctional relationships. For, no matter how petty or pernicious, whether a violation of law, or a violation of personal relationships, every crime is a case of trespassing across boundaries. Thus, ethics defined with a single word is *boundaries*.

Now, continuing our discussion of ethics, the Polaris of which is the traditional family: atop the very pinnacle of absurdity, the Marxist mind-bending saboteurs propose that male equals female and female equals male. These lies are, perhaps, the uttermost incongruity to nature. Perversion, as this, seems to geometricize like a disease, infecting all about it yet has no effect upon the ice-cold facts—the sexes are anatomically, chemically disparate. And, as we have seen, women and men are chromosomally distinct; the XX sex chromosome is present within a woman's cells, whereas men's cellular composition includes XY. Moreover, a higher infusion of testosterone causes most men to possess broader shoulders, greater height, strength, and stamina, allowing them to play sports faster, with superlative performance. If this were not so, why are there women's sports? Men and women should play these sports together if they are physiologically equal. But, according to elemental biology and sports statistics, they are decisively not. That is one reason Sylvanists enthusiastically applaud women's sports, encouraging strong, healthy athletic women. Women's tennis, for instance, is a well-watched women's sport because, in addition to testing the limits of endurance and mental strength, it simultaneously accentuates the fluid grace and beauty of the female physique. No doubt, some of the most thrilling matches are among the women.

Some tasks, however, require manliness. I recall when my squadron was on a maneuver through a heavily forested area, each man carrying a little over forty pounds of combat gear. We also brought along a machine gun weighing eighty-four pounds, which we took turns carrying. So, during his turn, each man carried over one hundred-twenty pounds of gear in that sweltering heat. It was not easy. But it was a fanciful waltz in the park compared to other as-signments. And, although some of our women are statuesque with beautifully defined muscularity and are aerobically fit, few women could have carried their weight, figuratively and literally, during that mission. The notion of women on that mission is preposterous simply because that assign-ment was testosterone-driven and, consequently, had no biological basis for them. So, such observations should not initiate debate about superiority or inferiority of one sex over another, unless the debater can first demonstrate the superiority of an orange above that of an apple.

Women attain astonishing heights, often excelling men in other areas. The works of Mary Ann Evans, known by the pen name George Elliott, are in the author's opinion, unsurpassed in their literary brilliance, most poignantly demonstrated in *Silas Marner*. The sheer intellectuality of her sentences, expressing delicate nuances and subtleties with vivid clarity, is simply breathtaking. Margaret Mitch-ell's *Gone with the Wind* transports the reader to the Antebellum culture of the deep South as though the reader is living within the story, reacting to the keenly animated pro-tagonist and complex array of personalities. Few authors, if any, have achieved more finely developed characters. Courageous aviatrix, Amy Johnson, CBE, was the first woman to fly solo eleven thousand miles from England to Australia in her open cockpit, Gipsy Moth biplane. Florence Nightingale fought for years against crushing opposition to finally triumph with her innovations, which vastly im-proved and eventually revolutionized nursing, medicine, and even the prevailing design of contemporary hospitals. And, Dr. Jane Goodall, DBE, has influenced society to think about urgent ecological challenges, influencing the world perhaps more than any other woman since Nightingale.

Yet, of all the women who have walked among this fallen race of humans, the finest, the bravest, the truest, the wisest, and one of the most beautiful that history affords is Joan of Arc, Deliverer of France. Her country was pillaged, humiliated, raped, and ransacked by invaders during ninety-six years of war. What could Joan do? She could neither read nor write and was only a little shepherdess from an out-of-the-way French village. Nonetheless, she sought to drive the intruders out of France and crown the rightful king.

Miraculously, in 1429, at the age of only seventeen, Joan became General in Chief of the Armies of France. It was the only time in history that a seventeen-year-old became the supreme commander of a nation's army. Thousands of hardened, brutal soldiers instantly obeyed her every soft-spoken word because she so dearly loved France and fought with them in the thick of the battle.

The events of her life—a sweeping saga of heroism, fantastic feats, and perfect goodness—could never stand to reason if not recorded meticulously in judicial records. Indeed, no person from medieval Europe was more closely scrutinized through the cross-examination of eyewitnesses under oath in a court of law. Many of these archived testimonies were recorded by her enemies, so we may assume they were unbiased. Therefore, we know that grievous wounds in the pitch of battle, false accusations in unlawful hearings, chains of a dungeon, even consuming flames could not affect her virtue.

Hundreds of paintings and sculptures portray Joan, and more than four hundred stage plays and operas about her, including those by Friedrich Schiller, Giuseppe Verdi, and Pyotr Tchaikovsky. Thousands of books illustrate her life. Perhaps the best known of these is *Personal Recollections of Joan of Arc* by Mark Twain, supported by twelve years of research. Twain considered it his finest work.

To be sure, Joan of Arc is a worthy role model for young women.

We have considered only a short list of heroines since numberless women throughout the ages can be extolled, as well. Yet, nature itself whispers ever so softly, softly to woman, beseeching with infinite mystical star-lights from within her every cell . . . I entrust you with my precious light, for I have chosen you to be the living nucleus of the family.

Now, let us turn our attention to an issue that seems to epitomize the fatuous rhetoric surrounding what we have come to, incorrectly, refer to as equal rights: the question of sex change. Should we analyze the subject logically, our first question might be this: If men and women are, indeed, equal, why would sex change be considered? Doesn't the need to change from one to the other imply that there is, to be sure, a sharp contrasting distinction between the two? And furthermore, doesn't such a dramatic preference of one over another imply that the prospective patient deems one to be better than the other, which, in turn, demonstrates discrimination against the rejected sex, an act forbidden by political correctness?

As we give further thought to the bizarre phenomenon of those who desire to change the sex given to them by nature, let's seek the counsel of specialists at Johns Hopkins Hospital, one of the foremost medical centers in the world. Psychiatrists there have concluded that cases in which a person wishes to change his or her sex are identical to cases in which patients seek to have healthy arms, legs, or other extremities amputated because of the patient's insistence

that the extremity is not theirs but alien. Similar cases involve patients who are "dangerously thin," although, when
looking in a mirror, they perceive themselves as unaccept-
ably overweight. These patients were, without exception,
placed under close psychiatric care. The prognosis of the
caring physicians was not to arrange for their "alien" extremities to be removed, nor was further dieting recommended in
cases of anorexia. Such Frankensteinian procedures would
have almost assuredly resulted in a physician's lifetime ban
from medicine, heavy financial penalties, worldwide dis-
grace in the media, and a prison sentence. Why, then,
would it be permissible for physicians to remove sex organs
from patients who, in like manner, perceive those organs as
alien?

Dr. Paul R. McHugh is the former Psychiatrist in Chief
for Johns Hopkins Hospital and presently Distinguished Service Professor of Psychiatry. He has authored over one
hundred twenty-five peer-reviewed medical articles, six
books, and an article published by *The Wall Street Journal*
titled "Transgender Surgery Isn't the Solution."

In this article, Dr. McHugh states that transgenderism is a
"mental disorder" requiring psychiatric treatment and that sex
change is "biologically impossible." Dr. McHugh explains
that transgender surgery is the improper solution for people
who suffer from a "disorder of assumption," the notion that
their maleness or femaleness is different from that assigned to
them biologically. He continues by saying that people who
advocate surgery for sexual reassignment are colluding with
and promoting a mental disorder. McHugh cited a study revealing that suicide rates among transgendered people who
had reassignment surgery are twenty times higher than suicide
rates of those who are not transgender. He discussed research
conducted at London's Portman Clinic of Children and Van-
derbilt University, indicating that, over time, seventy to eighty

percent of those who questioned their gender "spontaneously lost those feelings." Those who control the media, however, inundate their "programs" with covert and overt messaging, promoting lifestyles that Dr. McHugh deems "mental disorders" and which cause extraordinarily high suicide rates. The military refers to such mind-bending as "psychological operations," which they abbreviate as "PSYOPS." These are operations designed to confuse and destroy the enemy psychologically and, in turn, morally and spiritually.

So, rather than watching and listening to mind-bending messages from the media, Sylvans turn away from television, most movies, and all music with antisocial messages, many of which are cleverly crafted to warp the soul. Some of us do not listen to the radio in our cars, use cell phones, or hand-held devices.

Instead, we listen to tree leaves gently rustled to exaltation by the warm summer zephyr, the morning rejoicing of the cardinal atop the highest maple. We see the knowing smile of our lover after a kiss when to speak would be to transgress into a silent, sacred temple. We feel the morning Sun upon our uplifted faces, inhaling the mountain air as drunkards drink their wine. We know we are men. Our women know they are women.

Now, let us continue our inquiry into ethics by recognizing the uninvited brontosaurus sitting at our tea party.

It is the destiny of every species to succumb to periodic natural calamities or competition from other species; no species has permanent nightly reservations for dinner. Only those who are most vigorous and versatile have a place at the table. Yet, those who are not are swiftly grabbed by the collar and thrown cruelly into the street gutter by the *maître d.* These are the rules. They are acceptable to those who are willing to fight battles and win. Nature mandates that those unwilling to fight should be run over and crushed. Frankly, I wish it were not so. Nevertheless, Sylvans protect children, women, the elderly, the sick, and the disabled, and this without omission. While we are far from perfect, Sylvanists are chivalrous, protecting those who cannot defend themselves. However, I can tell you it is life-giving to fight battles and win, both figuratively and literally.

Now, my fair ladies, has there ever been a species that decided, in the Darwinian sense, to mysteriously stop surviving? Here, I am not speaking of individual members of a species committing suicide or a herd running over a cliff, but a significant percentage of a species choosing to cease the fight to survive, although there is no visible threat. The ancients of the ancients appeared to embrace Darwinianism long before Charles penned *On the Origin of the Species*, but we have no record of a race committing "specicide," as I call it, until now.

The laws of natural selection and survival of the fittest apply to you and, in tandem, therefore, to us, your masculine counterparts. It's a bit of a sticky wicket, isn't it? We are indissolubly intertwined, as is a double helix, because, should you decide to commit specicide, you increase the chances of collapsing our genetic heritage, as well. That is the genealogical "end of the line"—the irreversible termination of an individuated upward struggle of 1.9 million years, beginning when *Homo erectus* made his cameo appearance in this our "Pageant of the Masters." To be sure, you, dear lady, are the manifestation of your ancestors, who fought to live when a multitude of others succumbed to the rigors of frostbitten feet, left to die as the tribe trudged mercilessly onward. Bloody intertribal intrigues, disease that drug a thousand, thousand families to the eternal blackened pyres, the long-ago wars of nevermore—nothing stopped that fighting sword of light, living on within the shining tributaries, trickling inexorably to this precise moment and stead.

Why, then, have you inexplicably decided *en masse* to stop passing on the golden baton of life?

The decision was not yours, my dear and beautiful cousin, but a planted response repeatedly suggested to your unconscious by the Marxist mind benders. Who was the champion of this women's movement that "liberated" women? All ideologies have a leader, do they not? Indeed, they do. And this leader was not a woman, to be sure, but none other than the profoundly chauvinistic Karl Marx.

Let us remember that his poisonous ideas were propagated to a great extent by Leon Trotsky, who, as we noted earlier, was the former head of the communist Red Army and responsible for the mass murder of over thirty million people simply because they were of European descent and Christians. You'll recall that many of his victims were worked to death, others hideously tortured to death in unspeakable ways, but most were shot in the back of the head and dumped in mass graves.

And as we have seen, Marxism and its accomplices killed an estimated 370,000,000 innocent people, approximately half of whom were females, most of whom were viciously tortured and raped before being murdered. So, as we speak of Marxist, Trotskyite notions of women's rights, we are speaking of nothing more, nothing less, than a genocidal maniac's ideological weapon.

In her article "Women's Liberation: The Marxist Tradition," Sharon Smith writes, "The classical Marxists of the nineteenth and early twentieth centuries—Karl Marx, Frederick Engels, Clara Zetkin, Rosa Luxemburg, V. I. Lenin, Alexandra Kollontai, and Leon Trotsky—developed a theoretical framework tying the fight for women's liberation to the struggle for socialism. Women in and around the Communist and Trotskyist movements began to reexamine theories of women's oppression, with some incorporating the effects, not only of class inequality but also of racism. In so doing, they began to develop a political groundwork that helped to pave the way for the future fight for women's liberation."

Leon Trotsky said, "In order to change the conditions of life, we must learn to see them through the eyes of women." Trotsky elaborated, "All our domestic habits must be revolutionized before that [equality] can happen. And yet it is quite obvious that unless there is actual equality of husband and wife in the family, in a normal sense as well as in the conditions of life, we cannot speak seriously of their equality in social work or even in politics."

If these words came from the mind of a rational person, we would feel that they were an expression of empathy, even kindness. Yet, they came from the mind of arguably the most dangerous psychopath of all time, meant for mass ideological annihilation, which materialized in Trotsky's murder of thirty million women, men, and their children. To be sure, since Karl Marx and Frederick Engels published *The Communist Manifesto* in 1848, the West has been inundated with its toxic ideas of "women's liberation" by the communist-owned and operated media. Indeed, there can be little doubt that women's issues are inseparable from communism, which is why communist revolutionary leader Inessa Armand said, "If women's liberation is unthinkable without communism, then communism is unthinkable without women's liberation."

Now, should most women be asked, "What do you think about abortion," or any variation of this question, their answer would probably be, "It's a woman's choice," or a close resemblance of this response. That is the answer that most women, especially those most educated, would give in reply. Anyone with varying opinions, is confronted with trenchant dogma, void of the tolerance the self-same abortionists righteously pontificate. Yet is this answer true? Or is it misleading? Is it a woman's choice, cut and dried?

The facts are painfully obvious: abortion is a choice in which three people, not only one, are vitally involved in a matter of life or death: the woman, the man, and the baby. Of course, the baby, with unexceptional consistency, without the slightest alloy of variation, always chooses to live. So, why has this blatant lie, that abortion is only a woman's choice, been so seamlessly calculated to be heard and read repeatedly by millions of women who live in the Western World?

That one lie has brutally ended the lives of over sixty million babies in the United States alone, many of whom would have been the tall, beautiful men and women of our great and mighty tribe. Some may have been our tribe's most noble leaders. Yet that one lie led to their merciless deaths and has rampaged our ethical gyroscope. For these Marxists, these Leonardo da Vincis of duplicity, know our demise begins with the disintegration of our families, which, as we have learned, is the irreducible bedrock of our society. From this attack upon the family, we have seen the loss of our protection, our neighborhoods, our security, our national identity, and even our racial identity. As a whole, they have all but blinded us from the scintillating North Star of our ethics. For blinding us is the only work of their hand. Of course, their other hand grasps the pommel of a poison dagger, and this not in vain. *Or is it?*

V. The biologic determines the sociologic.

The sociologic does not determine the biologic. The biologic determines the sociologic. Our enemies, who are at war not only with us but with nature itself, bend society with socially engineered propaganda in a refined covertness, the premise of which is that nature shall not determine society, but that society shall determine nature. For, these mind benders perceive that it is *they*, not the ballet of the Universe, that determines what is natural; thus, in effect, they become pretenders to the throne omnipotent, and the fallout upon Western society has been unprecedentedly cataclysmic.

As we have discussed earlier, Trotskyite, Marxist communists, have employed classic methodologies of psychological warfare, turning social institutions upside down and backward. This *psycho-sociological reversal*, as I call it, was mastered to an art in their laboratories, from which their poisons radiate. With the orchestrated complicity of their close allies, the media, they attack the following five social structures in order to destroy the biologic with mind-bending sociological messages that, with grand calumny, they masquerade as being organic. In other words, it is presented as social change that was not planted but which came about evolutionarily in reaction to oppression from people of European descent, their favorite synthetic monster and make-believe enemy. When, in fact, we could only be perceived as an enemy by those who wish to destroy the family, which we lovingly defend. And, of course, we are plagued with political correctness, yet we shall soon be emancipated from this gag of free speech. Its poison roots may have never found fertile soil had it not been for an alloy of contamination sowed long ago into the foundation of our societies—

the injunction to love our enemies. We see that "a little leaven leaveneth the whole lump;" that madness begets madness, and this made brilliant with vivid clarity to thinkers; for, our existential threat of Marxism and Saracenism fits perfectly like pieces of a puzzle with loving our enemies. And so, many who are unwilling to think for themselves have welcomed the death-wish of political correctness, the prearranged thinking that virulently hates these five virtues of society:

1. The Family: The traditional family of a man, a woman, and children is the groundwork of every society, and, consequently, it has been targeted for destruction by Marxist ideology since its inception. Lies about and ridicule of the family have been replicated countless times in television, movies, radio, news outlets, magazines, textbooks, and music, all of which are made popular by their seamless repetition, rather than their virtuosity or the discriminating good taste of society. To be sure, they have transformed the word *discrimination* to have only one connotation: hating people because of the color of their skin, whereas the word formerly meant, "an act or instance of making a distinction; the power of making fine distinctions; discriminating judgment." This redefinition, and many other redefinitions similar to it, are of transcendental importance to them since the new connotation of the word is, in of itself, a penalization to anyone who might exercise "the power of making fine distinctions." In other words, our children typically may not make discriminating judgments regarding distortions to traditional families, particularly if they are in public schools. Thus, neither is there a moral compass with which to make judgments.

2. Motherhood: Just as motherhood had become an offensive word in *Brave New World*, Aldous Huxley's warning of the coming cultural apocalypse, so it has, surrealistically, become an offensive word in our society, instituted by the legacy of Marx. Unprecedented in history, women are bending to these poison messages and choosing to not carry on their unique genetic legacy that was begun forty thousand years ago amidst Herculean struggle of the Ice Age, famine, war, plague, and pestilence. And so, the ascent of our ancestors is stopped forthwith by young women "liberated" by the mind-bending Marxists; these young women choosing, by external, malicious, and calculated control, to become the genetic end of the line of their foremothers and forefathers, who hoped against hope for the future of these selfsame young women.

3. Christianity: This has been our religion for hundreds of years, and although not without critics, it has been a bulwark of the charitable ambiance of our homelands, by far more generous than all other societies in the world. Now, albeit, across the strata of beliefs within the church, political correctness is more revered than the teachings of Christ, and so the church, as a whole, has lost its "saltiness" or its preserving qualities. Tragically, churches are more politically correct than biblically correct.

4. Gender: Seeds of sexual ambiguity have been sown and cultivated with meticulous care, particularly in the minds of our youth and youngest children, until those who are raised in a weakened home environment, and so are most susceptible to repetitive messages, succumb to notions that defy their biological nature. And those who "choose" an "alternative sexual orientation," as they call it, may never

be criticized most lightly; indeed, they must be proactively respected, whereas heterosexuals may be ridiculed without any fear of retribution, whatsoever.

5. Nationalism: A critical mantra to the masses is "no national boundaries." These money-grubbing Marxists are internationalists, having no allegiance to the nations of the world, for their realm is *monetary*. Their political machinations are merely ramparts that support this banking cartel, which manipulates world currencies, rewarding those who acquiesce to their Marxist global agenda of marginalizing these five social pillars and crushing those who do not. The national pseudo-leaders, most of whom are marionettes of these puppet masters, genuflect before them, eagerly committing high treason, selling national security secrets, compromising national borders, placing their fellow countrymen at grave risk of death. Thus, they impose their socialistic ideas upon the masses with unending repetition until they gain mass acceptance of societal communism, thereby bending the biologic.

Yet, we are above these death-wish messages, for we know the sociologic does not determine the biologic, the biologic determines the sociologic, the natural human expression of which is a man, a woman, and their children, the principal determinant of robust, thriving social order.

## VI. The Homogeneous Society

The society comprised of a homogeneous race is the strongest and healthiest social structure, whereas a heterogeneous society imposes manifold damage upon its members.

This fact, which is abundantly and naturally obvious to us, has been proven through an exhaustive and unbiased study conducted by distinguished academic, Professor Robert Putnam of Harvard University. Dr. Putnam's research, the largest study ever conducted on social interaction in the United States, was based upon carefully collected data from interviews of almost thirty thousand people who lived in forty-one communities across the nation. His research concluded that the greater the diversity in a community, the less its members volunteer, vote, donate to charity, work on community projects, and engage with each other socially, even on a civil basis. He discovered that in neighborhoods with the highest racial diversity, people trust one another about fifty percent as much as those who live in neighborhoods with the lowest racial diversity. Indeed, Putnam says the United States has devolved societally since the 1960s, when the federal government introduced forced integration with the resulting loss of *social capital*— the social ambiance of neighborhoods and communities. The nearly thirty thousand respondents he sampled were categorized into four racial segments: White, Black, Hispanic, and Asian. They were asked a long list of questions regarding their feelings about their neighborhoods and the people who lived in them, all according to race. Upon meticulous and objective analysis of the data, the higher the diversity factors, the more consistently higher were indications of diminished social capital.

Putnam says those who live in diverse communities have been statistically proven to "distrust their neighbors, regardless of the color of their skin, to withdraw even from close friends, to expect the worst from their community and its leaders, to volunteer less, give less to charity and work on community projects less often, to register to vote less, to agitate for social reform more but have less faith that they can actually make a difference, and to huddle unhappily in front of the television."

And this is, perhaps, the most disturbing of all his findings. It involves the two prevalent theories of ethnic and racial diversity: the *contact theory* and the *conflict theory*. The contact theory proposes that increased association with those of dissimilar races creates understanding and harmony between them, whereas the conflict theory suggests that increased association with those of dissimilar races produces lack of understanding and further disharmony. Putnam accepts neither theory, suggesting that individuals withdraw from everyone in a diverse society, even those of the same race and background. This indicates that our neighborhoods and communities should never be racially diverse since no one benefits from them but suffers a degrading withdrawal from one another into lonely semi-hermitage.

Perhaps an additional set of bookend theories should be introduced regarding civic intercourse: the *engagement theory,* in which a homogeneous society precipitates open and trusting social interaction, emphasizing the worth of the individual and providing them with opportunities to grow to the fullness of their potential; the polar opposite is the *withdrawal theory,* in which a heterogeneous society precipitates social withdrawal, thereby degrading the individual and individualistic growth and consequently fomenting the hopelessness of realizing their potential.

Putnam conducted his seminal study in the year 2000 and has since, over the years, reanalyzed his findings, which have refined and reconfirmed his original conclusions. Incidentally, these conflicted with his socio-political preferences, so we may be sure he was, indeed, unbiased.

As the Putnam study shines ample light upon the proven facts of "diversity" in stunning contrast to its mythology, a fiction propagated by the Marxist media as a utopia, we see that the presumed happy racial integration that is vigorously promoted by the media has no basis in realism or historical fact. For, prior to the tyranny of mandated integration, there was less animosity in our communities toward other races. To be sure, I never heard the suggestion, even in the slightest allusion, that the failure of extra-racial communities, or the people within them, was desired. I did, however, hear many comments made by those in our local communities wishing them well. And, as Putnam unquestionably demonstrates that the homogeneous society is a happier one, so the homogeneously Black communities were, alike, happier. Their family nuclei assumed traditional definitions, and the men, standing independent of government subsidies and entitlements, were prouder.

So, without a scintilla of evidence that race mixing has any benefits, the Marxists, all the same, seek to challenge nature with yet another fanciful lie in what they term "celebrating diversity," "supporting diversity," etcetera. By this *doublespeak*, they mean that cultures and races should mix. Yet, any thinker can see that should this proposed mixing occur, diversity would literally disappear. A rather monotone, lackluster semi-society would result, wherein its deprived citizens would become painfully oppressed by the ensuing jungle. So, it is quite elementary, to those who give the notion a little *thoughtwork*, as I call it, that the mind benders seek the destruction of diversity, not its celebration as they claim.

And why, pray tell, is it unnecessary for the indigenous natives of Japan, China, Africa, India, Latin America, or Arabia to "celebrate" diversity? It is perfectly fine for them to remain Japanese, Chinese, African, Indian, Latino, and Arabian. However, they tell us it is the foulest of crimes for us to remain of European descent. Alas, not only is this nincompoop's lie thrust upon us, they demand that we joyously celebrate it or be called a racist; such a hollow slander, of course, should be casually laughed off since a racist hates people because of their God-given genetics, and we never do this. It is beneath us.

Contrary to their lies, we want all races to excel and prosper, and we will even help them to do so, as we have done endlessly in the past.

So, in concert with this Orwellian terminology, the Marxist mind benders program subliminal messages, weaponized to create guilt for being of European descent. Amongst other tribes, we may have the least cause for guilty. In addition to those incomparably rich gifts, we have bestowed upon humankind, a scant few of which are cataloged in the foreword of our book, we have given laws that have emancipated a vast multitude of men and women from oppression. Moreover, these laws have been the model of nations the world over. Much of the substructure of these laws were penned and passed by Englishmen, often against the stalwart opposition in parliamentary proceedings. Lord Denning tells us that the Magna Carta, for instance, is "the greatest constitutional document of all times—the foundation of the freedom of the individual against the arbitrary authority of the despot." The ancient English writ, *habeas corpus,* also known as unlawful detainer, prevents detainment without a lawful cause. The original Bill of Rights, which was also created by Englishmen, ensures freedom of

religion, speech, and the press. Its American emulation protects against unreasonable searches and seizures. Rights to
life, liberty, and property are also vouchsafed by this law,
which we freely gave to men. Now, suppose our people
never existed. These laws would probably neither exist, for
they all came from us, redeeming every creed and hue
from grinding slavery and oppression.

Yet, we have done other things for which we rarely, if
ever, receive credit. We will illustrate these deeds with accounts from Sir James Frazer's meticulously researched
work, *The Golden Bough*. Simultaneously, we will, by comparative antithesis, consider the advancement of our tribe
juxtaposed to other tribes. In so doing, we are not condescending but merely giving thought to a realism that is
purposely convoluted by the media, causing unmerited
guilt amongst some of our tribe. Please be aware that the
following description is quite savage, and the reader may
find it disturbing.

"A particular account has been preserved of the sacrifice of a Sioux girl by the Pawnees in April 1837 or 1838.
The girl was fourteen or fifteen years old and had been
kept for six months and well treated. Two days before the
sacrifice she was led from wigwam to wigwam, accompanied by the whole council of chiefs and warriors. At each
lodge she received a small billet of wood and a little
paint, which she handed to the warrior next to her. In this
way she called at every wigwam, receiving at each the
same present of wood and paint. On the twenty-second of
April, she was taken out to be sacrificed, attended by the
warriors, each of whom carried two pieces of wood which
he had received from her hands. Her body having been
painted half red and half black, she was attached to a sort of
gibbet and roasted for some time over a slow fire, then shot

to death with arrows. The chief sacrificer next tore out her heart and devoured it. While her flesh was still warm it was cut in small pieces from the bones, put in little baskets, and taken to a neighbouring cornfield. There the head chief took a piece of the flesh from a basket and squeezed a drop of blood upon the newly-deposited grains of corn. His example was followed by the rest, till all the seed had been sprinkled with the blood; it was then covered up with earth. According to one account the body of the victim was reduced to a kind of paste, which was rubbed or sprinkled not only on the maize but also on the potatoes, the beans, and other seeds to fertilize them. By this sacrifice they hoped to obtain plentiful crops."

This atrocity occurred in North America only one hundred eighty years ago, at a time when we had lived in the world's most urbane societies, preeminent in their charity, for thousands of years. Zurich, the oldest continuously inhabited city of all, enjoyed such urbanity and charity for over five thousand years. Had it not been for the European settlers in North America, we can only speculate as to when, or if, these barbarities would have ceased. Yet, we know with certainty that these materialized phantasmagorias abated and finally stopped through our intervention. Not only did we stop human sacrifice among the Native Americans, but among the indigenous natives of South and Central America, as well as Africa, to mention but a few.

Now that we have considered the results of racial integration based upon the most exhaustive quantitative research ever conducted, let's consider it from a perspective that is purely anecdotal, before the federal government unlawfully forced integration upon us, literally, from the point of a fixed bayonet. This was a time when it was not uncommon for people to, both day and night, leave their

keys in the ignition of their car with the doors unlocked for
convenience. I recall it quite vividly. The milkman delivered
milk to almost everyone's front door, leaving a few bottles
of fresh milk on their porches before the sunrise, and I never
heard of anyone stealing or disturbing them. It was inviolable. The doors of every Catholic and Episcopal church, and
many others, remained open at all hours, a perpetual welcome to anyone in all our nation to come in, to rest and
pray. Over the years, a multitude came, often in the middle
of the night, with never a violation befalling that sanctum
from worldly troubles.

In the summertime, my childhood friends and I
would spend all day at a spotlessly clean amusement park
where we would swim in an Olympic-size pool, ride the
rides, test our skill at games, and play miniature golf. There
was never the slightest concern for our safety. Summer holidays were sometimes celebrated with yard parties or street
parties in a cul-de-sac, where families with members of
every age would gather and share a neighborhood meal
together, the same way our people have had common meals
for centuries. Sunday evening was a time when friends,
neighbors, or relatives might drop by, unannounced, for dessert and coffee.

These were rich with laughter, the latest news about
the kids, and even singing old-timey songs accompanied by
piano, causing more laughter, tears of affection, and expatia-
tion of the soul that increased so greatly as to include and
envelope everyone with life-giving light. This was neither
excitation nor mild hysteria but, with our feet planted firmly
on rational ground, a "fellowship divine." We shall restore
such joy to our friends and families in the coming years.

Once my father, mother, sister, and I called on my
aunt Kathryn and uncle Galen on a Saturday afternoon,

which was also common to do unannounced. They didn't know we were coming and weren't home, but had left a note on the front door in case anyone did drop by: "Be back in an hour or so. Come in. Door's open." Such were those safe and innocent days. Dear cousins, these exalted times can return to our neighborhoods and communities.

VII. The Importance of the Individual

The equilibrium of our society rests upon several ideologies. Two of the most vital are the importance of the individual and the willingness of the individual to sacrifice for the greater good of society.

Before we expound upon these ideas, let us consider the related words of Aristotle and Bertrand Russell, respectively: "A political society exists for the sake of noble actions, not of mere companionship." "The aim of the state, in this view, is to produce cultured gentlemen who continue the aristocratic mentality with love of learning and the arts." This is a society in which the individual may flourish without limit and is worth any sacrifice.

So, we will examine it with a keener eye. The individual is the most influential element of a neighborhood, a community, a nation, or a society. For it is the individual who leads and manages society as a whole because, of course, only the individual can think, reason, and take action upon thoughts and rationale, whereas a group, particularly a large one, is limited to reaction. Thus, often a group will react in a non-thinking, irrational way, sometimes even assuming the character of a mob whose default leader becomes the lowest common denominator, that is, the person with the least integrity, morals, or intelligence. Others may follow such persons simply because their ideas exceed normal boundaries, which may have a visceral appeal to the masses, who are typically frustrated by their lot in life and eager to blame anything or anyone outside of themselves. Indeed, a group will always be prone to behave in this manner without a virtuous leader.

By contrast, the rare Alfredian leader, who is truly virtuous, will be devoted to educating his followers, which is to be distinguished from programming them with propaganda or disinformation. This is, possibly, the foremost reason he is so unique, since he is unafraid of the people, they being *his* people, and, therefore, he possesses a singular desire to present the unadulterated facts to them. Contenders for control of the group will commonly try to undermine this act of virtuosity by telling the people a fanciful version of what they wish to hear, rather than what the urgent evidence bears. Such an undermining is quite easy to instigate within a democracy, wherein a pseudo-leader simply lies to the people, gaining a majority who are gullible enough to be compromised by this mendacity, a *coup d'état* from the shadows that is replicated with astonishing frequency in democracies across the globe. And so, we have little more than mob rule, usually cloaked most with religious and patriotic robes. After many decades of this charade, a nation slowly loses its sovereignty, and its citizens correspondingly lose their individual freedoms while, nevertheless, parroting their imagined democratic liberty. So, we see, from a leadership position, that the individual, particularly the virtuous, individual leader, is of paramount importance.

Of equal importance—perhaps even more important than the indispensability of the individual leader—is the individual thinker. A group, as we have noted, cannot think. So, it is the most exceptionally gifted individual who becomes the recognized logistician, the philosopher, the poet, the painter, the musician, the architect, the ecologist, and the mathematician, acclaimed as the consummate artist within a society. These create a vivid delineation, a ceiling, if you will, that governs the expertise of all who dream of contributing to the excellence of their art and, in turn, to their fatherland. We may recoil in aversion from the idea of a ceiling with its limitations. But even the Athenians created such invisible ceilings, for these are merely an inadvertent standard, albeit those of Athens were the loftiest of mankind. We shall exceed them. Should individuals, however, who think original thoughts become a rarity because of ineffectual education or orchestrated tyranny, a society may limp along for some time but will eventually implode. Yet, if individual thinkers are chosen and rewarded because of their true merit, society will advance steadily.

Notions of each individual having inherent value were somewhat unique to our people. This rationality set them apart from the uncivilized throngs in their midst, and that is why, over two thousand years ago, Herodotus said, "Of old, the Hellenic race was marked off from the barbarian as more keen-witted and freer from nonsense."

This sensibility, this worth of the individual, was manifested in the statues of the ancient Greeks, accenting the free-flowing natural grace of our beautiful cousins; their sculptors were inspired by a young lady seen shopping in the market or a muscled athlete hurling a discus at the local games. It was the same familiarity apparent in their gods, who were immortal and powerful yet as fallible as any human, and this sometimes quite comically. The ancient Greek needn't shudder with dumb trembling before Zeus but stand tall and state his case simple because their gods weren't perfect. Yet a member of another race might fall on his face before his terrible, all-consuming god, whose perfection would paralyze his mortal imperfection, hitherto unrealized. The Sphinx may have caused a similar response in the primitives who stood before that alien structure, for, after all, it was a thing wholly unnatural. But the Greek was comfortably reconciled to his gods, and should he have seen that grotesque monstrosity, half-man, half-lion, created from a grotesque mind, he would have been appalled and may have laughed in derision, and this appropriately so.

"The Greeks made their gods in their own image," said Edith Hamilton in *Mythology*. "That had not entered the mind of man before. Before then gods had no semblance of reality. They were unlike all living things. In Egypt, a towering colossus, immobile, beyond the power of the imagination to endow with movement, as fixed in the stone as the tremendous temple columns, a representation of the human shape deliberately made inhuman. Or a rigid figure, a woman with a cat's head suggesting inflexible, inhuman cruelty. In Mesopotamia, bas-reliefs of bestial shapes unlike any beast ever known, men with bird's heads and lions with bull's heads and both with eagle's wings, creations of artists who were intent upon producing something never seen except in their minds, the very consummation of unreality.

"These and their like were what the pre-Greek world worshiped. One need only place beside them in imagination any Greek statue of a god, so normal and natural with all its beauty, to perceive what a new idea had come into the world. With its coming, the Universe became rational. This was not a Hebrew idea, it was Greek."

Odysseus personified those concepts. He was the catalyst for the heroic, rugged individual of Western man. Within his story are consoling messages of our human predicament of long suffering, human weaknesses, redemption, the triumph of justice, and even a similitude of resurrection and a second coming.

All these messages are, together, a microcosm of our animated struggle for completion as individuals. And so, we wishfully identify with Odysseus, who faced and overcame hardships with cunning versatility. Indeed, he endured manifold, hideous trials, some by miscalculation, others by the malevolent providence of Poseidon, on his arduous return from the Trojan War to his kingdom of Ithaca and his queen, Penelope. He did not try to transcend his pain-filled, yearning love for Ithaca and Penelope. He completed his love for them through progressive suffering. Homer's crystalline message: we too will endure much suffering in our quest for individual completion. So, we admire Odysseus for many reasons, yet I feel these are the two primary reasons: first, he suffered magnificently, as we often suffer alone in silence, and so he becomes special kin to us; and, secondly, he overcame his hideous trials through longsuffering in ways that succeeded. He could have remained with hypnotically beautiful Calypso on her garden island. He could have remained with equally beautiful Circe in idylls of splendor. Rather, he chose Ithaca and Penelope, and we love him for this. Why? Should he have remained in either of these new lands with new wives, would we not love him still? No, we would not. Had he done so, he would not have completed himself as an individual. Self-completion, although painful, is singularly why Odysseus is the worthiest of heroes. Therein lies the story's immense value—this perennial epic, evergreen before millennia.

For, I believe Odysseus was a forerunner and catalyst of the Greek Miracle and later the Renaissance since his distinction is versatility and resourceful intellectuality. Thus, we see the profundity of his character. It brazenly defies slavery, peasantry, and commonness. It brazenly defies all else save fullness and individual completion. So, notwithstanding *The Odyssey's* stunning beauty, Odysseus' unyielding character is one of the compelling reasons each succeeding generation must be taught to revere and treasure this gift. For in many ways, it is the basis of our respect for the individual and, in turn, individual freedom.

Long ages after *The Odyssey* was written, a prince and future King of Sparta was born who saved his people and, to be sure, may have saved our people, as well. Had he not sacrificed his life for his fellow countrymen, all the grace and beauty, all the science of the Greek Miracle may have been swept away, never to be remembered, even by the coming next generation. And, we may have never been born. So, we humbly honor him as one of our greatest heroes—King Leonidas. We must never forget that he gave his life for us.

As were all Spartan boys in his era, little Prince Leonidas was drilled in the toughest mental and physical training to become a hoplite warrior, armed with a round shield, a long spear, and an iron cutlass. They perfected a formation known as the phalanx, in which rows of fellow hoplites stood shoulder to shoulder, their shields overlapping, thus providing significant protection to the warriors behind it, a typically irresistible tactic.

During this time, ancient Greece was comprised of many little city-states, Athens and Sparta being the largest and most powerful of these. They considered each other confederates against foreign invasion, such as when a united Greek force defeated King Darius of Persia at the Battle of Marathon. Ten years later, Darius' son, Xerxes, led an invasion against the Greeks with an enormous army that marched south through Greece; as the Persian army marched, their navy sailed parallel to them a short distance out to sea. But in order to reach Athens, the Persian army needed to march through the coastal pass of Thermopylae, a pass so narrow that only a few men could march through it at once, thus dramatically slowing their advance.

Meanwhile, in Greece, there was much argument and

debate about how this emergency should be handled and what military strategies should be implemented, during which precious time was running out. Finally, towards the end of the summer of 480 BC, King Leonidas led an army of a few thousand men from the city-states across Greece, converging on Thermopylae. The king knew they could not stop the Persians, but he believed he could defend the Thermopylae pass until the men of Greece could organize their defenses to repel this juggernaut of death and destruction. And so, Leonidas camped his army at Thermopylae, knowing the narrowness of the pass would funnel the Persian army into the readied blades and spears of his hoplite troops. Scouts brought this news to Xerxes, who then sent an emissary to negotiate with King Leonidas, offering freedom to him and his men along with landed estates far superior in value to their present homes. Leonidas flatly refused. The emissary demanded more emphatically that his troops lay down their arms, to this, the king replied laconically, as the Spartans were wont to do, "Come and take them."

The emissary was befuddled by this choice of certain, brutal death rather than life and riches, for such a sacrifice was deemed madness to those of his culture who dearly loved oriental pleasures.

As the seemingly inexorable Persian army marched onward, a local Trachinian warned General Dieneces, who served under King Leonidas' command, that "Such is the number of barbarians, that when they shot forth their arrows, the Sun would be darkened by the multitude." General Dieneces calmly answered, "Our Trachinian friend brings us excellent tidings. If the Medes darken the sun, we shall have our fight in the shade." Nonetheless, Xerxes waited, assuming that King Leonidas would retreat, fleeing for his life, but our king would never countenance retreat-

ing, and this was a thing inexplicable to the soft and cowardly Xerxes. Exasperated after having waited four days,
Xerxes finally gave the order to attack. For the next forty-
eight hellacious, long, and bloody hours, King Leonidas
and his men held their position against Xerxes' army,
thereby giving time and life to his Grecian brothers at
home. Eventually, a local civilian traitor led a company of
Persian archers to a trail that overlooked the flank of the
king's men. As King Leonidas fought forward, he and his
men were assailed by volley after volley of arrows until all
lay dying on the ground, which they secured for their blessed
fatherland made sacred by their blood.

The gallant King Leonidas lost the battle, as he knew he
would, yet we may say with military confidence that he won
the war, for a few weeks later, the Athenian navy defeated
the Persians at the Battle of Salamis, after which the Persian
army retreated following a quivering Xerxes, who had
abandoned his men fleeing in panic-driven fear. We and our
culture live on today thanks to King Leonidas.

Many years later, Charles Dickens characterized the
importance of the individual with the notion of sacrificing
for the greater good in the person of Sydney Carton, the pro-
tagonist of *A Tale of Two Cities*. Sydney's superior intellect
is apparent as he analyzes legal cases for his law partner,
but, for what we may presume are deep psychological
wounds, he seeks not his personal success. He is a troubled
alcoholic and social recluse. The noble light of his life is
his love for the young lady, Lucy, and his affection for her
family; yet, purely because of his low self-estimation and not
their aloofness, he feels their reciprocal affections are unat-
tainable. Seeing himself as a hopeless deviant, Sydney
seeks redemption by trading his life for that of Lucy's husband, Charles, who is sentenced to death by French

revolutionaries for nothing more than having an aristocratic heritage. Having drugged Charles during a visit to
him in the Bastille, Sydney's confederates spirited Charles
away to freedom, leaving Sydney in his place. A few steps
from the guillotine, his last Earthly thoughts are thus recorded:

"I see a beautiful city and a brilliant people rising from
this abyss, and, in their struggles to be truly free, in their
triumphs and defeats, through long years to come, I see the
evil of this time and of the previous time of which this is the
natural birth, gradually making expiation for itself and wearing out.

"I see the lives for which I lay down my life, peaceful,
useful, prosperous and happy, in that England which I shall
see no more. I see her with a child upon her bosom, who
bears my name. I see her father, aged and bent, but otherwise restored, and faithful to all men in his healing office,
and at peace. I see the good old man, so long their friend,
in ten years' time enriching them with all he has, and passing tranquilly to his reward.

"I see that I hold a sanctuary in their hearts, and in
the hearts of their descendants, generations hence. I see her,
an old woman, weeping for me on the anniversary of this
day. I see her and her husband, their course done, lying side
by side in their last earthly bed, and I know that each was
not more honoured and held sacred in the other's soul, than
I was in the souls of both.

"I see that child who lay upon her bosom and who bore
my name, a man winning his way up in that path of life
which once was mine. I see him winning it so well, that my
name is made illustrious thereby the light of his. I see the
blots I threw upon it, faded away. I see him, foremost of just
judges and honoured men, bringing a boy of my name, with

a forehead that I know and golden hair, to this place—then fair to look upon, with not a trace of this day's disfigurement—and I hear him tell the child my story, with a tender and a faltering voice.

"It is a far, far better thing that I do, than I have ever done; it is a far, far better rest that I go to than I have ever known."

Another story about the individual's importance is one that I feel you will agree, we would be wise to read to our children and is told by Mary Mapes Dodge in her book, *Hans Brinker*:

"One lovely autumn afternoon, when the boy was about eight years old, he obtained his parents' consent to carry some cakes to a blind man who lived out in the country, on the other side of the dike. The little fellow started on his errand with a light heart, and having spent an hour with his grateful old friend, he bade him farewell and started on his homeward walk. Trudging stoutly along the canal, he noticed how the autumn rains had swollen the waters. Even while humming his careless, childish song, he thought of his father's brave old gates and felt glad of their strength, for, thought he, 'If they gave way, where would Father and Mother be? These pretty fields would all be covered with the angry waters—Father always calls them the angry waters. I suppose he thinks they are mad at him for keeping them out so long.' And with these thoughts just flitting across his brain, the little fellow stooped to pick the pretty flowers that grew along his way. Sometimes he stopped to throw some feathery seed ball in the air and watch it as it floated away; sometimes he listened to the stealthy rustling of a rabbit, speeding through the grass, but oftener he smiled as he recalled the happy light he had seen arise on the weary, listening face of his blind old friend.

"Suddenly the boy looked around him in dismay. He had not noticed that the sun was setting. Now he saw that his long shadow on the grass had vanished. It was growing dark, he was still some distance from home, and in a lonely ravine, where even the blue flowers had turned to gray. He quickened his footsteps and, with a beating heart recalled many a nursery tale of children belated in dreary forests. Just as he was bracing himself for a run, he was startled by the sound of trickling water. Whence did it come? He looked up and saw a small hole in the dike through which a tiny stream was flowing. Any child in Holland will shudder at the thought of a leak in the dike! The boy understood the danger at a glance. That little hole, if the water were allowed to trickle through, would soon be a large one, and a terrible inundation would be the result.

"Quick as a flash, he saw his duty. Throwing away his flowers, the boy clambered up the heights until he reached the hole. His chubby little finger was thrust in, almost before he knew it. The flowing was stopped! Ah! he thought, with a chuckle of boyish delight, the angry waters must stay back now! Haarlem shall not be drowned while I am here!

"This was all very well at first, but the night was falling rapidly. Chill vapors filled the air. Our little hero began to tremble with cold and dread. He shouted loudly; he screamed, 'Come here! come here!' but no one came. The cold grew more intense, a numbness, commencing in the tired little finger, crept over his hand and arm, and soon his whole body was filled with pain. He shouted again, 'Will no one come? Mother! Mother!' Alas, his mother, good, practical soul, had already locked the doors and had fully resolved to scold him on the morrow for spending the night with blind Jansen without her permission. He tried to whistle. Perhaps some straggling boy might heed the signal, but his teeth chattered so, it was impossible. Then he called on God for help. And the answer came, through a holy resolution: 'I will stay here till morning.' The midnight moon looked down upon that small, solitary form, sitting upon a stone, halfway up the dike. His head was bent but he was not asleep, for every now and then one restless hand rubbed feebly the outstretched arm that seemed fastened to the dike—and often the pale, tearful face turned quickly at some real or fancied sounds.

"How can we know the sufferings of that long and fearful watch—what falterings of purpose, what childish terrors came over the boy as he thought of the warm little bed at home, of his parents, his brothers and sisters, then looked into the cold, dreary night! If he drew away that tiny finger, the angry waters, grown angrier still, would rush forth, and never stop until they had swept over the town. No, he would hold it there till daylight—if he lived! He was not very sure of living. What did this strange buzzing mean? And then the knives that seemed pricking and piercing him from head to foot? He was not certain now that he could draw his finger away, even if he wished to.

"At daybreak a clergyman, returning from the bedside of a sick parishioner, thought he heard groans as he walked along on the top of the dike. Bending, he saw, far down on the side, a child apparently writhing with pain.

"'In the name of wonder, boy,' he exclaimed, 'what are you doing there?'

"'I am keeping the water from running out,' was the simple answer of the little hero. "Tell them to come quick.'

" . . . that little boy represents the spirit of the whole country. Not a leak can show itself anywhere either in its politics, honor, or public safety, that a million fingers are not ready to stop it, at any cost."

VIII. Superior, Inferior Dynamics

Before reading this section, it is noteworthy to remember that as part of the Sylvan Pledge, we never treat someone condescendingly because of his or her race, creed, or religion. We observe and maintain that pledge here. Nonetheless, we must consider the facts without the slightest alloy of disrespect.

Now, whenever an inferior is treated as equal to a superior, the inferior will always try to destroy or at least usurp the superior. I can hear the harmonized howls of protesting Marxists, for this is a societal fact threatening their ideas from center to circumference since it greatly limits their ability to drain us of our resources and energy, of which they, themselves, are entirely bereft. So, while ignoring their harmonic screechings, which are comedically pathetic, we shall continue.

Of course, it is not only the Marxists whose *modus operandi* is sabotaging their superiors; a significant percentage of the population prescribes to this method of pseudo-competition. The Marxists, albeit adore fomenting this societal weakness, for they realize that most people are unwilling to expend the effort to improve themselves, finding it infinitely easier to focus their attention upon the make-believe faults of others, which reside as vain imaginings within the inferior's mind.

If you will, picture two people—Messrs. Chip and Dale. On a scale of zero to ten, Chip possesses a high self-estimation of nine, Dale a low self-estimation of only five. Let us also suppose that on a scale in which the highest is two hundred, Chip enjoys an intelligent quotient of one hundred sixty while Dale is heavily burdened with a lowly ninety. Should these individuals be told repeatedly and in dozens of ways from birth to death that they are equals, Dale will become intensely frustrated and angry that his efforts, compared to those of Chip's, appear to be unfairly rewarded. This will culminate in Dale's resentment and disrespect for Chip, which, over time, will become so deeply ingrained that Dale will justify any action to bring Chip beneath his level, be this sabotage or, quite possibly, violence.

Let us further suppose that, through government-imposed hiring quotas, Dale has replaced Chip, assuming his managerial role. Since Dale has a self-esteem of only five, he will never hire a co-worker with a self-esteem equal to or higher than his own, which means his department will become ever more woefully inept as they turn away the brightest and best candidates.

While this scenario is unadulterated madness, it is not a departure from the very dynamics that are being repeated on an immense scale in our present society. This was poignantly illustrated by a story that an acquaintance told me who is an airline captain. Upon approaching a major airport from the air, his copilot, from without our tribe, who at that time was responsible for duties that were critical for the safety of the many souls aboard, began sobbing uncontrollably and even refused to cooperate by radio with those on the ground who were responsible for guiding the plane to the appropriate docking station. As the ship's captain, he ordered his copilot to, "Stop blubbering and do your job." Later, the copilot made a written complaint about the captain. Although the copilot was unable to function, thereby jeopardizing the lives of many people, whereas the captain saved them all, the captain was summarily disciplined and ordered to attend sensitivity training, but the incompetent copilot was shortly thereafter promoted to captain.

These ditches dug for another's demise often might fig-uratively become the diggers' undoing. This is quite a shame. For diggers, like the copilot, assume a narcissistic fantasy of themselves that are substitutes for their factual deficiencies and, with this illusion of grandeur, they pretend to be free from self-critique, the sole threshold of their improvement. Laziness, such as this, is the root of all evil, which is commonly attributed to the "love of money," however, money is simply the favored tool of the lazy. So, we see that laziness is the principal disorder, the love of money being its manifested symptom.

This dark background, a wide curtain draped 'cross life's stage, sharply contrasts against the incomparable industriousness of our tribe, and this may appear blindingly dazzling to the lazy, yet it is nothing more than normality. And so, we are often detested for inventiveness and build-ing civilizations, which accents the drowsiness of our de-tractors. Acknowledging and then resolving this lethargy, especially the emotional genre, is a process that requires dis-comfort, even agony, which most of us attempt to postpone or avoid altogether. For when we have something in the forefront of our mind connected to an unbearable moment, we must take it out and look at it, although it is possibly tor-turous at the time, because if we do not, it assumes ridiculous proportions. Monsters appear. Yet, they merely appear monstrous, magnified by our unwillingness to re-solve them, at which time they become manageable and, if truly confronted, may become fuel for the vast super engine of the unconscious mind, thus helping us along our way. Oh, but we must be heroic. For years may be required to face our phobias and fears. Sincerely trying to do so, one small step at a time, will begin to slowly make a difference. The cowardly, on the other hand, refuse to slightly acknowledge these problems resulting in discomfort that inhibits the ability to grow emotionally, mentally, and spiritually.

I feel this denial is so profound that it retards some physical growth and, most clearly, physical appearance as well. I recall a political candidate whose autobiography was indelibly written upon his facial features; perhaps I should say it was absent, for here were not to be found the muscles of resolution molded while enduring soul-crushing struggle, from which is formed the mettle of manly hardihood. Here, instead, was the protagonist of a dark novel, indeed, who had never faced an honest test of battle. This is undeniable for the sabotaging diggers of ditches, though they expertly create unlimited ways to deny their flaws while relishing the discovery of an armorial kink in others.

Of course, we are quick to note that we, as individual members of our tribe, possess no immunity from lackadaisicalness. There are plenty of those who eagerly dig a ditch for the demise of others within our tribe. Herein, too, whenever an inferior is treated as an equal to a superior, the inferior will always try to destroy or at least usurp the superior.

IX. Friendly Cooperation

One of the tenets that King Alfred the Great taught his people was friendly cooperation. As in the days of old, when the greatest of all kings ruled Wessex, friendly cooperation is, at this very hour, not a luxury but a present and timely need. For, it is non-negotiable that we always work together, hand in hand, amongst our pan-European race. Never again may we allow globalists, rabid with filthy lucre, to push us into war with one another. May the love of our people forever stand as one living organism, sacrosanct and holy, inconceivable of violation.

Now, let's read the words about friendship penned by the greatest of all kings. As we do, let us remember that he attained the stratosphere of every achievement for which the most ambitious men have ever dreamt: fantastic wealth, the revered honor of world rulers, unmatched military heroism in which he saved his people, a happy family life, civic and societal advancements that were hundreds of years ahead of their time, the title of "Great," and the love of all who knew him and learn of him still. This is what the great king said:

"For some men think that the greatest happiness is for a man to be so rich as to need nothing more, and all their life long they yearn after this. Some think that the highest good is to be the most honoured by their fellows, and they strive thereafter with might and main. Others think it lies in sovereign power, and desire either themselves to rule or to attach to themselves the friendship of the powerful. Again, some are persuaded that the best thing is to be famous and widely known, and to have a good name, and they labour thereafter both in peace and in war. Many men account it the greatest good and the greatest happiness to be always merry in this present life, and to satisfy every desire. Some, when they seek wealth, seek it to get more power by it, so that they may with impunity enjoy these worldly pleasures and riches. Many again desire power to enable them to amass enormous wealth, or from a wish to spread abroad their name and fame. Such among others are the frail and corruptible honours that afflict the soul of man with yearning and ambition; he thinks he has acquired some notable good when he has received the flattery of the crowd, but I think he has purchased a very false distinction. Some men desire wives most earnestly, for the begetting of many children, and also for a pleasant life. Now I assert that the most precious of all this world's blessings is True Friendship, which must be accounted not a worldly good, but a heavenly blessing; for it is not false Fate that produces it, but God, who created natural friends in kinsmen. For every other thing in this world man desireth either because it will help him to power, or to get some pleasure, save only a true friend; him we love for love's sake and for our trust in him, though we can hope for no other return from him. Nature joins friends together and unites them with a very inseparable love; but by means of these worldly goods and the wealth of this life we oftener make foes than friends."[14]

Perhaps this story will also reveal, in some small way, this sovereignty from materialism we wish to emulate in our day-to-day lives: I recall an evening when, as a poor student, I wanted to have dinner with a friend in spite of an almost bare cupboard. We had spaghetti, water, and a cook-

---

[14] From King Alfred's translation of *Consolation of Philosophy* by Boethius.

ing pot, which was a good start. With a few pennies that we scraped together, we bought a head of iceberg lettuce and a loaf of French baguette bread that was on sale. Since we had no sauce, we took what little mayonnaise, ketchup, and olive oil that remained, and mixed them for our tomato paste. We laughed at our triumph and relished our unanticipated yet delicious meal more than if we had dined at Delmonico's. And the crowning touch—we were happily grateful to our gracious Lord for the humble meal bestowed upon us and, thus so without religiosity.

Now, my message goes beyond doing something fun with a friend. It might be more clearly understood, if we ask, "Why was this meal particularly delightful?" It was especially savored because our joy was not worldly but spiritual; we played a trick on the world, one might say, for, with a few pennies' worth of food, we were every bit as happy as if dining at an expensive restaurant. As an old Nordic proverb teaches,

> A man knows nothing if he knows not
> That wealth oft begets an ape.

The point, dear cousins, is that the world plays tricks on us almost seamlessly throughout our lives, enticing us in the most beguiling ways to love things and use people. While loving people and using things is the preeminent hallmark of sovereignty from worldly ways and the seat of friendship.

Beguiling worldliness is explicitly demonstrated in movies set in lavish locales, mansions appointed with opulent furnishings, and actors and actresses who wear Italian wardrobes costing more than the average moviegoer's annual income; for should the identical movie be set in a middle-class neighborhood, the audience would almost assuredly soon lose interest. Material intoxication, however, keeps us visually attuned to the kaleidoscopic cinematography and thus to the plot, which is a methodology often used by directors to mesmerize their viewers. Yet, it seems a good script would be more effective and less costly. Material intoxication in day-to-day life is normal to an extent; the desire to be wealthy enough to control things around us more completely is almost irresistible. And, enjoying beautiful clothes, a car, and a home are innocent.

Yet we might become quite friendless should we go through life loving things and using people, more starkly revealed as loving the nonliving and casually using living things, thus casting an exanimate cloud all about us. Should we love the nonliving at all, those things that are without life? For we may have a vault filled with bars of purest gold, yet these will not render one fleeting moment of honey sweet sleep. These cannot hear us weep, being silent, frozen, and vacuous of empathy before our longings. They, nor the things they might buy, will provide that cherished mellow contentment, that sublime moment of gentle rest when the depth of our soul is gratified, at peace with our deeds and the work of our hands. As a sheer ebony night without stars is to the unclouded Sun in all its brilliance, so is material intoxication to the simple beauties of life.

> "Oh! friendly to the best pursuits of man,
> Friendly to thought, to virtue and to peace,
> Domestic life in rural pleasures past!"

> William Cowper

To be sure, "there is a place of quiet rest" where a friend welcomes us, come day, come night, awaiting always to calm our fears. A place of awe before a temple of mosaic miracles infinitesimal, a vaulted cathedral ceiling ever-changing with many colors, of rejuvenating powers of blessed peace. A place where we can find unspoiled nourishment and inhale the pristine air as the desert wanderer drinks from the long-awaited oasis. The old-growth forests are these. A backyard in which nature has her ways, rather than neurotically mowing and trimming the life out of her, may become our little Xanadu, as well. And we are, of course, members of the fauna, and by befriending them, make no mistake about it, we befriend ourselves. Among them, we find many gurus, if you will, who are supra-religious, and this congenitally so. In other words, they were born in a state above and beyond the need for religion, for they are perfectly innocent in this respect, and the perfect teachers of this truth.

These, the flora and fauna, are gateways to the frequency enveloping us in vibrating waves of light, wave upon ceaseless wave in the eternal ocean of the spirit, exclusively received by a soul unspotted from this world. It seems those who nurture and protect their bodies and thus, in turn, protect their souls are naturally tuned to this frequency, as a radio is tuned, yet imperfectly, to a broadcasting signal. Although radio waves are sending signals all about us, continuously both day and night, we cannot receive them unless tuned into their various frequencies. Likewise, we cannot receive the light waves that enlighten us, enabling us to see what is invisible to others, unless we are reconciled to the flora and fauna; for this is, indeed, self-reconciliation. And, here, dear friends, I speak of a heart and mind more fully alive, which sees positive outcomes in the future and, therefore, more easily sees the good in others. Thus, as we have learned earlier, we are a people of great faith, for we, with a sanguine mind, believe our plans shall come true.

And so, we are alive from head to toe, rising early in the morning, working smarter and harder than those who might be less aware. This, the state of friendship itself, that spiritual state unconsciously manifesting a subtle expression of kindness from the light of our eyes, our free yet respectful deportment, an understanding tone of a single word, altogether of which magnetizes friendship.

> I once was young and traveled alone.
> I met another and thought myself rich.
> Man is the joy of man.
> Be a friend to your friend.
>
> Give him laughter for laughter.
> To a good friend's house.
> The path is straight
> Though he is far away.
>
> An old Norse poem

Indeed, the richest man among our tribe is he who has one good friend.

## X. A Good Deed Every Day

This was one of King Alfred's ideas, which made the Kingdom of Essex a wonderful place to live. It also improved the morality and spirituality of his people. Like our cousins who lived under Alfred's reign, we can find countless good deeds to do every day.

But before helping others or the environment, we should do a good deed for ourselves. And the best good deeds we can do for ourselves are having a grateful attitude, healthy relationships, sleeping well, vibrant energy, a positive work environment, and eating life-giving food.

Healthy food changes the way we think, how deeply we sleep, our energy levels, how we work with others, and even our appearance.

And, as we have learned, outward utopia begins within our bodies. So, let's look at a delicious and healthy menu for one day:

Breakfast

*Eco Smoothie*
Place the following organic ingredients in a blender: a frozen banana, spinach or kale, celery, blueberries, strawberries. Add 12 oz of filtered water. Blend. While blending, add one scoop of green pea protein powder sweetened with stevia. Drink and enjoy this extremely healthy smoothie.

*Buckwheat with molasses, almonds, walnuts, cinnamon*
After your smoothie, enjoy a bowl of organic buckwheat cereal. You may want to add four or five almonds, four of five walnut halves (more may cause weight gain), a tablespoon of molasses topped with a generous sprinkling of

cinnamon. This is a carbohydrate that will boost your energy all day long. The almonds and walnuts provide the healthy fat and protein your body loves; the molasses is rich in iron for stamina; the cinnamon is an anti-fungal. And buckwheat cereal is one of the healthiest breakfast foods we can eat. Altogether, it tastes marvelous.

Lunch

*Avocado Salad*
Using all organic ingredients, slice an avocado, mix with baby leaf spinach, cherry tomatoes, slices of red onion, shredded carrots, chopped celery, sliced red bell pepper, sprinkle with olive oil and apple cider vinegar. Enjoy with an organic apple or an organic orange along with a glass of organic carrot juice, organic apple juice, or another healthy organic juice not from concentrate.

Dinner

Here are three delectable dinner choices:

*Pasta Fusilli Rossellini*
Using all organic ingredients, cook gluten-free pasta fusilli, mixed with tomato paste, olive oil, fresh basil leaves, fresh spinach leaves, black olives, and red onion slices. The amount of each ingredient is up to you. Enjoy with a glass of organic grape juice, not from concentrate, in a beautiful wine glass. *Salute!*

*Enchilada Champs Elysees*
Two organic vegan enchiladas on a bed of organic Champs Elysees salad (green leaf lettuce, frisee, radicchio, and carrots). Sometimes you can find the organic vegan en-

chiladas ready-made and the organic Champs Elysees salad ready mixed at the local market.

### Taste of Old Kashmir
Organic brown rice mixed with Kashmiri curry, organic green peas, organic peanuts, organic baby spinach leaves, all topped with organic coconut flakes. Positively delicious!

Dessert

### Lime Sorbet
Organic lime sorbet served in a small, frosted dessert cup topped with a single mint leaf.

After eating healthy meals like those, you will probably think of plenty of good deeds to do. However, many people need suggestions, so here are a few that you might like.

### Your good deed might be driving less
According to the Environmental Protection Agency, motor vehicles in the United States produce approximately fifty percent of pollutants like volatile organic compounds, nitrogen oxide, and particulate matter. Also, seventy-five percent of America's carbon monoxide emissions come from automobiles. In urban areas, harmful automotive emissions are responsible for anywhere between fifty and ninety percent of air pollution.

Yet, motor vehicles create more ecological damage than the poisonous fumes from their exhaust; the factories that manufacture automobiles and the parts for them send poison into the air from the paint, plastic, and rubber products they make. And cars often leave puddles of antifreeze wherever they are driven. It is not uncommon for birds, dogs, cats, and other animals to mistake the antifreeze for water and drink it, only to die a torturous death. What is more, millions of us are killed and injured, and literally billions of animals are killed by cars year after year.

It is possible for some of us to emancipate ourselves from the multiple troubles of a car. Many cities in Europe, because they were designed before the advent of the automobile, are "walking cities." There are fewer in North America, but they exist and are a true joy to live in because, in this day and age, it is a wonderful feeling to be liberated from the oppression of a car. I believe that all who can live comfortably without a car would be happier by doing so, and, of course, leave much less negative impact upon the flora and fauna. They will save money, too. According to the American Public Transportation Association, families that use public transportation, rather than driving cars, can reduce their household expenses by $6,200 annually.

Walk more. Rather than getting in the car when you feel restless or the need to get out and about, try going for a walk instead. The fresh air and exercise may give you a new attitude about life. You may become more animated, pleasing, and even entertaining to those around you. If you do this regularly, your health will improve, too, whereas driving probably does none of these things and may cause stress and irritability. Of course, driving costs money, but walking is free. If you live within a mile or so from your grocery store, it's more fun and gratifying to put a backpack on your shoulders and walk there. I do this about twice a week. When you arrive, you'll feel more alive and appear healthier and friendlier to those you meet. If you have a few minutes, stop and share a cup of tea with a friend. Buy a few items, place them in your backpack and enjoy the walk home. Should you live in a city designed for cars, rather than humans, walking a mile or so to the store may not be feasible. In this case, you may want to think about moving to an area that is walking- friendly.

Ride a bike.

A boy, his dog, a bike.
The Universe.

I can pedal to a specialty health food market that is four miles from my home and arrive as quickly as by driving a car. I enjoy it much more than driving since I bike along a riverside park where trees and birds provide scenic beauty. Of course, riding a bike also boosts endorphins, increases mental alertness, exercising our circulatory, respiratory, and lymphatic systems.

Packing a picnic lunch for two and riding to a park is also more fun than driving because the food and companionship will be more satisfying after the fresh air and exercise. If logistically possible, some of us may be able to ride a bike to work; the physical and mental health benefits could be immeasurable. The Danes know this well. According to several studies, they are considered the happiest people in the world, and I suspect part of this may be due to riding bikes, which they do religiously.

Work Remotely. If you are an employer, eliminating an office and a parking space multiplied by several or many employees who begin working at home could have a significant economic impact on your bottom line. If you are the employee in this instance and commute to work by car, you will save money by using less gasoline, receive a discount on your car insurance, spend less on car repairs, and save considerable time, as well. Should you have a family with one or more cars, in this arrangement you may be able to sell one of the cars, eliminating all car expenses and possibly placing the profits from the sale in the bank.

*Recycling is a good deed that we all should do*

A compelling reason to recycle is the gargantuan swirling pile of trash between the United States and Hawaii, known as the Great Pacific Garbage Patch. It is presently three times the size of France. This was determined by a study conducted with aerial sensors that reconstructed 3D shapes of the debris, concluding that this blight upon the Earth is 1.6 million km2, weighs 80,000 tons, and contains 1.8 trillion pieces of plastic. This equates to 250 pieces for every human in the world.

So, please *never* use a plastic water bottle or purchase one. It may very well become part of this hideous blemish on the sparkling Pacific Ocean.

Here is another dramatic example of the need to recycle: according to the Environmental Protection Agency (EPA), should an office building of 7,000 workers recycle all its office paper waste for a year, it would be the equivalent of taking almost 400 cars off the road.

To be sure, recycling makes a difference. So as Sylvanists, we recycle paper. We recycle glass bottles. As much as possible, we avoid buying anything in plastic, but should we do so, we must recycle it too. And rather than using paper or plastic bags when shopping at the grocery store, we shop with reusable bags.

Recycle for the flora and fauna, recycle for the ocean.

"As the day breaks over the ocean,
Moonlight still on the sea . . ."
Mike Love

*You might try the good deed of composting*

Banana peels, orange peels, apple cores, avocado skins, and seeds, etcetera, etcetera, should be composted. Over the course of a year, one person's compost can easily weigh over one hundred pounds, so this is an important part of recycling.

Place compostable items in a bag. To avoid unwanted odors or the attraction of insects, it may be a good idea to place the bag in the refrigerator. When it is full, dig a hole and empty the bag there, returning its contents to the Earth. The soil will be particularly nutritious in your composting area and ready for your garden.

*Planting a garden is a rewarding good deed*

The taste of a homegrown tomato will most likely set a new standard for your idea of the taste of tomatoes, as well as most vegetables and fruits you grow yourself. Visit your local nursery or hardware store, where you may find seeds, planting instructions, and advice about starting your garden. While there, ask about planting trees, too.

*Planting trees is an excellent deed*

"The trees are drawing me near, I've got to find out why
Those gentle voices I hear, explain it all with a sigh,"

When Justin Hayward penned those words in his musical poem *Tuesday Afternoon*, he captured the oneness that we feel for trees, especially the deep woods. Of course, as we know so well, Sylvan means "of the forest or having to do with trees," so planting trees is dear to our hearts. And how poetically satisfying to sit "under the greenwood tree," as our cousin Shakespeare wrote, that we planted, as it spreads its branches and leaves in august wonder? Indeed, trees are a source of enchanting beauty that oxygenate our world while attracting an array of fauna, such as birds who bless us with their songs and visual charm.

To only begin to appreciate these ideas, imagine for a moment if all the trees were suddenly gone. How would our neighborhoods, parks, schools, businesses, and cities look? How would this make us feel? Besides depression, we also may find it decidedly more difficult to breathe. With this contrasting antithesis, we readily see their indispensability. Indeed, trees provide many benefits, including these.

Increase property value,
Retention of soil,
Cooling our homes during the summer with shade,
Reduction of our cooling bill,
Cooling the environment,
Protecting streets from Sun deterioration,
Providing a home and protection for birds,
Providing a home and protection for fauna,
Lowering blood pressure,
Calming us unconsciously,
Creating a subtle, unconscious happiness,
They generate oxygen for all members of the fauna.

If you have a yard or other land, visit your local garden nursery and seek their advice about which trees are best suited for your area. You may wish to consider planting a variety of tree species, not only for the purposes of exterior landscaping but also for the many birds who desperately need a home. Both objectives can be met by planting tall trees, medium-sized trees, and smaller trees. This will be aesthetically appealing and will attract a wider array of bird species. Adding shrubs to this variation of tree height will also increase the beauty of your property and give the birds a much-needed place to hide from predators, thereby saving their lives and, in turn, attracting more species. Remember, within our cities, we have taken almost all the habitat, so we must plant more trees for them to survive.

Should you not own property on which to plant trees, you may want to learn about the tree canopy of your city. Most cities need more trees, and helping to promote a wider spread canopy is an excellent way, as a Sylvan, to do your good deed every day. Meeting with your city forester is a good place to begin; if your city does not have a forester, determine who is responsible for forest husbandry in your city. Meet him or her with the intent of becoming a supportive volunteer. If no program for trees exists in your city or if an existing organization is not addressing a need to increase the city canopy, consider making this your vision. Several organizations may support you in such a campaign and may even give you free trees to plant. Contact them and start today.

*Feeding wild birds is a rewarding good deed*

> "Sing me a song no poet yet has chanted,
> Sing me the universal."

Walt Whitman

Eleven years ago, a flock of Purple Finches came to my feeders for dinner. Perhaps they had looked for food for quite a while and were overjoyed to find my all-you-can-eat buffet.

After eating, one of the males sang a robust yet most

delicate song, with the tenderest metallic melodies, clear as cut crystal. And as he sang, he swayed from side to side like a great Italian tenor, declaring his matchless love to the world. So, I named him Pavarotti.

Toward the end of his concert, a little female hopped over to kiss him on his cheek. Then she hopped back to listen. Soon, she skipped over again to kiss him, then bounced back. She kissed him a third time, and they flew away together.

I witnessed that identical mating dance on two occasions separated by two years.

Feeding wild birds is an awareness experience for us, and consequently, we benefit perhaps more than the birds we feed. For the more compassionately we care for the flora and fauna, the clearer we shall see their creator, and, therefore, the more vividly we will accurately see ourselves, the flora and fauna, as well as our responsibilities to them.

More birds will come to your feeders and, therefore, survive longer and more easily if we offer filtered water and different types of food placed in the noon and afternoon shade. Placing them in the shade is important because we don't want the water to be too hot to drink but cool and refreshing, nor do we want the feeders to be in the Sun where the birds must endure the pounding heat.

An excellent buffet in North America includes:

purified water,
hulled sunflower (this leaves no hulls that litter a lawn or deck),
safflower,
peanuts (these must be raw with no salt),
suet,

organic peanut butter,
organic fruit,
hummingbird nectar

Hummingbird nectar is easily made from the following recipe. Start with 1/4 cup of organic white sugar mixed
until dissolved with 1 cup of filtered water. Please, never use ready-mixed nectar that is dyed red. The feeder
must be cleaned, and new nectar added every other day or
so when the temperature exceeds 80 degrees. But it is worth
it.

Millet is not suggested since it is unpopular with
most birds; however, it does attract sparrows who kill
songbirds, which is one of the leading causes of wild bird
deaths.

Yet, the leading cause of wild bird death is feral cats,
or cats who are allowed to roam outside by their owner. It
is estimated that 2.2 million birds are killed by cats each
year in the United States alone, year after year. So, please
always keep your cats inside.

*Avoid commercial cleaning products as a daily good deed*
The US Geological Survey reports that water coming out
of nine wastewater treatment plants in the Northwest United
States contained chemicals from household cleaning anti-
bacterial agents from hand soap, sunscreen chemicals,
cosmetics, and a considerable number of pharmaceuticals.
Treatment plants are not required to remove this toxicity and,
consequently, it pours into our rivers.

The Environmental Protection Agency (EPA) has iden-
tified personal care products as "emerging contaminants
of concern" for fish and other wildlife in our rivers and
streams. These chemicals can cause endocrine system disruption in aquatic wildlife, which may further cause a

compromised immune system, neurological disorders, reproductive and behavioral maladies, and quite possibly cancer. As other animals consume fish that are poisoned with these chemicals, a biological accumulation occurs, moving up the food chain with increased toxicity. In other words, any animal who eats fish or drinks water contaminated by these chemicals also ingests the chemicals we pour down our drains.

This is painfully ironic because "personal cleaning products" do not efficiently clean the human body, nor are "household cleaners" necessary to clean dishes, countertops, the bathroom, or clothing. So, when considered as a whole, it is a global tragedy that most people spend money on these items that are unnecessary, inefficient, contaminate our water, and our bodies. For many of these products contain ingredients that are absorbed into the bloodstream within seconds, which, in turn, crashes our immune system. For instance, almost all shampoos contain *sodium lauryl sulfate* or *sodium laureth sulfate* (SLS), which causes their bubbling, sudsing action. This is nothing less than poison and attacks our immunity.

Yet, friction from scrubbing with water removes an equal number of bacteria and with equal effectiveness as scrubbing with soap or shampoo. And commercial deodorant, for example, can be replaced with baking soda mixed with a few drops of water. Toothpaste is available at health food stores that is free of the toxins found in conventional toothpaste. Dishes can be cleaned with hot water and without any detergents at all. Baking soda and apple cider vinegar will clean and remove odor from our laundry. Apple cider vinegar disinfects and cleans toilets and countertops. Most sinks and bathtubs can be easily cleaned with nothing more than a wet washcloth, leaving them sparkling white. If we feel the need for an abrasive cleaner for sinks and tubs, baking soda is an abrasive cleaner that never leaves a scratch.

So, let's live in a toxic-free home by avoiding commercial cleaning products and clean instead with water, apple cider vinegar, or baking soda. Let's enjoy cleaner, younger looking skin and hair by bathing in warm water with a little scrubbing. We'll save money. And we'll help keep our rivers, streams, ponds, lakes, and oceans cleaner.

*It's always a good deed to use less energy*

It is a good idea to examine our lives, seeking ways to use less electricity, gas, coal, and any other energy source. Here are only a few ideas.

Heating and cooling costs constitute nearly half of an average home's utility bills, so the easiest way to save energy at home is to lower our heat in the winter and use less air conditioning in the summer. Turn off the heat or air conditioning during temperate weather and open the windows, welcoming the fresh air. We can also wear a sweater during the day at home when it's cooler and wear pajamas in bed at night with an extra blanket, rather than turning up the heater. This is the Sylvan way since we are attuned to the natural elements. And, of course, we want to always turn off the heat or air conditioning when leaving home, unless we live in a severe clime.

We can save eighty percent of the electricity used to light our homes quite simply by using LED lightbulbs throughout them. For example, an LED bulb producing 1100 to 1499 lumens and using the equivalent of 75 watts, actually uses only 6 watts. Moreover, one LED bulb can last as long as eighteen years!

The electricity used by electronics when turned off or in standby mode, known as phantom loads, is a significant source of energy drain. It has been estimated that 75% of the energy for household electronics is used when they are turned off. So, let's unplug our electronic devices when asleep or away from home or use a smart power strip that will do this for us.

Using energy efficient appliances, heat and air conditioning units, and time regulated thermostats will help, as will weatherizing our homes by installing insulation, sealing doors, windows, and vents, all of which will retain heat in the winter and coolness in the summer.

Thaw frozen items overnight as this will require less cooking energy; and, after cooking during the winter months, we might leave the oven door open so the heat will help warm the house.

### Using less water is a good daily good deed

There are many ways to use less water. However, it is surprising to realize that *seventy percent* of all freshwater is used to produce our food. So, it is wise to eat all the food we prepare by saving uneaten portions for another meal.

A plant-based diet, incidentally, will reduce our water footprint by thirty-five percent.

XI. Leaving Good Works Behind Us

Life is not easy. Amidst all its glories of wonder, many episodes of ardent struggles await Everyman. Whatever the station we attain, or to which we are relegated, we must bear the well-known yoke of the human predicament.

This is, in and of itself, reason enough to leave good works behind us, which is another of King Alfred's admonitions to his people. For there is an endless series of longsuffering, then a brief joyous overcoming, which is part of this Earthly equation, and so we want to ease the burden of those who remain behind us, as did Alfred, who left his great legacy. Though we live long ages beyond his life, he yet reconciles us to our high potential by example, so let us follow in the wake of his abundant generosity. As we give thoughtful consideration to what the great king has given and what we, in turn, might give, no matter how modest or vast, whether spiritual or material or both, we may best approach this notion by asking: What is the most beneficial and intelligent way to leave good works behind us? This question may lead us to pose another: What is the most precious gift? I will answer both questions with what I feel is the singular response: *our progeny.*

Yes, the highest and best good work we may leave behind us is our blessed children. 'Tis the gift bestowed upon us by millions over millions of years of upward striving, fighting to lift our heads midst the primordial pandemonium unto starlight until we walked on stage in this our sweeping romantic role.

For the next four hundred centuries of battling against paucity, in which almost every villager starved, the plague that drug millions to the blackened grave, pillagers who left only a few alive, wounded, weeping, limping amongst the smoldering thatched huts, thus feebly arose our blood ancestors. Yet we see not the struggle. We see not the traveler afoot weighted down by a heavy bundle upon her back while the Sun beats her as with a rod, the lathered horses under the whip, heaving, straining uphill in the harness, the twelve-hour day of toil for pennies at the workhouse with only a blessed Sunday of respite. We do not see the hale and hearty young man, so lofty and bright-eyed after working his life away, become an elderly wanderer, bent and begging for a crust of bread, and this at only two score years when we have not reached our prime. We see not the sweat. We see not the anguish. We see not the struggle that bought our lot in life. Yet, this is their longsuffering gift to us, wherein each little child who became our forebearer was encircled by a vanguard against the storm.

Since our very lives were purchased at this cost far beyond price, should we not wish to return the same sparkling gift?

Second to leaving our children behind us as the ultimate good deeds, come *ideas and ideologies*.

Ostensibly, a few countries—two or three—presently rule the world due to their superior weaponry, yet this is somewhat misleading since these superior weapons are, themselves, controlled by ideologies that weld far greater superiority; as Victor Hugo said, "No army can withstand the strength of an idea whose time has come." We see rather clearly then that hard weaponry may be a simile of a glove, which is directionless and powerless, its inutility being fatuously obvious without the thing for which it was created, the hand within the glove, namely ideology.

Ideas, particularly those that are collectively accepted, overpower weaponry since foreign battalions and bayonets are typically met with far greater resistance at a nation's border; whereas these same borders become quite porous before regimented ideas. Of course, Sylvanists believe in clearly defined and sovereign borders that are protected by military might.

Yet, ideas supersede these. Indeed, the ideas of individuated worth and divine rights of the individual are exceptionally contagious across much of the globe, meeting with as little resistance as a floating cloud at borders. Therefore, foreign ideas can conquer a society through cultural insurrection. Their continuously repeated messages, for example, cause communistic behavior while the affected individuals simultaneously, with unconscious bewilderment, deny their Marxist bent. This is the preferred invasion methodology of contemporary communism, with its virtual invisibility, whereas the use of conventional weapons requires a forced penetration of national boundaries tantamount to rape and, though successful, will always be physically, emotionally, and spiritually rejected.

Thus, rule the ideas of men within our Earthbound plane. These ideas of seismic effect, their tremors felt internationally, typically derive from the mind of one man. Thus, the global jungle is ruled by many individual men warring with ideas, the ideas of men alive today and those long dead. For it is one man who changes things. This is why Lord Nelson despised councils of war. It seems that F. Scott Fitzgerald shared his distaste for huddling with conformists, "No grand idea was ever born in a conference, but a lot of foolish ideas have died there," he said. To be sure, the laboratory of world change is most often the single daring mind in spite of, rather than in concert with, the collective fecklessness of a blundering herd stampeding with confidence, with agreement toward the cliffs. There are, however, instances of ideas being managed, promoted, and implemented by a group; we, of course, have seen revolutionary ideas agreed upon by groups of men, such as the fifty-six gentlemen signers of the Declaration of Independence, who were inspired collectively after becoming the object of tyranny and threatened with almost certain death by hanging for their stance against it. Yet, the idea itself, almost without exception, is born within the independent mind.

So, let autonomous thought be daring and bold, unafraid of critique by peers or masses, as Gulliver was thoroughly unafraid of mere words spoken in a tiny squeakiness by the Lilliputians far beneath him. Yes, we must think of ourselves as giants who can never be stopped by small voices, for then we shall assume the physical, mental, and spiritual posture attuned to the vast bio-computer of our unconscious mind, unlimited in its authority. For these little voices of these little saboteurs are representational of their limited experience and self-esteem, both typical accompaniments of mental dwarfism; in other words, they live in a tiny world and project that same smallness to us, ascribing to us an experience and intelligence as narrow and uninventive as their own. We are, nevertheless, firm but not unkind to them, considering them as tall children.

Even so, when our original epiphany dawns upon the horizon of thought, we must test it against Aristotelian logic. And, as a boxer never shrinks back from a worthy opponent but heartily welcomes his challenge, we must welcome both positive and negative criticism, for this will assist our analysis of our idea's seaworthiness until fully battle-tested and sure. Then, as we present our ideas, our hand grasp shall be firm, our gait quick and efficient, and, before speaking a word, the light of combat readiness in our eye shall command others to follow our overwhelming lead. For then, we shall influence others to embrace our ideas, being adopted as their own, at which time they shall help and support us until we may find a network of adherents who will convince others. Therefore, our ideas, and even our physical appearance and personalities must become as attractive and strong as possible. For, the strongman is magnetic. Alfred was a successful ideologue for this reason and many others, the foremost of which was, perhaps, that he clearly understood an ideologue's tools of trade.

". . . I was desirous of materials for the work which I was commanded to perform; that was that I might honorably and fitly guide, and exercise the power which was committed to me. These then are a king's materials and his tools to reign with: that he have his land well peopled—he must have praying men, fighting men, and working men."

Many countries today are, of course, well peopled. Yet how many are peopled with praying men? How many of the men are fighting men, that is, men who would be disciplined soldiers? How many are working men? And how many of them are all three? These three elements are the Sylvanists' ideologue's sculpting clay, for only with them shall he build a statuesque monument we stand before in awe, in which our dreams and spirits remain congruent with and subject to nature, invulnerable to those seducing ideologies that compete for the very souls of our people. Exclusively with these three mediums can the ideological artist create a society sacred, extramundane. Hence, the able-bodied man who prays, who is willing and qualified to fight in a regiment, and who works, is of highest value to our tribe as a farm with loamy soil is to a farmer.

Now, a virtuous idea or ideology must be ignited with providential timeliness, in which the culmination of public opinion amongst only three percent of a nation shall prime a counterbalancing pendulum swing wherein one man becomes the people's *id*. This is presently to our advantage.

For, political correctness has moved the range of acceptable discourse, known as the *Overton window*, to the far radical left, which is nothing less than the stifling of free speech, the only environment wherein communism flourishes. "The tyrant to be feared is no longer a monarch but the tyranny of conventional public opinion, which hates and fears originality and the defiance of its prejudices as any Inquisition or Starchamber of old." This observation by David Churchill Somervell is a succinct description of the inflexibility that Marxists employ while proclaiming their tolerance. It is quite mad. Because of this psychological warfare, the pendulum has swung so far afield from nature that the precious few thinking men of our societies yearn night and day for it to be put aright. Only powerful ideas that spring forth from nature, that possess the impetus to exceed the gravitational pull of these enfeebled opinions, will allow us and our posterity to live in bold-blooded freedom. So, let us live them and teach them. And may this be our primer: *virtuous people are exclusively capable of living in freedom.* Indeed, only with well-defined moralities and humility before the Infinite may we enjoy sublime freedom.

If we have left well-bred children and heroic ideas behind us, we will have done well. After having done so, or if we have been unable to leave these legacies, *wilderness land* is the next most benevolent bequest.

In 1914, Ivan G. Borodin said, "Occupying a huge territory spreading out into two continents of the world, we in Russia are the possessors of unique natural treasures. They are as unique as, say, the paintings of Raphael—and they are as easy to be destroyed, but it is not possible to recreate them." This is an elegant, compelling reason to leave a trust behind us that protects the beauties of the wild. Old-growth forests, of course, might be our first choice since these are homes to the measureless flora and fauna whose biological ancestors have dwelt there for unrecorded ages; it is obvious that the seed falls not far from the tree; and, it is also not uncommon for many species of fauna to remain in the place of their birth or return to them should they migrate.

Russia is protecting such richness within 332 million acres of strict nature preserves called *zapovedniks,* wherein few humans are ever allowed to set foot. Because of zapovedniks, many species, such as musk oxen, polar bears, sable, European bison, and Siberian crane, have been saved. The last little islands of virgin steppe and vast, pristine forests have also been conserved. In the United States, although the National Wilderness Preservation System protects 109 million acres, this is only 5 percent of the US landmass, and half of this acreage is in Alaska. Yet, we continue to lose over 6,000 acres of open space each day to development. The Pew Charitable Trusts considers these to be the best reasons to bequeath wilderness land to future generations:

"Clean drinking water: Falls and rushing water accentuate the upper Bald River in Tennessee's Cherokee National Forest. Undisturbed ecosystems in wilderness areas produce clean water for thousands of communities. According to the US Forest Service, national forests and grasslands, including wilderness, are the nation's most important water source, providing drinking water to some 60 million Americans.

"Outdoor recreation: A view of Lake Pend Oreille greets a hiker descending Idaho's Scotchman Peak. From the clear rushing rivers of Washington's Wild Olympics to the beautiful mountains and lakes of Tennessee's Cherokee National Forest, the nation's wildlands offer some of the best places to enjoy fishing, hiking, camping, climbing, and paddling. These quiet areas also provide us opportunities for peace and solitude—a refuge from our busy lives.

"Economic engines: Outdoor recreation such as fishing and rafting generates $646 billion annually in consumer spending and supports 6.1 million US jobs. Safeguarded landscapes boost the bottom line for local economies, attracting visitors and adding to local residents' quality of life. Across the West, for example, counties with permanently protected public land report higher per capita income and above-average job growth.

"Wildlife habitat: A bull moose in Alaska's Steese National Conservation Area, is a treat for wildlife watchers. Undeveloped public lands are a haven for animals, fish, and birds of all types, providing them with safe places to live, raise off-spring, rest, and feed during migratory flights, as well as a way to traverse from one area to another along migration corridors."

As we have noted, over 6,000 acres of open land are lost daily in the United States to development. That is over 2,000,000 acres each year, or over 40,000,000 acres in 20 years. Therefore, Sylvans place a priority on preserving wilderness lands.

## XII. Good Works Cannot Fail

Who would know more about the nature of good works than our royal patron? For, as we have seen, it is widely agreed upon by men of greatness that few people throughout history have done more good works than he, a truth stated succinctly by Sir John Spelman: "A man beyond the hopes of emulation . . ."

So, it is curious that the great king should say, "good works cannot fail." Surely, he must have attempted a good deed or two without succeeding. And anyone amongst us who has set his or her hand to a mighty task knows the soul-wrenching pain of trying, failing, and trying yet again. Some of our enterprises may have failed utterly. How is it, then, that the great king should say that good deeds cannot fail? I do not pretend to be remotely as wise as the king, for in this respect and many others, he enjoys a hall of honor all his own. Yet, I offer my humble answers to this question, which may help in some ways to unravel the mystery:

First, these deeds, which might be described as infallible, are good by nature, and it is this honest feather that brings virtuosity, yielding protected dividends to the souls of those who attempt them. Whether we bring them to fruition or merely attempt to do so with all might and main, the honorable task strengthens our everlasting soul. The unfailing goodness of the deeds, notwithstanding, is predicated upon their altruistic character. Should we set about purely to make money as a profiteer, this deed may or may not manifest itself in the temporal world, enduring for a time only, but it shall never appear in the eternal realm, where such things do not exist. Whereas philanthropic deeds may or may not fully appear, or not appear at all, in the temporal realm, they will dependably manifest in the eternal. Perhaps, our deeds, whether carnal or altruistic, are attached to our unfailing souls, and therefore, the deeds everlastingly coexist with us. As we discussed earlier, Nikola Tesla said, "Everything that we once saw, hear, read and learn, accompanies us in the form of light particles." If this is true, our autobiographical aura is a cloud all about us, clearly visible to the unconscious mind to read and to the souls of men to divine. This is a sobering thought. It is one I hope will inspire us to take a clearheaded account of our lives.

What have we done thus far, dear friends, with this our gift of infinitesimal value? Secondly, these deeds mustn't be undertaken casually with an accepted option of failing, but matched with our full integrity, striving to the uttermost for their unqualified success.

Consequently, strengthening our bodies with rigorous exercise three or so times each week and passive exercise, such as walking in the fresh air every day, will prepare us to fight the good fight of the spirit. For we struggle in temporal bodies against worldly opposition.

Yes, we may be certain that should we build a sandcastle, there will be others who will line up to kick it down, relishing the destruction of our good work. The nobler the altruism of our dreams, the more vigorously we shall be besieged by metaphysical gravities, and so we must be ever vigilant. We must expect these attacks and be prepared to defend ourselves against them. We must be wise. Such preparedness and wisdom may be exercised by learning to play chess. "The game of chess is not merely an idle amusement; several very valuable qualities of the mind are to be acquired and strengthened by it, so as to become habits ready on all occasions; for life is a kind of chess," said Benjamin Franklin. And, Bobby Fischer, arguably the best chess player of our time echoed this idea when he said, "chess is life."

And to do deeds that cannot fail, it may be helpful to meditate on the words of one of the best tennis players in the world, Novak Djokovic. "Just believe in your dreams. If you have dreams, don't give up. Belief is the most common word to me, even more than hope. For one, to achieve his dreams, he needs to truly believe in them. I was dreaming of becoming number one. Wimbledon was in those dreams. Then, in a span of just two days—my dreams came true. For a long time after that, images were moving in my mind—clearer than ever before." So, with the great king and his unparalleled deeds before us, let us dream good dreams and believe, with exact specificity, in their positive outcome.

Dear cousins, now that we have considered our twelve societal laws, our "shield wall" of protection, let us be cognizant of them and stand by them, for they ensure our freedom and happiness. It may be wise, therefore, to reiterate them here, thinking about their importance.

I      The Law of Survival

II     Subjects of Nature

III    Love is a Positive, Constructive Force

IV     Ethics

V      The Biologic Determines the Sociologic

VI     A Homogeneous Society

# PART II

# CIVIC VIRTUE

Chapter One

# Civic Realism

*I wrote this chapter twelve years before writing* The Tribe of Sylvan; *so, you may notice a slightly different tone that is more academic. It is included here because it is positively vital to notions of a free government.*

IN this observation of contemporary America, we will consider the principle ways the United States has devolved into a less perfect state by discussing misconceptions and deliberate perversions of Jeffersonian ideology. We will also consider the sociological pendulum swing that, if given the opportunity, will open wide the door to Jefferson's vision and, consequently, America's zenith.

First, we will discuss Jefferson's idea of a republic balanced by a constitutional aristocracy with limited democracy. We will discuss Jefferson's idea of a decentralized government that acts as an agent of the sovereign states and, in turn, the sovereignty of the individual citizen. Next, we will discuss the centerpiece of our individuated freedom and, lastly, the plan to preserve it, which might simultaneously be our gateway to peaceful prosperity.

I. Jefferson's Idea of a Republic Balanced by a Constitutional Aristocracy and Limited Democracy:

The United States of America was founded as a republic balanced by a constitutional aristocracy with a narrowly defined democracy; only men who owned land could vote. Their new government was fashioned after the earliest republics of the ancient Greek city states, in which only the landed gentry attended debates, casting votes for the brightest and best leaders, who were called aristocrats. These aristocrats, especially in Athens, were well educated, extraordinarily articulate, and polished gentlemen who were trained with uncompromising discipline as soldiers from their earliest youth. And as America's Founding Fathers, the Greeks were mostly gentry farmers who also pursued professions in the arts and sciences but were, foremost, the homeland's fighting men.[1,2,3] The fact that the United States began as a constitutional aristocracy with qualified democracy is less surprising when we consider that each of the Founding Fathers were Englishmen accustomed to the aristocracy of the British Monarchy.

Yet this fact is all but lost amidst the extra-constitutional rhetoric of our leaders and the apparent reluctance of our educators to require their students to read the quintessential laws of our freedom, namely, the Articles of Confederation, the Declaration of Independence, and the Constitution, wherein the word "democracy" or its derivatives are unmentioned. Indeed, the idea that democracy alone is the best form of government was foreign to the Founding Fathers. In contrast to their original plan, we see that the United States Government has changed to what I call "hyperdemocracy" or democracy in which everyone may vote— an anomaly within world history that appeared in 1920 yet

was not enforced until 1966 within the new American exper-
iment. Indeed, it seems that hyper-democracy has gained the
perception of being the single lodestar of our freedom,
while less and less constitutional authority and quality
leadership have become the status quo. Should Aristotle
witness this shift in priorities, he might agree that these
changes may be somewhat of a political devolution. In *Politics*, Aristotle said the best form of government is a
monarchy, the perversion of which is a dictatorship; the
second best government is an aristocracy, the perversion of
which is an oligarchy; the least favorable form of government is a constitutional government, the perversion of which
is a democracy.4 And, in what may be a breathtakingly accurate commentary on America's very near future, Aristotle
also said, "When some people are very wealthy and others
have nothing, the result will be either extreme democracy or
absolute oligarchy, or despotism will come from either of
those excesses."5 That uniquely profound social scientist and
sage Victor Hugo apparently also agreed that naked hyper-
democracy is ominous. He said, "Theocracy is the beginning
of civilization, democracy is its end."6 George Bernard Shaw
said, "Democracy substitutes election by the incompetent
many for election by the corrupt few."7 So we see there are
some extraordinarily bright people who have questioned the
viability of democracy when it stands alone and on its own.
And, although democracy judiciously counterbalanced by a
constitutional aristocracy is best for us, it is not always best
for the world's multiplicity of culturally diverse societies, as
has been so poignantly illustrated in less than successful
attempts in implementing our foreign policy. Nonetheless,
it seems the federal government uses a subjective, self-
reliant criterion for determining that democracy is the
ubiquitous philosopher's stone for all human societies. Then,

with the brute authoritarianism of a common despot, neurotically commands the members of those societies to hold
"free, democratic elections" or face the consequences, such
as embargoes or military intervention.

What is more, implicit within the idea of democracy is
the notion of equality. Unfortunately, Jeffersonian ideologies of equality have also become exceptionally ambiguous.
Many contemporary ideologues, particularly those who are
part of the media, seem to promote the notion that all
people are precisely equal, whereas Jefferson said, "We
hold these truths to be self-evident, that all Men are created
equal, that they are endowed by their Creator with certain
unalienable Rights . . ." Many would agree that the emphasis
in this well-known excerpt from the Declaration of Independence is upon the word "rights" as man's common
denominator. Should Jefferson have meant that all are equal
at birth, he would also be obligated, by common sense, to
recognize that we would instantly begin a process wherein a lifelong comparison with others begins. More rights
will inevitably be given to those unequally endowed with
the most beauty, power, money, intellect, courage, wisdom,
talent, reputation, and, we hope, integrity. Only before the
Infinite are all humans heavenly equal. Yet, when compared with one another—as we compete with one another, as
we are beset with the painful longsuffering and sweat of our
terrestrial labor—equality of beauty, power, money, intellect, courage, wisdom, talent, reputation, and especially
integrity is the rarest phenomenon.

Notions of equality can best be congruent with reality
when contemplating this natural law: The sociologic does
not determine the biologic. The biologic determines the sociologic. Plethoric dissimilarities comprising human biology
preclude person-to-person equality. So, as we see, accord-

ing to the highest laws of our society, it is the rights, alone, of each person that are equal. And this point of equality must be vigorously emphasized, for without the proper emphasis squarely placed on individual rights, rather than emphasis upon a fanciful idea of individual equality, our precious rights will surely be abused, diminished, and tragically abolished. Such shall be the legacy of unfettered political correctness.

Another perversion of Jefferson's ideas is that, because we live in a democracy, someone else is duty bound to ensure our equal rights. Again, in Jefferson's words, ". . . all men are created equal . . . with certain inalienable Rights . . ." These words are commonly misinterpreted as meaning all people, wherever they may be born, by shear virtue of their birth, are born with an indelible writ of rightful, equal treatment, and someone else, particularly a breed of the English Founding Fathers, is responsible for conceiving, explaining, defending, and fighting for those rights. We need only recall the times we hear groups or individuals demanding rights to realize that many of them make this assumption. The critical question is, to whom are they making the demand? What is more, being created by God with equal rights at birth and enjoying the luxury of being treated equally are two separate ideas. God does not assure us that, after being created, others will respect the equal rights that were mystically transferred to us at birth. Jefferson's words presume that, after our creation, an effort—to be sure, a struggle—far beyond the ability to shout very loudly, must be exerted to ensure equal treatment. The Founding Fathers' struggle was manifested and most dramatically exemplified in the Revolutionary War. Indeed, to expect someone else to fight for and safeguard our freedom is anathema to nature. And nature cannot for long be defied.

Thus, asking another to ensure one's rights is a substitute for bearing equal responsibility. For instance, when the great lawgiver Lycurgus was asked how the Spartans would best oppose an invasion, he answered, "By each man continuing to be poor and not wishing to be greater than his neighbor."[8] His answer may seem odd at first. Yet upon examination, we see he was suggesting that all men bear identical responsibility to defend Sparta rather than delegating the responsibility to someone else. In this way, every man would be a combat ready, front-line fighting man. Thus, they sought not equal rights but equal responsibility; for those who fully assume equal responsibility rarely want for equal rights. Therefore, those who wish to remain free surely must pose the rhetorical question: What equal responsibilities have we assumed to ensure our freedom? Do we rest assured of our equal treatment because a piece of parchment with the Constitution written upon it has been archived in Washington? That is not enough. Unless we have equally borne many civilized responsibilities, especially the responsibility of electing leaders who will treat the Constitution of the United States of America with venerable respect, such a treasured document—such a sacred document—will never affect one human life. A person who wishes to be equal before the law never allows the presumptuous abnegation of equal responsibilities.

And then there is the false notion, given wide media attention of late, that democracies do not attack each other.[9] Let us give an abbreviated history lesson to those who propagate such ideas: democratic Sparta and democratic Athens waged a brutal war; the democratic Confederate States of America sought its constitutional legal right of succession and therefore became embroiled in a war with the democratic Union lasting from 1861 to 1865, in which well over one-half million people died. In 1914, democratic Germany, France, and Great Britain marched into one of the bloodiest wars in history. More recently, Israel, which boasts of being the only democracy in the Middle East, went to war with democratic Lebanon, leaving over 1,000 dead and 10,000 homeless. Ethnic cleansing and democratically elected dictators are also phenomena of democracies.10

Dear reader, please understand that, with its many weaknesses, democracy has redeemed us all one thousand times from tyranny. It is elemental to our freedom. Yet while it is elemental, it is not summational. Subtracted from our constitutional aristocracy, democracy loses all equilibrium; and, of course, this is the very reason the Founding Fathers wrote the Constitution.

Very well. So, we have changed since Thomas Jefferson's time, a political pundit may reply. At least the taxpayer has a say in the decisions of our government, they might quip. Do we? Our present hyper-democracy, or its illusion, merely allows us to elect officials who, only under immense pressure and even then, on the rarest of occasions, will honestly represent us. For implicit trust, a characteristic of which many elected pundits are unworthy, is presumed by the theorist of democracy. Yet, many of our "representatives" seek office without the motive of serving their constituency, but of their constituency serving them. All this while we, the taxpayers, are never given the opportunity to vote on issues rending our nation, such as birth control by abortion, intentionally opening our borders to massive illegal immigration, and deliberately leaving our borders vulnerable to what our leaders say is an almost certain terrorist attack. Not a single United States Citizen was given an opportunity to vote on the question of going to war against the many countries we have invaded over the years that have never attacked us, declared war upon us, or threatened us in any way whatsoever. Nor were we even given knowledge of many of the "secret wars," often referred to as "covert actions."[11]

To be sure, rather than our elected officials submitting to our will, are they not literally telling us how to conduct our businesses and personal lives when, as Jefferson might have phrased it, they should be merely representatives of our will? Dear reader, are these the ideas Jefferson proposed? Is this even democracy? And, since the United States was founded as a constitutional aristocracy balanced by democracy, how did we become a hyper-democracy in which little importance is placed upon our constitution and upon leadership by the best and brightest?

II. The Extra-Constitutional Centralization of the People's Government:

The United States had a sanguine beginning for the freedom of the individual, at least ostensibly; for, its beginning also had an underlying inauspicious element: an ideology propagated among the leaders of the time, led particularly by Alexander Hamilton, to centralize the power of the sovereign states within the federal government. Others felt this idea contradicted both letter and spirit of the freedoms vouchsafed by the Founding Fathers, who expressly limited government to being only an agent of the people's will. Passionate debates of decentralization and centralization dominated Washington, D.C. from our country's founding until the Civil War was fought. In fact, some people feel the Civil War was completely orchestrated by the centralists as the only means of implementing their

ideology. Particularly in question were internationalist ideologues and international bankers who employed Lincoln's
duplicitous contempt for the United States Constitution
while seeking increased power of the federal government.
This led to less and less state and individual sovereignty.12
It should come as little surprise, then, that Karl Marx
greatly admired Lincoln and even sent Lincoln a letter of
laudatory praise.

In his book, *The Constitution in Exile*, Judge Andrew
Napolitano says, "In order to increase his federalist vision
of centralized power, 'Honest' Abe misled the nation into
an unnecessary war. With very little regard for honesty, Lincoln increased federal power and assaulted the Constitution.
His actions were unconstitutional, and he knew it. Lincoln's view was a far departure from the approach of
Thomas Jefferson, who recognized states' rights above those
of the Union. Lincoln increased the power of the federal
government at the expense of the rights of the states and
civil liberties. This opened the door to more unconstitutional acts by the government in the 1900s through today."
Judge Napolitano also makes the argument that, without exception, every country in the world ended slavery
peacefully, and, likewise, a peaceful abolition of slavery
could have easily occurred in the United States.13

The Declaration of Emancipation was essential to
basic human rights and, obviously, a good thing. It was also
sociologically inevitable. England abolished slavery thirty-
five years before the United States did so, and abolition
was dawning upon America's social horizon. Lincoln, however, used the emancipation of slaves as a false pretense
for war and the slaves themselves as political pawns. The
neo-federalists needed these false flags to justify their
warmongering and their true underlying goal: to achieve

the centralization of political power in Washington and the corresponding erosion of citizen sovereignty. So, we see that the federal government assumed its power by extra-constitutional means. Indeed, the centralists trampled on the constitution and the lives of hundreds of thousands of people, under the Marxist regime of Abraham Lincoln.

General Robert E. Lee, the South's champion during the Civil War, knew that state sovereignty was integral to individual freedom. His sentiment was spoken with clarity in a conversation with Lord Acton on December 15th, 1866: "While I have considered the preservation of the constitutional power of the General Government to be the foundation of our peace and safety at home and abroad, I yet believe that the maintenance of the rights and authority reserved to the states and to the people, not only are essential to the adjustment and balance of the general system, but the safeguard to the continuance of a free government. I consider it as the chief source of stability to our political system, whereas the consolidation of the states into one vast republic, sure to be aggressive abroad and despotic at home, will be the certain precursor of that ruin which has overwhelmed all those that have preceded it."[14] General Lee's words, "aggressive abroad and despotic at home," seem remarkably prophetic.

Let's consider another expert opinion from Dr. Thomas DiLorenzo, professor of economics in the Sellinger School of Business and Management at Loyola College in Maryland. His book, *The Real Lincoln: A New Look at Abraham Lincoln, His Agenda, and an Unnecessary War,* is revealing. He says, "Before the [civil] war, government in America was the highly decentralized, limited government established by the Founding Fathers. The war created the highly centralized state that Americans labor under today.

The purpose of American government was transformed from the defense of individual liberty to the quest for empire . . . Lincoln thought of himself as the heir to the Hamiltonian political tradition, which sought a much more centralized governmental system, one that would plan economic development with corporate subsidies financed by protectionist tariffs and the printing of money by the central government . . . It was Lincoln's real agenda. For his entire political life Lincoln was devoted to Clay and Clay's economic agenda. The debate over this economic agenda was arguably the most important political debate during the first seventy years of the nation's existence. It involved the nation's most prominent statesmen and thus pitted the states' rights— Jeffersonians against the centralizing Hamiltonians. The violence of war finally ended the debate in 1861. . . A war was not necessary to free the slaves, but it was necessary to destroy the most significant check on the powers of the central government: the right of secession."[15]

It is also interesting to note that Lincoln has been deliberately "mythologized." Lincoln did not begin his law practice as an impoverished country boy, as the Department of Education would have us believe. He was the equivalent of today's Washington lobbyist, who makes deals with elected officials.[16] Lincoln was well paid for his deal-making machinations and married into a well-to-do family from Kentucky who owned slaves. The fact that his family-owned slaves was not a moral dilemma for Lincoln who said:

"I will say then that I am not, nor ever have been in favor of bringing about in anyway the social and political equality of the white and black races—that I am not nor ever have been in favor of making voters or jurors of Negroes, nor of qualifying them to hold office, nor to intermarry with white people; and I will say in addition to this that there is a physical difference between the white and black races which I believe will forever forbid the two races living together on terms of social and political equality. And inasmuch as they cannot so live, while they do remain together there must be the position of superior and inferior, and I, as much as any other man, am in favor of having the superior position assigned to the white race."17

Yet, from earliest elementary education, the federal government's Department of Education immersed our impressionable minds in Lincolnian mythological dogma, the religiosity of which was implicitly unquestionable. Lincoln was presented as the gentle hero, the champion of civil rights for black men and women. He was made semi-holy. He had to be. For with the government-fabricated robes of a false prophet, "Our father Abraham," hid the fact that he silenced the constitutionally lawful right of state citizens to secede from the Union by the willful genocide of 620,000 people and the grievous injuries of more than 412,000 others, all of whom he was sworn to protect as the president of their United States.

This image is congruent with those who must portray themselves as champions of good over evil, as nearly angelic to veil their hidden, darkened selves. Some people feel the recent false testimony of such people intensified the federal government's war on terror. These false testimonies came from those elected or appointed to the nation's highest offices. As a consequence, National Guard soldiers, who are stationed and live in specific states for the purpose of protecting state citizens in the event of emergencies, were ordered by the federal government to fight, endure grievous wounds, and die in a questionable foreign war. This was one reason Hurricane Katrina was America's worst national disaster. The Louisiana National Guard had been illegally sent to Iraq when Katrina hit Louisiana. They weren't there to come to the rescue. 18,19

Also, in direct violation of the United States Constitution, Amendment IV, effective December 15, 1791, the federal government's war on terror allows warrants to be issued by police, rather than a judge, to secretly enter, search, tap phones, and place listening devices in the homes of United State Citizens. 20, 21

Furthermore, the United States Constitution, Article IV, section 4, says, "The United States shall guarantee to every state in this Union a Republican Form of Government and shall protect them against Invasion . . ."

In direct violation of this law, the federal government has failed to protect our borders against invasions, especially from Mexico. It is estimated that as many as 20 million illegal aliens from Mexico are living in the United-States.22 Legal immigrants are checked for criminal records and numerous communicable diseases, including leprosy. But, of course, none of those who come to the United States illegally, many of whom are evading criminal prosecution and have serious diseases, are checked for disease at all.

Ironically, illegal aliens are killing more Americans than are dying in the Iraq War. According to Family Security Matters, some 2,158 murders are committed every year by illegal aliens in the United States, which they claim are more than 15 percent of all the murders reported by the Federal Bureau of Investigation that occur within the US.23,24 Perhaps we should rethink Theodore Roosevelt's words as he addressed the Knights of Columbus in 1915: "There is no room in this country for hyphenated Americanism . . . The one absolutely certain way of bringing this nation to ruin, of preventing all possibilities of its continuing to be a nation at all, would be to permit it to become a tangle of squabbling nationalities."[25]

Brice Hortefeux, Minister of Immigration for France, recently said, "We must put aside massive legalization. It does not work and it penalizes, even immigrants." He stated that the immigration policy of France would be guided by "firmness and humanism" with "lots of pragmatism." Moreover, Hortefeux says he plans to adhere to the policy of deporting illegal immigrants from France. The number of deportees is expected to reach some 25,000 each year, and he vowed to ensure that this figure is reached. If France can control immigration, surely, we can do so.[26]

And, it appears that the North American Free Trade Agreement will cause the very borders of our nation to become less significant. Public Citizen, a national, nonprofit consumer advocacy organization, says that NAFTA "requires limits on the safety and inspection of meat sold in our grocery stores; new patent rules that raised medicine prices; constraints on your local government's ability to zone against sprawl or toxic industries; and elimination of preferences for spending your tax dollars on US-made products or locally-grown food. In fact, calling NAFTA a 'trade' agreement is misleading, NAFTA is really an investment agreement. Its core provisions grant foreign investors a remarkable set of new rights and privileges that promote relocation abroad of factories and jobs and the privatization and deregulation of essential services, such as water, energy and health care. Remarkably, many of NAFTA's most passionate boosters in congress and among economists have never read the agreement. They made their pie-in-the-sky promises of NAFTA benefits based on trade theory and ideological prejudice for anything with the term 'free trade' attached to it. Now, over a decade later, the time for conjecture and promises is over: the data are in and they clearly show the damage NAFTA has wrought for millions of people in the US, Mexico and Canada."27

Ross Perot, one of the richest men in the world and for-mer presidential candidate who obtained nineteen percent of the popular vote, said this about NAFTA: "And you are going to hear a giant sucking sound of jobs being pulled out of this country."28 Was his prediction correct? And what should we think of a government that demonstrates such flagrant contempt for the United States Constitution, state sovereignty, state laws, including the federal laws it creat-ed, and its very national borders? Should we think it is a rogue government? Consideration of these thoughts de-mands a corresponding solution from all United States Citizens who cherish freedom. But how shall we recreate Jeffersonian state sovereignty and individual sovereignty from Lincolnian, centralized tyranny?

III. The Centerpiece of Our Freedom:

The centerpiece of our freedom is free speech; for with-out free speech, we can neither protest tyranny nor protect the other freedoms within the Bill of Rights: "freedom of religion, freedom of the press, freedom to peacefully assem-ble, freedom to petition the government, the right to keep and bear arms, freedom against unreasonable searches without supporting oath or affirmation, freedom from being held without a fair and speedy trial by an impartial jury under common law." (Amendments I through X to the Constitution of the United States of America)

Since free speech is the prerequisite to all freedom, it

may be beneficial to analyze its present state in the Western World by considering recent trends in Europe, where Lincolnian centralization is on the rise in many countries and, most strikingly, in the European Union. Participation in the European Union will directly, personally affect the lives of 728 million Europeans. The profundity of the EU's political, societal, and, consequently, personal implications will be so forceful that the rest of the world will be impacted, particularly each of the 327 million citizens of the United States. In other words, it is accurate and, indeed, responsible to say that it will, over time, and perhaps very quickly if left unopposed, change Western Civilization. Therefore, let us contemplate our sovereignty, mindful of the fact that German courts are sentencing people to prison for questioning or trivializing the government's official version of history. Included in those sentenced, were respected historians and authors, one of whose books are fully available in almost every American and European public library.29 But shouldn't all people have the right to freely examine and discuss unorthodox views of history without fear of prison? The question is not wether we agree or disagree with "official history," for most of us already agree with the German court's version. "History laws" merely accentuate our most pressing question: do we value the sovereignty of our very words? That is the question. Of course, the officials of the European Union think controlling individual speech is a good idea. In fact, they have proposed to make questioning or trivializing official history a crime punishable by prison throughout Europe.30 This is frightfully reminiscent of the Greek dramatist Euripides' words: "A slave is he who cannot speak his thought."31

John Stuart Mill also had insightful words about freedom of speech: ". . . it has been for centuries the pride of this country [England], and one of its most valued distinctions from the despotically-governed countries of the continent, that a man has a right to speak his mind, on politics or on any other subject, to those who would listen to him, when and where he will." Mill also said, "All silencing of discussion is an assumption of infallibility." Are governments now claiming infallibility? And in one of his most sagacious observations of free speech he further states, "If all mankind minus one, were of one opinion, mankind would be no more justified in silencing that one person, than he, if he had the power, would be justified in silencing mankind. But the peculiar evil of silencing the expression of opinion is, that it is robbing the human race; posterity as well as the existing generation; those who dissent from the opinion, still more than those who hold it. If the opinion is right, they are deprived of the opportunity of exchanging error for truth: if wrong, they have, what is almost as great a benefit, the clearer perception and livelier impression of truth, produced by its collision with error."[32]

Should the EU have the right to silence the free speech of 728 million people? What shall we do to preserve our freedom of speech in the United States? And, again, what shall we do to change our present centralized government to become more decentralized and, thus, more representative of the individual?

Of course, the United States government, although sometimes tyrannical, should not be overthrown—of course not! It should be reasonably but rigorously overhauled, subject to state sovereignty, as it was originally chartered, in orderly fashion under the auspices of the Articles of Confederation, the Declaration of Independence, and the United States Constitution. Rebellion or revolution is thoroughly

unnecessary and even an absurdity. And let us never entertain Lincoln's tyrannical behavior of multiplied high
treason, but let us consult the Declaration of Independence
for our authority in our proposed invigorating of state sovereignty and, consequently, our individuated freedom:

". . . Life, Liberty, and the pursuit of Happiness—That
to secure these rights, Governments are instituted among
Men, deriving their just Powers from the Consent of the
Governed, that whenever any form of Government becomes
destructive of these Ends, it is the Right of the People to alter or to abolish it, and to institute new Government, laying
its Foundation on such Principles, and organizing its Powers in such form, as to them shall seem most likely to affect
their Safety and Happiness. Prudence, indeed, will dictate
that Governments long established should not be changed
for light and transient Causes; and accordingly, all Experience hath shown, that Mankind are more disposed to
suffer, while Evils are sufferable, than to right themselves
by abolishing the Forms to which they are accustomed.
But when a long train of Abuses and Usurpations, pursuing invariably the same Object, evinces a Design to reduce
them under Despotism, it is their Right, it is their Duty, to
throw off such Government, and to provide new Guards for
their future Security."

We see that in accordance with the highest law of the
land, the people of the United States are fully authorized to
contemplate such a sea change. For, according to its founding documents, it is, by law, our government. But how shall
we begin? Anger is an appropriate beginning, but not madness. Our distant cousin Euripides said, "Whom the gods
would destroy, they first make mad."[33] Madness is the abnegation of thinking. Therefore, let us think. And let us

first think upon this question: where does the true power reside within the United States?

Hand-in-glove with the occasional tyranny of the United States Government is another enemy of our freedom that is more subtle and, perhaps, more dangerous: the media oligarchy. Doesn't the media, through magazines, radio, cinema, and television, strongly influence the fashionable thoughts of our young people, the clothes they wear, their most personal attitudes toward intimacy, and even their "sexual orientation?" Doesn't the media affect the passive or aggressive behavior of our youth? The Association for Psychological Science states that "Research on violent television and films, video games, and music reveals unequivocal evidence that media violence increases the likelihood of aggressive and violent behavior in both immediate and long-term contexts."[34] Aren't adults subject to the same principles of media influence in presidential elections? Today, we receive our knowledge of presidential elections almost exclusively from a television, before which we sit in non-reciprocal silence. We see and hear without being seen or heard. Yet, the vitality of the original United States government rested with much of its weight upon checks and balances and the rule of reason—and, perhaps most of all, upon the wisdom of a well-informed citizenry. The Founding Fathers took thoughtful care in protecting the interchange of ideas and knowledge by protecting the freedom of the printing press, the media of their time, with the First Amendment, which ensures our free speech.

But veteran talk show host Phil Donahue was told he could not feature war dissenters on his MSNBC talk show without having "two conservatives for every liberal." Shortly thereafter, Donahue was fired. A leaked NBC memo about his firing states that he "presents a difficult public face for NBC  in a time of war."35 Donahue was clearly guilty of blasphemy against Big Brother Media by committing flagrant "thoughtcrimes" and improper "newspeak."36

In another example of media machinations, William Safire wrote twenty-seven opinion pieces in favor of war. *The Washington Post* carried at least 140 front-page stories during the same time presenting the Bush administration's case for invasion. In the six months leading to the Iraqi invasion, *The Washington Post* also editorialized in favor of the war twenty-seven times or more; and, the evening news at NBC, CBS, and ABC broadcast 414 stories about Iraq, with almost all information coming directly from the Pentagon, the Department of State, or the White House, which, of course, favored war.37 But can we have free speech when only one voice is heard?

In his book *Assault on Reason*, Al Gore writes about a case in which the media apparently prevented United States Citizens from exercising their First Amendment rights: "And what if an individual citizen or group of citizens wants to enter the public debate by expressing their views on television? Since they cannot simply join the conversation, some of them have resorted to raising money in order to buy 30 seconds in which to express their opinion. But too often they are not allowed to do even that. MoveOn.org tried to buy an ad for the 2004 Super Bowl broadcast to express opposition to Bush's economic policy, which was then being debated by Congress. CBS told MoveOn that 'issue advocacy' was not permissible. Then, CBS, having refused the MoveOn.org ad, began running advertisements by the White House in favor of the president's controversial proposal. So MoveOn.org complained, and the White House ad was temporarily removed. By temporarily, I mean it was removed until the White House complained, and CBS immediately put the ad back on, yet still refused to present the MoveOn.org ad."38 How often have news organizations denied United States Citizens their First Amendment rights? Syndicated columnist Georgie Anne Geyer also laments the media's profound lapse in journalistic responsibility: ". . . where are we to go for any real legitimization of news? How can a government function? Citizens make judgments? Institutions plan? The sad fact is that the Iraq War was started essentially by thirty men and women in the Washington establishment. And they could do this because those old 'connects,' such as newspapers, between citizen and government had already been so seriously eroded."39

It is critical to note that solving the media problem is paramount and is, therefore, to be examined before attempting to change our federal government; indeed, the media solution will be, simultaneously, the solution for the United States government. For the media, rather than the government, is the crown jewel in our quest for freedom. To be sure, the government, though immensely powerful, is subservient to the media, merely acting as a conduit of media power. And because this strategic tool—this crown jewel— is depended upon with near singularity, contemporary warmongers have limited options to wage war without it.

Without wishful naivety, let us be reconciled to a fiat of nature: there exists no panacea to prevent war. That is why Peace is the most precious aberration within nature. For, we have Peace within the context of the natural condition of war. Notwithstanding, we can create the best possible barrier to war by implementing laws requiring the media to distribute only well-researched facts; I believe creating such laws is our only hope for this best possible barrier to war and for retaining our robust liberties.

IV. Proposed Solution to Preserve Our Constitutionally Guaranteed Freedoms:

In recapitulation of our discussion thus far, the United States of America was founded as a republic balanced by a constitutional aristocracy and limited democracy, and that this triune balance is a superb form of government. We have seen that Lincoln and the Hamiltonians, by extra-constitutional acts of oppression, commandeered the sovereignty of the states, centralizing the states' power within the federal government under the ruse of the War to Free the Slaves. Thus, we have discovered that the federal government has grotesquely transcended its authority, becoming a tool of tyrants in which democracy is greatly emphasized while constitutional law and wise, truehearted leadership is ignored. And, we have determined that the media has been most able to maintain that centralized, tyrannical control and thus became the government's master. Now we will consider a solution for this grandiose conundrum.

Before continuing, please allow me to present the historical and social scientific premise of my plan: As you are undoubtedly aware, the English created the Magna Carta, the Bill of Rights, *habeas corpus*, as we know it, and the Abolition of Slavery. These are what I call the Four Pillars of Human Freedom from which most of the world richly benefits. The Magna Carta set the precedence for human rights: In June of 1215, at Runnymede, King John reluctantly signed the Magna Carta, a document fundamentally guaranteeing certain rights and privileges to common men. This was quite possibly the most significant change ever to occur in human society. King John's signing the Magna Carta was a natural introduction to the Petition of Rights of 1628, which later introduced the Glorious Revolution, in which John Locke was central. This led to the English Bill of Rights and, eventually, to America's Bill of Rights. In addition, the Magna Carta also affected the ancient writ of *habeas corpus*. Formerly a tool of English courts, *habeas corpus* became a law of the people, protecting anyone from being unlawfully detained without charge; in turn, *habeas corpus* was included in the United States Constitution to vouchsafe our freedom. Then, in 1830, England became the first country in the modern world to abolish slavery. 40, 41

Many social scientists believe, as I do, that the Magna Carta was the catalyst to all contemporary human rights, the significance of which is that a single document can literally change the world. Today, however, we do not contend with the absolute rule of monarchs. . . or do we? No, today we contend with the near absolute rule of oligarchists who wield global media power of Atlantean proportions. Therefore, the media, and those who control it, must be governed by something more powerful—a Magna Carta of sorts. Implementation of ideas as a quasi-Magna Carta, causing sudden and sweeping social change, must ignite the hearts and minds of common men, for social regeneration has seldom occurred from the upper classes downward. History sufficiently demonstrates that social regeneration has most commonly occurred from the masses upward. Please remember that barons empowered by the people forced King John's recalcitrant signature of the Magna Carta. Consequently, the plan I present is class-inclusive, and therein lies its oceanic power.

This social contract, this powerful set of laws, must include the interests of common people, for they are, generally speaking, representational of Americans. And these Americans are vexed, as are many of us, by an *artful* media. Thus, by parlaying the yearning of the populace for a media that reports substantiated facts, we can create somewhat of a barrier to warmongering and a meddling big government. For nontruths, rather than facts, are most commonly used as a fraudulent call to arms and bureaucracy.

Mindful of these thoughts, I have learned, during a recent conversation with the Federal Communication Commission, that the media has little governance. With the exception of the FCC oversight of radio, network television and "some" cable television, little accountability is imposed upon the rest of the media; and so, Americans are, at times, subject to seamless machinations and false war propaganda. I believe the social contract of high laws I propose will champion their plight. It imposes restrictions on the media to safeguard the American people from harmful manipulation, particularly manipulation leading to frivolous war. And, because this declaration demands decency of the media, I feel that many Americans will readily sign a petition demanding its adoption as law.

This lawful, peaceful plan is appropriately audacious in scope. Likewise, America needs considerable changes, as a sports team might need when drastically losing to an opponent. Indeed, sweeping transformations are appropriate, for slight adjustments will be innocuous. Paradoxically, it is often easier to create societal innovations on a grand scale rather than modest adjustments. And most important, they should affect the central nervous system of our society— what I have referred to as the crown jewel of our struggle for civilized society—*the media*. To do so, we must introduce a Bill to be passed by the House and Senate and signed by the President, which becomes binding law and part of the United States Code. Before examining this Bill, let us reexamine that excerpt of the Declaration of Independence which we read earlier:

". . . Life, Liberty, and the pursuit of Happiness—That

to secure these rights, Governments are instituted among Men, deriving their just Powers from the Consent of the Governed, that whenever any form of Government becomes destructive of these Ends, it is the Right of the People to alter or to abolish it, and to institute new Government, laying its Foundation on such Principles, and organizing its Powers in such form, as to them shall seem most likely to affect their Safety and Happiness. Prudence, indeed, will dictate that Governments long established should not be changed for light and transient Causes; and accordingly, all Experience hath shown, that Mankind are more disposed to suffer, while Evils are sufferable, than to right themselves by abolishing the Forms to which they are accustomed. But when a long train of Abuses and Usurpations, pursuing invariably the same Object, evinces a Design to reduce them under Despotism, it is their Right, it is their Duty, to throw off such Government, and to provide new Guards for their future Security."

Freedom of Speech and Electoral Transparency Bill:

1. Any organization that broadcasts news by television, radio, newspaper, magazine, internet, or other forms of media in the United States shall be owned and operated by dedicated United States Citizens with no sworn loyalties to a foreign country.

A dedicated United States Citizen is a US Citizen who does not hold dual citizenship. Many of the media executives whose companies present news to Americans are citizens of foreign countries or have sworn loyalties to a foreign country. This piques interest in the question of whether we are receiving news with a foreign agenda. More importantly, it raises the question of national security. Should we trust a foreign national to present the news to us? By ensuring the owners and operators of news agencies that distribute news to America are dedicated United States Citizens, we have more hope of keeping the information with which we make decisions about national interests and security within patriotic American hands.

The caveat of dedicated citizenship is critical. For instance, a media mogul who controls thirty-nine percent of the media in the United States was born in a foreign country, swore allegiance to another country, became a U.S. Citizen, some say in order to consummate a business deal, and recently married a Chinese national and member of the Communist Party.

To ensure better clarity of this proposed law, the author's experience may be a helpful example: I belong to societies that celebrate English culture and promote international understanding through the English language. Yet, I would never salute the English flag or pledge allegiance to England. That exclusive patriotism is dutifully reserved for the United States of America, as should be the truehearted attitude of media owners who distribute news to 327 million Americans.

2. No one may own more than five percent of the newspapers, television and radio stations in the United States, and that ownership may not be concentrated in one state.

This will be a protective obstacle against oligarchs who may wish to control the United States government and its citizens. The present law allows thirty-nine percent ownership of television stations, which could allow only three people to control all the news that is broadcast to millions of United States Citizens. This, of course, places the entire nation at risk.42

3. News shall not be subject to national, corporate, or any other screening but shall be distributed freely from news company to news company, state to state, and city to city.

Presently, our local news stations do not decide if a story is newsworthy. Each station is subordinated as a corporate affiliate to its syndicate headquarters. The corporate executives determine what can or cannot be broadcast. For instance, New Zealand broke off high diplomatic ties with the State of Israel on July 15, 2004.43 I called a local station to ask why this news story was not being aired. The general manager of the local television news station said he would not air this story "unless directed to do so by New York." Local representatives of the Associated Press and United Press International said they adhere to the same centralized policy. The news relevance of this story, however, was extraordinarily high for the people of the United States because of these reasons: The American taxpayer gives the State of Israel three billion dollars each year in a lump sum to spend at their discretion without conditions or auditing. That is more than $4,600 for each Israeli citizen. In addition, we give them much more technical, materials, and diplomatic assistance than any other country. One economist estimated that we have given Israel more than 1.6 trillion dollars in cash, services, and material or approximately $5,700 from each American Citizen.44 And there can be no doubt that we have given her tremendous political capital. Indeed, it can be said with confidence that America has a vested financial, technical, material, political, and diplomatic interest in Israel. So, New Zealand's termination of diplomatic relations with Israel was clearly news of interest to the American people, yet it was blacked-out in the United

States, where, among all other countries, the story was newsworthy.

Another example of a media blackout is the Wichita, Kansas massacre in which two men raped, savagely tortured, and murdered five innocent young men and women.45 A similar crime occurred in Knoxville, Tennessee in which a young man and woman on a date were carjacked by four men and a woman. The victims were raped, barbarically tortured, and murdered. The young woman was kept alive through four days of rape and torture before she was shot to death, dismembered, and left in five trash bags.46 In one case, a professional football player with the National Football League was part of a cult, the purpose of which was the ritual killing of people of European descent.47 All three of the above cases, and many almost identical to them, were crimes committed by another race against people of European ancestry, none of which were reported to the nation. In a contradistinction, the media provides extraordinary press time, richly peppered with sensationalism, to the mere suspicion of those of European descent committing a crime against a person of color: there was absolutely no evidence presented to a court of law against the Duke lacrosse players except what the courts called "hearsay;" yet, for months it was reported to the nation as though the accused were guilty.48 Consequently, some people feel that these cases, and many others like them, support the argument that a double standard agenda exists within the media.

The media has never presented the nation with the fact that the General Accounting Office reported that the Pentagon was unable to account for 1.3 trillion dollars, the equivalent of approximately ten percent of our gross national product. Of course, the American taxpayer should be aware of this urgent story. But apparently, it was never reported nationally.49 Of course, the media has not adequately presented the facts about NAFTA to the American people. If the people were properly informed about NAFTA by the media, this so-called free trade agreement would probably cease to exist.

And how could the following earthshaking news from United States Senator Ernest F. Hollings be ignored by the national and international media? On Wednesday, June 23rd, 2004, Senator Hollings made this speech on the United States Senate Floor:

"In 1996, a task force was formed in Jerusalem including Richard Perle, Douglas Feith, and David Wurmser. They submitted a plan for Israel to incoming Prime Minister Benjamin Netanyahu called Clean Break. It proposed that negotiations with the Palestinians be cut off and, instead, the Mideast be made friendly to Israel by democratizing it. First Lebanon would be bombed, then Syria invaded on the pretext of weapons of mass destruction. Afterward, Saddam Hussein was to be removed in Iraq and replaced with a Hashemite ruler favorable to Israel.

"The plan was rejected by Netanyahu, so Perle started working for a similar approach to the Mideast for the United States. With the backing of Dick Cheney, Paul Wolfowitz, Stephen Cambone, Scooter Libby, Donald Rumsfeld, et al., he enlisted the support of the Project for the New American Century.

"The plan hit pay-dirt with the election of George W. Bush. Perle took on the Defense Policy Board. Rumsfeld, Wolfowitz and Feith became one, two and three at the Defense Department, and Cheney as vice president took Scooter Libby and David Wurmser as his deputies. Clean Break was streamlined to go directly into Iraq.

"Iraq, as a threat to the United States, was all con-trived. Richard Clarke stated in his book, *Against All Enemies*, with John McLaughlin of the CIA confirming, that there was no evidence or intelligence of 'Iraqi support for terrorism against the United States' from 1993 until 2003 when we invaded. The State Department on 9/11 had a list of 45 countries wherein al Qaeda was operating. While the United States was listed, it didn't list the country of Iraq.

"President Bush must have known that there were no weapons of mass destruction in Iraq. We have no al Qaeda, no weapons of mass destruction and no terrorism from Iraq; we were intentionally misled by the Bush administration.

"Which explains why President-elect Bush sought a briefing on Iraq from Defense Secretary William Cohen in January before taking the oath of office and why Iraq was the principal concern at his first National Security Council meeting—all before 9/11. When 9/11 occurred, we knew immediately that it was caused by Osama bin Laden in Af-ghanistan. Within days we were not only going into Afghanistan, but President Bush was asking for a plan to invade Iraq—even though Iraq had no involvement."[50]

Why was this story not brought front and center before the nation by our journalists? Is it because we are being de-liberately led to believe things that are untrue? And to echo Georgie Anne Geyer words, "How can a government function? Citizens make judgments? Institutions plan?"

Such news blackouts, news filtering, and manipulation will continue and, I believe, become far worse unless we demand that the news is distributed and broadcast freely, unencumbered by corporate syndication, from news company to news company, state to state, city to city, and person to person. This will be a giant stride in giving sovereignty back to the states and the individual. Receiving news that is truly "fair, balanced, and unafraid" will set us free. For then we can make sound decisions based on facts. Fact-based decisions about our foreign policies, making our cities and neighborhoods safe, investigating government fraud, and eliminating self-destructive trade agreements will finally allow us to make decisions that are best for us—the American people. Then, armed with the facts, we can make unfettered progress toward peace and prosperity.

4. When state and federal representatives are in session, their discussions and voting will be televised live. It has been rumored in Washington, D.C., and in most of the fifty states that many of our state and federal representatives do not read the bills they sign. Neither do they hear all discussions by the bill's authors because they often do not attend state or federal sessions; however, should they know their constituency is watching every session, they may be informed, accountable, and present. Obviously, portions of some sessions would need censoring for security.

5. It will be a felony crime for journalists, elected leaders, and those appointed to office by elected leaders to televise, broadcast, or print in any way information that they know is false. We deserve the confidence that the news we depend upon is factual. We deserve the confidence that the news executives and newscasters will responsibly research the facts before presenting them to 327 million Americans. We especially deserve, according to Constitutional law, that our state senators, governors, Congressional members, senators, and the President, and those they appoint to office, present facts to us that have been thoroughly researched. This law will inspire media executives, elected leaders, and poli-

ticians to circumspectly revere the American people to whom they speak.

6. News broadcasts must make an effort to present a balanced and unbiased presentation of the news.

All news media sources must begin by identifying themselves as a balanced and unbiased source of news. When a news presentation requires a debate, a moderator will conduct the debate in orderly, disciplined decorum, giving equal time to all sides. Those in debate will not shout out their opponent. No one will be interrupted or ridiculed for an unpopular opinion. Likewise, when an interview is broadcast, both parties will allow the other to speak without being ridiculed or interrupted. Implementing and enforcing this law will almost certainly require higher standards of news reporting for the American people, of which we are in most serious need.

Because facts are often unclear or a matter of opinion, particularly in editorial presentations, the opposing view may be given equal airtime or print time upon written request. But no regulation will be established by federal or state or any other level of government to watch and determine what newscasts are balanced and unbiased. That will be the responsibility of United States Citizens.

On the other hand, a media source that does not claim to present balanced news as unbiased professional journalists but presents only a liberal or conservative view would be exempt. Therefore, the very popular radio talk shows, for example, may be as liberal or conservative as they please, and United States Citizens may listen to the ones they desire.

As one can easily see, this is not a reinstatement of the Fairness Doctrine, which stated that an opposing view "must" be given equal time, whereas I suggest that the opposing view "may" request such equal time. What is more, biased bureaucrats regulated the Fairness Doctrine, but they will not regulate this process in any way whatsoever. Should there be any regulation, it will be done by United States Citizens who will voice opposition to unbalanced or biased media whenever they deem it necessary. Perhaps the greatest distinction from the Fairness Doctrine is the contemporary dynamics of a media balanced by the extraordinary free-flow and abundance of information and opinions on the Internet.

7. Freedom of speech on the Internet will not be regulated by the municipal, county, state, or federal governments or by any other government or any commercial or non-commercial entity.

The low costs and wide availability of communication, including video broadcasts via the Internet, are essential for the centerpiece of all our freedoms—the freedom of speech. This last bastion of free speech must remain easily accessible to all classes of citizens.

Consequently, the right to freely express our thoughts through the Internet must be intolerantly, vociferously guarded.

8. All those who seek elected office within the United States of America will be given an equal opportunity to be elected by eliminating all financial barriers to office.

This issue is critical to our ability to elect candidates based on their qualifications rather than their wealth. Matthew Mosk, a staff writer with *The Washington Post,* says, "Running for president is a pursuit of the wealthy, according to personal financial disclosure forms released yesterday

[May 16, 2007] that show at least 10 of the major candidates are millionaires and collectively, the field of contenders is worth at least a quarter-billion dollars."[51]

Frank Phillips and Brian Mooney, both staff writers for *The Boston Globe* said, "The record for self-financers is Republican Mitt Romney, who spent $6.3 million of his own money in an eight-month period, helping himself win the governorship [of Massachusetts] four years ago. His campaign was the most expensive ever, with total spending of almost $9.4 million. That year, Romney's running mate, Healy, spent nearly $1.8 million of her own cash. Her husband, Sean Healy, is a businessman with a net worth of at least $100 million who has cashed in at least $1.8 million worth of stock options in the past year."[52]

And then there is the issue of financial and criminal involvement in presidential campaigns. Many people feel that John F. Kennedy assailed the 1960 presidential election with numerous bribes made by his extraordinarily wealthy father, Joseph Kennedy. Sam Giancana, Joseph Kennedy's former business partner and Chicago mafia boss, who is credited with more than two hundred murders, also contributed excessive sums of cash as well as his unique style of political influence. His Eminence, Cardinal Cushing, of the Catholic Church, helped by laundering money.[53, 54]

The record reveals, ostensibly, that Kennedy received 34,220,984 votes while Nixon received 34,108,157, a difference of only 112,827 votes in a comparatively close election in which Kennedy was hailed as president.[55] Consideration of the infamous philandering of JFK, the nefarious company with whom he felt at ease, and the inexplicable appearance of thousands upon thousands of last-minute votes gives us little wonder that his opponent, Richard Nixon, repeated over and over during the campaign,

"We've run a clean and fair campaign."[56]

Was Kennedy elected President of the United States? Or did he rob the American people of one of their most precious rights—the right to choose their president? And are we to presume that all presidential elections since Kennedy's 1960 "campaign" have been free?

Bold new changes must be implemented to eliminate electoral corruption and ensure we have free elections. Those who seek the office of the United States Presidency will be qualified by acquiring a certain, significant number of signatures from eligible voters petitioning for their candidacy. During the time in which signatures are being acquired, individuals may make one-time donations of not more than $2,500 to the office seeker of their choice. Non-profit organizations, for-profit organizations, or any other entity or organization may not make any donations whatsoever to an office seeker.

Once the required signatures have been received, the office seeker will become an official candidate who will then be given identical and equal media coverage with the other qualified official candidates. The cost of media coverage will be paid by the local, state, or federal government. No contributions from individuals, organizations, or the candidates themselves will be made to the candidate's campaign. This will ensure that all qualified candidates will be given an equal voice to speak to the American voter, who can then make a fair assessment of the candidates.

Those qualified to lead the United States of America will also possess the ability to influence "grass roots" volunteers without a multibillion-dollar budget. Instead, they will motivate their supporters to make phone calls, knock on doors, host teas or dinners at their homes, and make campaign buttons and posters.

Presidential elections will last twelve months. During this time, the candidates will receive equal and identical media coverage, engage in six nationally televised debates, and be interviewed one-on-one on two occasions for one hour. These measures will prevent big business and wealthy candidates from buying the presidency. It will also prevent the media from manipulating the voter's perception of a candidate or giving one candidate more time than others.

In conclusion, let us visualize the benefits of the proposed Freedom of Speech and Electoral Transparency Bill: On the other side of creating a quasi-barrier to the war waged by media oligarchists is the opportunity of entering a new era of peace and prosperity, which was mentioned at the beginning of this discussion. For when we confidently receive news based upon researched factuality, we have the ability to trust our decisions and, especially, to be more trusting of the government. With implicit trust in the factual news, we can more easily ensure the safety of our cities and neighborhoods. With inherent trust in the media, we can make solid decisions affecting long range domestic and foreign policy. For this reason, trust is integral to every cog and gear within our socio-industrial dynamo. With trusted facts about national and international events, we can move beyond war, releasing the national grandeur of our immense talent reservoir with renewed and liberated energy.

I believe that sociological pendulum swing is poised to occur now within the United States. Social change, however, is not autocatalytic—it does not happen of its own volition. You and I must implement these bold changes today, for we are dangerously parallel to Edward Gibbon's description of

Rome in his *Decline and Fall of the Roman Empire*. As it sometimes seems to be in our government and media today, corruption was universal within the Great Mistress of the World toward her end. So vile was Rome's corruption that in AD 193, the Praetorian Guards, who were to protect the emperor, killed him and then, quite literally, auctioned the empire to the highest bidder. Didius Julianus won the bid with an astonishing sum of money and, thus, purchased his position as Emperor of Rome. Gibbon tells us that upon receiving crown and scepter, Julianus was almost immediately filled with remorse and paranoia.58 There remained not safety, not triumph, not a meal eaten without fear of poison, not sweet sleep. For all virtue had been murdered by Rome's warmongering, by her merciless cruelty, and by her lust for insatiable pleasures.

*Virtue—murdered by desiring beauty while despising the truth thereof.*

Do we behold, not a long-ago time and place, but a mirror? The mayor of one of our largest cities is reported to be contemplating a self-financed quest for the White House, in which he will spend one billion dollars of his fortune.59 Then let us remind all men that our allegiance shall never be purchased. And let us never regard the United States of America as Cicero regarded Rome: "Anything more corrupt than the men and times of today [in Rome] cannot be conceived. And since no pleasure can be got of politics, I don't see why I should fret myself. I find my pleasure in my literature and my favorite pursuits and the leisure of my country houses . . ." It seems Cicero grasped the rights of Rome while shunning its responsibilities, a symptom of corruption that we discussed earlier. Ten years after he made the above comment, the Roman Empire had all but ended, and Cicero was beheaded on the order of Caesar Augustus.60 It is an ice-cold fact that, "Nature is raw

material; so is that part of the human race that does not effectively participate in government."[61]

Beyond peace and prosperity, our ultimate objective is
the same dream that lives within the hearts of all good people: "the pursuit of happiness." And, beyond making us
happy, the author hopes these changes will make us a more
virtuous people. For we shall possess true happiness only
through virtuosity. As Aristotle said, ". . . a life of virtuous
activity will be essentially a happy life."[62]

Chapter Two

# The

# Sylvan Peace Model

W E have peace within the context of war. For, it seems as if all living things are devouring one another. The mockingbird, who delights us with the cleverest, oft times comical, orchestration of melodies, is yet mortal enemy of the butterfly. Should we examine a drop of water 'neath a microscope taken from the apparently tranquil pond, we see a life and death war struggle of embattled microbes. Even amidst our peaceful societies, quiet and serene, were it not for laws backed by deadly force, others would take all we own including the divine gift of our lives.

So, it is within ubiquitous war that we have the anomaly of precious peace; therefore, the desperation of catching hold of this elusive thing is well known to the author. Thus, I am neither overly optimistic nor overly pessimistic, yet somewhere between the two, being appropriately realistic as the architect of our hall dedicated to peace. Nevertheless, if we are tough as nails, as free men must be, and at the same time ever so gentle, this white dove can be coaxed to alight upon our outstretched hand, happy to remain with us of her free will.

Thus, mindful of the rarity of peace and without denying a world history of perpetual war, we will visit the Temple of Peace, supported by twelve columns; eight Doric columns, four on either side of the temple, and four Ionic columns that support the portico, each one a paladin upon which our plan for peace rests.

Approaching the temple from afar, we behold this elegant poem in white marble, awestruck by its alabaster brilliance against the deep, royal blue sky. We pause to admire the portico with its frieze of our family of beautified cousins, pleased and proud to be one with this great and mighty tribe. We climb the temple's twelve steps. Upon entering, we are awestruck by what we see—a panoramic vista of a spreading forest valley of pristine old growth woods, and beyond this, the "purple mountain's majesty." For, there are no columns at the end of the temple. It is open and free.

Yet presently, our attention is given to the manly voice of one of our young gentlemen, who recites the following words meaningfully and with perfect diction. So, let the savant listen as we begin with these four Doric columns supporting the temple's right side.

The First Pillar, Neutrality

There are currently over twenty neutral countries with a combined population of over five hundred million souls. Their citizenry benefits from the wisdom of neutrality in many ways. Physically, they are safe from war, which allows them to live somewhat comfortably in a state of bodily and psychological balance. Spiritually, they are not denied the friendship of others throughout the world, and this enrichment of the soul makes peace between their people easier; and, peace within each person, a self-serenity, is found with greater ease, no doubt. Intellectually, their travel is unrestricted by self-imposed conflicts, flinging wide the door of the wonderworld to every corner of Earth, thereby expanding their thinking, reducing preconceptions and prejudices. And, of course, they are free to welcome those from other nations, which would be limited by waging war. Economically, their business dealings are unaffected by sanctions or trade embargoes imposed by international conflict.

Neutral nations comprise small and medium-sized countries. Nonetheless, neutrality is possible in larger countries, as well. George Washington wished this for America, a desire he expressed with great care in his farewell address with these golden words. Those who seek peace may learn to become peacemakers by reading them attentively.

"Observe good faith and justice toward all nations. Cultivate peace and harmony with all. In the execution of such a plan, nothing is more essential than that permanent, inveterate antipathies against particular nations and passionate attachments for others should be excluded, and that in place of them just and amicable feelings toward all should be cultivated. The nation which indulges toward another a habitual hatred or a habitual fondness is in some degree a slave. It is a slave to its animosity or to its affection, either of which is sufficient to lead it astray from its duty and its interest. Antipathy in one nation against another disposes each more readily to offer insult and injury, to lay hold of slight causes of umbrage, and to be haughty and intractable when accidental or trifling occasions of dispute occur.

"So, likewise, a passionate attachment of one nation for another produces a variety of evils. Sympathy for the favorite nation, facilitating the illusion of an imaginary common interest in cases where no real common interest exists, and infusing into one the enmities of the other, betrays the former into a participation in the quarrels and wars of the latter without adequate inducement or justification. It leads also to concessions to the favorite nation of privileges denied to others, which is apt doubly to injure the nation making the concessions by unnecessarily parting with what ought to have been retained, and by exciting jealousy, ill will, and a disposition to retaliate in the parties from whom equal privileges are withheld; and it gives to ambitious, corrupted, or deluded citizens (who devote themselves to the favorite nation) facility to betray or sacrifice the interests of their country without odium, sometimes even with popularity, gilding with the appearances of a virtuous sense of obligation, a commendable deference for public opinion, or a laudable zeal for public good the base or foolish compliances of ambition, corruption, or infatuation.

"Against the insidious wiles of foreign influence (I conjure you to believe me, fellow citizens) the jealousy of a free people ought to be constantly awake, since history and experience prove that foreign influence is one of the most baneful foes of republican government.

"The great rule of conduct for us in regard to foreign nations is, in extending our commercial relations to have with them as little political connection as possible. So far as we have already formed engagements let them be fulfilled with perfect good faith. Here let us stop."

Thomas Jefferson agreed, echoing Washington's notions succinctly: "Peace, commerce, and honest friendship with all nations . . . entangling alliances with none." Yet, the nation once proclaimed free by the Declaration of Independence has caused untold misery to her people and the people of the wider world; she has been led away in double iron economic chains, the shackles of a tattered reputation, now a common slave, bewildered, and woebegone of countenance by ignoring the sage warnings of her founding fathers. Had she only remained neutral, she would have retained every radiant vestige of youthful vigor, every beauty, and rosy loveliness.

The Second Pillar, A Reserve Military

With the assumption of neutrality, the military can take a less prominent role in national affairs without lessening its responsibility for national defense. So, rather than a large standing military—one that is on active duty—a reserve military may fulfill this need. Mandatory service for young men may last one year, for example, followed by ten years or so of reserve service, which might involve two weeks of active duty each year.

The idea is this: If one does not own a weapon, one is less apt to use a weapon; likewise, if a country has no standing army, its leaders are unlikely to engage in venturesome military exploits.

The Third Pillar, No Dictatorship by War

Governing the politic by galvanizing them into one body, with one common mind, infused with false patriotism inspired by an arranged war, will rapidly bring a nation to rubble, even as the masses shout jingoistic slogans taught to them by the media. This is why Alexis de Tocqueville said, "No protracted war can fail to endanger the freedom of a democratic country . . . it must invariably and immeasurably increase the powers of civil government; it must almost compulsorily concentrate the direction of all men and the management of all things in the hands of the administration. If it does not lead to despotism by sudden violence, it prepares men for it more gently by their habits. All those who seek to destroy the liberties of a democratic nation ought to know that war is the surest and the shortest means to accomplish it. This is the first axiom of the science."

A long, ongoing war is, perhaps, equally as dangerous as its enemies. With every battle, whether overt or covert, the federal government increases its power, its invasive intrigues into our lives and those of our families; even the decision-making processes for the education of our children are likely to become centralized; protracted war is justification for monitoring our whereabouts and messages; and, religious leaders oft become the fount of every false blessing, being the most willing propagandists.

Therefore, should a national leader wish to go to war, he is most literally wishing war upon his people, possibly more so than his fabricated enemy. This is why *"no dictatorship by war"* should be a well-used mantra among Sylvanists. As we have noted, only three percent of the populace is needed to effect such change, guarding ourselves and our cousins against a self-conquering war.

The Fourth Pillar, A Limited Government Payroll

Government jobs mustn't differ from those that are commercial, with the exception that employees are civil servants.

They should be commensurate in every other way; their wages, retirement, benefits, performance expectations, performance accountability, and grounds for termination should be patterned after commercial enterprises. All government servants must understand, with perfect clarity, that customer service means they serve the taxpaying customer, not that the taxpayer serves them. By using these standards, the government's payroll will be strictly limited, yet adequate to complete the overall task without wasted motion or duplication.

Now, on the left side, we find these Doric pillars.

The Fifth Pillar, High Qualifications for Politicians

1. Anyone who wishes to serve his country shall begin with military service. No one will be allowed to seek any elected position without having completed an honorable tour of duty of at least two consecutive, uninterrupted years. For to hold office without the willingness to serve in the military is an insult to every soldier.

2. While serving in an elected office, a moratorium must be imposed on all other business dealings of any kind, including lobbying, and enforced by heavy penalties.

3. Term limits must be imposed, allowing only two terms in office.

4. Those seeking elected office must pass a battery of psychological tests, as well as a criminal background investigation.

5. Lobbying on behalf of a foreign nation is strictly outlawed while holding office and after leaving office.

The Sixth Pillar, Sound Economic Principles

The first of these must be currency issued by the central government and never by a private bank. This is constitutional law in the United States. But the Federal Reserve, a private bank with a "governmentesque" name, issues currency in the form of paper money, which they refer to as a "note," similar to a note a parent might pin on his child's collar for its teacher to read. As we have learned, printing money randomly, or whenever the Federal Reserve feels particularly greedy, is the Keynesian school of economics in which the issued currency always deteriorates until worthless. Keynesianism is an economic weapon by nature, especially under the auspices of a private bank with no accountability to the government, even the government's president.

By contrast, for peace, stability, and monetary longevity, the currency must be issued by the central government and backed by gold, which is Austrian economics. Pegging the value of a nation's money to gold is, perhaps, the most elementary and safest of economic strategies.

It is also of importance, in this time of multi-trillion-dollar wars, to stress that although certain industrialist warmongers have become extraordinarily wealthy, and that the oil reservoirs of the Middle East may be the most significant material prize in all of world history, fantastic riches are unequal to one single drop of our blood.

After all, a robust economy is entirely possible without war, exampled by the nation of Japan, the largest of neutral countries with one hundred twenty-seven million souls. Yet, according to the International Monetary Fund, it has the third largest economy in the world, generating over five trillion dollars annually.

The Seventh Pillar, Nationalism

The necessity of this pillar is abundantly axiomatic. For example, the definition of the word "nation" is, "a large body of people, associated with a particular territory, that is sufficiently conscious of its unity to seek or to possess a government peculiarly its own; the territory or country itself." It seems this definition would gain agreement among all parties, but it does not. This is purely because the enemies of peace want to eliminate the borders of our nations. Which brings us to the foremost point about nationalism: it is predicated upon boundaries. These must be protected with force from military invasion; interlopers must be stopped and turned away; and even those who cross a sovereign national border with a proper passport must be welcomed but regulated.

Nationalism's most fundamental prerequisite is the blessed freedom to pursue happiness, to fall in love, to marry, to see one's sons and daughters grow to be men and women. And, in turn, the delight of their children—all far from the slightest shadow of inhibition. To stand upon fertile land that is your land, in your beloved fatherland, and to know that you are free is the very essence of nationalism.

The Eighth Pillar, No Fifth Column

In addition to overt war, is covert war, waged from both stages, left and right, by the Marxists who have run every aspect of the United States government since the Civil War. President Kennedy found himself in a turf war with this shadow government, and though he may have been less than honest in his campaign for president, he yet boldly spoke the truth about this usurping monster.

"For we are opposed around the world by a monolithic

and ruthless conspiracy that relies primarily on covert means for expanding its sphere of influence—on infiltration instead of invasion, on subversion instead of elections, on intimidation instead of free choice, on guerrillas by night instead of armies by day. It is a system which has conscripted vast human and material resources into the building of a tightly knit, highly efficient machine that combines military, diplomatic, intelligence, economic, scientific, and political operations.

"Its preparations are concealed, not published. Its mistakes are buried, not headlined. Its dissenters are silenced, not praised. No expenditure is questioned, no rumor is printed, no secret is revealed. It conducts the Cold War, in short, with a war-time discipline no democracy would ever hope or wish to match."

Now, let us again stand before the portico of this hall of peace in alabaster white. Here we gaze anew at the frieze of one of our tall men, lean and muscular, who holds the hand of his wife. She is beautifully athletic yet ever so feminine. On either side of them are their children, the little girl holding her father's hand, the tall adolescent boy holding hands with his slightly taller mother.

Supporting the portico are four stately Ionic columns, each topped with a spiral scroll capital known among architects as a *volute* that welcomes our citizens to peace. These are the Four Pillars of our People.

Architecturally, these share the same load-bearing weight as the other eight columns. Yet, sociologically, they symbolize the principal columns of the temple, without which it cannot stand. Their solid state of perfectly matched white marble is without alloy, however, and so the hall is well supported to last many thousands of years.

The Ninth Pillar, Our Forefathers

This graceful Ionic column represents and is dedicated to the upward struggle and triumphs of our ancestors who fought to vouchsafe our homeland—a source of towering pride for us, the descendants of these pioneers. While this is a source of our satisfaction, can this same feeling well up within the breast of someone whose people evolved in a region geographically remote from the United States, far from the events celebrated by this column and, therefore, had nothing to do with them in any way?

Let us be candid. Multiracial societies are disastrous. The perspicuous research of Dr. Robert Putnam of Harvard indicates this in the most comprehensive quantitative analysis ever conducted of its kind, the ongoing replications of which have reconfirmed the original findings with ever increasing accuracy. The results clearly confirm that multiracial neighborhoods, communities, towns, and cities are socially and individually devastating.

While Dr. Putnam's findings are quite valuable and genuinely appreciated, most of us don't need such studies to know the blatantly obvious. It is common sense that harkens this message from on high, as a clap of thunder rolling cross hill and valley of the thinking mind.

For racial heterogeneity dilutes and divides heritage even among the ambient highways and byways of a nation, a reflection of a raging conflagration to come. In *Common Sense*, Thomas Paine speaks of this chaos "which hath stirred up the Indians and Negroes to destroy us, the cruelty hath a double guilt, it is dealing brutally by us, and treacherously by them." And, ". . . tampered with Indians and Negroes to cut the throats of the freemen of America." Such interracial strife continues. According to statistics published by the US Department of Justice, fifty-six percent of all rapes, robberies, and assaults are committed by one race, although it represents only thirteen percent of the population. And this criminal element is even smaller when segmented by gender and age; then we find that it is only *three percent* of the American population who commits the majority of all rapes, robberies, and assaults. Of course, the Marxian media moguls purposefully hide this obstreperous, rampaging subculture.

And, what of national loyalties? Race always answers that question. As British Prime Minister Benjamin Disraeli said, "All is race; there is no other truth, and every race must fall which carelessly suffers its blood to become mixed." And also, "No man will treat with indifference the principle of race. It is the key to history, and why history is often so confused is that it has been written by men who are ignorant of this principle and all the knowledge it involves. . . Language and religion do not make a race— there is only one thing which makes a race, and that is blood."

As has been said on several occasions in this book of ours, we want all races to do well and to prosper in every way. For them to do so, each must have their fatherland. We simply want this for ourselves, as well.

The Tenth Pillar, Custom and Culture

Here, we honor the splendid expressions of our lives. These are principally Anglo-Saxon, British, Celtic, Gaelic, Germanic, Scandinavian, and Slavic customs and cultures.

Many of our customs are folkish and close to the loamy soil of our fatherlands. Perhaps, this is why we love the customary festivals of the changing seasons. In Eastern

Europe around February, *Maslyana* is celebrated with sledding, dancing, elaborate snow castles, snowball fights, and eating an abundance of pancakes. 'Tis time to go "a Maying" in Western Europe among the new flowers, with picnics and singing in that month, which brings the hope of warmer days. Summertime affords picnicking in the park as a prelude to an outdoor play by one of the ancients, and in the evening, barn dances last late into the long, romantic, warm nights. Oktoberfest animates revelers with irresistible Germanic cheer as polka music and dancing bring out the best in everyone. Then comes Father Christmas, and, although all the leaves and flowers are gone until next year, our spirits compensate with double joy. Yes, we are a folkish people. These are the yearly folkish customs we fancy all the more when there is peace. In a way, we have peace because of them, for in no small part they are an expression of our freedom.

Now, beyond custom, how shall we describe our culture? It will be unnecessary to list again some of the noble works of our artists, scientists, and thinkers, which we reviewed in the foreword. Nor shall we mention the cultural gifts of many more of our cousins, the heroic stories of whom could fill a great many libraries. Perhaps, instead, our culture can be expressed in vignette.

I once lived in the quiet little village of Harbledown, on the immediate outskirts of the old cathedral city of Canterbury. This, they call the Garden of England. My bedroom window was not more than twenty feet from the ancient Pilgrim's Pathway, traveled by countless souls to the place of St. Becket's martyrdom within the great cathedral. This pathway, of course, was the setting of Chaucer's *Canterbury Tales*.

Each morning, the milkman, driving a quiet electric cart to not awaken the villagers, left fresh milk and butter on everyone's doorstep. The efficient postman rode a bicycle and was ever so cheery and polite when one had the pleasure to meet him. Otherwise, he quietly went about his business, too.

In the garden of Harbledown's only church, near its front door, stood a statue of one of our tall, handsome young men, cut down in the budding flower of his youth while battling to defend the weak. Beneath the statue was inscribed, "Greater love hath no man than this, that a man lay down his life for his friends."

The village boasted of one inn, the Old Horse and Coaches, where so many of our cousins had stopped to rest. On a midsummer day, one could enjoy a ploughman's lunch in its gardens that overlooked the spreading valley, a multicolored checkering of farm crops as though a giant had cast his patchwork blanket upon the Earth for miles and miles. The droning of humming bees, the melodies of birds, a faint barking of a faithful farm dog in the faraway distance protecting his master's home, were all one might hear on such a halcyon summer's day.

There was one lovely red phone booth in the village, emblazoned in understated elegance with "GR" for George Regina, for it had been there since the reign of King George VI. Many villagers made use of the phone booth in those days. And each and every week of the year, an anonymous, dear ole soul would place a fresh bouquet of flowers in that red phone booth to brighten the hearts of all who made a call there.

To be sure, Harbledown was a microcosm of our cultures. Yet, to fully appreciate this Garden of England, where so many flowers and great oaks of our tribe have blossomed and grown so high, let us consider our present condition by comparative antithesis, by comparing its opposite.

Though inundated with it, our culture is not rock-and-roll, which is a euphemism for a vulgarity that originated among another race that is profoundly different from ours. Neither is our culture jazz nor is it rap. These three sounds, rock-and-roll, jazz, and rap, are often cultural digressions. Scholar of Greek antiquity, C. E. Robinson, said this about the ancient Greeks. They "believed that the development of character was greatly influenced by the type of tunes which were employed. Plato, in sketching the institutions of an idea city-state, lays great stress on this; and it is clear that modern ragtime and jazz would have been completely banned." However, some upbeat, resonant orchestration with a hint of jazz, and certain folk music performed by pop bands is alive with pleasing charm.

At the same time, musicologists have proven that the seamlessly reoccurring dissonant drumbeat of these three African tune-types exacerbates restlessness and, not uncommonly, attracts drug dealing, prostitution, crime, and violence. Whereas the music of our culture, especially the genre of Bach, Beethoven, and Brahms, calms the human spirit and quite literally disperses criminals. Forty train stations across the London Underground play classical music. Elm Park on the District Line, for instance, has been occupied by criminal gangs. Yet, in less than eighteen months of playing classical music there, robberies were reduced by thirty-three percent, assaults on train staff were reduced by twenty-five percent, and vandalism by thirty-seven percent.[15] [16]

---

[15] "5 things to know about fighting crime with classical music." (Washington, D.C., PoliceOne.com, 2018)
[16] Gersten, Jennifer, "Is Classical Music Actually Effective in Fighting

Nonetheless, it seems that in contemporary society, we are besieged by the ill effects of the dissonance of the rhythm and rhyme, which Plato discussed in *The Republic*: verse is compelling, although its lyrical message may be destructive. That is a valid point. And, today it is possible, and the norm, to repetitively deliver an alluring message to the masses that is individually and socially destructive. The insistent beat of the three aforementioned tunes is literally pounding self-destructive messages into our young people's minds. The weak respond with surrender. Along with this trance-inducing messaging is a subculture in which participants behave with half-witted mannerisms and dress the part, as well.

Having said this, Sylvanists are not prudish or boring. Yet we must ask, is it permissible to allow our custom and culture to be replaced with an alien one created by another race of men whose religion was, and in many cases still is, voodoo? Upon investigation, we will discover that the big beat rhythm of "popular music" originated in such primitive ceremonies wherein were unspeakable rituals. Let there be no mistaking it, dear cousin.

In proper response, a good percentage of us are drawing away in repulsion, which is the normal reaction to evil, embracing ever more tightly our virtuous customs and culture. Here, every generation of a family celebrates festivals together, rather than separating to a diverse culture where the presence of certain family members is literally taboo. This is a shame.

So, let us wholly reject this alien music, along with its

Crime?" (New York City, wqxr.org, 2019)

customs and cultures born in the basest savagery. Let us return to our first loves: the irresistible happiness of our folk music and dancing, which is equally stimulating as "pop music" while exuding health to the whole family. Let us return to the grandeur of Tchaikovsky, Dvorak, Wagner, Chopin, and the heavenly host of great masters like them. Their work is culturally heroic. For, how the soul towers when hearing their symphonic miracles. Let's hike to our favorite picnic spot with family and friends in the month of May. Let our summer times be remiss without camping in the woods, picnicking, and Shakespeare in the park. Let's welcome the fall with crackling fires, pumpkin pies, and barn dances 'neath a harvest moon. And when all the leaves and flowers are gone, replaced by fields of silent white, let's be our merriest, as is our ancient custom.

Let us rebuild our societies upon this pillar of Custom and Culture and our other supporting pillars. Then our fatherlands will become, once again, like that little Camelot of kindly neighbors called Harbledown.

The Eleventh Pillar, Our Language

This stately Ionic column represents the splendid beauty of our language, of which each word was once a poem, for upon its christening, one word expresses what may have formerly required two, three, or more words. For you see, rather than saying, "in a secretive, unauthorized way," you can say *surreptitiously*; instead of explaining that something is "a catalysis of a reaction of one of its products," you merely say it is *autocatalytic*. If something is "capable of indefinite continuation," which differs from autocatalytic, you can use the adjective *self-perpetuating*.

Thus, although often unaware of the nuance of this prin-

ciple, our words symbolize a precision and fineness of
feeling that is poetic. We shall explore the value of verse
later. But now, we will give thought to other aspects of our
language.

First, it is invaluable, for it was handed down to us at an
inestimable cost. As we have seen, thousands of years of
poetic cultivation preceded the dialectical victory of our
language until the simple yet empowering creation of vowels, the profundity of which one cannot overstate. At that
time, long-forgotten years of upward refinement were further required until our language became the premise of our
incomparably evolved society. However, it was not until
1755 that the English language was supported by a dictionary recognized as authoritative by the prevailing readership.
So then, we see that English rests on a foundation that only
recently made this vital advancement. Yet, its greater bedrock is "conventionally, if perhaps too neatly, divided into
three periods usually called Old English (or Anglo-Saxon),
Middle English, and Modern English. The earliest period
begins with the migration of certain Germanic tribes from
the continent to Britain in the fifth century A.D., though no
records of their language survive from before the seventh
century, and it continues until the end of the eleventh century or a bit later. By that time, Latin, Old Norse (the language
of the Viking invaders), and especially the Anglo-Norman
French of the dominant class after the Norman Conquest of
1066 had begun to have a substantial impact on the lexicon .
. ."[17] Yet, as we have seen, even this monumental ground-

---

[17] Merriam-Webster, Inc., *Merriam-Ebster's Collegiate Dictionary*,
Springfield, Massachusetts, 1999.

work was built upon millennium after millennium of intense desire to communicate, one man to another.

Secondly, it unifies us. Because of this linguistic unification, which is the lifeblood of our societies, we enjoy universal agreement among the fraternity of our tongue.

Thirdly, it creates peace, for agreement is peace. Albeit seemingly innocuous to blessed concord, there exist no unity without conversations. Consequently, our language is perhaps the irreducible precept of internal peace among citizens.

Fourth, without this unifying element of language, a nation is subject to internal threat from fifth column insurrectionists, more precisely Marxists, and no less insidious external enemies, many of whom they control. It is quite simple. We tend to associate and form groups with those we easily understand, and who understand us most clearly, rather than forming subcultures where there should be one. Such factions cause disunion that communists wish to exacerbate for a Tower of Bable effect, in which several segments of the population cannot communicate in the language used by the founding fathers of a nation.

Fifth, and less obvious, language has an unconscious effect upon morals. Here, I speak of an organic notion of some things being correct, others being incorrect, such as the elementary building blocks of a language in which there is a decided idea of proper and improper spelling, grammar, word usage, pronunciation, diction, etcetera. Of course, in many cases, the science of language is mixed with artistic liberties to excellent effect by masters such as Victor Hugo, Mark Twain, Thomas Hardy, Guy de Maupassant, and many others.

Notwithstanding, the early scholastic emphasis on proper language is a subtle yet effective defense against a nihilistic philosophy that presently ravages the West. Nihilists argue that life is without objective meaning, purpose, or intrinsic value, except the life of the nihilist, of course, whose purpose is quite well-defined and targeted: to rape and pillage their host society. For these progenitors of philosophical poison come to us, especially in our schools and universities, not by happenstance, but by the organized, systemic cacophony of sour notes orchestrated by none other than the legacy of Karl Marx.

Such "moral" nihilists assert that there is no inherent morality since socially accepted moral values, they claim, are abstractly contrived. Nihilists, masquerading as artistic authors, sometimes call themselves "Dadaists" who reject the rationalism and aestheticism of our societies. Instead, they seek to replace them with the irrationality and ugliness of their works, which they claim to be *avant-garde* but are not. And so, they cravenly hide behind the false notion that language is subjective. Whereas, Sylvanism states that language is an objective science attuned to truth and beauty; if this were not so, we must dispose of all dictionaries.

The science of other fine arts may help us appreciate the objectivity of speech and the written word. Nicolas Poussin, a leading painter of the classical French Baroque style, agreed with the idea of artistic objectivity, teaching that there is a science to beauty; his paintings are a living testimony to this school of thought. His predecessors, the sculptors of ancient Greece, also agreed with this notion. Polykleitos, for instance, developed a set of aesthetic principles known as the *canon* or *rule,* based upon mathematical ratios, the expression of which the Greeks called *symmetria,* from which they created statues of surpassing beauty. The Parthenon, of which our hall is but a faint wisp of a fleeting dream, is magnetic to the human eye because of the objectivity of beauty, in which its architects, Iktinos

and Kallikrates, perfected an architectural science em-
ploying curvilinear lines rather than purely linear. By
eliminating the monotony of straight lines and exact perpen-
dicularity, seen rarely, if at all, in nature, the Parthenon is
attuned to the living landscape, and, therefore, we find it
mystically appealing. Because of artistic objectivity, the
masterworks of Poussin, Polykleitos, Iktinos, and Kallikrates
remain unequaled standards as the rolling centuries come
and go with all its artists, a truth the Marxian Nihilists and
Dadaists are unwilling to admit.

Not only do they want us to accept and even praise
their markedly disturbing work as art, but they also want us,
particularly us among all other people, to adopt the character
of a snowflake. Yet, this is merely a way for these psychological assassins to disarm their imagined enemies, whom
they assail with implacable hatred.

All the same, we and our languages shall prevail over
these insurrectionists. For, the intellectuality and depth of
soul, exercised and expanded by reading the literary virtuo-
sos, propel our progress, edify our defense. Indeed, reading
the masters strengthens our cognitive skills, which, in turn,
enriches the national repository of thinkers. Those authors
who lived before the twentieth century have a uniquely positive effect upon such thoughtwork since this era held
substantially higher literary standards and society was un-
subjected to political correctness. Decoding such a series of
ideas that flow in Aristotelean logic helps us to, in turn, dis-
criminate clearly between soundly logical thinking and
contradictory thoughts, such as the Marxian genre. Thus,
we learn to think sophisticatedly, the objective purpose
being the attainment of wisdom, that rarest virtue without
which a peacemaker is utterly bankrupt.

Now we come to that dimension of language exalted
above all others, the finest expression of words. Many thou-

sands of years ago, as artists sought to reveal the secret
subtlety and nuance of the heart that common speech would
not yield, they sang stories in rhythm and rhyme, often accompanied by harp.

Thus, poetics became the wordsmith's state of the art.
For, verse is background to Everyman's chivalry, the he-
roine's given grace. At once luxurious and laconic, it releases a thousand details of conscious process unto knowing imagination—that conscious permission of our original
self to catch things unknown and give them names.

These are those ideas expressed with marvelous precision and efficiency attained by the poet, of whom there are
precious few living among us. To be certain, simply because someone writes a few verses or even a great deal of
them, does not make him a poet. For the poet's call is the
highest of beckonings, which scarcely any can answer.

We may further understand the nature of a poet by re-
calling the second coming of Odysseus, wherein he drinks
vengeance deep and to the dregs, unleashing his just wrath
upon those besieging his home, plundering his wealth, plot-
ting to murder his son, and prevailing upon his wife to
remarry.

> Now, there remained two quivering on knees,
> Priest Leiodes, poet Phemius, these,
> "I have only burnt incense and made prayer!"
> "If you've prayed," Odysseus grabbing priest's hair,
> "Prayed I'd ne'er return so you'd take my wife!
> For thy filthy lust, I take now thy life!"
>
> With his flashing bronze blade took off priest's head,
> Which rolled in dust still speaking words he said,

Yet turned to poet saying, "Peace be still,
Poet ne'er hurt anyone, fear no ill."

As was the nature of Phemius, true poets are humble seekers of the truth whose only quest is virtue, and even more dearly, they yearn for the virtuous greater good of society. They neither flatter nor fawn upon the powerful to ingratiate themselves. They flee not before the murderous glare of the tyrant, and, for this reason, tyrants fear them, perhaps, above all others. Thus, upon the culmination of a nation's star-crossed events, one, true poet is possibly the most important citizen.

This seems to be forgotten by the West, heavily burdened 'neath our interminable Marxist occupation. Even so, our cousins, the Russians, have always been faithful to the poet. I love them for this. And so, we look to that blessed and coming Sunrise, dazzling, whereupon we shall conquer the Marxists, as have the Russians, and the poet will again be esteemed in his place of high honor, from whence he might speak his living words. Then the miswoven tapestry will oft be granted divine juxtaposition.

God grant us speed.

And so, we see that our language came to us with a sacrifice beyond price. It unifies us. That subliminal friendship begets internal peace. The unifying nature of one language also defends us from domestic and external threats. It is an unconscious defense against moral decay. And its highest order is bequeathed to us by the poet, who are heroic leaders in a natural and free society.

Thus, within our Temple of Peace, we dedicate this tall Ionic column unto our blessed language.

The Twelfth Pillar, Our Philosophy

Everyone and their dog has a philosophy. And, if you must choose between the two, always choose your dog's. Although we may learn much from canine wisdom, their philosophies transcend our abilities to emulate them since they are unsubject to the human condition, our inherent nemesis. So be it, we will strive to reach higher heights with our best friend as faithful confidant and consultant.

Yes, it is true that everyone has a philosophical view of the world, his individuated living pattern helping him negotiate what e'er befalls him. It seems, however, this interpretive filter of the chaos all about us is, for the most part, woefully inadequate. And Sylvanism is also imperfect, beautifully imperfect as the Universe in which we live is all sublime imperfection. This is consoling. For, as exact right angles were omitted from the Parthenon to align it with the natural landscape, so Sylvanism's imperfection is attuned to Earth's exquisite nonlinearity. To wit, we are synchronized to nature in ways imperfect which is, itself, nature's way in contrast to religions that fraudulently claim infallibility.

Yet, I dare say that Sylvanistic thought may well be an expedient philosophy as we stand upon this culmination of forty thousand years of ascent. We shall continue as a race, not perish from the Earth. So, let us speak as men of clear Sylvan logic:

First, as we speak of saving the imperiled flora and fauna, we speak of redeeming ourselves, whereas some people feel we are commanded to subdue the Earth. This admonition is a double folly, for it implies that man must subject nature unto himself, a gross vulgarity and a hideously plasticine notion, which is the precept of alienation from

God and the world He created—the very murder of His blessed personification. Thus, men abdicate the dignity of kingly thought to follow Nimrod.

Secondly, as we speak of our emancipation from *societal Marxism*, we speak of deliverance from the ongoing ethnic cleansing of our race; whereas, some teach us to love our incorrigible enemies who systemically, tirelessly devote themselves to our genocide. Is that not the Stockholm syndrome?

Homer's contrast of the lascivious priest and virtuous poet is not without lesson. Shall we remain ensconced in priestly philosophical madness? Must we cling ever so tightly to these religious Orientalisms, which are extra-cultural and, let us be truthful, extra-coherent? What is the logical justification for doing so? Is it papal pontifications that are aligned ever more with Marxism? Do costly robes and opulent palaces and slow-motion amblings about bear any authority?

Should we ascribe a trace of spiritual royalty to this luxurious masquerade, then we must plunder the Earth and the very face of God within its mirror—we must allow our enemies to invade our fatherlands and, leaving not a vestige, wipe us from the face of the Earth.

Now, in light of these suppositions, let us further rightly divide the word of truth. Sylvanism is neither anti-Christ nor anti-Christian. Should anyone be against Christ, particularly if he hates Christ, showing open disdain, something is dreadfully wrong. Such a person is likely communistic, for there is only one thing they despise more than our race and that is Christianity; they loathe Christianity because it represents love, kindness, forgiveness which accent their *modus operandi* of deception and hatred. Moreover, they deem Christianity to be our societal and kindred cohesion and thus desperately wish its destruction. It has, indeed, given us a sense of community that has also been an antidote to communism over the years. But time changes things. If Christianity had retained its saltiness, in other words, its integrity, even with its contradictious and suicidal messages of plundering nature and loving one's enemies, it still would have been a bulwark against Marxism. Sanity would have prevailed before the immigrating armies of militant, military-aged men we face today.

This has not been the case. Through a slow, insidious poisoning over many years, Christianity as a whole is now more politically correct than biblically correct. Now, many of those who frequent what once were churches are fraught with ambiguity about whether to admit they are Christians for fear of offending someone. And thoughts from the putrid mind of Karl Marx have shape-shifted into social laws upheld by wolves in sheep's clothing, which may not be transgressed, especially by our children. Thus, is communism's triumph over Christendom. Shall we then follow the teachings of Christ, who in Matthew 5:13 said, "Ye are the salt of the earth: but if the salt have lost his savor, wherewith shall it be salted? It is thenceforth good for nothing, but to be cast out, and to be trodden under foot of men." It deeply saddens me to see the Bride of Christ in this drunken, bewitched condition. I take no pleasure in it.

Yet, all is not lost. If we liken the world to a combat zone with parameters wherein soldiers live, eat, and sleep, which must be protected at all costs, then where is the parameter of Christianity? Since their liberation from communism, Russians have rebuilt over thirty thousand churches that were destroyed by the 1917 invaders. Yet, another forty thousand must be rebuilt to return to the community of eighty thousand churches that thrived under the reign of Czar Nicholas. This spiritual revival is background to imposed atheism in which believers were beaten and murdered, in which seventy thousand churches were destroyed, amidst the mass rape, torture, and murder of over thirty million people. And so, Sylvans stand with Russia in this resurgence of Christian values, authentic and free of mind-bending Marxist and Leninist ideologies.

Onward as a race, we share a specific overarching philosophy that has been replicated rather consistently throughout our history, in a word, *goodwill*. We find it intermittently, however, between war. This goodwill toward men has been influenced to no small degree by Christianity. If Sylvanity were in its place over the last two millennias, would we see less fratricidal strife among Sylvans than Christians? We shall never know, of course. Yet theoretically, it seems a philosophy without pretensions of perfection would be less incendiary among its adherents.

Perhaps, more influential than Christianity upon us as a race has been our genetically driven behavior. Albeit, the two have melded socially somewhat, but the genome has triumphed because it is only our social behavior that religion has affected, not our genetics; this forever fount cascading in crests within our unconscious shall always have its way, manifesting itself within irresistible norms and mores. Though its course be redirected temporarily amidst this groping, slothful era of religiosity, the fount ever flows upward. Here, I speak not of man's lower nature but his higher. And so, whilst one thing passes away, another is born in its time.

Moss covered ruins are peacefully redeemed by nature's ineluctable greenery, yet with sweet melancholy.

Thus, I have become unintentionally iconoclastic. Never, dear cousins, for the sake of being so. For, this would not be Sylvanistic. Neither to harm nor to destroy, as the Marxian mind is wont to do. I am so purely because Sylvan's time has come . . . come that it might set the captives free.

Notwithstanding my tendentious feelings, Sylvanism is, indeed, the philosophic lifestyle that shall redeem us from genocide, from ecological collapse and, moreover, within the coming generations, prepare us to transcend the Athenian Miracle. For, within this melodramatic and vast novel of which we are the protagonists, after forty millennia we are poised before a redeeming page unto an epoch hitherto undreamt. As if it were a grand window open to alpine air and morning Sunlight, we see our answer vouchsafed before us. These light waves expand in widening concentric circles, to an audience awakening from slumber, for even at this bleak and darkened hour, the frequencies, the vibrations are clearer. And one is this: we needn't do anything to commune with our creator; but only to see, hear, smell, taste, feel the green and blue miracles all about us. These wonders are vessels of light far above our understanding, yet within the simplicity of knowing . . . inexplicably knowing. And so, the culmination of our lives within this pinpoint in time is a privilege divine. For, we may stand upon the threshold of an era of mankind in which our creator is esteemed above religion.

Now, we have visited the Twelve Pillars, upon which rests our Hall of Peace.

| | |
|---|---|
| Neutrality | Nationalism |
| Reserve Military | No Fifth Column |
| No Dictatorship by War | Our Forefathers |
| Limited Government Payroll | Custom and Culture |

High Qualifications for Politicians     Our Language

Sound Economic Principles       Our Philosophy

Standing upon the threshold of the temple's open vista, we behold the green wonderworking of the gardens and the spreading valley of virgin woodland beyond; for the temple is but a gateway to these alluring freedoms, liberties, and joyous opportunities we see within nature's awaiting grandeur. Let us, therefore, dwell in this new world as good stewards of such divine gifts.

# PART III

# THE

# SYLVIAN LIFESTYLE OF HEALTH

Chapter One

# Our Well-Being

*Please note that I am neither a physician nor a medical professional. While the following remedies worked for me, they might not be the best choice for you. Therefore, always rely on your doctor's advice for your health.*

S HOULD we hope to break asunder the double iron shackles that societally bind our people hand and foot, we must first emancipate ourselves from poor or mediocre health.

Lethargy and gluttony are handcuffs and leg-irons that must be thrown away and replaced with vitality of life. It is free for the taking. As King Alfred taught us with his actions, we must replace weakness with hale heartiness, despondency with a bright vision of victory, ambiguity with definitive plans for the future.

Moreover, there is yet another manacle we must break and castaway—the corpse gray prisons we are building all about us that are replacing the flora and fauna. For, are we not replacing life with death, the living for the non-living?

Ecological collapse shall be our just reward. Reversal of

this death wish begins with inner ecology, our health. To be certain, if we do not care for our bodies, we shall not care for the flora and fauna, the three being indissolubly inter- twined. So, this chapter is not only essential to our bodies but to the world around us.

Therefore, let us now begin this march to tomorrow with these life-changing health solutions, all of which I've used to great effect. To be sure, I take my own medicine: I perform much more than the suggested workout routine with heavier weights and beyond the recommended repe- tition three times each week and walk, run stair laps, and sprint daily. I've done this for many years. I'm the ap- propriate weight for my height according to the chart I've included, and for several years I've enjoyed the life-giving diet I recommend. Indeed, every nuance of the lifestyle I suggest, I live fully. Of course, I am not a physician. So, I strongly recommend discussing these ideas with your doctor before trying them.

These health solutions are arranged in alphabetical or- der except self-esteem, which I feel is paramount to our overall health, and so we will now discuss raising it and maintaining its high level.

*Self-Esteem*

Should we believe that we can be successful at work and are worthy of love, we will enjoy high self-esteem. In turn, we will be good stewards of our health. If we believe that we cannot be successful at work and are unworthy of love, we will almost invariably neglect our health. For, con- fidence in our ability to succeed at work and our worthiness of love is the undeductible foundation of high self-esteem. It is obvious that those who highly esteem themselves will possess more dash and daring than those with low self-estimation, making it easier for them to succeed at work. Yet, why would worthiness of love be part of the formula of healthy self-esteem? As we have seen, it is simply this: *love is the recognition of value.* And, if we value something, we nurture and care for it, especially the precious vessel we have been given, which we call our body, home to our soul and spirit.

Now, suppose we have low self-esteem. How do we raise this poor self-evaluation? There are many ways to accomplish this. Yet, it should first be understood that all of us struggle with the way we feel about ourselves from time to time and, perhaps, day to day; for, just as we don't eat one meal and expect to never need nourishment again, we must continuously re-nourish the way we feel about ourselves.

The quickest and easiest way to raise our self-esteem is extraordinarily simple yet equally powerful. Although this method may seem innocuous, even meaningless, its power to protect and raise our self-esteem cannot be overstated. I am speaking of *detachment.*

As Tennyson said, "Self-reverence, self-knowledge, self-control; these three alone lead life to sovereign power." That type of detachment does not mean numbness to an urgent situation, nor does it mean being disengaged from others. It is not giving someone the silent treatment. Neither is it irresponsibility of any kind, whatsoever. By sharp contrast, detachment means being appropriately engaged, being fully alive to the situation at hand and our reaction to it, or non-reaction to it, rather than being attuned to the reactions of others. It means being the uncompromised, original you—the highest and best version of yourself, fully adequate to overcome any challenge. Detachment in this sense is never aloof in a condescending way. Rather, it is what might be called *self-sovereignty*. This self-containment is, indeed, emancipation from circumstances and the negative influence of others.

Yet, detachment and self-sovereignty are not easy for anyone, even for those who are the most well-adjusted members of society. And it may be impossible to become detached when grieving for a lost loved one, an unavoidable process that can sometimes seem hellishly lonely and unending.

Now, the first principle of detachment is to halt. If we are Hungry, Angry, Lonely or Tired, we must halt and take care of our needs. Just as we are instructed by airlines in a case of emergency to secure our oxygen mask before trying to help anyone else, we must also put our needs first, finding our place of stability.

Learning detachment can also begin by memorizing and practicing the following twelve sayings. You most likely have heard and said them. Yet, you may not have realized their extraordinary power to protect and raise your self-esteem. Indeed, the influence of the following words on our feelings about ourselves might be vital. So, consideration for memorizing and practicing them is advisable.

*But for the grace of God, there go I.*

We may say this to ourselves when encountering someone for whom we have an aversion and, therefore, remind ourselves that we may be equally offensive to others or possibly to that very person who offends us. We may choose to say this aloud or to ourselves when among those who are gossiping or back-biting, which is something we should never do; for, gossiping or backbiting is a sign of being unhealthily attached. *But by the grace of God, there go I,* also reminds us that we are not better than others.

*Easy does it.*

We often try too hard, which many times leads to mistakes and wasted energy. This saying, although profoundly elementary, could save us from woeful suffering, ill health, failure, and a poor image of our self. Be good to yourself. *Easy does it.*

*First things first.*

When faced with many things to do, we must stop and ask ourselves—what urgently needs our attention? What is the first priority? What is the second priority, etcetera? In this way, we'll put *first things first.*

*How important is it?*

When the driver in front of you is mindlessly talking on a cell phone, oblivious to the green light until it turns red, it is irritating. But how important is it? The light will turn green in another minute or two. Will that extra wait truly make any difference in your life? If someone calls you a bad name, is it any more important than if he said you have green hair? You know you don't have green hair, so if someone said you have green hair, it probably wouldn't threaten your self-esteem. Neither should we be disturbed by someone calling us a bad name. For, if we know who we are, being called a derogatory name will be purely immaterial. We should simply make it a point to avoid such a person politely. So, when we encounter an irritating situation or person, we must ask *how important is it?*

*Is he or she, my responsibility? / Is this situation my responsibility?*

Each man and woman are their responsibility. When this self-responsibility is truly assumed, he or she has all that can be managed. We, of course, assume responsibility for our children and the elderly. Yet even our responsibility to them is sometimes limited. The gist is that we must avoid the co-dependency of trying to fix someone else; should we do so, we forfeit our sovereignty, much as a king would abdicate his divine right to rule; likewise, in such a case, we would lose our divine right to rule over our self.

So, we mustn't give away our power by trying to fix someone outside of our responsibility. We must ask, *Is he or she, my responsibility? / Is this situation my responsibility?*

*Just for today.*

I will not try to tackle all my life's problems in one day. Just for today, I will be happy. Just for today, I will not try to make everyone, and everything adjust to my liking but instead take life as it comes to me. I will not try to regulate anyone but myself. Just for today, I will exercise my mind with intellectual stimulation and my body with exercise, preferably in the fresh air. Today, I will act and dress in an attractive way. I will not be disrupted by hurry, indecision, or fear. I will enjoy the beauty of the world alone for thirty minutes. I will not worry about trying to do these things for the rest of my life or even tomorrow, but *just for today.*

*Keep it simple.*

Simplicity—it is often a characteristic of truth and beauty. At the same time, the beautiful and truthful can be expressed with extraordinary complexities. Yet, they commonly derive from a simplified idea. Sir Isaac Newton's book *The Principia* begins by establishing elementary thoughts upon which notions of profound intricacies are based. And as a builder begins with four bricks to erect an architectural wonder, Beethoven began with four notes to build *The Fifth Symphony,* that sparkling city of musical grandeur.

Likewise, rather than beginning with the complex, let us reduce our challenges through their simplification. Keep it simple. Indeed, we all tend to make life too complicated, although it seems the best solutions are simple, exampled by these twelve sayings. Memorizing them will help to clarify our lives and *keep it simple.*

*Keep an open mind.*

Open-mindedness allows learning, innovation, and progress, virtues that are stopped by a closed mind. Being open to new ideas is a youthful characteristic and a hallmark of high self-esteem. This does not imply that we should accept all ideas. Some ideas are quite bad. Open-mindedness simply means that we might want to consider ideas that are new to us. We will make progress in our lives if we *keep an open mind.*

*Let it begin with me.*

Let the virtues you wish to see in others, begin with you. Think about the good you wish to see in the world, particularly the immediate world in which you live. Then think, *let it begin with me* followed by meaningful action.

*Live and let live.*

Aristotle offered sage advice to his fellow citizens and did so succinctly by kindly saying, "Mind your own business." What others do is their problem. We may not like it. Yet, unless it adversely affects us, we should be independently detached. The foremost exceptions being our underage children, the sick, and elderly; and, even then, as hard as it may seem, we should be healthily detached from them, as well. In other words, we should not enable their codependency by allowing them to control or manipulate us. This detachment will draw them closer to us, and us closer to them.

Of course, this does not absolve us from standing against the salient threats we have discussed earlier, for these adversely affect us and our posterity. All the while, let us never become busybodies, so unconsciously obsessed with our weaknesses and flaws that we project them into the lives of others rather than mustering the courage to gaze into our autobiographical mirror with honesty and, there, own and manage them. By sharp contrast, the best way is to *live and let live.*

*One day at a time.*

The belief that we are divinely beckoned toward something bigger than ourselves allows us to patiently engage this present day since our destiny is immeasurably valuable and, therefore, worth waiting to realize. This is not any shade of negligence of our responsibilities but a visualization of a good outcome that we patiently await one day at a time while striving to take another step each morning. Although we may not fully understand delays and setbacks, we continue to live only one day at a time with our vision ever before us. As a wise man once said, "Steady plodding brings prosperity." It is similar to our cousin Sir Edmund Hillary's reply when asked how he became the first man to ascend the summit of Mount Everest. He answered, "One step at a time." It would have been laughably absurd to envision climbing atop Everest in a single day; likewise, we design plans to achieve our goals and pursue them intelligently as we meet all challenges *one day at a time.*

*Think.*

If we are thinking dispassionately, how will we act during a disagreement with a friend or a loved one? If we are cerebral rather than overly emotional, how will we react to any problem? As the martial artist knows, the master uses the opponent's energy rather than his own. For, it is self-defeating to expend one's energy, particularly that which is unchanneled. Such is emotional banter. Let us, therefore, think and keep our power.

Thinking, nevertheless, has limits. Toward the end of the day, it becomes weaker, less accurate. So, it is typically best to slow down our thoughtwork in the evening, surrendering unto rest at night before bedtime, and finally to honey sweet sleep. Here, we may let the unlimited creativity of our unconscious mind unravel and reorder the day's challenges. In the morning, the path may be clearer. As the Russian fairy tale, *The Little Humpbacked Horse* teaches us, "the morning is wiser than the evening." The morning, therefore, might be the best time to *think.*

Try practicing these exercises of detachment. You may find that they raise and protect your self-esteem when applied to challenging circumstances, yet they require practice and are not altogether easy. You may notice that those with phlegmatic personalities will find detachment easier than others. Those with choleric personalities may have somewhat of an easier success, as well. Yet, those who are melancholy and sanguine by nature will have the greater challenges remaining detached.

So, if you are melancholy or sanguine, be patient and forgiving to yourself. Remember, these personalities are integral to art, science, success, and triumph throughout the world. Every great composer, painter, sculptor, every great scientist, physician, and inventor were melancholy. And the world would be far less positive and, therefore, less accomplished without the essential visionary sanguine temperament. What is more, our personalities are congenital; consequently, we must not try to change them but simply modify them slightly by developing habits of detachment, one day at a time.

As we practice detachment to raise our self-esteem, it is important to distance ourselves from those who undermine our self-image. An excellent way to judge this is sensitivity to our feelings immediately after spending time with such a person. If we have a feeling akin to roller-coaster-stomach, if our gut feels upset, although we may not be able to identify precisely why, we have probably been in the presence of someone who was attempting to vicariously drag our self-esteem to the deplorable level of their own. Another warning sign is lying. If someone lies to us once, he or she will probably do so again and again, the lies becoming more sinister and malicious. You may be certain of it. So, while getting to know people, it might be best to avoid those who lie to you, even once. Should we detect either of these warning signals, we will invariably begin to create an inner dialogue with that person, somewhat of an internal debate about things we dislike about him or her. This is not hearing voices. It is mentally repeating what we would like to say to reconcile legitimate grievances. Such inner dialogues can be time-drains and emotionally exhausting. These are not unimportant issues. If we are in a fixed relationship with such a person, a relative or coworker, for example, these issues must be resolved by talking to him or her. This should be done in a reasonable, rational way without making accusations but by telling the person how we feel. Because our feelings are authentic, they cannot be disputed. If, however, we feel that such a discussion would be fruitless, impossible, or even dangerous, we must avoid that person. For inner dialogues that are repetitively troubling are unhealthy, telling you something is wrong. If you feel you cannot cope with them, and the person they involve, seek the help of a qualified counselor, preferably a psychiatrist, which is an M.D. whose specialty is psychiatry. Set this book down and make the call right now. You'll feel better simply knowing that you've reached out to someone who is imminently qualified to help you through the very challenges you are facing.

Also, keep things in perspective by bearing in mind that maintaining healthy self-esteem is not easy for anyone. At times it may be fine, other times not particularly good. So, do not be too discouraged should you experience high and low episodes of the way you feel about yourself. This is normal. Albeit these highs and lows should not be too extreme or erratic but should occur over time and be self-manageable or, perhaps, manageable with a relaxed chat with a friend. Should you feel these episodes of elation and depression are too frequent and their highs and lows too disproportionate for you to manage on your own, seek the advice of a qualified counselor, preferably a psychiatrist. Your physician will kindly refer you to the right professional who can give you the help you need. So, set this book aside and contact him or her right now.

While waiting to see your recommended counselor, you might receive some benefit by reading the upcoming section on depression. Even if you don't feel depressed, it may open windows to clear vistas and intoxicatingly fresh air.

Finally, remember two things: you can be successful at work, and you are worthy of love. Always behave as though it were true because it is, dear cousin.

Before we continue the discovery of ideas that may improve our health, please know that simply because these ideas have worked wonderfully for me does not mean they will work for you, or that they are even appropriate for you. You, and preferably your physician, must make these decisions. So, my first suggestion is to make an appointment to see your physician for a thorough physical examination. You may even wish to discuss some of these ideas during that visit.

With that thought in mind, let us learn more ideas that might improve and maintain our health.

*Acid Reflux Disease (heartburn)*

Also known for many years as simply acid indigestion, Acid Reflux Disease is a "disease" that, it would seem to some casual observers, was largely invented by the pharmaceutical industry. For, this condition is almost always quite easily resolved by eating a healthy diet in which an organic salad is eaten every day. This salad should be made with dark green leafy vegetables, such as kale and spinach. Using all organic ingredients, chop up a few celery sticks, a cucumber, a few slivers of a red onion, a tomato, and carrots, add them to a large salad bowl. Sprinkle it with apple cider vinegar and olive oil. Toss it up and enjoy. All your body, especially your stomach, will be appreciative.

Drink purified water. Avoid juices made from concentrate and avoid all processed food.

Should you, even so, have episodes of an acidic, upset stomach, mix one-half teaspoon of baking soda (which does not contain aluminum) with eight ounces of purified water. Drinking this may ease all acidic discomfort.

If you still have an upset stomach after eating organic salads, avoiding processed foods for a day or two, and using the above baking soda remedy, contact your doctor without delay.

Avoid non-prescribed antacid medicine. I met a pastor of a church who glowingly testified that God had miraculously intervened into the affairs of his life to save him from near death. He told the story of eating whatever he wanted, which was mostly processed junk food, followed by antacids at every meal to ease the pain. Finally, he was rushed to the emergency room, where it was discovered that these antacids had eaten a hole in his stomach. He narrowly survived emergency surgery in which a portion of his stomach was removed. Now, for the remainder of his life, he must eat small portions equal to half a normal meal.

Had he simply eaten healthily, consuming fresh green salads or smoothies rich with dark green leafy vegetables, along with a balanced diet, this near-death episode would have been avoided. So, don't be as foolish as this man, who, for the remainder of his life, must live with half a stomach. Treat your stomach wisely.

*Age Spots*

Perhaps, these darkened spots that sometimes appear on our face with age would be more appropriately called Sun spots, since exposure to the Sun exacerbates their occurrence. They most commonly appear on the left side of the face of those who drive on the left side of the road, the more direct exposure to the Sun resulting there, and vice versa amongst the British, for example, who drive to the right. I developed such a spot that was about one-quarter inch in diameter. After checking to ensure that it did not fall within the parameters of the characteristics of skin cancer, which are described in the section titled *Skin,* I began applying undiluted apple cider vinegar to this spot for three weeks, at which time it peeled off.

Of course, my skin may differ significantly from yours. So, if you try this idea, you may want to dilute your dosage with water to test your reaction.

To avoid age spots, be certain you are taking vitamin-C every day, which helps protect the skin against such dermal abnormalities. Take only genuine vitamin-C, rather than an ascorbic acid derivative. Sunscreen may help to avoid age spots, but most of them contain harmful chemicals, some of which are carcinogenic. It is possible, however, to find sunscreens that do not contain these harmful ingredients.

*Allergic Reactions to Pollen and Hay Fever*

*Rhinitis*, sometimes referred to as *coryza*, is an irritation and inflammation of the mucous membrane of the nose. Typically, symptoms include difficulty breathing through the nose, excess mucus, sneezing, and drainage affecting the throat. This annoying inflammation of the mucous membrane is triggered by viruses, bacteria, or irritants caused by airborne allergens such as pollen and dander. This may lead to other symptoms: sneezing and itchy nose, coughing, sinus headaches, marked fatigue, and mental dullness. The eyes may be affected, too, with wateriness, redness, itchiness, or puffiness. Allergic rhinitis causes histamine and other chemicals to result in inflammation. But infectious rhinitis, however, occasionally leads to viral pneumonia or bacterial pneumonia.

To protect ourselves from these maladies, we must maintain a strong immune system. When the immune system is free to fight allergic battles, it can win in many cases. This means not putting anything on one's skin or eating anything that contains toxins of any kind. Eating organic food is mandatory for this reason, as well as cautiously reading labels. If we are unable to pronounce an ingredient, we must give careful thought about placing it in or on our body. Processed food and fried food also place a strain on our body because it demands more effort to digest. Freeing ourselves from these poisons is merely a matter of forming new habits, which only requires three weeks. Take heart, for we all can do this.

Cayenne pepper has been a boon for me in the fight against allergies, which I take all year round. I sprinkle it on super-firm tofu and add two tablespoons of olive oil. Using this remedy, I have not had an allergy problem in nine years, whereas I formerly was crushed by them every year.

The key to remember is that cayenne alone probably won't protect us against allergens, but your immune system is the perfect match for them. Free it of toxins so it can fight this battle.

### Apple Cider Vinegar

The medicinal powers of this natural elixir are extraordinary. And so, we refer to its health benefits often as we discuss our remedies and suggest that it become a staple in every home.

### Arthritis

Nine years ago, I awoke with a painful stiffness in my hands and the ball of my right foot. Lasting approximately forty-five minutes, it caused difficulty in moving my hands, and the pain in my foot caused limping for about the same amount of time. These symptoms continued for several days and were bewildering to me for I had athletic heartbeats per minute and had been a vegetarian for over ten years. Yet, I was diagnosed with degenerative arthritis.

At this same time, I stopped eating wheat altogether in order to lose weight, and, as a by-product of doing so, in three weeks all the discomforts disappeared from my hands and foot, never returning since. Had I continued eating wheat, I may have been crippled with arthritis by now.

This is why: gluten, which is found in wheat, is valued for its viscosity, which gives elasticity to dough, helping it rise, maintaining its shape, often giving bread, pizza, or the dough of other items a pleasingly chewy texture. Yet, this *viscoelasticity* has a tenacious quality that lines the digestive tract, inhibiting digestion, in turn, causing weight gain, fatigue, arthritis, and other problems. Anyone who wishes to lose weight, enjoy robust energy, and avoid arthritis should also avoid gluten.

Another arthritic culprit is soda. This is neither a food nor a liquefier. It is so incomplete that it must take lipid acids from our joints to travel through our body, destroying hands, back, elbows, neck, hips, and knees on its rampaging journey. Coffee, it appears, is not much better and is possibly the most acidic consumable besides pure grain alcohol.

*Aspirin*

For many decades, the US Federal Drug Administration (FDA) recommended taking an aspirin daily to lessen the risk of heart attack or stroke. Consequently, an estimated forty million Americans take aspirin daily for these reasons. This recommendation has now been withdrawn for those "who have not had a heart attack, stroke, or cardiovascular problems."

According to information published on their website, "FDA has concluded that the data do not support the use of aspirin as a preventive medication by people who have not had a heart attack, stroke, or cardiovascular problems, a use that is called 'primary prevention.' In such people, the benefit has not been established but risks—such as dangerous bleeding into the brain or stomach—are still present."

So, we see that the FDA says that taking aspirin is accompanied by the risk of "dangerous bleeding into the brain or stomach." This is rather shocking. Expounding upon further dangers of aspirin, Neena Abraham, M.D., reported in *The New York Times,* ". . . it is important to remember that even small doses of daily aspirin—including 'baby aspirin,' at a dose of 81 milligrams daily—can increase your risk of ulcers and bleeding. It is important to remember that all nonsteroidal anti-inflammatory drugs (NSAIDS), including over the counter aspirin, have the potential to damage the tissue of the gastrointestinal tract. Damage can occur anywhere, from mouth to anus."

It seems that thinking men would be loath to expose themselves to this danger.

Pain, such as a headache, can be remedied by placing a package of frozen green peas on one's forehead and another on the back of the neck while lying in bed. Relax, maybe even fall asleep, and literally chill out. Pain from inflammation can be reduced by eating celery, plain celery soup, or plain white onion soup. Be sure not to dilute the medicinal powers of these natural remedies by adding any ingredient other than purified water to the soup. Cayenne pepper and turmeric are also powerful anti-inflammatories.

Always remember RICE:

Rest: Don't try to work an injury out, or work around your injury. It could be worse than you think, and not listening to your body could invite permanent damage. Be patient. Use a cane, if needed, to take the weight off your legs and feet even while getting around the house. For example, tennis elbow takes time to heal, and an irritated rotator cuff takes even more time. Yet, your body will heal itself if you let it.

Ice: Applying ice to an affected area is one of the quickest ways to reduce swelling. If you have a package of green peas in your freezer, you have what might be a perfect ice pack. Place it on the injury, let the ice do its work and be cool.

Compress: An array of compresses specifically designed to treat inflammation are available at many stores and pharmacies. They may also keep muscles, tendons, and ligaments aligned to some degree, as well, while you are healing.

Elevate: Rest the affected area in a way so that it is above the heart. This will lessen blood flow to the injury and, consequently, lessen inflammation.

*Back*

Our spinal column, a stunning work of divine architecture, is comprised of thirty-three individual bones, called vertebrae. These are stacked one atop the other, providing the main support for our body, allowing us to stand upright, bend, and twist, while miraculously protecting the spinal cord from injury. Well-developed muscles, strong bones, flexible tendons and ligaments, and nerve sensitivity are integral to a healthy spine. The neck, or *cervical*, and lower back, or *lumbar,* have a slight concave curve. The broad part of our back, or *thoracic* region, and base of our back, the *sacral* region, have a gentle convex curve. These curves, forming a slight S-like shape, work as a coiled spring, absorbing shock, maintaining balance, and allowing a range of motion throughout the spinal column. If you don't have this S-curve, something is wrong.

Good posture places the least amount of strain on our back, as we stand, walk, sit, and even when we lie down. But excess body weight and weak muscles can cause a misalignment of the spine and possibly a host of other problems. The principal muscles affecting the spine are *extensors* and *flexors.* Extensors, attached to the back of the spine, enable us to stand up from a sitting position and to lift objects. The flexor muscles are in front of the spine, including our abdominal muscles, so one of the best ways to have a flexible, pain-free back is to strengthen the flexors.

There are many stomach exercises, so find different ones by searching online or asking a friend who is in excellent shape. Most people will be complimented and delighted to tell you how they maintain their trimness. Talk with a professional trainer or your physician before beginning.

Try a few exercises. Find one you prefer, and then start slowly. I prefer the "crunch." If you'd like to try it, lay on the floor, pull your knees up toward your chest, cross your legs at the ankles, and, while also crossing your arms at the wrists over your chest, draw your chest and head toward your waist. Repeat until fatigued. Once again, start slowly, and later, if you wish, hold fifteen-pound dumbbells in each hand for added effect.

Good posture and a good bed to sleep on are essential. But there is another trick that I suggest: hang from a chin-up bar for two sets of thirty seconds every day. Most of us sit interminably, and, in the process, our spine becomes somewhat compressed and may even be pulled to one side or the other. Hanging from a chin-up bar allows the vertebra to open up ever so gently, achieving alignment. Chin-up bars that fit in a doorway can be set up inside your home and are available at most sporting goods stores. I do not recommend using an *inversion table* for bodily alignment since the Mayo Clinic reports that inversion tables slow the heart rate and increase blood pressure. It can also upset the crystals associated with the equilibrium system, possibly requiring days or longer for recovery, during which time severe vertigo, headaches, and nausea may be experienced.

Those with high blood pressure, head injuries, proneness to episodes of dizziness, or migraine headaches should never use an inversion table.

If you are a little overweight, look at the section on weight because excess weight can keep your spine in a perpetually stressful condition. And remember, losing weight and maintaining your appropriate weight is simply a habit. Bad habits can be broken and replaced with good habits in only three weeks. You, dear friend, can do this. Be encouraged and envision it.

*Heartbeats Per Minute (BPM) and Blood Pressure (BP)*

Let's measure our pulse rate. You'll need a watch with a second hand or a stop-watch. Find a quiet place where you are not distracted, sit down, and after relaxing at least ten minutes to ensure you obtain a resting pulse, count your pulse by gently placing your index, middle, and ring fingers on the inside of your other wrist below your thumb. Count your pulse beats for thirty seconds. You then double this figure to determine your resting pulse.

Inexpensive digital wrist watches are also available that can read your pulse rate and blood pressure.

Your heart beats per minute should usually be between 60 and 85 beats per minute.

Low 40 to 60

If you are vigorously athletic, this is normal. However, if you are not athletic, this may indicate low blood pressure, and you should see your doctor right away.

Normal 60 to 85

Try to bring this number to around 72, through a daily exercise program such as walking and a diet rich in organic fruits and vegetables. Also, avoiding alcohol and tobacco will help substantially.

High 86 +

This indicates a problem, and you should see your physician without delay.

Generally speaking, your blood pressure should be approximately 120 over 80.

$$\frac{120}{80}$$

However, your doctor must determine what blood pressure is healthy for you based upon your age and other factors. So, I recommend meeting with your physician for a professional analysis.

Knowing your BPM and BP is important because high blood pressure, or hypertension, is known as the "silent killer." So, knowing the health of your heart by the numbers is essential, illustrated by the fact that the European Heart Network says, "Each year cardiovascular disease causes 3.9 million deaths in Europe and over 1.8 million deaths in the European Union. It accounts for 45% of all deaths in Europe and 37% of all deaths in the EU. Cardiovascular disease is the main cause of death in men in all but 12 countries of Europe and is the main cause of death in women in all but two countries." According to the American Heart Association, "Common hereditary and physical risk factors for high blood pressure include:

"Family history. If your parents or other close blood relatives have high blood pressure, there's an increased chance that you'll get it, too.

"Age. The older you are, the more likely you are to get high blood pressure. As we age, our blood vessels gradually lose some of their elastic quality, which can contribute to increased blood pressure. However, children can also develop high blood pressure.

"Gender. Until age 45, men are more likely to get high blood pressure than women. From age 45 to 64, men and women get high blood pressure at similar rates. And at 65 and older, women are more likely to get high blood pressure.

"Unlike the traits you are born with, the risk factors related to how you live are things you can change to help prevent and manage high blood pressure, including:

"Lack of physical activity. Not getting enough physical activity as part of your lifestyle increases your risk of getting high blood pressure. Physical activity is great for your heart and circulatory system in general, and blood pressure is no exception. Learn more about getting regular physical activity.

"A diet that is too high in salt consumption, as well as calories, saturated fat and sugar, carries an additional risk of high blood pressure. On the other hand, making healthy food choices can actually help lower blood pressure. Learn more about improving your diet.

"Carrying too much weight puts an extra strain on your heart and circulatory system that can cause serious health problems. It also increases your risk of cardiovascular disease, diabetes and high blood pressure. Learn more about managing your weight.

"Regular, heavy use of alcohol can cause many health problems, including heart failure, stroke and an irregular heartbeat (arrhythmia). It can cause your blood pressure to increase dramatically and can also increase your risk of cancer, obesity, alcoholism, suicide, and accidents. Learn more about alcohol, high blood pressure and the importance of moderation. In addition to the known risk factors, there are others that may contribute to high blood pressure, although how is still uncertain. These potential contributing risk factors include:

"Using tobacco can cause your blood pressure to temporarily increase and can contribute to damaged arteries. Secondhand smoke, exposure to other people's smoke, also increases the risk of heart disease for nonsmokers. Stress is not necessarily a bad thing in and of itself. But too much stress may contribute to increased blood pressure. Also, too much stress can encourage behaviors that increase blood pressure, such as poor diet, physical inactivity, and using tobacco or drinking alcohol more than usual. Learn more about managing your stress."

*C Vitamin*

For several years, I was taking daily doses of ascorbic acid, which is sold as vitamin C by well-known grocers and supplement companies. Yet, I was exhibiting signs of vitamin C deficiencies, especially dry skin, and sports injuries of joints, simply because ascorbic acid is not vitamin C but its synthetic impostor. Nature, of course, creates vitamin C with ascorbic acid, but merely as an antioxidant protective coating that envelops vitamin C's four other integral ingredients:

1. Vitamin P is considered the anti-pneumonia vitamin and helps our lungs inhale oxygen proficiently, which is essential for asthma sufferers.

2. Vitamin J, a bioflavonoid, protects the tissues around the arteries and veins and most noticeably prevents spider veins on the face.

3. Copper is another component of vitamin C, that helps to build adrenal hormones, the repository of vitamin C.

4. Vitamin K is necessary for blood coagulation. Deficiency of vitamin K may also weaken bones, potentially leading to osteoporosis, and may promote calcification of arteries and other soft tissues.

So, there is a significant difference between ascorbic acid and vitamin C, and it seems quite criminal to misrepresent the two when we consider the pivotal health role of this life-giving vitamin. For instance, when I stopped taking ascorbic acid and replaced it with a quality vitamin C derived from organic fruits and vegetables, the dry condition on my legs and feet, which had been present for over nine years, was subsided within two weeks. Here are some fruits and vegetables rich in Vitamin-C, measured in milligrams and daily value:

| | | |
|---|---|---|
| Kiwi<br>1 cup | 164 mg | 273% DV |
| Bell Peppers<br>1 cup, raw | 120 mg | 200% DV |

| | | |
|---|---|---|
| Orange | 95.8 mg | 160% DV |
| Strawberries 1 cup | 89.4 mg | 149% DV |
| Papaya 1 cup | 86.5 mg | 144% DV |
| Pineapple 1 cup | 78.9 mg | 131% DV |
| Grapefruit 1 cup | 71.8 mg | 120% DV |
| Broccoli ½ cup, cooked | 50.6 mg | 84% DV |
| Brussels Sprouts ½ cup, cooked | 48.4 mg | 81% DV |
| Mango 1 cup | 45.7 mg | 76% DV |
| Tomatoes 1 cup | 18.9 mg | 32% DV |
| Spinach 1 cup, cooked | 17.6 mg | 29% DV |

### Cancer Prevention

The World Health Organization's International Agency for Research on Cancer states, "It is estimated that almost half of all deaths due to cancer in Europe could be avoided if everyone followed these recommendations.

"Do not smoke. Do not use any form of tobacco. Make your home smoke free. Support smoke-free policies in your workplace.

"Take action to have a healthy body weight. Be physically active in everyday life. Limit the time you spend sitting.

"Have a healthy diet: Eat plenty of whole grains, pulses, vegetables and fruits. Limit high-calorie foods (foods high in sugar or fat), and avoid sugary drinks. Avoid processed meat; limit red meat and foods high in salt.

"If you drink alcohol of any type, limit your intake. Not drinking alcohol can prevent cancer.

"Avoid too much sun, especially for children. Use sun protection. Do not use sunbeds.

"In the workplace, protect yourself against cancer-causing substances by following health and safety instructions.

"Find out if you are exposed to radiation from naturally high radon levels in your home. Take action to reduce high radon levels.

"For women: If you can, breastfeed your baby. Breastfeeding reduces the mother's cancer risk. Limit use of hormone replacement therapy, which increases the risks for certain cancers.

"Ensure that your children are vaccinated against: Hepatitis B (for newborns) Human papillomavirus (for girls).

"Take part in organized cancer screening programs for: Bowel cancer (men and women), Breast cancer (women), Cervical cancer (women)."

In addition to this sage advice, perhaps, the safest lifestyle that ensures one is taking all precautions against the incidence of cancer is a gluten-free, processed-food-free, substance-free, dairy-free, plant-based diet with a big daily dose of fresh air and exercise.

A gluten-free diet is suggested since gluten causes

weight gain, which increases the incidence of cancer. Processed food is artificial and, consequently, alien to our bodies, requiring extra work to digest and, in some cases, is only partially digested, which causes a multiplicity of damage, some that might be irreversible, such as cancer. Substance freedom includes freedom from tobacco, alcohol, drugs, many prescription drugs, coffee, soft drinks, and a host of other synthetic things misinformed people consume. Dairy freedom markedly reduces inflammation and removes a host of chemicals, not to mention unimaginable misery to cows and calves. The plant-based diet is also recommended since many people feel it is the healthiest diet for it excludes meat, which, with its many chemicals and digestive challenges, causes a higher risk of cancer. And, daily exercise in the fresh air renews and cleans the whole body, lessening the risk of cancer.

Assuming such a lifestyle may seem somewhat impossible. If this is the case, just take one step at a time, then when you are ready, take another. After all, time will elapse anyway, and by steady plodding, we may achieve many things that others dismissed as utter impossibilites.

### Cartilage

Two years ago, while peddling ten miles round-trip from the grocery store with about twenty pounds of groceries in my backpack and riding into a strong headwind, I overdid it. I had been running stair laps, running on a riverside trail three times a week, and walking three miles in the fresh air daily, so I was expecting quite a lot of my dear cartilages. The ride from the grocery store, however, exceeded the limits. An MRI revealed a torn cartilage. My doctor said, "Once it's gone, it's gone." Yet, I wanted to give it every chance to heal, so I used the RICE method, Rest,

Ice, Compress, Elevate.

I stopped all the work outs of my lower body. I ate onion soup, celery soup, and cayenne pepper for their powerful anti-inflammatory benefits. Since I was eating a plant-based diet, I was already on a healthy diet, and this, of course, made an enormous difference in my recovery, along with *glucosamine*, a supplement requiring no prescription. As I mentioned earlier in this section, simply because a solution was helpful to me, does not mean it will help you. Therefore, I do not recommend that you take glucosamine since you may have allergic reactions or side effects to it that I did not experience. You may, albeit wish to read a little about glucosamine or seek your physician's opinion about it.

During this recovery, I never took one aspirin, ibuprofen, or anything similar; these are anathema to a strong, healthy life-style. I was patient, not running or even riding a bike for two years.

Now, my right knee is perfect. I run stair laps, ride my bike, and run on the trail just as before with no pain. Of course, now I am more respectful of my cartilages.

*Hyraluronic acid* may also be a supplement to consider, with your doctor's advice, since it is in every tissue of the body, especially the connecting tissues of the skin and cartilage.

*Cholesterol*

The Harvard School of Medicine reports that, "Oats are an easy first step to improving your cholesterol . . . having a bowl of oatmeal or cold oat-based cereal . . . for breakfast. It gives you 1 to 2 grams of soluble fiber. Add a banana or some strawberries for another half-gram. Current nutrition guidelines recommend getting 20 to 35 grams of fiber a day, with at least 5 to 10 grams from soluble fiber.

"Barley and other whole grains can help lower the risk of heart disease, mainly via the soluble fiber they deliver. Beans are especially rich in soluble fiber. They also take a while for the body to digest, meaning you feel full for longer after a meal. That's one reason beans are a useful food for folks trying to lose weight. With so many choices—from navy and kidney beans to lentils, garbanzos, black-eyed peas, and beyond—and so many ways to prepare them, beans are a very versatile food. Eggplant and okra are two low-calorie vegetables and good sources of soluble fiber.

"Almonds, walnuts, peanuts, and other nuts are good for the heart. Eating 2 ounces of nuts a day can slightly lower low-density lipoprotein (LDL) by 5%. Nuts also have additional nutrients that protect the heart in other ways."

Nuts are, indeed, a good source of healthy fat that helps lower cholesterol. Walnuts, in particular, are a superb choice since they contain omega-3 fatty acids that lower triglycerides and raise high-density lipoprotein (HDL). Be certain you eat only organic walnuts; otherwise, they are loaded with pesticides. The *Journal of Nutrition* reported that pistachios, which are also a source of monounsaturated fats, help lower LDL cholesterol, too.

Olive oil also contains monounsaturated fat that helps lower LDL cholesterol, whereas butter, for example, is higher in the saturated fat that increases cholesterol. Like olive oil, avocado is rich in monounsaturated fats and should be in-cluded in a healthy diet. Both olive oil and avocados are excellent additions to a salad, as well.

*The Journal of Agricultural and Food Chemistry* published the results of a study of apple cider vinegar's effect upon cholesterol, indicating lowered VLDL (very low-density lipo-proteins) levels and lowered triglycerides when apple cider vinegar was a regular part of a diet.

There is some evidence that soluble fiber lowers LDL cholesterol by blocking the absorption of cholesterol and fats into the bloodstream. Apples, strawberries, grapes, and other citrus fruits are rich in pectin, a type of soluble fiber that lowers LDL. Yet, it is generally agreed upon by clinical lipidologists that any fruit or vegetable contains antioxidants, which normalize cholesterol levels. So, these should be the greater portion of a healthy diet.

Let's enjoy the wonderful benefits of the above health-giving foods while eliminating these:

1. Anything that is fried.
2. Anything containing hydrogenated oil. We must read labels of products before purchasing them at the grocery store and, if a product contains hydrogenated oil, do not buy it.
3. Meat and dairy products should be greatly lessened or eliminated.

*Colds*

All my life, I would become debilitated two to three times each year, unable to do little except lie in bed, suffering, waiting for my cold to take its course and leave. It was not uncommon to lose three weeks in this miserable condition, often with a throat so swollen I could barely swallow. Painful fever blisters would also break out on my lips, causing embarrassment in public. Ironically, I felt as though I was eating a healthy diet. But the colds persisted, and so I was resigned to the regularity of this wretched annual agony, accepting it as part of life.

Yet, at this writing, I have not had a cold for nine

years—a veritable miracle—which has freed me from weeks and weeks of miserable immobility.

The common cold occurs because of our compromised immune system. But while uncompromised, it can overcome virtually any conventional alien assault. It must be understood, however, that almost all of these assaults, rather than deriving from viruses or bacteria, come from things we place *on* our body or *in* our body.

The chief menace in my case was cologne. Inhaling cologne is nearly worse than second-hand smoke. It destroys the bio-mechanism needed to transfer oxygen to the bloodstream, as well as leaching through the skin to attack our immune system. I wore cologne every day for decades, but when I discovered the harmful effects from its many toxic chemicals, I threw it away. In three weeks, I noticed that my ability to deeply inhale increased. This was rather startling because I had never assumed that I had a limited breathing ability since I was vigorously athletic.

This improvement convinced me to rid myself of any other contaminants that I put on my skin, for I learned they are quickly absorbed into the bloodstream, in turn, crashing the immune system. I replaced deodorant, for example, with aluminum-free baking soda mixed with a few drops of water. I found a toothpaste free of the toxins typically found in conventional toothpaste. I discovered that the friction from scrubbing with water removes an equal number of bacteria and with equal effectiveness as scrubbing with soap or shampoo. So, I quit using soap several years ago. I stopped using shampoo, also, since almost all shampoos contain Sodium Lauryl Sulfate or Sodium Laureth Sulfate (SLS), which cause the bubbling, sudsing action. This is nothing less than poison and will clearly crash our immune systems. So, for the last nine years, I have simply scrubbed my skin and scalp vigorously with water. My skin and hair improved noticeably. And my physician, with whom I have enjoyed a friendly doctor-patient relationship for fifteen years, tells me I have no body odor at all.

Proportionate to using wisdom about what I placed on my skin, although I was vegetarian and drank only water, I began to use greater judgment about what I *ate*. I had stopped eating fried foods and sweets years before. Then, a significant improvement began by eating only organic food.

This made a profound difference, poignantly illustrated by an occasion when I bought a fruit plate for lunch and returned home to enjoy it. It was then I realized it was not organic. At that time, I had eaten only organic food for three years and debated whether I should eat this delicious fruit. I decided it would be inconsequential.

Within fifteen minutes of eating it, however, I felt as though I had the flu. The effects lasted two hours, during which time I lay in bed, quite sick. This experience underscores the fact that toxins used in foods will crash our immune system, causing marked susceptibility to colds.

My triumph over colds, flu, sore throats, fever blisters, and hay fever changed my life. This triumph didn't come from drugs, dear cousins, but from everyday common sense.

*Conscious Awareness*

"Arthur, looking downward as he past, Felt the light of her eyes into his life Smite on the sudden, . . ."[18]

---

[18] From *Idylls of the King* by Lord Tennyson.

You have probably felt the light of another's eyes or soul touch you, even inexplicably knowing the source and direction of that subtle radiance. Light emanating from another's soul, indeed, recently entered my being; for I sensed this instantly, and even knew the direction of that esoteric light, for I turned to see the lost daydream of an admirer amongst a crowded room. It seems we possess this sensitivity to light because we are, in fact, light.

Some of those who apparently understand quantum physics feel that all matter, including matter comprising the human body, is composed of light waves. Interestingly, the foremost inventor in world history believed that all our life episodes are light recordings, which become permanent physical characteristics unperceived save by the unconscious or, more probably, the soul: "Everything that we once saw, heard, read, and learned, accompanies us in the form of light particles," said Nicola Tesla. Our unvarnished autobiography in a mosaic of metallic glistenings all about us and for all to see, at least to see unconsciously or spiritually, is a supposition that might inspire us to live responsibly.

Rather than studying quantum physics, I went to my dog for lessons about conscious awareness, he being an accomplished guru of the higher virtues. I learned more from him about the fruits of the spirit—love, joy, peace, patience, kindness, gentleness, and self-control—than all the priests and prophets of this terrestrial dimension could ever hope to teach me. And, whereas all these swamis I have met wanted money, he wanted nothing but water, food, and love.

Other than my dog's teachings, eating organic fruits and vegetables and drinking mostly purified water seems to have increased my awareness. But, in this life, I shall never attain the consciousness of my blessed Blackjack.

*Depression*

Dear cousin, this section is for those who are situationally depressed or periodically depressed and, to a lesser degree, for those who are chronically depressed without knowing why. If your depression includes thoughts of suicide, particularly if you think of specific ways, you might carry out this act, please seek help—right now—from a professional counselor, one who is genuinely empathetic to your plight.

A few symptoms of depression are:

- Overeating or appetite loss
- Lack of direction in life
- Lack of normal energy
- Difficulty concentrating and making decisions
- Feelings of guilt, worthlessness, or helplessness
- Feelings of hopelessness and negativity
- Insomnia or excessive sleeping
- Irritability and restlessness
- Loss of interest in activities once enjoyed
- Lack of interest in sex
- Chronic aches or pains, headaches, cramps
- Digestive problems, unresponsive to normal treatment
- Persistently sad, anxious, or feeling emotionally lost
- Thoughts of suicide or suicide attempts

All of us become depressed from time to time. Yet, we can take concrete steps to adjust their frequency and intensity. One elemental way is by eating healthy food. You see, our mind, as a whole, is indivisibly comprised of our brain and our digestive system. For, we make what might be called "hard and fast" decisions drawn from a repository of episodes stored within our conscious mind; we make innovative decisions drawn from the limitless reservoir of creativity within the unconscious; and, we make intuitive decisions, which are commonly drawn from our gastrointestinal tract, our gut.

This should come as no surprise when we consider that the enteric nervous system within our digestive tract contains around one hundred million neurons, more than is found within the spinal cord or the peripheral nervous system. The enteric nervous system uses more than thirty functional types of neurone, and approximately ninety-five percent of our serotonin is found within our digestive tract. We know the vagus nerve connects the brain to our gastroregion, but the infinite complexity of these biomechanisms is not vividly understood, especially the manner in which they communicate.[19] As Alfred Adler said, "We know more than we understand." In other words, we may know things intuitively, or even empirically, yet they remain consciously inexplicable. This pioneering work of our mind's interactivity is presently of keen interest to both the medical and psychiatric community. However, it appears to be a rediscovery, for the ancient Egyptians knew that the seat of the mind was the gastrointestinal tract rather than the brain.

Nevertheless, I know this: As a man eateth, so thinks

---

[19] Karen McConalogue, John B. Furness, "Bailliere's Clinical Endocrinology and Metabolism," Elsevier, (January 1994)

the man. Consequently, we must be wise about what we eat, particularly since we are, quite literally, feeding our mind and this directly. So, after reading the above paragraph, highlighting the extraordinary sensitivity of the gastrointestinal tract and its vital relationship to the brain, together forming the mind itself, it is easy to see that drinking clean, filtered water, eating mostly organic fruits and vegetables while avoiding other food is indispensable for a positive mental attitude. Depression, on the other hand, is exacerbated by sugar and sugar substitutes, margarine and other butter substitutes, deli meats, non-organic fruits and vegetables, salted nuts and seeds, canola oil, soda, caffeine, all processed "foods" and, of course, alcohol.

Realizing the gastro-system is a subset of our mind also underscores the importance of taking probiotics, which contain live bacteria, replacing or adding to the beneficial bacteria normally present in the gastrointestinal tract. This derives from kefir, which is typically a fermentation of dairy products, coconut milk, or other sources. I use a coconut-based probiotic, which is readily available at most health food stores and contains over one hundred million living bacteria in a single tablespoon. Their effervescent presence significantly increases our chance for happiness. Of course, this benefit is predicated upon a clean, wholesome diet enjoyed in unselfish moderation.

As we age, the corresponding daily need for probiotics increases proportionately. Another juncture when it is vitally needed is during illness, especially during colds. Rather than taking antibiotics, which kill much or most of the life-giving bacteria in the gastro-system, I take probiotics should I sense the possibility of a cold, for I want a super-abundance of friendly bacteria to fortify my immune system at such a time. I've been cold-free for the last nine years. Yet, I take it every day, principally for a positive state of mind and antidote to low spirits.

Another countermeasure for depression is vitamins in general, and vitamin B specifically. It is important to note that the B-vitamin group works synergistically and are, therefore, best taken together since high doses of one B-vitamin can deplete another B-vitamins. I feel that B-1, 2, 3, 6 and 12 are healthy anti-depressants, of sorts. But visit with your doctor about adding a B complex supplement because, although rare, there can be side effects and interactions with B-12 may occur with certain medications.

Another tonic for the mind is exercise. Even a short walk will invigorate the heart, lungs, and lymph nodes, at which time, the flow of thoughts is stimulated to move our focus away from fixations, their monstrous immensity resuming a normal size once again. Depressed folk usually feel little energy; but to possess energy, we must expend stored fuel. In normal situations, exercising gives us more than enough energy to complete a busy, daily schedule. Most achievers begin the day with exercise.

Beginning the day early in the morning is also a way to overcome depression. If you want to awaken early enough, watching the Sunrise gives us hope. Whether we see the Sun come over the eastern horizon or not, we know we have new opportunities with the new day; yet, it is a hope-giving gift actually to witness the coming of the King of the East, and oftentimes his arrival is adorned with majesties of pink, magenta, and orange which forever escaped the hand of Sandro Botticelli.

Arising early may also increase the chances of meeting others who will help you overcome depression. Do not, however, unload your problems upon them or they will flee. But if you show up every day or so over the period of a month at a local coffee shop, for example, eventually others will accept you as part of the ambiance and begin to nod hello, and later maybe you can become friends. The local prevailing climate, however, has great influence upon this, as do many other factors. All the same, early morning rising is clearly an antitoxin for depression.

Should you spend time at the market early in the morning, for instance, you will notice that more positively minded, successful people are among you; if you go to the same place as the day wanes on into the afternoon, less positive and less successful people will be there; late in the evening you will find still fewer positive, successful folk. For, those who are depressed often remain in bed, fraught with ambiguity about what to do. Two answers to that question are get up and stay busy.

Another way to overcome depression is to journal. Your journal needn't be expensive. A spiral-bound notebook will be fine. This is your private journal, which contains intimate experiences, many of which may have been deeply troubling to you over the recent past or even decades ago. It may be best never to share it with anyone. Let the pen have its way, taking you to places you may have forgotten consciously yet that are strikingly relevant to your present moment. Write. Write. Write. Let the pen find its path. Let it all out. This is your journal, unique amongst all others in the world. Few exercises are equal to this supertherapeutic unburdening of the heavy weight upon your shoulders.

Edify yourself with affirmations such as those discussed at the beginning of this chapter. If you believe you will overcome depression, you will. Force yourself to believe this if necessary.

Listen to upbeat, positive music rather than sad, melancholy songs. Some of the Broadway musicals from the 50s and 60s are endlessly clever and funny. Polka music is designed to create happiness. Even if you are only able to connect with the humor remotely, this is one step forward, which will lead to one more step forward.

Avoid those who tend to create a negative or troubling inner dialogue within your mind. These inward commit-tee meetings of interminable replayings of conversations may indicate that the person who ignited them within you might be someone to avoid. Go with your gut. As we have seen, that is your intuitive mind, wise beyond conscious analysis.

*Diabetes*

Ask your doctor about these ideas to avoid diabetes.

Eliminate sugar, sugary foods, and processed foods from your diet and replace these artificial foods with fresh, organic fruits, vegetables, nuts, and grains to avoid diabetes.

Eat only the number of calories that corresponds to your height.

Exercise for at least 20 minutes each day.

Stay active. Go for a walk with a friend, or if you have the extra time, volunteer at a worthy organization rather than watching television or playing computer games, which are two things you should avoid. Besides being mind-numbing traps, such inactivity as these lead to more sedentary behavior, which is the poison soil wherein diabe-tes finds a root.

Should you have diabetes, dear friends, your doctor might suggest following the above advice. But seek his or her directions.

It is also important to note that apple cider vinegar may help control diabetes. In fact, several studies have demonstrated a distinct correlation between apple cider vinegar and lower blood sugar levels. In one study, participants took two tablespoons of apple cider vinegar before bedtime, and by the morning, they reported that their blood sugar had dropped 4 to 6 percent. It was deduced that the antiglycemic properties of the acid in apple cider vinegar affect insulin sensitivity.

The American Diabetes Association says, "There are many foods rich in vitamins, minerals and fiber that you can make part of your daily eating plan that are good for your health.

"Some of these include non-starchy vegetables, fruits, legumes, nuts, seeds, and whole grains. The list of foods below is rich in vitamins, minerals, antioxidants, and fiber that are good for overall health and may also help prevent disease.

"Beans—kidney, pinto, navy, or black beans are packed with vitamins and minerals such as magnesium and potassium. They are high in fiber too. Beans do contain carbohydrates, but ½ cup also provides as much protein as an ounce of meat without the saturated fat. To save time you can use canned beans but be sure to drain and rinse them to get rid of as much added salt as possible.

"Dark Green Leafy Vegetables—Spinach, collards, and kale are dark green leafy vegetables packed with vitamins and minerals such as vitamins A, C, E, and K, iron, calciumand potassium. These powerhouse foods are low in calories and carbohydrates too. Try adding dark leafy vegetables to salads, soups and stews.

"Citrus Fruit—Grapefruits, oranges, lemons and limes or pick your favorites to get part of your daily dose of fiber, vitamin C, folate and potassium.

"Sweet Potatoes—A starchy vegetable packed full of vitamin A and fiber. They are also a good source of vitamin C and potassium. Craving something sweet? Try a sweet potato in place of a regular potato and sprinkle cinnamon on top.

"Berries—Which are your favorites: blueberries, strawberries or another variety? Regardless, they are all packed with antioxidants, vitamins, and fiber. Berries can be a great option to satisfy your sweet tooth and they provide an added benefit of vitamin C, vitamin K, manganese, potassium, and fiber.

"Tomatoes—The good news is that no matter how you like your tomatoes, pureed, raw, or in a sauce, you're eating vital nutrients like vitamin C, vitamin E and potassium.

"Nuts—An ounce of nuts can go a long way in getting key healthy fats along with helping to manage hunger. In addition, they offer magnesium and fiber. Some nuts and seeds, such as walnuts and flax seeds, are a good source of omega-3 fatty acids.

"Whole Grains—It's the whole grain you're after. The first ingredient on the label should have the word "whole" in it. Whole grains are rich in vitamins and minerals like magnesium, B vitamins, chromium, iron, and folate. They are a great source of fiber too. Some examples of whole grains are whole oats, quinoa, whole grain barley and farro."

*Digestive Health*

A plant-based diet that is free from gluten, processed food, and junk food, accompanied by about four to six glasses of purified water (depending upon our climate and physical activities) and daily exercise, virtually assures good regularity. Regularity could be one to three times daily, depending upon what we eat and the quantity. Should irregularity become a problem, we might take larger than average doses of vitamin C (not ascorbic acid) until becoming regular again. It's the best laxative since it is also excellent for our overall health. However, do not depend on it for regularity. Approximately 1000 mg of vitamin C is a good daily dose. Seek your doctor's advice.

Eliminating alcohol, tobacco, salt or sodium, and sugar will improve our colon health. The University of Pittsburgh Medical Center suggests limiting animal fats from meats and fatty dairy products to reduce our risks of colon polyps. Whereas the University of Michigan Health System reports that tomatoes and cruciferous vegetables like Brussels sprouts, broccoli, and cabbage, will improve colon health.

It is also important to understand the relationship between colon health and regularity with a positive mental attitude, which was discussed in the section on depression.

*Drinking*

Now, since we are members of the animal kingdom, it may be helpful to try to see ourselves, with any possible degree of objectivity, standing in an enormous group among its manifold subjects. We may note that, save for ourselves, all of them drink only water, with the exception of their mother's milk during infancy. Our fellow subjects drink to quench their thirst; we, on the other hand, drink many things for many reasons.

It is healthy to follow our fellow animal's lead, however, for up to 60% of the human body is water; our hearts and brains are 73% water, our lungs are about 83% water, our skin is 64% water, our muscles and kidneys are about

79% water, and even our bones are composed of water—31%. To be certain, water is a building block of the 37 trillion cells of our bodies.[20] The indispensability of water is self-evident but let's consider some of the reasons to drink clean, purified water:

- Acts as a thermostat, regulating our body's temperature
- Metabolizes carbohydrates and proteins
- Principle component of saliva and necessary to swallow
- Needed to manufacture neurotransmitters and hormones
- Keeps mucus membranes moist
- Lubricates our joints
- Shock absorber for vital organs and spinal cord
- Insulates and cushions the fetus
- Delivers oxygen to all parts of the body
- Flushes waste and toxins from the body

Reward your body with a crystal-clear glass of purified water first thing in the morning. After all, it's been busy all night maintaining your body from head to toe. Depending upon our local climate and our diet, we should typically drink four to six glasses of water each day.

––––––––––––––––––––––

[20] Mitchell, H.H., Hamilton, T.S., Steggerda, F.R., and Bean, H.W., 1945, "The chemical composition of the adult human body and its bearing on the biochemistry of growth," *Journal of Biological Chemistry*, v. 158, issue 3, p. 625-637.

Alcohol, by contrast:

- Causes difficulty in maintaining normal temperatures
- Interferes with metabolizing carbohydrates and proteins
- It thickens our saliva and interferes with swallowing
- Interferes with neurotransmitters and hormones
- Dehydrates mucus membranes
- Deteriorates our joints
- Compromises protection of brain, organs, and spinal cord
- Critically harms the fetus
- Significantly slows delivery of oxygen to all the body
- Deposits toxins throughout the body
- Increases the chance of stroke
- Increases the chance of high blood pressure
- Increases the chance of obesity
- Increases the chance of breast cancer
- Increases the chance of suicide
- Increases the chance of accidents
- Poisons the liver and kidneys
- Kills cells
- It is profoundly addictive

Despite these facts, some people advocate drinking wine for the health of their hearts. It appears this is a myth. For, surprisingly, no research has been conducted to substantiate this idea. According to the American Heart Association, "No direct comparison trials have been done to determine the specific effect of wine or other alcohol on the risk of developing heart disease or stroke."

If we drink, we should pose the question: Can I enjoy a meal or an evening out without alcohol? If the answer is no, or if the answer is yes but it doesn't align with your actions, you may be addicted, ever so mildly or monstrously.

How do we know if we are drinking too much? According to Alcoholics Anonymous, a woman who has more than seven drinks per week or more than three drinks per occasion is drinking too much. For a man, the limit is fourteen drinks per week or more than four drinks per occasion. For those older than sixty-five, seven drinks per week or more than three drinks per occasion is too much.

*Energy*

Why run the race of life with a heavy boat anchor chained to one's neck? If we aspire to have buoyant energy, wheat is an anchor that must be heaved overboard. Eliminate all wheat, which is gluten, from your diet. Gluten counterbalances energy by creating weight gain, general fatigue, mental fog, and arthritis.

Energy begets energy. Exercise compliments the work of our respiratory, circulatory, and lymph node systems, giving them a boost. So even a walk will add zest to our lives.

Be certain your walk is in fresh air, when the weather permits, since oxygen also enlivens us. We can workout at an indoor gym and eat a supremely healthy diet yet, without deep breathing clean, fresh air, we will never attain optimal health.

It is important to note that the potassium and enzymes in apple cider vinegar energize us. You might add apple cider vinegar to a glass of water and drink it during a workout to prevent fatigue. The amino acids in apple cider vinegar combat lactic acid that accumulates after exercise;

doing so may help us feel fresher and stronger.

Positive friends, even casual friends, family, and sociability energizes us. It must be positive, however.

Sunlight invigorates. Even a few minutes of sunlight makes a difference, yet it is best to spend as much time outside as possible. Those who live in regions with less sunlight time, will benefit from lighting up daytime hours with artificial light and bright colors.

But let the night be the night. As we will discuss in the section on sleep, we want zero light in our bedrooms.

Deep breathing—one way to ensure we are completely expanding and filling our lungs with fresh air is to run a mile or so three days each week with a day between runs to allow recuperation. We can also achieve deep breathing by walking and holding our breath. Every time our left foot hits the ground, is one count. After counting to ten, which would be twenty steps, exhale thoroughly. This will start the deep breathing cycle that you might use two or three times during each walk.

Of course, you should consult with your doctor before trying this routine.

Noise is stress. And stress saps our strength. Therefore, doctors so often recommend quiet rest to their patients. We would be wise to use discriminating taste about what comes into our bodies via soundwaves. Rather than welcoming radio gibberish into our minds, bodies, and souls, we would be foresighted to allow our whole person to resonate with Vivaldi, Schubert, Paganini, Chopin, or a panoply of other masters.

Coffee, alcohol, tobacco, and processed "food" markedly deplete energy.

B-complex supplements that include B-1, B-2, B-3, B-6, and B-12 enhance energy and are a necessity for those who eat a plant food diet.

Finally, nothing is more essential to living an energy-filled life than a diet that is principally based upon sparkling clean water, fresh organic vegetables, fruits, nuts, grains, and inhaling plenty of fresh clean air.

## Eye Health

In this, the Information Age, we place profound stress on our eyes, so we must care for them daily. Afterall, they give us light, every shade of color, they express an infinite array of emotions and clever wit, they help us read books, and see the boundless glories of our realm. All this work requires maintenance. Eight hours of non-stimulated rest in darkness, while we sleep, is essential. A bedroom darkened by curtains, shutters, or blinds gives our eyes the rest they crave and a quality sleeping mask will provide near total darkness.

After a long day, it may be helpful to place a warm compress on our eyes. Soak a washcloth in warm water, wring it until only damp, lay down in bed, placing the compress over your closed eyes, and relax for at least five minutes. This process tends to keep the tear ducts open so that your eyes can remain moist and properly lubricated. In addition, it will also help to avoid a stye and shorten its duration should one occur. Our eyes will be protected, relaxed and our whole being will be calmer, as well.

Another eye care technique is using eye drops made with *colloidal silver*. Please note that you must use the correct type of colloidal silver. There could be side-effects, one of which is a condition known as *argyria*, which causes the skin, nails, and gums to have a bluish-gray to gray-black pigmentation, and it is irreversible. This is due to the ingestion of colloidal silver, which is composed of silver particles that are too large to exit the body.

Should you decide to use colloidal silver, you must talk to your physician first and, with his or her approval, use a type that contains particles smaller than a nanometer.

I mention colloidal silver because it improved my eyes dramatically. I had used an expensive, Swiss-made homeopathic eye drop for years, and my eyes suffered the consequences. They were noticeably red. I had also been diagnosed with *blepharitis*, bacteria, and flaky skin residing at the base of eyelashes, a condition that interrupted my sleep, for at night I felt as though my eyes were full of sand. My ophthalmologist told me blepharitis was essentially incurable.

I decided to stop using the homeopathic eye drops and try colloidal silver eye drops three or four times each day. After these at-home treatments, a surprising amount of white substance would gather at the corners of my eyes. At the end of three days, the discharge stopped, and my eyes improved markedly. My general physician commented on the improvement the moment I saw him without my inquiry, and a recent exam by my ophthalmologist revealed no blepharitis. The type of colloidal silver I use is ninety-eight percent positively charged with silver ions and nanoclusters, a feature that effects its rehabilitative performance; and, its particle size is smaller than a nanometer, 0.8 nanometers/0.0008 microns. If this composition is taken seven times a day for seventy years, the ingestion range still falls below the Environmental Protection Agency's (EPA) Reference Dose (RfD) for silver.

Very gently cleaning our eyelids with tearless baby shampoo while showering is also an effective way to manage blepharitis.

Another key eye aid is lutein, which is extracted from marigold petals. Lutein is an antioxidant carotenoid that occurs in nature along with zeaxanthin, which is a closely

related carotenoid and protects the macula from degradation and cataracts normally associated with aging and
oxidative stress. The critically important macula helps our
eyes focus and differentiate colors. I take forty milligrams
each day.

Spinach, peas, avocados, broccoli, and collard greens
are also rich in lutein and zeaxanthin. Oranges, lemons, berries, and grapefruits are excellent sources of vitamin C, which
may also guard against macular degeneration and cataracts.
Sunflower seeds, which are excellent sources of vitamin E
and zinc, may also be a healthy choice for eyes.

Not long ago, I feared I must abandon writing because,
after working particularly long and hard on a project, my
very eyeballs ached as though they were swollen. I listened
to this cry of my overwrought eyes, turning away from
my computer screen for two weeks; and, since I haven't
owned a television for twenty-five years, wasting my eyes
on this programmed nonsense was not an issue. During this
time, I employed the eye care techniques described above.
Yet, after this fortnight of rest, I was disappointed that
looking at a computer screen, even for fifteen minutes,
still caused an ache that required me to stop. I was crest-
fallen.

Yet, my eyes regained their fortitude almost overnight from one small change: I began including a handful
of organic kale in my morning smoothie. These mega-
doses of kale, naturally enriched with vitamin A, healed and
strengthened my eyes, returning them to a condition in
which they were better than ever. Kale also made my eyes
brighter and more attractive.

If you don't have a blender, you may want to consider
purchasing one. It needn't be expensive.

Here is a kale smoothie suggestion: Purple Kale Smoothie

- One frozen organic banana (peel and freeze overnight).
- One cup of organic blueberries.
- Carrot Juice, 8 to 10 oz., organic, not from concentrate.
- One big handful of organic kale.
- Vanilla vegan protein powder from peas and no sugar.

Drink this for breakfast as you take your daily vitamins and supplements before eating anything else since fruit may interfere with the digestion of other foods. Give your body time to digest this super healthy drink before eating a second breakfast or lunch. Your eyes will sparkle!

*Exercise*

Exercise is a tonic for the mind and the whole body. So, if you are not exercising regularly, start today.

Begin by talking with your physician before starting an exercise regimen, asking for his or her advice about the best workout for your age and health. If your doctor determines that you are healthy and able to pursue a full exercise program, you might follow these suggestions.

Let's assume you're new to exercising. In this case, walking is probably the best place to start. First, buy a quality pair of walking or running shoes that give you good support. The cushion of quality athletic shoes will absorb the rhythmic shock that ordinarily would be absorbed, not only by your feet, ankles, shins, knees, thighs, and hips, but also your spine, chest, back, shoulders, neck, and head.

If all these body parts, and more, are receiving hundreds or thousands of shocks in a concentrated amount of time, it could cause debilitating fatigue; this is particularly true when we are over the age of fifty. By contrast, the extra shock absorption afforded by high-quality athletic shoes alleviates this trauma, allowing us to recover faster from a workout that includes walking or running. This will help us feel stronger and more vigorous rather than tired after a workout.

Take it easy at first. Don't overdo it. You should, however, be able to walk one mile each day in around 30 minutes. This is the minimum time that you should maintain an elevated heart rate needed to give your heart, lungs, circulatory system, and lymph nodes an elementary workout.

With the assumption that you are walking in the fresh air, breathe deeply during your walks. After walking a quarter of a mile or so, you may try inhaling and then holding your breath for anywhere from ten to twenty seconds. Each time your left foot touches the ground, count until reaching the number you choose, up to twenty. This will help you breathe more deeply, invigorating your whole being, especially your lungs, heart, and brain.

When you feel the need to expend more energy, try running an eighth of a mile on Mondays, Wednesdays, and Fridays. Once you've consistently run an eighth of a mile, try a quarter of a mile until you are able to run one full mile three times a week. The health and mental rewards will be astonishing.

After you feel comfortable with this exercise level, you may want to add an isometric routine to walking. Isometrics are excellent for the results they offer as well as the fact that they can be completed without equipment or a gym. Push-ups are an example. This exercise develops:

1. the *pectoral* (chest) muscles
2. the *latissimus dorsi* (muscles beneath the shoulders on either side of the rib cage and often called "lats")
3. the *deltoid* (shoulder muscle),
4. *triceps* (on the back of the arms between the shoulder and elbow),
5. the *trapezius* (the muscles above the shoulders extending towards the neck),
6. the abdominal or stomach muscles.

Men and boys who are in shape and within their height/weight ratio (see the section on *Weight* for the height/weight chart), should be able to do two sets of thirty push-ups for a total of sixty.

This may seem impossible. Maybe you are unable to do even one push-up. But in a week, by trying each day you work out, you will be able to do one push-up. You will be surprised that by trying one more push-up each workout day, you will be able to do two sets of ten push-ups in three or four weeks, and two sets of twenty in six weeks, and two sets of thirty in eight weeks. Your schedule may vary, of course.

Here's an important tip: never do push-ups every day. Do them only three times a week—Monday, Wednesday, and Friday, for example. This allows your muscles to rest and recuperate; for once you tear them down with a workout, they must have time to rebuild. Therefore, consistent workouts with intervals of rest cause muscles to grow.

Another excellent isometric workout is stomach crunches. These are essential to keep a flat stomach, as well as strengthening the muscles to keep your spine in the flowing S curve necessary for healthy posture and a pain-free back.

Lay on your back with your legs crossed at your ankles. Draw your knees toward your chest, and while holding your knees in this position, cross your arms over your chest. Now, lift your upper back off the floor while lifting your chest and head forward. Avoid rocking back and forth as this will negate the stress on your stomach. This strengthens:

1. the *rectus abdominis* (stomach muscles) and
2. various muscles in the neck.

Start slowly, adding more crunches each time you work out. A man or woman who is in shape should be able to do two sets of 75 for a total of 150 or more of these.

If you cannot do even one crunch, do not let this discourage you. Let it encourage you!

By steadily adding one or more crunches to every workout, you will be able to do more than 100 crunches, maybe 150 crunches, in a few months. Be sure of it. You may even want to hold thirty pounds on your chest as you do them. Just take one small step at a time. This is how every weakling became a muscle-bound brute—one little bit at a time. It will work for you, too.

Now, you might want to buy a set of dumbbells. Start with those that weigh about fifteen pounds each.

Try curls. While standing, hold them in each hand and, alternating from one hand to the other, bring one up toward your shoulder, taking turns. Set a goal to do two sets of fifty for a total of 100 curls. As with the other exercises, begin with a few repetitions and add more weight and reps each time you work out.

I suggest exercising early in the morning before eating. You may first wish to drink a glass of room temperature water, for most people receive better results by not eating or drinking more than this before exercising. Immediately after your workout, you must recover. Consider drinking a smoothie. Here's one I love, the Green and Purple Smoothie:

- One frozen organic banana
- Big handful of fresh organic kale
- Chopped celery
- Chopped cucumber
- One-half cup of organic blueberries
- Eight to ten oz. of purified water
- Vanilla vegan protein powder without sugar

Another positively delicious smoothie is the Carrot, Strawberry Smoothie:

- One frozen organic banana
- Big handful of fresh organic spinach
- One cup of organic strawberries
- Three stalks of organic celery, chopped
- Eight to ten oz. of carrot juice
- Vanilla vegan protein powder made without sugar

While enjoying your smoothie, it is an ideal time to take your vitamins and supplements. Follow your smoothie by carbing-up with a healthy breakfast. This is one you may like:

- One-half cup (before cooking) of organic buckwheat cereal
- One tablespoon of organic cayenne pepper
- Three tablespoons of organic olive oil

You may want to try a smaller portion of cayenne pepper to test its heat.

This will not only provide plenty of carbs to help you recover from your workout, but the cayenne pepper and olive oil will serve as a powerful anti-inflammatory, as well. It will also help to reduce sports injuries.

Of course, if you are running eight miles each morning and bench pressing three hundred-fifty pounds thirty times, you will need more carbs to recover. We must find the workout and recovery routine that is best for us. The important thing is to start today.

*Face*

It is unnecessary to have what is generally considered a pretty or handsome face to be uniquely attractive. Our facial features, in fact, can be quite incidental to facial attractiveness.

A glow emanating from a clean, happy soul is magnetic, and this magnetism can be wonderfully enhanced by a few glasses of purified water each day and a diet of mostly fruits and vegetables. Certain vegetables can even give us a tan without the Sun; the carotene from carrots, for example, will cause the face to have a beautiful, Sun-kissed blush, making our teeth appear a little whiter, the whites of our eyes a tad more blanche. This may be a motivation to eat carrots and drink carrot juice. Adding carrot juice to a smoothie may be something to try. Should we exercise vigorously every day, all the above benefits will be enriched, giving our face the unmistakable appearance of salubrity. Add a generous smile, and we will look fully alive, a trait that will draw others to us.

Also, vitamin A is a natural skin potion and is, therefore, good for our face. Vitamin A-rich-foods, in order of potency, are sweet potatoes, winter squash, kale, collards, turnip greens, carrots, sweet red peppers, Swiss chard, spinach, and romaine lettuce. Do something nice for your face today: toss a salad with these life-giving foods.

But the Sun will age and wrinkle our faces. Even one sunburn will accelerate aging in only a few hours. So, avoid direct Sunlight, especially between10 am and 4 pm, when the Sun's rays are most damaging. If you must be in direct sunlight, wear a hat that protects your face and sunglasses that protect you against UV rays. Sunscreen may be needed, too. But avoid rubbing toxins into your face that are in most Sunscreens; find one that is free of them. More about protection from the Sun is found under the section *Sunburn*.

Most of our women know many ways to keep their faces beautified, so I may not have anything new to tell them about facial care. Men, however, usually don't subscribe to facial care, possibly because it seems unmanly to them. It did to me until I aged a little. But, gentlemen, we are only issued one face. It is how we are judged most often, and it must serve us all our lives, so we are better served by taking care of our face each day. If you are an alpha male, such a notion will not be intimidating.

I testify that witch hazel (without toxic chemicals) is a superb way to keep the face clean, smooth, soft, and glowing; it is the best way I've found to tighten pores, remove dirt, and excess oil, too. I use it morning and night, and, after each use, I massage about one quarter teaspoon of organic coconut oil into my face; this is a particularly good moisturizing routine after a shave. But without a moisturizer, our faces may look dry, pale, and old rather than the true ruddy, peach color of our complexion.

Above all, our faces are animated by a clean body.

*Feet*

If we are to enjoy robust health, we must care for our feet since walking, running, and, general liveliness depends on them.

Our first concern is cleanliness. Therefore, we should change socks three or four times each day. This is especially important to those of us who exercise five to six days each week. Socks must be removed after every workout. Our feet should be soaked in warm water daily or at least several times each week. Soaking them in apple cider vinegar is ideal. Yet, if we shower rather than bathe, soaking our feet for a minimum of five minutes in a foot tub is necessary. Allowing our feet to air-clean without shoes or socks is important. But it is suggested that this is enjoyed at home rather than outdoors, for many harmful parasites may be contacted in nature. These often enter the body through our feet so be wise and wear shoes and socks while outside. Clipping our toenails is essential to cleanliness and provides the appropriate room within our shoes, too.

Shoes profoundly affect our posture, energy level, and freedom from injury. So, we are wise to wear high-quality running and walking shoes with appropriate cushion and lateral support. Cushion literally protects us from head to toe. For, when we run or even walk, shock waves jolt our feet, ankles, shins, knees, thighs, hips, pelvis, back, shoulders, neck, and head. These are the eleven main points of potential injury. However, high-quality shoes protect these vulnerable points from damage. Moreover, shoes that are properly designed will preserve our vitality since these eleven connecting points needn't compensate for thousands of small concussions they absorb daily particularly during vigorous exercise. So rather than missing out a single day or sometimes several days of exuberant life caused by energy drain, wear the right shoes and thrive.

*Fever Blisters*

Should you feel a tingling, itchiness on or around your lips, this could be the onset of a fever blister, especially if you have experienced undue stress in the last few days . That stress may have compromised your immune system, breaking down the gates guarding your lips against hostile bacteria.

Without delay, take an ice cube and, with a washcloth to protect your fingers from the cold, hold the ice directly on the suspect place. You might need to go through several ice cubes, but this may save you from weeks of discomfort and embarrassment in public.

One of the key points is to ice it down immediately. Once it begins to fester, it will enlarge and spread rapidly. By acting right away, you may be able to freeze it before it can make a noticeable appearance.

But fever blisters are a strong virus. So, you might want to ask your doctor about a prescription that you can keep on hand when such a breakout occurs.

And if you are a man and you shave, you may want to stop shaving until you have overcome this little malady because a razor can spread the infection to other parts of your face.

*Fatigue*

If we are eating a diet without fried foods, processed foods, or dairy products but one that is rich with organic fruits and vegetables, particularly leafy green vegetables, and exercising regularly in the fresh air, we should have plenty of energy.

Yet even while doing all the above, we may still feel drained of pep, and the reasons could be myriad. A significant drain on our energy is walking in shoes that have insufficient support. Wearing high-quality shoes is especially crucial the more we age since the cushions throughout our bodies begin to weaken. This is why I suggest wearing only the best quality shoes constructed with plenty of cushion. Insoles may also be a solution. And when we walk for exercise or run, it is essential to wear athletic shoes. This will alleviate the great stress that runs all through our body, and causes debilitating fatigue.

If we are feeling drained of energy, one important question we might ask is this: with whom are we spending the precious moments of our life? Are these successful, happy people? Or are your associates unsuccessful and unhappy people who drain your energy? Find people who are succeeding and enjoying life; listen to them, emulate them, and decide that you will also be successful.

One cause of fatigue may be depression. If you have any of the following feelings, reread the section on depression.

- Overeating or appetite loss
- Lack of direction in life
- Lack of normal energy
- Difficulty concentrating and making decisions
- Feelings of guilt, worthlessness or helplessness
- Feelings of hopelessness and negativity
- Insomnia or excessive sleeping
- Irritability and restlessness

- Loss of interest in activities once enjoyed
- Loss of interest in sex
- Chronic aches pains, headache, or cramps
- Digestive problems, unresponsive to normal treatment
- Persistently sad, anxious feelings

If you experience these feelings, they can be replaced with positive thoughts. So, read the section about depression and believe you will turn things around. Simply believe, believe, believe.

Another reason for fatigue is gluten.

### Gluten

Gluten, which is found in wheat, is valued for its viscosity, which gives elasticity to dough, helps it rise, maintains its shape, and often gives the final product a chewy texture. Yet, this viscoelasticity has a tenacious quality that lines the digestive tract, inhibiting digestion and, in turn, causing weight gain, fatigue, and arthritic symptoms. Anyone who wishes to lose weight, enjoy robust energy, and avoid arthritis should also avoid gluten.

### Grieving

I was told I would never again see my dearest love. The soul-cleansing embrace was forever and ever gone, the cheery, childlike smile would never again cast life cross my face.

I involuntarily fell to my knees and cried one thousand times, *"No!"* There, with my face in my hands upon my neighbor's couch, I wept for two hours, calling the name that would never again answer. I lost ten pounds in four days, and friends said I aged a decade overnight. There was no sleep for three weeks. During this time, to keep a morsel of my sanity, I went to a local coffee shop and wrote a screenplay about our lives together. As waves swamping a drowning man, grief came upon grief. Then there was a lull. Then I was viciously swamped, yet again. Over the months, the waves came less frequently and less violently. Upon the end of the ninth month, I had completed my grief.

Though six years have passed, tears filled my eyes when I wrote this. Yet, I also smile when the sweetness of that precious gift visits my heart as though a butterfly flitters through a garden lattice, and I whisper, *I love you.*

*Hair*

Eating green leafy vegetables every day may possibly slow down graying or even stop it from happening at all, whereas fried and processed foods will probably hasten graying.

Another way to keep hair healthy is to use a filter in our showers that eliminates chlorine and other harsh chemicals in our water. And, as you may have read, I discourage the use of shampoo since almost all shampoos contain Sodium Lauryl Sulfate or Sodium Laureth Sulfate (SLS), which cause the bubbling, sudsing action. This is nothing less than poison and will clearly crash the human immune system. For, the last nine years, I have simply scrubbed my scalp vigorously with water, and from the beginning, my hair improved noticeably.

I use shea butter on my hair, and this keeps it shiny and in place. Apple cider vinegar can be used as a rinse and may also give our hair a shiny, healthy appearance. These foods might help your hair, too:

- Pumpkin seeds
- Strawberries
- Almonds
- Beans
- Shiitake Mushrooms

*Headaches*

A migraine or a severe headache requires the examination of a physician. In such cases, we always make the right decision by seeking the advice of our doctor right away.

While there are many different types of headaches, including cluster, sinus, migraine, and chronic, the most common is a tension headache triggered by stress, anxiety, or depression. The discomfort is usually mild to moderate and may feel as though a band is squeezing around our head, which is simply because a headache is inflammation, especially across the forehead.

I suggest keeping a few bags of frozen green peas in the freezer for a quick, healthy remedy for such headaches. Lie on your bed and place a bag behind your neck; this will affect the inflammation in your forehead. You may also want to place another bag directly on your forehead, but because it may be difficult to endure the cold, you first might want to allow it to warm a little.

Lie there in silence for an hour or so if you wish. Falling asleep is recommended. This is a way to literally, and figuratively, chill out.

Avoid aspirin and other headache pills. Aspirin can cause stomach and brain bleeding, and a host of other maladies, including, irony upon irony, headaches if used repeatedly. Ibuprofen attacks the liver and kidneys so never use this toxin.

Ensuring that prescription lenses, if you wear them, are the correct strength may eliminate headaches since an inaccurate strength will cause eye strain and headaches.

Keeping the head and neck in the same position over time can cause headaches. Holding a phone to our ear, working on a computer, or working at a desk and from a chair that are not ergonomically designed, and doing so in a sustained position may induce headaches. In such cases, the *upper trapezius* and *levator scapulae* muscles become shortened, tightened, and inflamed, leading to a headache.

Dehydration will cause a throbbing ache in our heads. One of the first things we should do each morning is drink plenty of purified water. At least 16 ounces are needed to help our body begin its holistic cleansing process; for example, 8 ounces of pure water followed by 8 ounces of a fruit smoothie. Coconut water is a superb hydrator, too. Even while remaining indoors, dehydration can sneak up on us quickly, so drink several glasses of clean water if you begin to feel light-headed or even slightly disoriented.

*Height Loss*

I have always been six feet tall, but recently I measured my height and was dismayed to discover I had lost almost two inches. But I regained this lost stature by doing something very simple.

I purchased a chin-up bar designed to be set in the top of a doorway and, while grasping it with both hands, would hang there for thirty seconds, three or four times each day. From the first experience, I could feel the invigoration of my spine extending and straightening. After about six weeks, all my height was regained, and my posture improved as well.

## *Ibuprofen and Pain Killers*

"Taking common painkillers can raise heart attack risk by half after just one day, a major study warns," says Nick McDermott, Health Editor for the *Sun*. "Experts looked at nearly 450,000 adults given non-steroidal anti-inflammatory drugs (NSAIDs). They include popular over-the-counter pills such as ibuprofen, and prescription-only drugs such as diclofenac. Both are taken by millions for conditions such as headaches, back pain, and arthritis.

"The study, published in the *British Medical Journal*, said their effect on heart attack risk was almost immediate. But it was not long-lasting and wore off over time. Past studies have found the common painkillers increase risk of cardiac arrest by up to a third. Scientists fear the drugs may cause blood vessels to narrow, increase fluid retention and alter blood pressure. Canadian experts found taking any regular dose of ibuprofen for between one to seven days raised chances [for heart attacks] by 48 percent. For diclofenac it went up 50 percent, and naproxen 53 percent."

The National Kidney Foundation states, "Heavy or long-term use of some of these medicines, such as ibuprofen, naproxen, and higher dose aspirin, can cause chronic kidney disease known as chronic interstitial nephritis."

These dangerous drugs are often taken to ease the pain caused by inflammation, which can be more effectively reduced with the medicinal powers of celery, white onions, or cayenne pepper. A soup made from these natural

painkillers is also suggested. Of course, celery, white onions, and cayenne pepper have no side effects and,
depending upon the severity of the pain, usually act reasonably fast.

*Inflammation*

The most intelligent way to avoid inflammation is to
not eat inflammatory foods, such as those that are fried,
processed, have too much salt or sugar content, or are derived from animals. These fake foods harm and
prematurely age our bodies, even turning our hair gray, and
so they should be replaced with a diet of predominantly
life-giving organic fruits and mostly vegetables, particularly the green, leafy variety.

Sugar may be the leading cause of inflammation as it
permeates modern diets and releases small secreted proteins known as *cytokines*, which are essentially inflammatory
messengers. Table sugar and high-fructose corn syrup are
the two types of sugar in most people's diet, and are often
disguised on labels as any word ending in "ose," such as
fructose or sucrose.

Although some sugar is integral to our bodies, if we eat
too much, we will experience an inordinate amount of inflammation, which is profoundly damaging. This occurs
when eating fake foods processed with added sugar and refined carbohydrates, such as soda pop, drinks sweetened with
sugar, drinks made with concentrated juices, white rice,
white bread, white flour, cookies, crackers, potato chips,
cake, and ice cream. These destructive fake foods can lead to
heart disease, poor mental health, diabetes, obesity, Alz-
heimer's, aches, and pains incorrectly attributed to aging.
Rather than suffer from these maladies and the high cost of

fake medicines to cure them, which are often maladies in themselves, they can be prevented by simply eating healthily.

We will probably receive enough sugar by eating two or three servings of fresh fruit each day; so, sprinkling sugar on our food or adding it to recipes is nothing more than an unhealthy habit, and this can be broken in three weeks.

Another of the foremost causes of inflammation is sodium, which is an ingredient in salt. Sodium is needed, however, to maintain our electrolyte balance, which allows healthy transmission of nerve impulses such as normal contraction and relaxation of muscles. Without sodium, we would be unable to maintain our appropriate fluid equilibrium, experienced most notably when dehydrated on a hot day.

Our kidneys are the central repository of sodium, releasing it into our bloodstream upon demand while excess sodium is secreted in urine. Yet, when our kidneys are unable to eliminate excess sodium, it accumulates in our bloodstream, causing our blood volume to swell since sodium retains water. In such cases, a greater demand is placed upon our heart, for it must pump with increased force to keep the excess sodium moving through our veins and arteries. This is the cause of high blood pressure.

As we can see, swelling of our veins and arteries may affect our joints, causing or exacerbating arthritic conditions. A swollen, puffy face, pleurisy, and tinnitus, or ringing in our ears, are also complements of excess salt. Indeed, over time, sodium imbalance commonly leads to a host of health maladies, the most serious of which are congestive heart failure, chronic kidney disease, and cirrhosis of the liver.

Most of us can maintain the proper level of sodium without sprinkling salt on our food or adding it to recipes, for sodium is already in much of our food. I stopped adding salt to my meals several years ago and benefitted by eliminating pleurisy, tinnitus, puffy eyes, and occasional dry throat.

Alcohol is also an aggressive inflammatory, particularly affecting the pancreas, joints, accelerating the graying of hair, and aging of skin. Drinkers, considered those who take only two drinks a day, will over time exhibit loss of facial collagen since alcohol subtracts fluid from the skin, most readily observed in a sagging, wrinkled, pale complexion accompanied by red blotches on the nose and cheeks. Coffee dehydrates and inflames the skin, as well. Rather than drinking these toxins, maintain hydration by drinking plenty of purified water—the amount depends upon diet and climate—to avoid inflammation.

If, however, you experience inflammation from a strain or twisted ankle, for example, make an appointment with your physician, think twice before taking aspirin or ibuprofen, and remember RICE—Rest, Ice, Compress, Elevate. Your physician might suggest that you use RICE at least one week after your affected area assumes its healthy appearance and feels as though it is healed. Be especially nice to your body, giving it ample convalescence. In addition to RICE, your doctor might suggest avoiding the foods and drinks described at the beginning of this section and enjoying the following anti-inflammatory recipes:

Breakfast:
*Cayenne Buckwheat:* One of my favorite anti-inflammatory dishes is buckwheat cereal mixed with cayenne pepper and olive oil. This is ideal for breakfast since it not only fights swelling but is also a good clean carbohydrate burn, meaning it is a carbohydrate that is easily assimilated

into energy, whereas processed carbs require significantly more energy to burn, giving us a tired sleepy feeling after eating them. By contrast, one-half cup of buckwheat cereal will provide the needed energy throughout much of the day.

Cayenne pepper is a powerful anti-inflammatory that helps reduce inflammation in the sinuses and throughout the body. If, however, you are unaccustomed to it, I suggest testing a tiny portion with a quarter cup of cooked buckwheat cereal before adding it to your full serving of buckwheat.

Olive oil is also an ingredient we want on our inflammation-fighting team because one of its compounds is *oleocanthal*, which inhibits the production of pro-inflammatory COX-1 and COX-2 enzymes, similar to the method of ibuprofen. By the way, you may find that the olive oil helps tone down the heat of the cayenne rice.

Lunch:

*The Sylvan Salad:* For a delicious anti-inflammatory salad, using all organic ingredients, mix fresh spinach leaves in a bowl with chopped walnuts, chia seeds, flax seeds, blueberries, and strawberries. Pour on coconut oil and mix. Together, all the ingredients taste marvelous, and each one reduces inflammation. Enjoy the wonderfully healthy, anti-inflammatory Sylvan Salad and relax.

Dinner:

*Celery Soup:* Chop up a stalk of fresh organic celery, place in a blender, and add filtered water. After it is blended into a soupy substance, pour it into in a bowl, and enjoy this cool idea that is especially refreshing on a summer day. Be sure to eat it plain without adding ingredients such as spices, oils, dairy products, and salt, which destroys the medicinal properties of the celery.

Or, you may prefer *White Onion Soup.* Peel a white onion, chop it up, place it in a pan of filtered water and heat for thirty minutes or so. Eat it plain also and enjoy the power of this natural anti-inflammatory.

*Irritability*

Please read the section about depression.

*Knees*

Our knees are a major load-bearing part of our body, and should they become compromised, we may lose our mobility; if this happens, the rest of our health might rapidly deteriorate since we cannot rejuvenate ourselves through vigorous daily exercise. So, it is not an exaggeration to say that to a large extent, our health depends upon our knees.

Consequently, it is critical to avoid any drinks, even fruit drinks, that are made from concentrate. They, like sodas and coffee, are so acidic that they subtract lipid acids from our body, and knees in particular. Eventually, they wear away knee cartilage. Acidic and processed foods can also be a knee threat.

Glucosamine may be a way to recover lost knee cartilage (see the section titled *Cartilage*). However, it is not a good choice for everyone. So, I do not recommend that you take glucosamine since it may cause allergic reactions or side effects. Yet you may wish to read a little about glucosamine or seek your physician's opinion about it. You may also want to ask your doctor about hyaluronic acid's ability to protect the cartilage of your knees.

Health writer Derek Bryan says, "Leafy green vegetables, such as collard greens, spinach and kale, tend to be moderately high in calcium and high in vitamin C and selenium. Vitamin C is an essential vitamin for the protection and function of cartilage in the body because it provides cushioning and support for major joints. Selenium, too, is thought to support bone and joint health, because it has antioxidant properties that protect against damage and plays a critical role in producing new cells. One cup of cooked collard greens contains more than 250 milligrams of calcium, about 25 percent of your Recommended Daily Allowance, and 35 milligrams of vitamin C, more than 30 percent of your RDA."

Should your knees become inflamed, you may also wish to read the section about inflammation.

*Lungs*

Our lungs must be filled with fresh air each day during exercise such as walking in the outdoors. Even a short walk will revitalize our lungs and, therefore, our heart, mind and, indeed, the whole body. This holistic enlivening from so little movement illustrates the extraordinary effect of oxygen on our body and the need to protect its single portal of oxygenation—our lungs. As we consider the complexity of the biomechanics of our lungs, many of us will appreciate the importance of protecting them.

*Alveoli,* which in Latin means "little cavities," are the hollow cavities within our lungs, exclusively responsible for respiration, the transport of oxygen to our blood as we inhale, the elimination of carbon dioxide when exhaling. There are approximately 700 million alveoli in our lungs, suggesting their intense intricacy and preponderance; for, without them, we would quickly suffocate. It is notable that they can be compromised by something as innocuous as lack of activity; in such cases, they can be partly smothered by excess phlegm or simply weakened as any other part of the body becomes with insufficient use. This may cause immediate symptoms such as coughing, a dull, lifeless complexion, lack of energy, the absence of alacrity, or a mental fog, along with many other maladies.

Smoking, albeit, is supremely destructive of the alveoli, covering it with black, sticky tar, limiting and eventually ruining the tobacco user's ability to inhale or exhale. A slow asphyxiation ensues, extending over several months or even years, in which the victim's skin may assume the deathly hue of a cadaver.

And because the alveoli absorb gaseous toxins at an isotopic rate, it is imperative to avoid aerosols such as perfume, cologne, hair spray, deodorant, and air fresheners that almost unexceptionally contain poisonous chemicals. So, it is wise to eliminate any gaseous household substances or grooming products that we might inhale.

Instead, we fill our lungs and, in turn, our entire body, with fresh, life-giving oxygen from walking in the mountains, the woods, the seaside, or riverside, holistically invigorating ourselves until we are sleek with radiant health.

While on such a walk, we may try inhaling deeply, holding our breath, then counting to ten, counting each number as our left foot strikes the ground, then exhaling completely. This helps us breathe deeply, clearing, and enlivening our lungs. As was previously recommended, discuss this routine with your physician before trying it.

Running, of course, is possibly the best way to achieve oxygenation of the lungs and the whole body.

*Nightmares*

Dreamless sleep markedly improves our lives, as we shall see in the section on *Sleep*. Yet, finding ourselves in surrealistic emotional traps in the middle of the night from which no escape seems possible drains us of energy and the necessary recuperation we must have during deep sleep. To avoid these traumatic episodes, take these steps:

First, never eat salty food or food that contains sodium after lunch. And, if we eat food containing salt or sodium during the day, its content must be low. This is critical since salt induces nightmares.

Secondly, excess sugar can also cause nightmares, so read labels of packaged foods to avoid them. There is, of course, sugar in fruit; for this reason and because it can require time to digest, it is recommended that fruit is not eaten after lunch.

Third, think about the amount of dietary fiber you are consuming; if you are eating one-half cup of buckwheat cereal at breakfast, for instance, and having vivid dreams or nightmares, you may want to reduce it to one-quarter of a cup. This way your body will not be preoccupied with digestion when it should be receiving the nourishment from deepest sleep.

Fourth, it might be helpful to not eat after 6 pm. This will allow the completion of basic digestion before bedtime, which is ideally at 10 pm; in this way, your body will have finished the hard work before going to bed, allowing rest and release unto deep sleep.

If nightmares persist after following these three steps, talk with your physician to resolve this issue.

*Oral Hygiene*

Five basics comprise the minimum of oral hygiene:

- A tongue scraper to clean the tongue,
- A quality, soft toothbrush to brush teeth and gums,
- Toothpaste that is free from harmful ingredients,
- Mouthwash,
- A water flosser

Tooth paste that is edible and, therefore, harmless if accidentally swallowed is recommended. And, perhaps the best mouthwash is apple cider vinegar, since it kills bacteria and treats halitosis, or bad breath. This natural mouthwash may also help to whiten teeth.

Brushing the tongue with a mixture of baking soda and apple cider vinegar will cleanse it from *fungus Candida albicans*, which causes a white appearance of the tongue.

*Pleurisy*

Pleurisy is a condition affecting the *pleura*, a membrane consisting of a layer of tissue lining the inner side of the chest cavity and a layer of tissue surrounding the lungs. Should it become inflamed, we may feel a sharp chest pain (pleuritic pain) which worsens during breathing.

If you suspect you have pleurisy, contact your physician right away, as it could develop into a serious condition.

Occasionally, I would have bouts of pleurisy after overcoming a cold or episodes of acute stress that lasted a day or two. After eliminating salt from my diet, however, I also eliminated pleurisy. You see, when sodium levels rise, our body retains water to dilute the blood, which increases the blood volume and blood pressure. This, in turn, leads to inflammation throughout our bodies, including the pleura.

Plenty of salt is in the food we typically eat every day, so we needn't sprinkle more on our meals for any reason other than seasoning. This is an acquired taste and habitual. We can, of course, break a bad habit, such as sprinkling salt on all our meals, in only three weeks and be healthier for having done so.

*Posture*

Our posture affects our self-esteem. This is a dynamic that I call Holistic Reciprocal Causation (HRC). For example, when standing erect, our mind and whole body respond with vitality, and, consequently, positive thinking becomes easier. If we sit with the base of our backbones against the back of our chair, our body responds similarly.

Besides the mental benefits of HRC, good posture allows our body to function more easily and freely. Blood flow to our vital organs opens, our breathing expands, and we are, in turn, more fully alive.

A superb way to improve posture is by hanging from a chin-up bar. This allows the spinal cord to slightly expand from a compressed state induced by hours of sitting. Hang for about thirty seconds, two times each day. You'll stand taller, walk with greater ease, and exude an aura of attractive self-confidence.

Now is the time to start. Buy a chin-up bar that fits in a doorway and begin standing taller today.

*Protein*

Our body must have protein to repair tissue and produce hormones and enzymes. In fact, protein is more multi-faceted than any of the other macronutrients since it's also necessary for cell growth and repair and allows our immune system to repel infection. Our body also needs protein for energy. And so, we must eat enough protein to keep our body healthy and operational. However, we most likely don't need as much protein as many people assume. Generally speaking, we eat far too much protein, which simply becomes fat. Overeating protein can also place unhealthy demands upon our kidneys and even increase calcium loss.

Our protein requirements can be based upon our ideal weight, which is based on our height, as the chart in the section titled *Weight* reveals. Based upon our ideal weight, the World Health Organization (WHO) suggests that the medium protein requirement for the average person is .50 gram of protein for each pound of body weight. Remember, this is your ideal body weight. So, the WHO recommends 75 grams of protein for a person whose ideal weight is 150lbs. This, I feel, may be too much. And so, I join the many opinioned discussion of the subject. I seem to function quite well on about .25 grams of protein for each pound of body weight.

Of course, it would be shortsighted extrapolation to assume this would be appropriate for anyone else. So, I suggest you ask your physician what would be right for you.

In the meantime, you might find a good protein powder for smoothies that does not contain sugar or dairy products, since these are inflammatory. There are excellent protein powders providing 20 grams of protein per serving, which is derived from a combination of green peas, hemp seeds, and cranberry seeds, for instance. You might want to try some of these protein sources, too:

| Food | | Grams of Protein per Serving Beans |
|---|---|---|
| Tempeh | 8 oz. | 18 g |
| Sprouted Tofu | 6 oz. | 20 g |
| Lentils, cooked | 1 cup | 18 g |
| Garbanzo Beans | 1 cup | 14 g |
| Black Beans | 1 cup | 15 g |
| Black Eyed Peas | 1 cup | 14 g |
| Kidney Beans | 1 cup | 15 g |
| Pinto Beans | 1 cup | 15 g |
| Cannelini Beans | 1 cup | 17g |
| White Northern Beans | 1 cup | 15g |

Grains

| Brown Rice | 1 cup | 5 g |
|---|---|---|
| Quinoa, cooked | 1 cup | 8 g |
| Amaranth | 1 cup | 7 g |

Vegetables

| Lima Beans | 1 cup | 15 g |
|---|---|---|
| Green Peas | 1 cup | 9 g |
| Kale, steamed | 1 cup | 2.5 g |
| Spinach, steamed | 1 cup | 5 g |
| Chard, steamed | 1 cup | 3.3 g |
| Mustard Greens, steamed | 1 cup | 3.6 g |
| Collard Greens, steamed | 1 cup | 5 g |
| Dandelion Greens | 1 cup | 2.1 g |
| Broccoli, steamed | 1 cup | 2.6 g |

| Brussel Sprouts, | 1 cup | 4 g |
|---|---|---|

Nuts

| Almonds | 1/4 cup | 7 g |
|---|---|---|
| Walnuts | 1/4 cup | 4.5 g |
| Cashews | 1/4 cup | 4 g |
| Pistachios | 1/4 cup | 6 g |
| Pine Nuts | 1/4 cup | 4 g |
| Pecans | 1/4 cup | 2 g |
| Brazil Nuts | 1/4 cup | 5 g |
| Hazelnuts | 1/4 cup | 5 g |

Seeds

| Sesame Seeds | 1/4 cup | 7 g |
|---|---|---|
| Sunflower Seeds | 1/4 cup | 8 g |
| Pumpkin Seeds | 1/4 cup | 7 g |
| Hemp Seeds | 1/4 cup | 10 g |
| Flex seeds | 1/4 cup | 8 g |
| Chia Seeds | 1/4 cup | 12 g |

### Rest

We should rest at the end of each day as a prelude to sleep. Yet, one full day each week should be given exclusively to rest. On this day, it is suggested that we do not seek the latest news on the internet or watch any television at all, and that we don't work or exercise but simply rest. Although we may have undertaken big projects that we have pursued twelve hours a day during the work week, we will probably reach these goals more effectively by forgetting about them for at least one day each week.

At times, we may have overloaded ourselves with so much datum—music, news, videos, study, work information, social media, emails, and texts—that, for basic emotional health, we might need to completely disengage from them. For those reasons, I own neither a television nor any hand-held devices nor a cell phone.

Should turning off the television and putting away the cell phone for one weekend seem uncomfortable and even frightening, we undoubtedly need detoxification.

If restful disengagement seems difficult, engage with nature as a replacement of data. An early morning walk in a park rich with a heavy canopy of tall green cathedral ceilings will be a living substitute for the non-living data with which we are barraged throughout the week. Maybe we can spend all morning or all day there with a loved one, enjoying a picnic and a book of classic poems. This one-day vacation each week will help us work with keener concentration and vigor when returning to work. We will also feel better, sleep better, have better interactions with others, and look better, too.

*Skin*

There are at least eight things we should do to maintain healthy skin:

- Avoid Sun exposure, especially from 10 am and 4 pm.
- Wear wide-brimmed hats, long sleeves, and trousers.
- Don't use tanning beds. These are unsafe.
- Use a moisturizer such as organic coconut.
- Eat plenty of green leafy vegetables rich in vitamin A.
- Place a quality filter on our shower.
- Take a high-quality multivitamin.

- Take a high-quality organic vitamin C.
- Know the A, B, C, D, and E of melanoma.
- Receive an annual examination by a dermatologist.

The following ideas are compelling reasons to begin these skin care tips today: A recent report by the American Cancer Society states that melanoma accounts for a mere one percent of all skin cancers in the United States but causes almost all skin cancer deaths. Therefore, it is essential to be able to recognize this deadly killer quickly. Skin irregularities due to melanoma may be raised or flat and are often dark brown or black, yet their color may include variant shades of red, brown, black, blue, and, in some cases, even white. These are the five alphabetic signs that the American Cancer Society suggests are suspect:

Asymmetric:  If you draw a line through a mole, the two halves will not match.

Border:  The borders of an early melanoma tend to be uneven. The edges may be scalloped or notched.

Color:  Having a variety of colors is another warning signal. A number of different shades of brown, tan, or black could appear. A melanoma may also become red, blue, or some other color.

Diameter:  Melanomas usually have a larger diameter than the size of an eraser on a pencil (1/4 inch or 6 mm), but they may sometimes be smaller when first detected.

Evolving:  Any change — in size, shape, color, elevation, or another trait, or any new symptom such as bleeding, itching, or crusting — points to danger.

If you discover a suspicious spot on your skin that meets these criteria, seek medical treatment without delay. Melanoma is deadly. It spreads with surprising rapidity. So, if you are unsure of a spot, always err on the side of caution and meet with your doctor today.

By using these ideas, we can enjoy a more attractive body and possibly avoid serious illness.

Of course, the skin that seems to be most important to us is our face. All those we meet judge us to a great extent by its condition. So, a continued discussion of caring for our facial skin is in the section titled *Face* and the coming section titled *Sunburn.*

*Sleep*

One-third of our lives is spent sleeping. Sweet sleep is where we reorder the banter of the day, reconciling the dissonance, finding an equilibrium of the conscious and unconscious and, finally, blessed forgetfulness. Though we dream continuously, journeying often amongst bizarre symbolic images, we forget all or virtually all these psychological adventures upon waking, for we have been living in a land of no recollection. In this deepest stage of sleep, our eyes dart roundabout their full orbital limits, and, thus, it is appropriately called *rapid eye movement* (REM). Those dreams we recall are experienced in a stage in which we sleep less deeply and more closely aligned with our conscious, and, therefore, we are able to remember them. REM, this deepest stage, is essential to optimal health. For, here, the anabolic process attains the apex of metabolism, in which simple substances are synthesized into the complex materials of living tissue, repairing the pineal gland, pituitary gland, pancreas, thyroid gland, parathyroid gland, ovaries, testes, and adrenal glands. For these reasons, we will consider ways to enhance our sleep with the intent of remaining in REM for as long as needed each night. Foremost among these is the essence of light and darkness.

The day is for wakefulness, the night repose. For, light stimulates a nerve pathway from the retina in the eye to an area in the brain called the *hypothalamus,* where the *suprachiasmatic nucleus* (SCN) signals other parts of the brain that control hormones, body temperature, and other functions, making us feel alert. The SCN acts as a clock powered by light reception, stimulating a miraculous sequence of events affecting the body as a whole; the body's temperature rises and stimulating hormones are released; simultaneously, the SCN delays the release of other hormones, particularly melatonin, anticipating the dark night where, in the absence of light, it will induce slumber.

"Melatonin," says the National Sleep Foundation, "is a natural hormone made by your body's pineal gland. This is a pea-sized gland located just above the middle of the brain. During the day the pineal is inactive. When the sun goes down and darkness occurs, the pineal is 'turned on' by the SCN and begins to produce melatonin, which is released into the blood. Usually, this occurs around 9 pm. As a result, melatonin levels in the blood rise sharply and you begin to feel less alert. Sleep becomes more inviting. Melatonin levels in the blood stay elevated for about 12 hours— all through the night—before the light of a new day when they fall back to low daytime levels by about 9 am. Daytime levels of melatonin are barely detectable."

This natural clock suggests the ideal time to sleep is between 10 pm and 6 am, based upon the fact that the Sun rises as early as 5 am in the summer and as late as 7 am during the winter months; therefore, 6 am is a medium time to arise throughout the year.

Good sleep commences upon waking, ironically, for this is the time we begin making decisions affecting our bodies sixteen hours later, when it is time for slumber. In other words, if we avoid sleep inhibitors during the day, we will prepare ourselves for quality sleep. Sleep inhibitors include salt, sugar, and sugar substitutes, margarine and other butter substitutes, deli meats, non-organic fruits and vegetables, salted nuts and seeds, canola oil, soda, caffeine, and, of course, alcohol. Excessive salt eaten during the day and any salt before bedtime will interfere with the descent to REM. Consequently, Sigmund Freud consumed salt before sleeping, for he wanted to block his dreaming entrance to REM, thereby inducing vivid nightmares, that would serve as a laboratory for dream analysis. Should you have problems with nightmares, simply reduce or eliminate your salt consumption, with no salt or salty foods at least six hours before bedtime.

By contrast, there are organic foods that improve our sleep: Walnuts contain tryptophan, a sleep enriching amino acid that manufactures melatonin, which, as we've seen, is the hormone that sets our cycles of sleep. Green leafy vegetables are loaded with calcium, which assists in the brain's use of tryptophan to manufacture melatonin. Almonds are rich in magnesium, a mineral that allows us to remain asleep deeper and longer.

Temperature is also a sleep determinant. Generally, a cool bedroom of approximately 67 to 70 degrees is most conducive for sleep; yet our age, body heat, and the local climate will affect this, as well.

In addition to a quality mattress protected by a clean mattress cover and clean sheets, a memory foam pad atop these might be helpful. This may allow us to lay in one position longer, without the need to change positions, increasing our time spent in the anabolic depths of REM.

Quietness, of course, is necessary. Earplugs or a "white noise" machine may be a solution to noise we are unable to control. Our snoring or that of a partner is a common challenge, too; yet, this is so varied in its nature that it is best to find the appropriate solution meeting your needs rather than attempting for us to list all the possibilities here.

Listening to music or the television during the night will reduce the multiplied benefits of your sleep, so spend the night with blessed silence instead. If you are in the habit of background music of television banter, you can break this unhealthy habit in only three weeks.

Once again, should all other factors be normal, the essence of sleep is the absence of light, for this beckons the whole of our body to sleep. Thus, a dark bedroom is a must. Window blinds and curtains must block outside light. And to truly allow our bodies to receive a strong SCN signal, we might consider wearing a sleeping mask. Such a mask must be comfortable and easily washed before wearing.

But even with a bedroom of total blackness, unless we are eating and drinking clean, organic living food during the waking hours, sleep may yet evade us.

*Smoking*

This odd habit causes skin to wrinkle prematurely, destroys vocal cords until the voice becomes coarse, drastically increases the incidence of stroke, lung cancer, heart attacks, is repulsive, and causes one's breath to be unbearably offensive. The American Lung Association tells us that, "Cigarettes, cigars, smokeless tobacco and almost all e-cigarettes contain nicotine. People who use tobacco products quickly become addicted to nicotine and thus have a very hard time stopping their use of those products.

"During pregnancy, nicotine exposure harms the developing fetus, and causes lasting consequences for the developing brain and lung function in newborns, according to the Surgeon General. Nicotine exposure also can result in low birth weights, preterm delivery, and stillbirth. Nicotine also negatively impacts brain development in children. Human brain development continues far longer than was previously realized, and nicotine use during adolescence and young adulthood has been associated with lasting cognitive and behavioral impairments, including effects on working memory and attention. In high enough doses, nicotine is also a poison—children have been harmed or even died from drinking e-cigarette liquid. Research suggests that nicotine is as addictive as heroin, cocaine, or alcohol."

Despite these well-known facts, humans are the only animals who *intentionally* inhale toxic fumes.

It is best if we have no part of this toxin. However, if you smoke, you can stop. Although it may seem altogether impossible, you can quit. So, take heart and be encouraged, dear friend. And, if you have not already, you may wish to read the section about lungs.

*Sore Throat*

Gargle equal parts of warm water and apple cider vinegar at the first sign of a sore throat and repeat this every hour or as needed. Gargling with saltwater helps sometimes, as well. It may be good to wrap one's throat and neck with a thick scarf. Quiet rest is also indispensable for healing to

ensure this condition does not become more complicated.
Do not hesitate to see your doctor.

### Suntan Appearance

Drinking a smoothie with strawberries, blueberries,
and carrots can give our skin the glowing flush of life that
is so attractive. Also, cantaloupe, olive oil, bell peppers,
tomatoes, Brazil nuts, peaches, pineapple, sweet potatoes,
and almonds will give our skin a beautiful ruddy glow.

### Sunburn

Our six-billion-year-old Star, which we have named
the Sun, can be quite hard on those of us of European descent since we have fair hair and skin. Should we receive a
mild sunburn, organic apple cider vinegar will ease the pain,
keep the burn from peeling, and increase the chances of the
redness turning to a golden tan. If the burn is a concern, especially if blisters appear, see a doctor right away.

The UVA and UVB rays are most intense between 10
am and 4 pm so it's best to avoid Sun exposure during
these hours. It is also strongly suggested that we wear a
wide brimmed hat and sunglasses when spending time
outside within this time of ultraviolet intensity. For a
sunburn always damages our largest vital organ, the epi-
dermis, accelerating the aging process with deep wrinkles
and sagging skin and can even deplete the vigor of our
immune system, a phenomenon experienced as weakness
and tiredness after receiving too many harsh sunrays within
the burning hours. It's wise to remember that although the
Sun is our friend, like Icarus who flew too close to its blinding smile, sunrays can be deadly. UV radiation is con-

sidered the main cause of non-melanoma skin cancer, which includes *basal cell carcinoma* and *squamous cell carcinoma*. These are mutations of the skin that can be rather grotesque. Yet, melanoma skin cancer can be quite deadly, too, and kills many thousands of people every year. One of its deadly traits is that it will often metastasize rapidly. So, we must seek a doctor's examination without delay when noticing a suspect irregularity on our skin.

In general, it is best to:

- Never allow yourself to be sunburned.
- Never use tanning booths.
- Avoid the Sun from 10 am and 4 pm.
- When outside wear a cap or a broad-brimmed hat.
- Wear sunglasses that block UV rays when outside.
- Use a Sunscreen without harmful ingredients.
- Self-examine your skin every two weeks.
- Ask your doctor to examine your skin during check-ups.
- Know the signs of skin cancer and seek medical attention without delay should a suspect irregularity appear. (See the section titled *Skin*).

*The Plant-Based Diet*

Plant-derived food supports robust human health, particularly in the following seven ways: because of these benefits and several others, after two or three weeks on a plant-based diet, many people experience a new life from which they never wish to return.

1. Energy. Less work is required by our bodies when eating only vegetables, fruits, grains, and nuts. This, of

course, means we have more energy for other activities throughout our lives. As a rule, we are decidedly lighter than those who eat meat, both literally and figuratively; in other words, we are typically within our weight to height ratio and we feel lighter in the sense of agile mobility. And of course, a plant-based diet holistically revitalizes the body with nutrient-rich foods, whereas meat and processed foods are often deficient in these health requirements while placing energy-consuming demands upon us.

For athletes, a plant-based diet is likened to rocket fuel. We can exert unusual energy over time and yet remain energized. Some of the top athletes in the world have discovered this and attribute their success in part to a diet that is strictly plant-based.

2. Longevity. Because our bodies are working less to digest food, our longevity is probably increased since the digestive bio-mechanisms (the throat, stomach, digestive tract, and bowels) last longer as they undergo the least wear.

3. Nutritional. Plant-based diets are rich with fiber, anti-oxidants, potassium, magnesium, and vitamins A, C and E.

4. Skin and hair. The vitamin A, C, and E rich plant-based diet noticeably improves our skin and hair and may even slow the graying of hair.

5. Disease prevention. Eating red meat, chicken, or fish exposes us to the risk of parasites that can cause dramatic health complications, including death. By contrast, a plant-based diet is free from these threats and contains fewer saturated fats and more fiber, phytonutrients, antioxidants, carotenoids, and flavonoids. Consequently, it

statistically reduces the incidence of obesity, skin disorders, type 2 diabetes, coronary heart disease, hypertension, chronic constipation, diverticulitis, and many other health maladies, including cancer. In an article titled, "No Amount of Alcohol, Sausage or Bacon is Safe According to Cancer Experts," *The Daily Mirror* reported that "Even small amounts of processed meats and booze increase the risk of a host of cancers outlined in World Cancer Research Fund (WCRF) guidelines updated every decade."

6. Headaches and Migraines. Because a proper plant-based diet is essentially a diet of anti-inflammatory meals, it may reduce the occurrence of headaches and even migraines since these are often associated with inflammation. For instance, the absence of dairy products in the plant-based diet reduces swollen sinus passages, which exacerbates headaches and migraines that may originate from tension and stress.

7. Weight loss. Because a plant-based diet typically entails fewer calories, vegans may find it easier to maintain their recommended height-to-weight ratio.

It is important to note that those who eat a strictly plant-based diet should take (1) a daily, high-quality protein supplement, (2) a vitamin B complex supplement, and (3) foods rich in Omega-3.

You may want to read the section on protein if you begin the plant-based diet. But always talk with your doctor before beginning a vitamin B regimen. Vitamin B is essential to a positive mental attitude. Without it, we may become chronically depressed, so we must compensate by taking vitamin B. An example of B complex is:

| Thiamin | 100 mcg | 6,667% of Daily Value |
|---|---|---|
| Riboflavin | 100 mcg | 5,882% |
| Niacin | 100 mcg | 500% |
| Vitamin B-6 | 100 mcg | 5,000% |
| Folate | 400 mcg | 100% |
| Vitamin B-12 | 100 mcg | 1,667% |
| Biotin | 100 mcg | 33% |
| DV Pantothenic Acid | 100 mcg | 1,000% |

Omega-3 is needed for our health, and some plant-based sources include chia seeds, flaxseeds, walnuts, and soybeans. However, the absorption rates for Omega-3 from plants are low. For example, two tablespoons of ground flaxseed contain 3,590 mg of Omega-3, however, only ten to fifteen percent is absorbed, which equals only 359 to 538.5 mg. So, that should be considered when depending upon plants for Omega-3.

*Weight*

The following chart uses the National Institute of Health's body mass index tables to determine the healthy weight according to height for both men and women.

| Height | Normal | Overweight | Obese |
|---|---|---|---|
| 4ft 10" | 91-115lbs. | 119-138 | 143-186 |
| 4ft 11" | 94 -119lbs. | 124-143 | 148-193 |
| 5ft | 97-123 lbs. | 128-148 | 153-199 |
| 5ft 1" | 100-127 lbs. | 132-153 | 158 -206 |
| 5ft 2" | 104-131 lbs. | 136-158 | 164-213 |
| 5ft 3" | 107-135 lbs. | 141-163 | 169-220 |
| 5ft 4" | 110-140 lbs. | 145-169 | 174-227 |
| 5ft 5" | 114-144 lbs. | 150-174 | 180-234 |
| 5ft 6" | 118-148 lbs. | 155-179 | 186-241 |
| 5ft 7" | 212-153 lbs. | 159-185 | 191-249 |

| | | | |
|---|---|---|---|
| 5ft 8" | 125-158 lbs. | 164-190 | 197-256 |
| 5ft 9" | 128-162 lbs. | 169-196 | 203-263 |
| 5ft 10" | 132-167 lbs. | 174-202 | 209-271 |
| 5ft 11" | 136-172 lbs. | 179-208 | 215-279 |
| 6ft | 140-177 lbs. | 184-213 | 221-287 |
| 6ft 1" | 144-182 lbs. | 189-219 | 227-295 |
| 6ft 2" | 148-186 lbs. | 194-225 | 233-303 |
| 6ft 3" | 152-192 lbs. | 200-232 | 240-310 |

Being overweight, obese, or very obese places us in a higher risk category for cancer, heart attack and heart disease, diabetes, arthritis, joint failure, lack of mobility, and an array of other deadly maladies. It also makes us less attractive, lowers our self-esteem, and wastes food and money.

Losing weight may seem difficult or even impossible, *but it isn't*. In fact, you can start right now. The first step toward normal weight is understanding that losing weight is merely a mindset that can be changed with a small amount of willpower. Changing a mindset, or habit takes only about three weeks. So, follow these simple suggestions for three weeks, and they will become habitual; after three weeks, the more you follow them, the more strongly they will become formed within your mind until they become your normal lifestyle.

1. Enjoy one-half cup of buckwheat cereal for breakfast every morning, and you may find this helps you lose weight. You might try four or five almonds and four or five walnut halves (more than this amount may cause weight gain) mixed with cinnamon and molasses. Some people prefer blueberries, bananas, or strawberries.

2.  Eat a gluten-free diet. Going one hundred percent gluten-free will allow you to drop several pounds in one week, and you'll be able to keep it off as long as you're gluten-free. As we have seen, gluten causes arthritis, gas, bloating, extreme fatigue, and, of course, excess weight. Forget gluten.

3.  Weigh yourself every morning before drinking or eating and without wearing any clothing at all. Think of the scales as your friend. Seek their advice without fail each morning since they will suggest what you should eat that day to adjust your weight if needed.

4.  Drink plenty of purified water, starting with a glass of room-temperature water first thing in the morning after weighing. The amount you need depends on your climate and diet. Generally, most of us need about four to six glasses of fresh water each day. This helps digest our food, keeps our system cleansed, and increases our metabolism, all of which helps us lose weight.

5.  If you have a television, you might consider removing it from your home by selling it or giving it away. This may seem like a peculiar suggestion to lose weight; however, most people overeat while watching television. I theorize this occurs because watching television is a non-reciprocal event; in other words, the television watcher gives their presence, sight, hearing, and many emotions to the event; yet the television does not, and cannot, since it is an inanimate object. Therefore, to endure, the

illusion of interacting with a mindless machine that cannot return the presence, seeing, hearing, and an array of emotions one gives to it, one must compensate by eating. The more one watches, the more one must compensate by eating. Along with the unconscious desire to compensate by eating while watching television, the viewer is subject to many food commercials meticulously crafted by Madison Avenue marketing executives to entice their audience to do the very thing a dieter hopes to avoid, overeating. So, by not owning a television, you'll almost assuredly eat less, become more active, and, most likely, lose weight.

6. Carb up in the morning, carb down in the afternoon, toward the end of the day, and at dinner. We need carbohydrates for energy throughout the day, so eat them in the morning. One-half cup of organic buckwheat cereal gives us plenty of fuel for the average workday. Yet too many carbohydrates eaten later in the day will probably turn into fat.

7. Avoid sugary foods, and do not put sugar on your food. Sugar becomes fat if not burned up and it is almost impossible to burn the sugar consumed in today's average diet. Besides, we receive plenty of the sugar we require by eating fruit. So, enjoy two or three servings of fresh organic fruit every day.

8. Forget table salt. It's purely a habit. Read labels to avoid foods with high sodium content, as this will cause water retention and weight gain. Too much salt is also inflammatory and damages many func-

tions and parts of our body.

9.  Never eat meals or snacks after 6 pm. This habit will make losing weight and keeping it off much easier. All it takes is a minimal amount of willpower for three weeks—the time required to break a bad habit and replace it with a new healthy one. So, think about eating dinner this evening before 6 pm.

10. Avoid meat. This is a fat producer, particularly when mixed with potatoes and other starchy foods. One of the unpleasant reasons that meat causes obesity is that it causes constipation.

11. Avoid fried foods, which are also fat producers, primarily because our bodies do not know what to do with them and so they are stored as detrimental fat.

12. Avoid any food that is processed. Again, this is a nonfood that becomes fat and, by the way, is sometimes dangerous carcinogenic.

13. Forget alcohol. It causes fat. If you feel that you cannot give up drinking, dear cousin, you may have a drinking problem. If interested, Alcoholics Anonymous can help with this, as it has helped millions of others. You may want to reread the section titled *Alcohol* to learn why it is so anti-life.

14. Exercise daily and vigorously. Of course, exercise alone is insufficient to lose weight; only a healthy diet can do this. Yet, exercise is an integral part of maintaining our ideal weight. Ask your doctor about

an exercise routine that is best for you and start to-day.

15. Count calories. First, we must determine the number of calories we need. This depends upon various factors such as our height, weight, and physical activity. There are a few equations that determine our caloric needs, yet their results vary. A resting metabolic rate (RMR) test is, perhaps, more accurate. The long-time recommendation, however, is about 2,300 calories per day if you are a sedentary adult male, and about 1,800 if you are a sedentary adult female. If you are an unusually active adult, these values are as high as 3,000 for men and 2,400 for women. Use these figures as guidelines until finding the number that allows you to maintain your ideal weight established by the previous chart. Many bottled, canned, and packaged foods are labeled with their caloric content, while many fruits, vegetables, seeds, nuts, and grains are not. Therefore, the following chart will help track your caloric intake of these items and may be a good reason to keep this book in your kitchen, too.

*Fruits*

| | | |
|---|---|---|
| Apple | 1 apple | 95 cal |
| Applesauce | 1 cup | 167 cal |
| Apricot | 1 apricot | 17 cal |
| Avocado | 1 avocado | 320 cal |
| Banana | 1 banana | 111 cal |
| Blackberries | 1 cup | 62 cal |
| Blueberries | 1 cup | 84 cal |
| Cantaloupe | 1 wedge | 23 cal |

| | | |
|---|---|---|
| Cherries | 1 cherry | 4 cal |
| Cranberries | 1 cup | 46 cal |
| Dates | 1 date | 20 cal |
| Figs | 1 fig | 37 cal |
| Grapes | 1 cup | 104 cal |
| Jackfruit | 1 cup | 143 cal |
| Kiwi | 1 kiwi | 112 cal |
| Lemon | 1 lemon | 17 cal |
| Lime | 1 lime | 20 cal |
| Mandarin | 1 orange | 47 cal |
| Mango | 1 mango | 202 cal |
| Mulberries | 1 cup | 60 cal |
| Nectarine | 1 nectarine | 66 cal |
| Orange | 1 orange | 62 cal |
| Papaya | 1 fruit | 215 cal |
| Peach | 1 peach | 59 cal |
| Pear | 1 pear | 101 cal |
| Persimmon | 1 fruit | 32 cal |
| Pineapple | 1 pineapple | 453 cal |
| Plum | 1 plum | 30 cal |
| Pomegranate | 1 pomegranate | 234 cal |
| Raisins | 1 cup | 434 cal |
| Raspberries | 1 cup | 64 cal |
| Rhubarb | 1 stalk | 11 cal |
| Starfruit | 1 star fruit | 28 cal |
| Strawberries | 1 cup | 49 cal |
| Tangerine | 1 tangerine | 47 cal |
| Watermelon | 1 wedge | 86 cal |

*Vegetables*

| | | |
|---|---|---|
| Artichoke | 1 artichoke | 60 cal |
| Arugula | 1 leaf | 1 cal |
| Asparagus | 1 spear | 2 cal |

| | | |
|---|---|---|
| Bell Pepper | 1 pepper | 15 cal |
| Black Olives | 1 olive | 2 cal |
| Broccoli | 1 bunch | 207 cal |
| Bru. Sprouts | 1 sprout | 8 cal |
| Cabbage | 1 head | 227 cal |
| Carrot | 1 carrot | 25 cal |
| Cauliflower | 1 floweret | 3 cal |
| Celery | 1 stalk | 6 cal |
| Chard | 1 leaf | 9 cal |
| Cherry Tom. | 1 cherry tom. | 20 cal |
| Chives | 1 tbsp, chopped | 1 cal |
| Collard Grns. | 1 cup, raw | 12 cal |
| Corn | 1 cup | 132 cal |
| Courgette | 1 courgette | 33 cal |
| Cucumber | 1 cucumber | 66 cal |
| Eggplant | 1 eggplant | 115 cal |
| Endive | 1 head | 87 cal |
| Fennel | 1 bulb | 73 cal |
| Garlic | 1 clove | 4 cal |
| Green Beans | 1 cup | 34 cal |
| Green Olives | 1 olive | 2 cal |
| Green Onion | 1 green onion | 5 cal |
| Horseradish | 1 tbsp | 7 cal |
| Kale | 1 cup, chopped | 33 cal |
| Leek | 1 leek | 54 cal |
| Lettuce | 1 head | 90 cal |
| Mushrooms | 1 mushroom | 1 cal |
| Okra | 1 pod | 4 cal |
| Olives | 1 olive | 2 cal |
| Onion | 1 onion | 34 cal |
| Parsnips | 1 parsnip | 128 cal |
| Peas | 1 cup | 79 cal |
| Potato | 1 potato | 164 cal |

| | | |
|---|---|---|
| Pumpkin | 1 pumpkin | 51 cal |
| Radishes | 1 radish | 1 cal |
| Red Cabbage | 1 leaf | 7 cal |
| Rutabaga | 1 rutabaga | 147 cal |
| Shallots | 1 shallot | 18 cal |
| Spinach | 1 bunch | 78 cal |
| Squash | 1 squash | 88 cal |
| Sweet Potato | 1 potato | 112 cal |
| Tomato | 1 tomato | 20 cal |
| Turnip Grns. | 1 turnip green | 34 cal |
| Turnips | 1 turnip | 34 cal |
| Zucchini | 1 zucchini | 33 cal |

*Seeds and Nuts*

| | | |
|---|---|---|
| Almond | 1 cup | 546 cal |
| Beechnut | 1 oz. | 161 cal |
| Brazil Nuts | 1 cup | 872 cal |
| Breadfruit | 1 oz. | 53 cal |
| Butternut | 1 cup | 734 cal |
| Cashew | 1 oz. | 155 cal |
| Chestnut | 1 cup | 309 cal |
| Chia Seeds | 1 oz. | 136 cal |
| Coconut | 1 coconut | 1405 cal |
| Flaxseed | 1 cup | 897 cal |
| Hazelnut | 1 cup | 471 cal |
| Hickory Nuts | 1 cup | 788 cal |
| Macadamia | 1 cup | 962 ca |
| Peanuts | 1 cup | 828 cal |
| Pecans | 1 cup | 684 cal |
| Pine Nuts | 1 cup | 909 cal |
| Pistachios | 1 cup | 691 cal |
| Poppy Seeds | 1 tbsp | 42 cal |
| Pumpkin Sds. | 1 cup | 721 cal |

| Safflower Sds. | 1 oz. | 145 cal |
| Sesame Seeds | 1 cup | 825 cal |
| Sunflower Seeds | 1 cup | 818 cal |

*Grains*

| Barley | 1 cup | 556 cal |
| Barley Groats | 1 cup | 31 cal |
| Brown Rice | 1 cup | 757 cal |
| Buckwheat | 1 cup | 583 cal |
| Cornmeal | 1 cup | 442 cal |
| Cornstarch | 1 cup | 488 cal |
| Couscous | 1 cup | 650 cal |
| Flaxseed | 1 cup | 897 cal |
| Oat Bran | 1 cup | 231 cal |
| Walnuts | 1 cup | 523 cal |
| Quinoa | 1 cup | 626 cal |

Once again, dear cousin, losing weight may seem like a hopeless cause. But it isn't. You can lose weight. And you *will* lose weight by beginning these fifteen good habits today. It may seem too difficult to remember all fifteen steps, but after three weeks, they'll become an almost unconscious routine. And soon afterward, they'll become a lasting lifestyle.

# PART IV

# EXPATIATION OF THE MIND

Chapter One

# Inspiration for
# Young Men and Women

SOMETIMES, when we are young, we see beauty so easily, especially when we are in love. The world all about us seems a beckoning friend, laughing when we laugh, miraculously seeing the same beauty we see, crying when that happens, too.

Other times, within reason, we may lose a sense of impossibility, for everything seems possible. This is when we may accomplish much. Many years hence, we may look back upon these times with some wonder of how we did so many things, the greatest of which was superseding the gravitational pull of adolescence unto adulthood without losing our youthfulness.

On the way to this eminent goal, it helps to fill our minds with virtuous thoughts, for then, goodness will naturally spring forth from them.

Maybe these are a few of such thoughts. Here, within this little anthology, you may find a word-painted message written directly to you. You might discover the right word—just the thought—that will be the perfect antidote to the challenges you face. There may be some lines you feel are uniquely clever and entertaining; poems and poetic prose needn't be all deadly serious, of course.

You might be one of the fortunate ones who finds exquisite truth and beauty within a line or two that becomes a sparkling oasis, offering refreshment to your whole being. So soothing its living waters, you may return to the same crystal-clear pool again and again for the rest of your life.

Here, you will find a minuet of the masculine and feminine with its swirling, eternal dance of virtuous splendor, forever apart and separate while yet coming together, becoming as one.

Maybe these words will even help you see into the future—your future and the good it holds for you. Because it does, you know.


## IF—

If you can keep your head when all about you
   Are losing theirs and blaming you;
If you can trust yourself when all men doubt you,
   But make allowance for their doubting, too;
If you can wait and not be tired by waiting,
   Or, being lied about, don't deal in lies,
Or, being hated, don't give way to hating,
   And yet don't look too good, nor talk too wise;

If you can dream—and not make dreams your master;
  If you can think—and not make thoughts your aim;
If you can meet with triumph and disaster
  And treat those two imposters just the same;
If you can bear to hear the truth you've spoken
  Twisted by knaves to make a trap for fools,
Or watch the things you gave your life to broken,
  And stoop and build 'em up with worn out tools;

If you can make one heap of all your earnings
  And risk it on one turn of pitch and toss,
And lose, and start again at your beginnings
  And never breathe a word about your loss;
If you can force your heart and nerve and sinew
  To serve your turn long after they are gone,
And so hold on when there is nothing in you
  Except the Will which says to them: "Hold on";

If you can walk with crowds and keep your virtue,
  Or walk with kings—nor lose the common touch;
If neither foes nor loving friend can hurt you;
  If all men count with you, but none too much;
If you can fill the unforgiving minute
  With sixty seconds worth of distance run—
Yours is the Earth and everything that's in it,
  And—which is more— you'll be a Man, my son!

RUDYARD KIPLING

## TO CELIA
*the first eight lines*

Drink to me only with thine eyes,
  And I will pledge with mine;
Or leave a kiss but in the cup,
  And I'll not look for wine.
The thirst that from the soul dost rise,
  Doth ask a drink divine:
But might I of Jove's nectar sup,
  I would not change for thine.

BEN JOHNSON

## OPPORTUNITY

This I beheld, or dreamed it in a dream:
There spread a cloud of dust along a plain;
And underneath the cloud, or in it, raged
A furious battle, and men yelled, and swords
Shocked upon swords and shields. A prince's banner
Wavered, then staggered backward, hemmed by foes.
A craven hung along the battle's edge
And thought, "Had I a sword of keener steel—
That blue blade that the king's son bears—but this

Blunt thing—!" He snapt and flung it from his hand,
And, lowering, crept away and left the field,
Then came the king's son, wounded, sore bestead,
And weaponless, and saw the broken sword,
Hilt-buried in the dry and trodden sand,

And ran and snatched it, and with battle-shout
Lifted afresh, he hewed his enemy down,
And saved a great cause that heroic day.

EDWARD ROLAND SILL


## IN THE MOONLIGHT


Well merited was the name "soldier of God" by the Abbe Marignan. He was a tall, thin priest, fanatical to a degree, but  a just and exalted soul. All his beliefs were fixed, with never  a waiver. He thought he understood God thoroughly, that he  penetrated His designs, His wishes, His intentions.

Striding up and down the garden walk of his little country parsonage, sometimes a question arose in his mind: "Why  did God make that?" Then in his thoughts, putting himself in  God's place, he searched obstinately and nearly always was  satisfied that he found the reason. He was not the man to  murmur in transport of pious humility, "O Lord, thy ways  are past finding out!" What he said was, "I am the servant of God, I ought to know the reason of what he does or divine it if I do not."

Everything in nature seemed to him created with an absolute and  admirable logic. The "wherefore" and the "because" were always balanced. The dawn were made to rejoice you  on waking, the days to ripen the harvests, the rains to water them, the evenings to prepare for sleeping and the nights  dark for sleep.

The four seasons corresponded perfectly to all the needs of  agriculture, and to him the suspicion could never have come  that nature has no intention and that all which lives has accustomed itself, on the contrary, to the hard conditions of different periods, of climates and of matter.

But he hated women; he hated them unconsciously and despised them by instinct. He often repeated the words of Christ, "Woman, what have I to do with thee?" and he would add, "One would almost say that God himself was ill pleased with that particular work of his hands." Woman for him was indeed the "child twelve times unclean" of whom the poet speaks. She was the temptress who had ensnared the first man who still continued her damnable work; she was the being who is feeble, dangerous, mysteriously troublous. And even more than her poisonous beauty he hated her loving soul.

He had often felt women's tenderness attack him, and though he knew himself to be unassailable he grew exasperated at this need of loving which quivers continuously in their hearts.

To his mind God had only created woman to tempt man and to test him. Man should not approach her without those precautions for defense which he would take, and the fears he would cherish, near an ambush. Woman, indeed, was just like a trap, with her arms extended and her lips open toward a man.

He had only toleration for nuns, rendered harmless by their vow; but he treated them harshly notwithstanding, because, ever at the bottom of their chained-up hearts, their chastened hearts, he perceived the eternal tenderness that constantly went out to him although he was a priest.

He had a niece who lived with her mother in a little house nearby. He was bent on making her a sister of charity. She was pretty and harebrained and a great tease. When the abbe sermonized she laughed; when he was angry at her she kissed him vehemently, pressing him to her heart while he tried involuntarily to free himself from her embrace. Notwithstanding, it made him taste a certain sweet joy, awaking deep within him that sensation of fatherhood which slumbers in every man.

Often he talked to her of God, of his God, walking beside her along the footpaths through the fields. She hardly listened but looked at the sky, the grass, the flowers, with a joy of living which could be seen in her eyes. Sometimes she rushed forward to catch some flying creature and, bringing it back, would cry: "Look, my uncle, how pretty it is; I should like to kiss it." And the necessity to "kiss flies" or sweet flowers worried, irritated, and revolted the priest who saw, even in that, the ineradicable tenderness which ever springs in the heart of women. One day the sacristan's wife, who kept house for the Abbe Marignan, told him very cautiously that his niece had a lover!

He experienced a dreadful emotion, and he stood choking, with the soap all over his face, in the act of shaving. When he found himself able to think and speak once more he cried, "It is not true; you are lying, Melanie!"

But the peasant woman put her hand on her heart. "May our Lord judge me if I am lying, Monsieur le Cure. I tell you she goes to him every evening as soon as your sister is in bed. They meet each other beside the river. You have only to go there between ten o'clock and midnight and see for yourself."

He ceased scratching his chin and commenced to pace the room quickly, as he always did in his hours of gravest thought.

When he tried to begin his shaving again he cut himself three times from nose to ear.

All day long he remained silent, swollen with anger and with rage. To his priestly zeal against the mighty power of love was added the moral indignation of a father, of a teacher, a keeper of souls, who has been deceived, robbed, played with by a child. He felt the egotistical sorrow that parents feel when their daughter announces that she has chosen a husband without them and in spite of their advice.

After dinner he tried to read a little, but could not attune himself to it and he grew angrier and angrier. When it struck ten he took his cane, a formidable oaken club which he always carried when he had to go out at night to visit the sick.

Smugly he regarded the enormous cudgel, holding it in his solid, countryman's fist and cutting threatening circles with it in the air. Then suddenly he raised it and, grinding his teeth, he brought it down upon a chair, the back of which, split in two, fell heavily to the ground.

He opened the door to go out, but he stopped upon the threshold, surprised by such a splendor of moonlight as you seldom see.

Endowed as he was with an exalted spirit, such a spirit as must have belonged to those dreamer-poets, the Fathers of the Church, he felt himself suddenly softened and moved by the grand and serene beauty of the pale-faced night.

In his little garden, bathed in the soft brilliance, his fruit trees, all arow, were outlining in shadow upon the walk their slender limbs of wood scarce clothed with green; while the giant honeysuckle climbing on the house wall exhaled delicious sugared breaths which hovered through the warm clear night like perfumed soil.

He began to breathe the deep, drinking the air as drunkards drink their wine and walking slowly, ravished, surprised and almost oblivious of his niece.

As he stepped into the open country he stopped to contemplate the whole plain, inundated by this caressing radiance and drowned in the tender and languishing charm of the serene night. In chorus the frogs threw into space their short metallic notes, and with the seduction of the moonlight distant nightingales mingled the fitful music of theirs which brings no thoughts but dreams, a light and vibrant melody which seemed attuned to kisses.

The abbe continued his walk, his courage failing, he knew not why. He felt, as it were, enfeebled and suddenly exhausted; he had a great desire to sit down, to pause right there and praise God in all His works.

Below him, following the bends of the little river, wound a great line of poplars. On and about the banks, wrapping all the tortuous watercourse in a kind of light, transparent wadding, hung suspended a fine mist, a white vapor, which the moon rays crossed and silvered and caused to gleam.

The priest paused yet again, penetrated to the depths of his soul by a strong and yet growing emotion. And a doubt, a vague uneasiness, seized on him; he felt that one of those questions he sometimes put to himself was now being born. Why had God done this? Since the night is destined for sleep, for unconsciousness, for repose, for forgetfulness of everything, why, then, make it more charming than the day, sweeter than dawns and sunsets? And this slow, seductive star, more poetical than the sun and so discreet that it seems designed to light up things too delicate, too mysterious for the great luminary-why had it come to brighten all the shades? Why did not the sweetest if all songsters go to rest like the others? Why set himself to singing in the vaguely troubling dark? Why this half veil over the world? Why these quiverings of the heart, this emotion of the soul, this languor of the body? Why this display of seductions which mankind never sees, since the night brings sleep? For whom was this sublime spectacle intended, this flood of poetry poured from heaven to earth? The abbe did not understand it at all.

But then, down there along the edge of the pasture, appeared two shadows walking side by side under the arched roof of the trees all soaked in glittering mist.

The man was the taller and had his arm about his mistress's neck; from time to time he kissed her on the forehead. They animated the lifeless landscape which enveloped them, a divine frame made, as it were, expressly for them. They seemed, these two, a single being, the being for whom this calm and silent night was destined; and they approached the priest like a living answer, the answer vouchsafed by his Master to his question.

He stood stock-still, overwhelmed and with a beating heart. He likened it to some Bible story as the loves of Ruth and Boaz, the accomplishment of the will of the Lord in one of those scenes talked of in Holy Writ. Through his head ran the versicles of the Song of Songs, the ardent cries, the calls of the body, all the passionate poetry of that poem which burns with tenderness and love. And he said to himself, "God perhaps has made such nights as this to clothe with his ideals the loves of men."

He withdrew before the couple, who went on arm in arm. It was really his niece, and now he asked himself if he had not been about to disobey God. For does not God indeed permit love, since He surrounds it visibly with splendor such as this?

And he fled in amaze, almost ashamed, as if he had penetrated into a temple where he had no right to enter.

GUY DE MAUPASANT

## CHERRY RIPE

There is a garden in her face
  Where roses and white lilies grow;
A heavenly paradise is the place,
  Wherein all pleasant fruits do flow.
    There cherries grow which none may buy
     'Till "Cherry-ripe" themselves do cry.

Those cherries fairly do enclose
  Of orient pearl a double row,
Which when her lovely laughter shows,
  They look like rosebuds filled with snow;
    Yet them nor peer nor prince can buy
     'Till "Cherry-ripe" themselves do cry.

Her eyes like angels watch them still;
  Her brows like bended bows do stand,
Threat'ning with piercing frowns to kill
  All that attempt with eye or hand
    Those sacred cherries to come nigh,
     'Till "Cherry-ripe" themselves do cry.

THOMAS CAMPION

## IT COULDN'T BE DONE

Somebody said that it couldn't be done
  But he with a chuckle replied
That "maybe it couldn't," but he would be one
  Who wouldn't say so till he'd tried.

So he buckled right in with the trace of a grin
  On his face. If he worried he hid it.
He started to sing as he tackled the thing
  That couldn't be done, and he did it!

Somebody scoffed: "Oh, you'll never do that;
  At least no one ever has done it;"
But he took off his coat and he took off his hat
  And the first thing we knew he'd begun it.

With a lift of his chin and a bit of a grin,
  Without any doubting or quiddit,
He started to sing as he tackled the thing
  That couldn't be done, and he did it.

There are thousands to tell you it cannot be done,
  There are thousands to prophesy failure,
There are thousands to point out to you one by one,
  The dangers that wait to assail you.

But just buckle in with a bit of a grin,
  Just take off your coat and go to it;
Just start in to sing as you tackle the thing
  That "cannot be done," and you'll do it.

EDGAR A. GUEST

## MY LIFE

My life is a bowl which is mine to brim
   With loveliness old and new.
So, I fill its clay from stem to rim
   With you, dear heart,
                    With you.

My life is a pool which can only hold
   One star and a glimpse of blue.
But the blue and the little lamp of gold
   Are you, dear heart,
                    Are you.

My life is a homing bird that flies
   Through the starry dusk and dew,
Home to the heaven in your true eyes,
   Home, dear heart,
                    To you.

MAY RILEY SMITH

## THE MANLY MAN

*This poem describes the manliness of Alfred as though it were written about him and his time in history which he caused to be momentous—a fitting hymn to his triumphs.*

The world has room for the manly man, with the spirit of manly cheer;
The world delights in the man who smiles when his eyes keep back the tear;
It loves the man who, when things are wrong, can take his place and stand

With his face to the fight and his eyes to the light, and toil
with a willing hand;
The manly man is the country's need, the moment's need
forsooth,
With a heart that beats to the pulsing troop of the lilied
leagues of truth;
The world is his and it waits for him, and it leaps to hear the
ring
Of the blow he strikes and the wheels he turns and the
hammers he dares to swing;
It likes the forward look on his face, the poise of his noble
head,
And the onward lunge of his tireless will and the sweep of
his dauntless tread!
Hurrah for the manly man who comes with sunlight on his
face,
And the strength to do and will to dare and the courage to
find his place!
The world delights in the manly man, and the weak and evil
flee
When the manly man goes forth to hold his own on land and
sea!

AN UNKNOWN AUTHOR

## EPITAPH TO BOTSWAIN

Near this Spot
are deposited the Remains of one
who possessed Beauty without Vanity,
Strength without Insolence,
Courage without Ferocity,
and all the virtues of Man without his Vices.

This praise, which would be unmeaning
Flattery if inscribed over human Ashes,
is but a just tribute to the Memory of Boatswain,
a Dog who was born in Newfoundland May 1803
and died at Newstead Nov. 18th, 1808

*He continues . . .*

To mark a friend's remains these stones arise;
I never knew but one—and here he lies.

LORD BYRON


## MY GARDEN IS A PLEASANT PLACE

My garden is a pleasant place,
Of Sun glory and leaf grace,
There is an ancient cherry tree,
Where yellow warblers sing to me,

And an old grape arbor, where
A robin builds her nest, and there
Above the lima beans and peas
She croons her little melodies,

Her blue eggs hidden in the green
Fastness of that leafy screen.
Here are striped zinnias that bees
Fly far to visit; and sweet peas,

Like little butterflies newborn,
And over by the tasseled corn
Are sunflowers and hollyhocks,
And pink and yellow four-clocks.

Here are hummingbirds that come
To seek the tall delphinium—
Songless bird and scentless flower
Communing in a golden hour.

There is no blue like the blue cup
The tall delphinium holds up,
Not sky, nor distant hill, nor sea,
Sapphire, nor lapis lazuli.

My lilac trees are old and tall;
I cannot reach their bloom at all.
They send their perfume over trees
And roofs and streets, to find the bees.

I wish some power would touch my ear
With magic touch, and make me hear
What all the blossoms say, and so
I might know what the winged things know.

I'd hear the sunflower's mellow pipe,
"Goldfinch, goldfinch, my seeds are ripe!"
I'd hear the pale wistaria sing,
"Moon moth, moon moth, I'm blossoming!"

I'd hear the evening primrose cry,
"Oh, firefly! come, firefly!"
And I would learn the jeweled word
The ruby-throated hummingbird

Drops into cups of larkspur blue,
And I would sing them all for you!
My garden is a pleasant place

Of moon glory and wind grace.
O friend, wherever you may be,
Will you not come to visit me?
Over fields and streams and hills,

I'll pipe like yellow daffodils, And every little wind that
blows Shall take my message as it goes.

LOUISE DRISCOLL

## THEN LAUGH

Build for yourself a strongbox,
Fashion each part with care;
When it's strong as your hand can make it,
Put all your troubles there;

Hide there all thought of your failures,
And each bitter cup that you quaff;
Lock all your heartaches within it,
Then sit on the lid and laugh.

Tell no one else its contents,
Never its secrets share;
When you've dropped in your care and worry,
Keep them forever there;

Hide them from site so completely,
That the world will never dream half;
Fasten the strong box securely—
Then sit on the lid and laugh.

BERTHA ADAMS BACKUS

## HOW TO BE HAPPY

Are you almost disgusted with life, little man?
I'll tell you a wonderful trick.
That will bring you contentment, if anything can,
Do something for somebody, quick!

Are you awfully tired with play, little girl?
Wearied, discouraged, and sick—
I'll tell you loveliest game in the world,
Do something for somebody quick!

Though it rains, like the rain of the flood, little man,
And the clouds are foreboding and thick,
You can make the Sun shine in your soul, little man,
Do something for somebody, quick!

Though the stars are like bars overhead, little girl,
And the walks like a well-heated brick,
And our Earthly affairs in a terrible whirl,
Do something for somebody quick!

AN UNKNOWN AUTHOR

## THE VILLAGE BLACKSMITH

Under a spreading chestnut-tree
The village smithy stands;
The smith, a mighty man is he,
With large and sinewy hands;
And the muscles of his brawny arms
Are strong as iron bands.

His hair is crisp, and black, and long,
His face is like the tan;
His brow is wet with honest sweat,
He earns whate'er he can,
And looks the whole world in the face,
For he owes not any man.

Week in, week out, from morn till night,
You can hear his bellows blow;
You can hear him swing his heavy sledge,
With measured beat and slow,
Like a sexton ringing the village bell,
When the evening sun is low.

And children coming home from school
Look in at the open door;
They love to see the flaming forge,
And hear the bellows roar,
And catch the burning sparks that fly
Like chaff from a threshing-floor.

He goes on Sunday to the church,
And sits among his boys;
He hears the parson pray and preach,
He hears his daughter's voice,
Singing in the village choir,
And it makes his heart rejoice.

It sounds to him like her mother's voice,
Singing in Paradise!
He needs must think of her once more,
How in the grave she lies;
And with his hard, rough hand he wipes
A tear out of his eyes.

Toiling,—rejoicing,—sorrowing,
Onward through life he goes;
Each morning sees some task begin,
Each evening sees it close
Something attempted, something done,
Has earned a night's repose.
Thanks, thanks to thee, my worthy friend,
For the lesson thou hast taught!
Thus at the flaming forge of life
Our fortunes must be wrought;
Thus on its sounding anvil shaped Each burning deed
and thought.

HENRY WADSWORTH LONGFELLOW

## THE WOOING OF SIR KEITH
from *The Merry Adventures of Robin Hood*

King Arthur sat in his royal hall,
And about on either hand,
Was many a noble lordling tall,
The greatest in the land.

Sir Lancelot with raven locks,
Gawaine with golden hair,
Sir Tristram, Kay who kept the locks,
And many another there.

And through the stained glass windows bright,
From o'er the red tile eaves,
The sunlight blazed with colored light
On golden helms and greaves.

But suddenly a silence came
About the Table Round,
For up the hall there walked a dame
Bent nigh unto the ground.

Her nose was hooked, her eyes were bleared,
Her locks were lank and white;
Upon her chin there grew a beard;
She was a gruesome sight.

And so with crawling step she came
And kneeled at Arthur's feet;
Quoth Kay, "She is the foulest dame
That e'er my sight did greet."

"O mighty King! of thee I crave
A boon on bended knee;"
'Twas thus she spoke. "What wouldst thou have."
Quoth Arthur, King, "of me?"

Quoth she, "I have a foul disease
Doth gnaw my very heart,
And but one thing can bring me ease
Or cure my bitter smart.

"There is no rest, no ease for me
North, east, or west, or south,
Till Christian knight will willingly
Thrice kiss me on the mouth.

"Nor wedded may this childe have been
That giveth ease to me;
Nor may he be constrained, I ween,
But kiss me willingly.

"So is there here one Christian knight
Of such a noble strain
That he will give a tortured wight
Sweet ease of mortal pain?"

"A wedded man," quoth Arthur, King,
"A wedded man I be,
Else would I deem it noble thing
To kiss thee willingly.

"Now, Lancelot, in all men's sight
Thou art the head and chief
Of chivalry. Come, noble knight,
And give her quick relief."

But Lancelot he turned aside
And looked upon the ground,
For it did sting his haughty pride
To hear them laugh around.

"Come thou, Sir Tristram," quoth the King.
Quoth he, "It cannot be,
For ne'er can I my stomach bring
To do it willingly."

"Wilt thou, Sir Kay, thou scornful wight?"
Quoth Kay, "Nay, by my troth!
What noble dame would kiss a knight
That kissed so foul a mouth?"

"Wilt thou, Gawaine?" "I cannot, King."
"Sir Geraint?" "Nay, not I;
My kisses no relief could bring,
For sooner would I die."

Then up and spake the youngest man
Of all about the board,
"Now such relief as Christian can
I'll give to her, my lord."

It was Sir Keith, a youthful knight,
Yet strong of limb and bold,
With beard upon his chin as light
As finest threads of gold.

Quoth Kay, "He hath no mistress yet
That he may call his own,
But here is one that's quick to get,
As she herself has shown."

He kissed her once, he kissed her twice,
He kissed her three times o'er,
A wondrous change came in a trice,
And she was foul no more.

Her cheeks grew red as any rose,
Her brow as white as lawn,
Her bosom like the winter snows,
Her eyes like those of fawn.

Her breath grew sweet as summer breeze
That blows the meadows o'er;
Her voice grew soft as rustling trees,
And cracked and harsh no more.

Her hair grew glittering, like the gold,
Her hands as white as milk;
Her filthy rags, so foul and old,
Were changed to robes of silk.

In great amaze the knights did stare.
Quoth Kay, "I make my vow
If it will please thee, lady fair,
I'll gladly kiss thee now."

But young Sir Keith kneeled on one knee
And kissed her robes so fair.
"O let me be thy slave," said he,
"For none to thee compare."

She bent her down, she kissed his brow,
She kissed his lips and eyes.
Quoth she, "Thou art my master now,
My lord, my love, arise!

"And all the wealth that is mine own,
My lands, I give to thee,
For never knight hath lady shown
Such noble courtesy.

"Bewitched was I, in bitter pain,
But thou hast set me free,
So now I am myself again,
I give myself to thee."

"It hath oftentimes seemed to me," said Will Scarlet to Robin Hood, "that it hath a certain motive in it, e'en such as this: That a duty which seemeth to us sometimes ugly and harsh, when we do kiss it fairly upon the mouth, so to speak, is no such foul thing after all."

HOWARD PYLE

## SONNETS

### I

From fairest creatures we desire increase,
That thereby beauty's rose might never die,
But as the riper should by time decease,
His tender heir might bear his memory:
But thou, contracted to thine own bright eyes,
Feed'st thy light'st flame with self-substantial fuel,
Making a famine where abundance lies,
Thyself thy foe, to thy sweet self too cruel.
Thou that art now the world's fresh ornament
And only herald to the gaudy spring,
Within thine own bud buriest thy content
And, tender churl, makest waste in niggarding.
Pity the world, or else this glutton be,
To eat the world's due, by the grave and thee.

### II

When forty winters shall beseige thy brow,
And dig deep trenches in thy beauty's field,
Thy youth's proud livery, so gazed on now,
Will be a tatter'd weed, of small worth held:
Then being ask'd where all thy beauty lies,
Where all the treasure of thy lusty days,
To say, within thine own deep-sunken eyes,
Were an all-eating shame and thriftless praise.
How much more praise deserved thy beauty's use,
If thou couldst answer 'This fair child of mine
Shall sum my count and make my old excuse,'
Proving his beauty by succession thine!
This were to be new made when thou art old,
And see thy blood warm when thou feel'st it cold.

### III

Look in thy glass, and tell the face thou viewest
Now is the time that face should form another;
Whose fresh repair if now thou not renewest,
Thou dost beguile the world, unbless some mother.
For where is she so fair whose unear'd womb
Disdains the tillage of thy husbandry?
Or who is he so fond will be the tomb
Of his self-love, to stop posterity?
Thou art thy mother's glass, and she in thee
Calls back the lovely April of her prime:
So thou through windows of thine age shall see
Despite of wrinkles this thy golden time.
But if thou live, remember'd not to be,
Die single, and thine image dies with thee.


### IV

Unthrifty loveliness, why dost thou spend
Upon thyself thy beauty's legacy?
Nature's bequest gives nothing but doth lend,
And being frank she lends to those are free.
Then, beauteous niggard, why dost thou abuse
The bounteous largess given thee to give?
Profitless usurer, why dost thou use
So great a sum of sums, yet canst not live?
For having traffic with thyself alone,
Thou of thyself thy sweet self dost deceive.
Then how, when nature calls thee to be gone,
What acceptable audit canst thou leave?
Thy unused beauty must be tomb'd with thee,
Which, used, lives th' executor to be.

## V

Those hours, that with gentle work did frame
The lovely gaze where every eye doth dwell,
Will play the tyrants to the very same
And that unfair which fairly doth excel:
For never-resting time leads summer on
To hideous winter and confounds him there;
Sap cheque'd with frost and lusty leaves quite gone,
Beauty o'ersnow'd and bareness every where:
Then, were not summer's distillation left,
A liquid prisoner pent in walls of glass,
Beauty's effect with beauty were bereft,
Nor it nor no remembrance what it was:
But flowers distill'd though they with winter meet,
Leese but their show; their substance still lives sweet.

## VI

Then let not winter's ragged hand deface
In thee thy summer, ere thou be distill'd:
Make sweet some vial; treasure thou some place
With beauty's treasure, ere it be self-kill'd.
That use is not forbidden usury,
Which happies those that pay the willing loan;
That's for thyself to breed another thee,
Or ten times happier, be it ten for one;
Ten times thyself were happier than thou art,
If ten of thine ten times refigured thee:
Then what could death do, if thou shouldst depart,
Leaving thee living in posterity?
Be not self-will'd, for thou art much too fair
To be death's conquest and make worms thine heir.

## VII

Then let not winter's ragged hand deface
In thee thy summer, ere thou be distill'd:
Make sweet some vial; treasure thou some place
With beauty's treasure, ere it be self-kill'd.
That use is not forbidden usury,
Which happies those that pay the willing loan;
That's for thyself to breed another thee,
Or ten times happier, be it ten for one;
Ten times thyself were happier than thou art,
If ten of thine ten times refigured thee:
Then what could death do, if thou shouldst depart,
Leaving thee living in posterity?
Be not self-will'd, for thou art much too fair
To be death's conquest and make worms thine heir.

## VIII

Music to hear, why hear'st thou music sadly?
Sweets with sweets war not, joy delights in joy.
Why lovest thou that which thou receivest not gladly,
Or else receivest with pleasure thine annoy?
If the true concord of well-tuned sounds,
By unions married, do offend thine ear,
They do but sweetly chide thee, who confounds
In singleness the parts that thou shouldst bear.
Mark how one string, sweet husband to another,
Strikes each in each by mutual ordering,
Resembling sire and child and happy mother
Who all in one, one pleasing note do sing:
Whose speechless song, being many, seeming one,
Sings this to thee: 'thou single wilt prove none.'

## IX

Is it for fear to wet a widow's eye
That thou consumest thyself in single life?
Ah! if thou issueless shalt hap to die.
The world will wail thee, like a makeless wife;
The world will be thy widow and still weep
That thou no form of thee hast left behind,
When every private widow well may keep
By children's eyes her husband's shape in mind.
Look, what an unthrift in the world doth spend
Shifts but his place, for still the world enjoys it;
But beauty's waste hath in the world an end,
And kept unused, the user so destroys it.
No love toward others in that bosom sits
That on himself such murderous shame commits.

## X

For shame! deny that thou bear'st love to any,
Who for thyself art so unprovident.
Grant, if thou wilt, thou art beloved of many,
But that thou none lovest is most evident;
For thou art so possess'd with murderous hate
That 'gainst thyself thou stick'st not to conspire.
Seeking that beauteous roof to ruinate
Which to repair should be thy chief desire.
O, change thy thought, that I may change my mind!
Shall hate be fairer lodged than gentle love?
Be, as thy presence is, gracious and kind,
Or to thyself at least kind-hearted prove:
Make thee another self, for love of me,
That beauty still may live in thine or thee.

## XI

As fast as thou shalt wane, so fast thou growest
In one of thine, from that which thou departest;
And that fresh blood which youngly thou bestowest
Thou mayst call thine when thou from youth convertest.
Herein lives wisdom, beauty and increase:
Without this, folly, age and cold decay:
If all were minded so, the times should cease
And threescore year would make the world away.
Let those whom Nature hath not made for store,
Harsh featureless and rude, barrenly perish:
Look, whom she best endow'd she gave the more;
Which bounteous gift thou shouldst in bounty cherish:
She carved thee for her seal, and meant thereby
Thou shouldst print more, not let that copy die.

## XII

When I do count the clock that tells the time,
And see the brave day sunk in hideous night;
When I behold the violet past prime,
And sable curls all silver'd o'er with white;
When lofty trees I see barren of leaves
Which erst from heat did canopy the herd,
And summer's green all girded up in sheaves
Borne on the bier with white and bristly beard,
Then of thy beauty do I question make,
That thou among the wastes of time must go,
Since sweets and beauties do themselves forsake
And die as fast as they see others grow;
And nothing 'gainst Time's scythe can make defence
Save breed, to brave him when he takes thee hence.

### XIII

O, that you were yourself! but, love, you are
No longer yours than you yourself here live:
Against this coming end you should prepare,
And your sweet semblance to some other give.
So should that beauty which you hold in lease
Find no determination: then you were
Yourself again after yourself's decease,
When your sweet issue your sweet form should bear.
Who lets so fair a house fall to decay,
Which husbandry in honour might uphold
Against the stormy gusts of winter's day
And barren rage of death's eternal cold?
O, none but unthrifts! Dear my love, you know
You had a father: let your son say so.

### XIV

Not from the stars do I my judgment pluck;
And yet methinks I have astronomy,
But not to tell of good or evil luck,
Of plagues, of dearths, or seasons' quality;
Nor can I fortune to brief minutes tell,
Pointing to each his thunder, rain and wind,
Or say with princes if it shall go well,
By oft predict that I in heaven find:
But from thine eyes my knowledge I derive,
And, constant stars, in them I read such art
As truth and beauty shall together thrive,
If from thyself to store thou wouldst convert;
Or else of thee this I prognosticate:
Thy end is truth's and beauty's doom and date.

## XV

When I consider every thing that grows
Holds in perfection but a little moment,
That this huge stage presenteth nought but shows
Whereon the stars in secret influence comment;
When I perceive that men as plants increase,
Cheered and cheque'd even by the self-same sky,
Vaunt in their youthful sap, at height decrease,
And wear their brave state out of memory;
Then the conceit of this inconstant stay
Sets you most rich in youth before my sight,
Where wasteful Time debateth with Decay,
To change your day of youth to sullied night;
And all in war with Time for love of you,
As he takes from you, I engraft you new.

## XVI

But wherefore do not you a mightier way
Make war upon this bloody tyrant, Time?
And fortify yourself in your decay
With means more blessed than my barren rhyme?
Now stand you on the top of happy hours,
And many maiden gardens yet unset
With virtuous wish would bear your living flowers,
Much liker than your painted counterfeit:
So should the lines of life that life repair,
Which this, Time's pencil, or my pupil pen,
Neither in inward worth nor outward fair,
Can make you live yourself in eyes of men.
To give away yourself keeps yourself still,
And you must live, drawn by your own sweet skill.

## XVII

Who will believe my verse in time to come,
If it were fill'd with your most high deserts?
Though yet, heaven knows, it is but as a tomb
Which hides your life and shows not half your parts.
If I could write the beauty of your eyes
And in fresh numbers number all your graces,
The age to come would say 'This poet lies:
Such heavenly touches ne'er touch'd earthly faces.'
So should my papers yellow'd with their age
Be scorn'd like old men of less truth than tongue,
And your true rights be term'd a poet's rage
And stretched metre of an antique song:
But were some child of yours alive that time,
You should live twice; in it and in my rhyme.

WILLIAM SHAKSPEARE

## THE WARMTH OF THE SUN

*Now that we have considered the wisdom and beauty of having children, so meaningfully word-painted by Shakespeare, we will now think about caring for them.*

Imagine a family as a glowing, living life source. In your mind, see it as a little Sun, radiant and life-giving as you might see the Sun at daybreak. It is warm and rich in coloring.

Envision that from this pulsating nucleus, beams of golden light shine in every direction, enlivening others with vibrations of health and goodwill. Its beams abound. The far

reach of its healing rays can touch even cold and dark cre-
vasses where never a light visited. Its radiance ever
increases until, at last, it fades yet, not before its beams become little Suns themselves.

You have just visualized the ideal relationship of a family
to society. There are precious few of these living nuclei.
Yet, as we shall learn, there can easily be more of them.
That may seem like an oversimplification, yet, let us begin
at the beginning, and we shall see. Where, however, is this
determining point in time, this alpha moment? Where within
the meandering cavalcade of human society, stretching out
over forty millennia, does this parade start? It is the instant
of inception—the union of male and female gametic nuclei—for, as these two living pulsations become divinely
one life, the long parade begins anew. Yes, upon this infini-
tesimally small flash of sparkling light, which is a living
vibration from both parents, the critical path commences
that is the subject of our inquiry, the journey toward the
warmth of the Sun.

This cameo appearance of conceived light stands alone
among all those who came before or after it since it is utterly exclusive, being precisely one within the Universe and
neoteric among all existence; in other words, its uniqueness
is absolute. And because the newly conceived child, even in
its zygotene stage, is an embodiment of unexampled characteristics, its contribution to the world shall be a benefaction
that no other may offer. The paramountcy of its full development is, therefore, obvious.

Like the birth of an oscillating star that knows only eternal
future without a single yesterday, this new light wave grows
with an expiation that geometricizes boldly, rapidly. Beckoning light floods its being "without shadow of turning," for
it has no concept of dark, only welcoming brightness, and

so, it is angelic—a messenger of light.

Indeed, it is a power unto itself. But, only to a point. For even in its blossoming primitiveness, it yearns to receive messages and acts of loving-kindness from its procreators. The magnitude of these parental gestures is all-consuming to this microscopic yet ultrasensitive new life. For like Zeus, the Sky Ruler, who possesses unfathomable powers to hurl lightning bolts or heal with exceeding strength, father welds life and death with his presence and upon his tongue. And as Hera, Queen of Olympia, can bless with validating tenderness or curse with mere neglect, so can mother give abundant livingness or spiritual, physical degradation. Thus, as strands of homologous chromosomes line up and become pairs to form this new person, it thrives to fullness of being or cringes and withers within the realm of its parents' making.

Now, for comparative antithesis, rather than imagining a warm little Sun, let us envision a different scene. With your mind's eye, see two frightened orphans lost in a howling snowstorm. They shiver from the intense cold, for their clothes are moth-eaten and ragged. They beg passersby to show them the path home, but all look away and hurry on their several ways as though the woebegone orphans are invisible. Indeed, the lost children receive neither mercy, nor the slightest concern, from the well-to-do people who rush by them. This passive abuse turns the tortuous minutes into hours as they are preoccupied with only two things: warmth and food. One of the orphans breaks the window of a grocery store to satisfy the never-ending gnawing within his stomach, and so that criminal act indelibly defines the word "success" within his mind. The other child finds that she can effortlessly control men with animal attraction. Thus, they discover paths of escape, yet those leading to death-dealing traps.

Dear reader, should we despise these lost children? Of course, we should disdain their crimes, yet does this preclude extending mercy to them as lost and frightened orphans? After all, their parents ignored them, and, consequently, they missed each of the warming rays of a family. They were born into a frigid, desolate world. Be assured of it. Yes, whenever we see children or adults in similar conditions, particularly homeless people, it is because of active or passive parental abuse; it matters not if the parents were wealthy or poor, successful or unsuccessful. To add meaning to the metaphor of lost orphans, one must understand that the victims of neglect may be neither orphans nor lost, yet may suffer as such. They may be princes and princesses dressed in ermine and robes of golden threads, yet they are within themselves, like orphans tossed about in a raging storm, while those lovingly validated by their parents may face the same hardships with the highest nobility, although born into the lowest class.

How do we escape the freezing wastelands, wherein is starvation, and draw nearer to the warmth of the Sun with the abundance it affords? We cannot expect perfection, of course, yet we can come closer to its life-giving Sunbeams. It is a process beginning within the parents, for although the mother carries the baby in her womb, both parents are parenting consciously, yet predominantly unconsciously, unaware of the countless lessons taught to the child by indirect, everyday examples. Yes, subliminal emulation of the parents by the child is inevitable. Moreover, the notion that rearing the child starts within each parent's body is essential and a prerequisite to comprehending excellent parenthood, for what is within the woman's and man's bodies manifests in the world about them determining their child's destiny. That is why Plato said, "Utopia begins within the body of man."

It is, therefore, only logical to eat living food and drink sparkling clean water, for these natural elixirs are fuel for what the French call the *elan vital*, "the creative force within an organism that is responsible for growth, change, and necessary or desirable adaptations." The appropriate fuel for this adaptive creativity is vegetables, especially the cruciferous and dark green, leafy varieties, accompanied by one or two daily servings of fruit, nuts, and seeds. Quality vitamin B-12 and multiple vitamin supplements are advisable, along with protein sources such as protein powder and perhaps high-protein tofu. These are the choice fuels to improve health, and you may be sure that they also upgrade our thinking to a higher sense of awareness. In turn, this diet may improve our relationships with others and the environment around us, the dynamics to which the newly conceived child is keenly observant and reactive. *Let everything I want to see begin with me*, one might say; in other words, let all I wish to see in myself, others, my immediate surroundings, the ecosystem, and *my child* start with me.

By glaring contrast, pregnant women who eat food that is highly processed, fried, sugary, salty, or considered junk food increase the risk of prenatal damage to their fetus; smoking or drinking any alcohol while pregnant are especially heinous crimes against the child. Birth abnormalities are derivatives of ingesting such poisonous foods, alcohol, and tobacco. To be sure, we must nurture our inner ecology before caring for our genetic counterpart and offspring; doing so is healing to our bodies, minds, and souls, of which our child is an integral part.

Beyond eating life-giving food, the attitude and behavior

of parents affect the unborn child, as well. As we have noted, should the home tremor with waves of dissonance and
vibrations of discordant tones, the child in its embryonic
stage shall not feel the freedom of relaxation wherein it rests
from the near-continuous hard labor of upward struggle
from a primitive state unto the higher upon higher stages of
evolution. This anabolic process of rest necessarily rejuve-
nates the child, without which robust development is
improbable. Indeed, the child must hear and feel the resonance of parents who, more often than not, mentally and
verbally recognize the value of persons and things around
them. These are acts of love. Such symphonic reverbera-
tions encourage the baby while fighting to grow and cast
him or her into blessed deepness of sleep when that noble
work is complete for a time. Moreover, even during this
nascent stage, the child begins to assemble its unique intellectual and emotional language by coding and decoding
what it feels and hears from its parents. This linguistic composition has a particular motif: *The Universe is hostile,
friendly, or any variation on the scale between the two ex-
tremes.* Mother and father are the composers. They must
acknowledge and assume accountability for that ice-cold
fact, for much of the irrevocable vibrational score is writ
indelibly upon the child's mind before its birth.

Once the epoch of healthy pregnancy is complete, the next
giant stride of the child's life begins upon its birth. It is not
an overemphasis to stress that the next sixty days of its life
determine how it will negotiate all challenges henceforth.
Should the child live to 120 years of age, it will continually
react to the precise psychological language it learns during
these first two strategic months. Consequently, loving care
must attend the child during this irreversibly formative juncture. For, without the tender touch and voice of mother and

father, a physician's assistance, feeding, bathing, and changing diapers are woefully inadequate for the child to develop emotionally and physically. Undoubtedly, the baby must receive loving touches to grow correctly. Throughout the day, father and mother must hold the baby often, and in intervals lasting at least fifteen minutes, accompanied by validating comments and, perhaps, singing; for, after all, singing is a vibration, something to which babies are readily attuned.

To further comprehend the profundity of this sixty-day patterning of the child's mind and body, we must recognize that of all the things that humans endeavor, acclimating to a new world as an infant is the most heroic. Should the child grow to be a soldier, who one day charges uphill under heavy enemy fire to take out a machinegun nest, it will be only secondary in courage to venturing into a foreign world as a newborn baby. This wholly alien terrain of colossal sizes, bizarre shapes, and sounds is often terrifying as giants laugh at us or ignore us while we desperately cry for help. The soul-crushing awkwardness of a wholly uncoordinated and sluggishly heavy body saps all strength and willpower from the tiny new citizen of Earth. And, dear parents, you must know that, although they may appear innocuous, your baby's squirms and wiggles are frenzied cries for a rescue that only you can perform. Thus, soft-spoken affirmations are essential, such as, "There, there, my precious baby. Daddy is right here with you, and he's taking care of you because daddy loves you." Gently rocking the baby in your arms while sweetly saying something like, "Mommy loves my little baby more than anyone in the whole wide world!" Gingerly kissing the baby with tiny kisses is particularly reassuring that everything is all right in the baby's "brave new world."

Therefore, it is altogether necessary that we never ignore our baby's cries or answer them with impatience or anger. Remember, your newborn infant is in a boundaryless state, for within its mind, there exists no delineation between itself and all things surrounding him or her, especially you. Yes, the infant possesses little spatial concept except the ethereal oneness experienced when touched by mother or father and the unbearable absence of their transcendent grace, for they are its only lifeline. And so, obviously, we must never leave our baby alone while it fights the most valiant sixty-day battle of all its life upon Earth; for, the victory or defeat you hand to your child during these two months shall be repetitious throughout his or her life.

Now let us revisit what we have learned. Should you wish to become parents, begin that journey before inception by nurturing your bodies with life-giving food. As you recall, these are primarily vegetables, particularly those that are cruciferous and dark leafy greens, fresh fruit, nuts, and seeds. All should be organic. I also suggest quality B-12 vitamins and protein supplements. Avoid alcohol, tobacco, drugs, and junk food or food that is highly processed. Such healthy eating habits will open new vistas, allowing you to experience the world with increased strength and clarity, which, in turn, will create the highest and best environment for your newborn. Cognizance of the emotional vibrations you exude in the home and their effect upon the unborn child is preeminent among your home life. Remember, even within the womb, you are programming your child's destiny, a program without the option of rewriting.

After the child is born, the next two months are also vital. Never let your baby cry without easing its distress by holding the child, gently rocking it, and singing softly to calm its fears. Hold your baby often for at least fifteen-minute intervals and much longer. Tell your baby how much you love him or her, for although a newborn cannot understand your mother tongue, it will be encoded and decoded super-linguistically by the knowing soul of your child. Be assured that your son or daughter shall remember it forever, and as a family, you will draw ever closer to the warmth of the Sun.

P. H.


## A SONG OF SYLVAN

*We might easily imagine little Prince Alfred reciting this poem while walking among the fields above the sea in his Wessex homeland. Since he loved poetry so dearly and memorized poems as a child, I am certain he would agree that this poem would be good for our children to memorize.*


The little cares that fretted me
I lost them yesterday,
Among the fields above the sea,
Among the wind at play,

Among the lowing of the herds,
The rustling of the trees,
Among the singing birds,
The humming of the bees.

The fears of what may come to pass,
I cast them all away,
Among the clover scented grass,

Among the new mown hay,
Among the husking of the corn
Where the drowsy poppies nod,
Where ill thoughts die and good are born,
Out in the fields with God.

LOUISE IMOGEN GUINEY

Chapter Two

# Our Legacy

S HALL the astonishing achievements of the Athenian Miracle and King Alfred the Great be the extent of our august work? Shall we ever look to a bygone age to enjoy the truly sublime masterworks of paintings, sculpture, music, literature, theater, architecture, math, and science? Is it museum or mausoleum that shall house our greatness?

Has the Sun of the days of our lives passed its noonday arch, we as a people forevermore living in the pales of gloomy Sunday evening? Shall we not see the flashing splendor of the gold-gilded sunrise fashioned anew every morning beckoning, always beckoning, "I am Greatness. Come unto me. You need only give yourself permission to come, to take all my riches. Come unto me."

No, my dearest friends. We shall not look to Athenian and Alfredian miracles as glories to be unrivaled, but as high columns yearning to be crowned with our capital and cornice, adorned with a flourish of leafage and ornamentation stunning in its grace. We shall build, and we shall build more 'til our legacy becomes Civilization Builders. We'll throwback our heads in roaring laughter, lift our women in the air, and dance with our children.

Although it is right that we should be happy and sanguine as we march forward toward our triumph, we've much work to do before we celebrate. Sylvanistic philosophy is the Polaris that shall guide us to that glorious day.

## I. The Law of Survival

All other laws are parenthetical to this overarching law.

## II. Subjects of Nature

We are members of the flora and fauna and subject to nature's ways. This is absolutely pivotal to creating a society that is natural and, therefore, normal in opposition to the abnormalities imposed upon us by communist mind benders.

## III. Love is a Positive, Constructive Force

By contrast, hate is a dysfunctional force, and because we hope to be highly functional, we choose to love. Remember, it was Alfred's love of his people that drove his victories. At the same time, we do not claim to be great lovers in the religious nor romantic sense. Yet, we go forward, one step at a time, with love as our beacon.

## IV. Ethics

Anything that harms the family, or the flora and fauna is wrong, except when receiving what we need, principally from the flora.

### V. The Biologic Determines the Sociologic

Our biological identity manifests itself in society, rather than society determining our biological identity, as the mind benders pretend.

### VI. A Homogeneous Society

As Dr. Putnam of Harvard University demonstrated with his exhaustive quantitative research, racially homogeneous societies are the most functional societies, whereas racially heterogeneous societies are profoundly dysfunctional.

### VII. The Importance of the Individual

The society in which the worth of the individual is promoted is also the best society.

### VIII. Superior, Inferior Dynamics

Every man is equal before the law. Yet when society pretends that a person of superior abilities is equal to a person of inferior abilities (a marked difference in IQ, for example), the inferior will always seek to sabotage or undermine the superior in an attempt to equalize himself.

### IX. Friendly Cooperation

As Sylvans, we help one another whenever needed. And, we believe that the richest man is he who has a good friend.

### X. A Good Deed Every Day

This was an important part of Wessex society that Alfred

introduced, making his homeland a place of blessedness, a social dynamic we hope to emulate.

## XI. Leaving Good Works Behind Us

The best good works are our children, who have been well parented and are, therefore, well-adjusted to society. The next best good works are legacies of virtuous ideologies and wilderness land, especially old growth forests, since this provides habitat for the largest array of species.

## XII. Good Works Cannot Fail

Though we may not see the materialization of our plans, as Alfred taught us, the purity of intent is equally virtuous.

As we embrace Sylvanism, it is foremost that we love our people dearly as Alfred loved his people. Although facing the behemoth heathen army with only a few farmers to fight with him, he never considered abandoning his people but saw victory ever more clearly. Likewise, the more we love our people, the vision of our coming victory shall appear spot lit before us with vivid brightness; 'tis then we will see their salvation. So now is the time to, as Charles Kingsley said, "Do noble things, not dream of them."

Then, we shall see the full extent of our existential threats: ecological collapse, the predatory media, the global economic hegemony, the dangers of loving our enemies, and Marxism. For like Beowulf, once we begin confronting them collectively as a tribe, we may discover that most of them, like Grendel, will retreat after a battle.

Albeit one of these Grendel-like beasts, namely ecological collapse, will not retreat so easily since it is principally caused by global overpopulation, which is racing toward 11 billion with a high estimation of 16 billion. Almost all of this growth will come from Sub-Sahara Africa, which is the only demographic region of the world that is not stabilized and where the population will quadruple by 2100 to over 4 billion people. Presently, its hungry, thirsting souls live in the poorest conditions on Earth, and many of them will seek to live in Europe. Yet, as we fight together as one tribe with the life-and-death urgency with which ecological collapse must be met, we may see that we can reverse even this specter of death. So, I urge everyone to read *The Hathaway Equation: The Plan to Halt and Reverse Ecological Collapse.*

As we discussed earlier in this journey, our victory over Marxism might be aided with the use of blockchain technologies, for it will decentralize power and authority, returning it to the people perhaps more than at any time in human history. For decentralization strikes at the very hearts of both the global economic hegemony and Marxism, centralization being their common and essential strategy. This hitherto unexperienced method of transactions afforded by blockchain may possibly liberate us from oppressive governments and the international bankers who manipulate them. In turn, blockchain's historical authentication will also reveal the names of contemporary authors of Marxist ideologies, such as political correctness and critical race theory, allowing us, the people, to directly challenge such antisocial nonsense. Along with sovereign currencies, blockchain may provide more liberty for our children than we have ever dreamt. One of its highest liberties being transparency, the benefit to us being accessibility to facts that will, in turn, allow us to more easily discern the truth about our most desperate dilemma—ecological collapse.

This gold-gilded window of opportunity, and the

grandeur of its limitless vista, will be ever surer as we treasure our health by nurturing our bodies. Great achievements will come easier if we are physically strong and healthy; moreover, a clean, healthy body is most often the gateway to emotional and spiritual health.

So, as our cousin Hippocrates said, "Let thy food be thy medicine, and thy medicine be thy food." While nurturing ourselves, we will naturally wish to nurture the flora and fauna; and this most virtuous of desires will open spiritual door after spiritual door; for the more we care for the flora and fauna, the more we shall see their creator. This is our future. Our only future. There are not two roads before us. Only one. The single road is subordination to nature as one of her subjects. Here, we find our true position and posture.

Now, dearest cousin, as you follow the Sylvan North Star, always and ever be mindful of this supreme fact: united as one great and mighty tribe, following our motto of *work and love*, we shall triumph.

## OUR LEGACY

And did he fight vaingloriously,
With face like flint at Thermopylae,
That day he left his home for last,
Of which his noble birth was cast?

He caressed his love with ten thousand kisses,
And she blest him with ten thousand blisses,
Her cascading tears a vale did make,
Their last wedding day for him to take.

How he kissed his little lady 'n' lord,
With all tenderness man could afford,
For he so loved them more than being,
Yeah 'mongst all these beloved things.

"Marry good men," bade he his darling wife,
And marched away to give his life,
With broken hearted dignity,
Brave face set toward Eternity.

For homeland 'twas being invaded,
'Twas all he needed to be persuaded,
Stand for his blood 'gainst onslaught,
Surrender freedom he thought naught.

'Twas Leonidas with a few brave men,
Stopped Darius multitude of Persians,
For unprepared Achaeans to regroup,
Her navy and Spartan Hoplite troop.

And once again the day was won,
But not by goddess Pallas Athenian,
But Achaean men of blood and flesh,
And we their posterity now flourish,

So, mark these words young lad 'n' lass,
Forever to your heart hold them fast,
The sacrificial battle of Hell's Gate,
Truly ransomed your most precious fate.

But for his sacrifice at great cost,
Greek Miracle would be lost,
And all constitutional aristocracy,
Seasoned by honest democracy.

And desire of the ages—Liberty,
Stolen from all men left unfree.
Yeah, in Leonidas' blood preserved,
Passed unto you these lovely words:

Azure eyes with flaxen hair,
Sublime music from the lyre,
Luxus fluidity of a thousand pen,
Erudite thoughts of sagacious men.

Rich culture gentility and grace,
Bequeathed from his Promethean race.
So, what say ye men of now,
Shall we bear the yoke, the plow?

Shall we stand as Leonidas the Best,
And place our mettle to the test?
Shall we bend knee to cabal hex,
Or favor Leonidas the Rex?

And now my friends harken dear,
To treasure wise words you hear,
For I speak them as my honest duty,
Our garland legacy must be Truth and Beauty.

And so much more than only we,
'Tis for Everyman's fidelity.
Yeah, for all races to be free,
We must stand individually.

For though it seems a paradox,
Nature gave us diverse lots,
And Nature's mantle fell to us,
To nobly bear magnanimous.

Mandate to lead with humble grace,
All breed of men all hue of face,
For all the world would be enslaved,
Should our blue blood be betrayed.

All monotone, lifeless grey,
A backdrop for a crimson day.
So, oh mine love listen sweet,
To these pure words I shall repeat.

And as ye hear them cast your mind,
To King Leonidas and his kind,
For they are writ with solemn duty,
Our garland legacy shall be Truth and Beauty.

P. H.

# PART V

# ESSENTIAL SYLVANISM

Chapter One

# Our Maxim:
# Work and Love

WE work to improve our character. We work to maintain excellent health and our ideal height-to-body weight ratio by eating life-giving food, drinking pure water, and exercising regularly in the fresh air. We work to think clean, positive thoughts and a mentality of goodwill to all men. We work to exercise our talents, bring value to the world, and provide for ourselves and our families.

We love nature and the magnificent world given generously and freely to humankind. We love our families and our people. We love freedom and want people everywhere, of every race, creed, and religion, to be free. We love our homelands. We love expressions of truth and beauty, which is our definition of art.

The premise of our maxim is the notion that *anyone who works and loves is normal*. As Sylvans, we should work and love every day, even at leisure and rest, which requires the effortless work of relaxation and the love that so easily flourishes there. To be sure, our work-a-day world and love life should be balanced by fun, which we cannot live with-

out. That is why Voltaire said, "Superfluity is a very necessary thing."

Indeed, workers and lovers are among the most positive
and, therefore, happiest people because of the soul-cleansing
nature of this dual virtuosity. They are the bedrock of our
advanced urbane societies merely because work solves every problem, even the need to give and receive love. To be
sure, before we can love, we must work.

Now, if you have a job and are lovingly providing for
your family, I heartily commend you. You are living the
Sylvan maxim. Perhaps, however, a curiosity about your
profession and family life will beckon you to read further.

So, we will now discuss two genres of work: endeavor-
ing to develop character and integrity, which begins as an
infant and continues throughout our lives, and secondly, labor for compensation, with which we may be generous.

A prerequisite to this is the realization that we are not
paramount to all conversations, that the feelings of others
are equally meaningful. With this series of epiphanies, we
step across the threshold of well-adjusted adulthood. This
process often requires years of challenge. During this
growth, if we work intelligently, diligently, we may discover our niche within society, from which we have triumphed
by reconciling the dichotomy of labor and our unique talent.
The degree to which we excel depends upon our willingness
for thoughtwork, the highest order of industry.

It is immaterial whether ours is a labor-intensive job or
one that is pure thinking. It only matters that we enjoy our
work and have a gratifying sense of completion at the day's
end. From this point, we more readily perceive the worth of
ourselves, others, and the world around us. That subtle perception is *the recognition of value*, which is my irreducible
definition of love.

Taking a further step, in which we give ourselves to another person, extending our most tender emotions, is, therefore, comparably easier. We can afford the freedom to be hurt or disappointed a little without threatening our emotional balance. Ideally, this may blossom into a partnership of mutual validation, forgiveness, understanding, and lifelong companionship, upon which our societies thrive.

So be it, some people we love from afar, others we courteously avoid. For, we are not obligated to love everyone, especially those who actively seek our demise. We neither love nor hate them, for hate is a dysfunctional force, and we hope to be highly functional. Remember, it was King Alfred's love of his people, not hate, that drove his victories. At the same time, we do not claim to be great lovers in the religious or romantic sense. So, we go forward, one step at a time, imperfectly, with love as our true north.

Let us give further consideration to the notion of work and love, with perhaps a similar yet more critical observation.

Some people propose that we are little more than savages—lazy savages, mind you—who tolerate one another from weaknesses and cowardliness so that we might benefit from agreed-upon laws and societal norms. These safeguards, however, are regularly, selfishly disobeyed.

Yet some see a grander vista; these are the heroes amongst the rabble of human tragedies, for they sacrifice for the greater good of our race. And from them evolves our salvation and destiny—cultured society, which is a manifestation of our spirit, the condition of our soul.

Perhaps, we are still base and crude, and our self-accolades do little to beautify us. Yet should we glimpse the light of dawn, we do a thing most uncommon. We think.

Tribe of Sylvan

That is the highest order of work.

How then, we must ask, should we commence this thoughtwork? We might consider ourselves as a single sprocket within a giant locomotive, as an individual is to society. As a gear, we may be small but integral to producing avalanching power. We might further pose the question, shall our energies be consumed and forever lost for self-centered reasons? Or will our lives be one of the precious few that genuinely count? Will it be one life that soldiered onward despite the weeping, the bloody sweat, the soul-crushing pain?

It seems there is only one way to overcome these Odyssian obstacles: we must find something worthy of our cognitive prowess, which necessarily corresponds in intensity to our intellect. The brighter we are, the more compelling the need for thoughtwork. Resisting this is neurotic. As we discussed previously, Carl Jung said, "All neurosis is a substitute for legitimate suffering." The legitimate suffering to which Jung refers is honest, smart, and hard work.

Should we be blest, we find a way to reconcile the need to labor with our idiosyncratic talent; we work in ways that we enjoy. We experience the equilibrium of the unconscious and conscious mind. Although a series of fleeting episodes, the profundity of that interchange can reorder our thinking. These psychological moments empower us. Indeed, more than superficial pleasantries, discovering our workplace in society allows us to attain self-sufficiency drawn from within ourselves. We become self-contained. We find that we grasp less and less for people and things outside of ourselves, for our strength and stay comes from a clean soul, one that needn't make the slightest excuse.

Looking outward from the ramparts of this fortress, we

slowly begin to see things that were once mundane but are now bright with vivid coloring and clarity. We know we have seen them when standing stone still in hushed awe before the limitless beauties of nature. Over the years, little by little, we observe the axis upon which the Universe spins and swirls through space—the recognition of value, namely love. So, we find work's reward.

And though we may be imperfect, should we have made this journey, whether over a few years or one hundred, we are normal, for we have worked and loved, which is the fusion of cultivated society from which we aspire to rise above barbarism unto the stars. So, work and love, dear friends, with all your heart.

Chapter Two

# The Sylvan Pledge

I solemnly pledge to:

**D**enounce hatred of every kind.

**D**enounce and avoid unlawfulness.

**D**enounce and avoid violence.

**N**ever treat others condescendingly because of their race, creed, or religion.

**R**ecognize that love is the highest power and my source of strength.

**A**sk, what would King Alfred the Great do?

**K**now and follow the twelve Sylvan tenets.

**B**e grateful for the flora and fauna and treat them as representatives of their maker.

**W**ork and love with all my heart.

For the sake of clarity, it may be helpful to look closer at the separate points of this pledge.

*Denounce hatred of every kind.*

We denounce hate because it is psychologically, socially, spiritually, and physically dysfunctional. This universally damaging emotion is self-hatred turned outwardly. Consequently, it grotesquely distorts our thinking and harms others. Once given a tiny foothold, it spirals downward, collecting speed as it goes, and is difficult to stop.

Should you be challenged by this supremely negative emotion, you may wish to read the section on depression in Part III, The Sylvan Lifestyle of Health. You may also discover that junk food and too much sugar can trigger uncontrolled anger. Another accelerator is foul language.

Incidentally, anger and hatred differ significantly. "A man can be angry and sin not." In other words, anger is appropriate at times, but not too often. It is when we lose our temper that anger becomes hateful. If we lose our temper every day, something is wrong and must be adjusted as soon as possible.

*Denounce and avoid unlawfulness.*

As Sylvans, we are law-abiding people. The law protects us, our family, our community, and our nation. Therefore, we humbly respect the majesty of the law, treating authorities and police officers with esteem and appreciation. Yet even they are subject to established principles and regulations.

There is a caveat to denouncing and avoiding unlawfulness; in a rare circumstance, peaceful civil disobedience may be appropriate for an individual. But remember, if you are a Sylvan, you are held to noble standards of behavior and represent Sylvanism and our patron, King Alfred the Great.

I don't envision organized protests by Sylvans. Yet, should such an extraordinary protest be appropriate, the proper permits and approvals from the police and authorities must be obtained well in advance. Any type of protest organized or attended by Sylvans must be peace-loving and quiet, without shouting, loud music, disruption of businesses, pedestrians, traffic, or disturbing or annoying others.

Please note that I have never participated in a demonstration of any kind, so, generally speaking, I don't feel that it is the Sylvan way.

*Denounce and avoid violence.*

That is one of the essential principles of Sylvanism.

Wisdom and commonsense will usually lead us away from most violent encounters. However, those who cannot abide by our doctrine of non-violence have no place whatsoever within Sylvanism.

At the same time, there are unusual exceptions such as unavoidable self-defense, defending one's family, the sick, or those too weak to protect themselves. A state of national emergency, such as an officially declared and justified war, is another exception.

*Never treat others condescendingly because of their race, creed, or religion.*

We are above such offensive and ignorant behavior. Let it not once occur among us. For some of the finest people on Earth are those of other races, creeds, or religions.

*To recognize that love is the highest power and my source of strength.*

The absence of love is evidence of low self-esteem, from which every malady takes root. The vacancy of love is death.

But the presence of love is the polar opposite, wherein every virtue flourishes, giving health to our mind, body, and soul. Love is vitality, courageousness, durability, magnanimity, generosity, and endlessly energetic. Make no mistake about it, love is life.

*Ask, what would King Alfred the Great do?*

Before posing this question to yourself, you may wish to reread the biography of King Alfred in Part I, and possibly more of his life story from other sources. When we know him and ask what he would do in our various circumstances, we will always have the wisest, noblest behavior and solution before us. And emulating his example, we may become noble ambassadors of Sylvanism.

*Know and follow the twelve Sylvan tenets.*

It is axiomatic that we know our tenets. And it is good to read them anew occasionally, keeping them in the forefront of our minds.

*Be grateful for the flora and fauna and treat them as representatives of their maker.*

The infinite generosity of the Universe and the magnificent wonder and beauty of the Earth, which we have been freely given, should inspire daily gratitude. After all, they are the source of our next sip of water, morsel of food, breath of oxygen, all of which are freely, abundantly given to us.

*Work and love with all my heart.*

Half-heartedness brings out the worst in you. Whereas soaring standards and visions accent your splendid characteristics, which you may possess to your surprise.

You will undoubtedly encounter many hardships, but don't be fainthearted. Fatigue, calamity, and suffering will cleanse your soul. Of course, we do not seek these misfortunes. They appear when anyone sets out to accomplish something worthy. It is a fiat of the Universe, as if the cosmos were taunting us by saying: You have no right to enter the pantheon of greatness until you fight and suffer for it! To that, I answer boldly:

*The key to every lock is a fearless heart!*

Chapter Three

# The Sylvan Interview

*Please note that redundant and inarticulate expressions, often used during informal conversations, are edited from this interview, making it pleasanter to read.*

Hardcastle:
Our guest is Phillip Hathaway, author of *The Tribe of Sylvan, Threshold of European Man's Ascendance.*

Thank you, Phillip, for being with us for our third interview.

Hathaway:
It's always a pleasure to be with you.

As you know, I like tough questions, so please feel free to ask anything you wish.

Hardcastle:
I have some of those questions coming later. First, I want to thank you for something else—for the chapter on health.

I started using the suggestions that you make in the section about the common cold. I am amazed, but I can breathe bet-

ter, more deeply, and feel better. So, maybe I've also overcome the common cold, which would be a big improvement
for me.

Hathaway:
That's what I like to hear. I hope it works for you, as well as
it has for me.

Hardcastle:
And, I regained an inch in height! I would have never
guessed that was possible. So, many, many thanks!

Now, let's get into the interview. If I wanted to, how do I
join the Tribe of Sylvan?

Hathaway:
Ah, good question.

By design, no one joins the Tribe of Sylvan.

Sylvans are, and behave according to the lifestyle described
in this book. Consequently, there is nothing to join. There
are no national headquarters, divisions, or local chapters of
Sylvanism.

Sylvans might socialize together in private lunches, dinners,
picnics, or in other such gatherings in their homes. But nothing official.

Perhaps it would be helpful to think of it in this way:

One may be a Stoic through dispassion and virtuousness, yet
one does not join Stoicism.

Someone can join a church, but that does not make one a Christian; one can read the Bible, but, again, that does not create a devotee of Christ.

Jesus said, "Ye shall know them by their fruits," not by membership, or what one reads, or the songs one sings, or the rituals and ceremonies one participates in.

Likewise, neither would joining the Tribe of Sylvan, if that were possible, nor reading this book make one a Sylvan because Sylvanism is a philosophy and way of life; and, so, the only union to Sylvanism is how one behaves and lives.

That's why Sylvanism is not something you join and then you say, "Now, I'm a Sylvan," but do nothing. I've seen this lackadaisicalness far too often in religion.

Therefore, I wanted something that is alive and renewed each day. Not something one joins and almost instantly becomes stagnant.

Sylvanism is alive and vitally attuned to the power of nature and the threats and challenges of life. The Sylvanist life is one that is fully awake, fully alive.

Hardcastle:
Would taking the Sylvan Pledge make me a Sylvan?

Hathaway:
[Laughter.] It's not that easy. You see, making the pledge is the *second* step of the Sylvan lifestyle. The first step, of course, is reading the book.

Only living the Sylvan life makes one a Sylvan. To be sure, the pledge is empty rhetoric unless acted upon for, Sylvanism is a natural series of actions based upon right decisions established in the volume of Sylvanist philosophy.

But the many decisions one makes in a lifetime are extra-Sylvanistic. In other words, by far, most decisions that one makes are the responsibility of the individual, whereas Sylvanism provides a track to run on for only some basic life choices.

We want people to lead their own personal lives, rather than being overshadowed by Sylvanism.

That should never happen. And, I feel it is unlikely to occur for Sylvanism is not domineering. It is free and natural.

Hardcastle:
Suppose someone who is of European descent wanted to marry someone of a different race. What would you say to that?

Hathaway:
I would say that is up to the individual.

At the same time, our schools and the media are not leaving the decision to that individual. He or she is bombarded with subliminal and overt messages to intermarry with those of other races.

That happens thousands and thousands of times before his graduation from high school.

So, while I leave such decisions up to the person, communist propaganda does not. They are actively, almost seamlessly, promoting the idea of interracial marriage among our people.

Therefore, I would say to that person, think for yourself.

I would ask that individual, why is it unnecessary for those of African descent, Chinese descent, Arabic, Japanese, and all the other races to intermarry?

Ask why.

Hardcastle:
I want to read the Sylvan Pledge.

Let's see. Here it is. Reading right out of your book.

"I solemnly pledge to:

Denounce hatred of every kind.

Denounce and avoid unlawfulness.

Denounce and avoid violence.

Never treat others condescendingly because of their race, creed, or religion.

Recognize that love is the highest power and my source of strength.

Ask, what would King Alfred the Great do?

Know and follow the twelve Sylvan tenets.

Be grateful for the flora and fauna and treat them as representatives of their maker.

Work and love with all my heart."

Now, it seems like a pledge that, well, it seems like anyone would say, that's the kind of person I would want as a neighbor, a work colleague, or particularly a spouse.

Yet, because *The Tribe of Sylvan* is written to those of European descent, the Marxist communists and their puppets, will call you a racist.

How do you respond to such false accusations?

Hathaway:
I'm glad you asked. Like you, I came prepared with notes about that topic.

But first, let me say that of all the people upon the face of the Earth—I dedicated *The Hathaway Equation* to a beautiful girl whom I met while traveling in India whose skin is ebony, almost jet black.

It was appropriate for me to dedicate my book to her because I wrote it to help millions who share her plight.

Her image seared my memory, and when you read her noblest story, you will understand why, and perhaps, you too will shed tears for dearest Nidhi.

I remember a Black teacher who helped me when I was a confused teenager. Had it not been for his kindness and big-heartedness, I might not have graduated from high school. I think about him often and richly bless him.

Now, I suggest responding to someone who falsely calls you a racist or makes an unfounded allegation of racism in this way.

I'm reading from my notes.

I hope you don't mind that I read this. I don't feel that it will slow down the interview, besides the information is vital.

Hardcastle:
Go right ahead. I think your listeners will want to know.

Hathaway:
Thank you. [Reading.] While never using foul language or losing your temper, politely, calmly tell the accuser:

*Since you are assuming a position of the moral high ground, I challenge you to take the Sylvan Pledge. I took it as a solemn oath. Will you?*

Politely recite the pledge to him or hand him a card with the pledge written on it.

He probably won't make the pledge because doing so would mean that he couldn't treat you hatefully. It might be best to leave the conversation at that moment unless it is a rearranged public debate.

Mark Twain has good advice about dealing with communist hatemongers who call people racists. "Never argue with a fool, onlookers may not be able to tell the difference."

He also said, "Never argue with stupid people, they will drag you down to their level and then beat you with experience."

However, if you are in a public debate or panel discussion, for instance, and you are assaulted with the word racist, you might respond in this way. It is essential to use these words verbatim. So, I'll read them again.

*Since you are assuming a position of the moral high ground, I challenge you to take the Sylvan Pledge. I took it as a solemn oath. Will you?*

If you're in a public forum, it's best to present a large printed version of the pledge, perhaps four feet by six feet, so your audience can see it clearly. Read the pledge aloud distinctly, taking time to emphasize each sentence.

Once again, he probably won't make the pledge because doing so would mean that he couldn't treat you hatefully. If he won't take the pledge, ask him why.

*You can skip the last three parts of the pledge. So why won't you make this pledge?*

If he refuses, ask him why again.

Continue with these questions:

*A Marxist communist named Magnus Hirschfeld coined the*

*word "racist." He lived in Germany and died in 1935.*

*So why would you use a word created by Marxist communism, a criminal organization that murdered over 120 million innocent defenseless men, women, and children, many of whom were kidnapped, raped, and tortured to death?*

Stop and wait for a response. He will probably try to avoid the question. Don't let him off the hook.

*What do you hope to gain by hating people of European descent?*

Stop and wait for his reply and ask again if needed.

*Is it because you cannot win a reasonable, rational argument without making hateful accusations?*

Stop and wait for the answer.

*Those of European descent are labeled racists because of their immutable racial features.*

*It doesn't matter that they are hardworking, kind-hearted, law-abiding citizens.*

*Isn't that profound hatred of a race?* [End of Reading.]

I feel those who accuse one of us of being a racist will be unable to answer those questions.

Hardcastle:
I agree. There is simply no sensible, logical response from a communist accuser. Very good!

Now, is it fair to call the Tribe of Sylvan, the people who embrace the philosophy, is it accurate to call them a society?

Hathaway:
Is communism a society?

Perhaps, but Marxism is overwhelmingly a social theory, a political philosophy, an ideology, a culture, but most of all a tribe. It is somewhat similar with Sylvanism.

Of course, Sylvanism is not a secret society like the very clandestine Marxism. Everything we believe is stated un-ambiguously for all to read in this tome of Sylvanist thought.

There are no secrets. Nothing to hide. Everything is there in the broad light of the noontide Sun.

But more than a society, much more, it is tribal since the word tribe carries the connotation of taxonomy, which is categorizing those who seek their natural relationships. Thus, we are, indeed, a tribe.

Hardcastle:
Is taxonomy, did I pronounce it correctly? Is it one of the poems within a word that you discussed in the, I believe it was the Sylvan Peace Model?

Hathaway:
Well done! I see you've read the book. Right, taxonomy is a fine example of a poem within a word.

Hardcastle:
In other words, instead of saying, I just looked up the definition, instead of saying "the orderly classification of animals according to their presumed natural relationships," I only need to say taxonomy.

Hathaway:
Yes. After reading the definition, you can appreciate the poetic efficiency of the word taxonomy. What is more, it is an appropriate and accurate definition of our tribe.

After all, there is the ancient Han Chinese tribe, who speak [the] Sino-Tibetan language, the several tribes of Native Americans, the Maoris of New Zealand, and many other tribes around the globe.

These are taxonomic tribes, and we admire their tribalism. Our tribe is taxonomic, as well; for we are a distinct classification with natural relationships to one another.

Thus, more than a society, we are a tribe with unmistakable, similar characteristics.

Hardcastle:
For the sake of our listeners, is it analogous to a religious sect or cult?

Hathaway:
[Laughing.] Not at all. Sylvanism is not a religion. This is

explained with unmistakable clarity in many passages of the book [*The Tribe of Sylvan*].

Something else I should say. Sylvanism is not oppressive or guilt-provoking like some religions. Sylvanism is comfortable and natural.

We don't pretend to be right about everything, an unbearable weight to carry through society that overburdens many of our religious friends.

It is wonderfully liberating to not feel as though you must be right about everything; but at the same time, we have high standards of behavior.

Like everyone else, we have good and bad urges. That is normal. All people struggle with the inward contradiction of our lower natures.

> "Can heavenly natures nourish hate
> So fierce, so blindly passionate?"

Hardcastle:
That's beautiful. What's it from?

Hathaway:
*The Aeneid of Virgil*.

Now, the second part of your question. A cult? The prevailing connotation of the word cult is some authoritarian commune where members are brainwashed, forced to do things against their will, are persecuted, and can't escape.

They usually have initiations and lots of secrets. Who in their right mind would want to be a part of that? [That's] madness.

We think highly of King Alfred the Great, as do many distinguished historians, yet they are not a cult of Alfredians. Neither are we.

[I have] something else I'd like to read to further answer your question. It's from the chapter Sylvanist Thought:

". . . Sylvanity is something one does. Consequently, we do not rely upon sacraments or rituals, holy men, or priests, which are religious substitutes for our own legitimate work and love.

"Neither have we anything, whatsoever, to do with magic nor the occult for these, too, are always substitutes for honest, wholesome, hard work and love."

Hardcastle:
Excellent. Now, what inspired you to write *the Tribe of Sylvan*? Was it one thing that was an epiphany or a series of events or both?

Hathaway:
That's a good question.

I guess it's been a growing inspiration that started very early in my life. I recall a Celtic folk song by Donovan. Let's see, it's. It's ah . . . "Wear Your Love Like Heaven."

It is a stunningly beautiful song that describes vivid colors as though a brightly painted oil painting becomes a song.

In that song are the lines.

"Cannot believe what I see,

All I have wished for will be,

All our race proud and free."

That touched a tender place in my heart when I heard [it] so many years ago. Why would it find a delicate longing there?

Because I, and, I feel, many people knew what we were enduring, an invisible oppression. From whence did it come? Most of us didn't know then. But we know now.

Hardcastle:
Marxism.

Hathaway:
Precisely.

You know, I suppose you might call it the animating action of growing up in a society that, here and there, seemed oddly oppressive.

And, little by little, that passive persecution became salient and frequent until, lo and behold, our children are taught critical race theory in our schools, in which those of European descent are blamed for all social problems in our society.

Our children are taught to hate themselves for the immutable, God-given color of their skin. They are taught that
everyone has a safety network where they may seek refuge
and assistance, except for boys of European descent.

And, that atop decades and decades of hiring and promotion
quotas for all, except males of European descent, and the
countless portrayals of our people as evil in news, movies,
and throughout the media.

The way the communists portray us, you'd think we were all
slave traders.

Hardcastle:
You made a good point in your book about that, and I'd like
to read it. Just a moment. I have it marked here.

Right. Here it is.

"Yet, let the truth be known, I am unaware of any case of
our tribe venturing to Africa to enslave the natives of that
continent. This was principally done by slave traders from
without our tribe and whose members were in league with
the Ashanti Kings of West Africa who made extraordinary
fortunes by enslaving and selling their people. As we have
previously noted, it is also intriguing that while over eleven
million slaves from West Africa were sent predominantly to
the Caribbean, Brazil, and North America, over fourteen
million were enslaved in East Africa and sent to Arabia.
There, the men were castrated upon arrival, bespeaking of
the heartlessly cruel way in which both men and women
were mistreated by those Saracen slave traders. We hear
nothing, however, of this Saracen enslavement simply because the media cannot cast blame upon us for this tragedy,

as they incorrectly blame us for those who were enslaved in West Africa and brought to the colonies and, later America."

Hathaway:
Those facts are buried by the media because they're terrified of the truth. Like Count Dracula would wither and die if exposed to sunlight, they wither and die when exposed to the ice-cold facts.

And, Sylvanism is a *response of truth and love, which are the two almighty powers given to us on Earth.*

Hardcastle:
The federal government puts out most or all of those programs, like affirmative action. Do you feel that the government should be replaced with something different?

Hathaway:
Positively not.

Anyone who wishes to subvert or overthrow the government may not be a Sylvan.

However, we hope to lawfully, peacefully restore our present government to the robust version that it was founded upon, so "that government of the people, by the people, for the people, shall not perish from the earth."

Ironically, I wonder if the US president that made these words famous stated them sincerely. Nonetheless, they are eloquent.

Now, to more accurately answer your question, the government is not the problem, but those we elect to office. So, the government does not need to be replaced, but the elected bureaucrats [need] to be voted out of office.

Hardcastle:
Are Sylvans pacifists?

Hathaway:
We denounce all violence. No one can be a Sylvan without embracing this non-violent stance.

The *rare* exception, and it would be a very rarified case, would be when self-defense, the defense of one's family, or the weak is *absolutely unavoidable*. Most people would agree that is a universal right.

We don't go around breaking things, burning anything, or being rude and disrespectful. We simply do not do such things. It's not our way. Anyone who would behave like that is definitely not a Sylvan.

Hardcastle:
May I read something?

Hathaway:
Please do.

Hardcastle:
*Merriam-Webster's Dictionary* defines conscientious objector as someone who "refuses on moral or religious grounds to serve in the armed forces or to bear arms in a military conflict."

Are Sylvan's conscientious objectors?

Hathaway:
We will fight in a war. But we must be existentially threatened, all avenues of peace must be exhausted, it must be
justified, and inescapable. Those are the main prerequisites.

But war is not the glamorous version depicted by Hollywood, where a soldier barely gets his fatigues dirty, skips a
day or two of shaving, but is well-fed and full of gung-ho
spirits and make-believe bravery.

War is a hideous nightmare that cannot be conceived by
those who have not been in that interminable hell. I thank
God that I never had to fight in combat.

A soldier may not have food or clean water for weeks, enduring temperatures fifty degrees below zero without proper
clothing or barely any clothing at all. That sounds impossible, but there are records of it happening.

No warmth, dirty water, no food, no medicine, or safety for
weeks and weeks. Living in a hell-hole with rats and ver-
min.

And, then there is the combat, which I've never had to endure.

It's far worse than I wish to talk about. That's only one of
the reasons I desire peace. That's why I wrote the Sylvan
Peace Model. Nevertheless, we'll fight for our country.

Hardcastle:
Do you plan for Sylvans to hold protests?

Hathaway:
I don't see that ever happening.

As I mentioned earlier, I've never participated in a protest. It's just not my style. And, I don't envision Sylvans protesting. That would be a most exceptional instance.

If such a protest was somehow appropriate, it would be silent, without blocking pedestrians or road traffic, and it would be planned well in advance and in accordance with all authorities.

But Sylvans should never participate in an unruly demonstration that is loud and obnoxious, or disrespectful to others or law enforcement officials. Such pugnacious behavior is anathematic to our philosophy.

By contrast as bright as life and death, the paragon of Sylvanism is King Alfred the Great, whose noblest bearing we hope to emulate.

*And so, we are never, never aggressors, offenders, or those who make threats.*

Part of the Sylvan Pledge is the denouncement of all unlawfulness. Thus, we humbly respect the majesty of the law.

The unusual caveats to this are the unlikely circumstances of civil disobedience, which would be, for example, unconstitutional laws. In such an extraordinary case, we must act with dignity, courteously, and without violence.

Hardcastle:
How do Sylvans interact with those of other races?

Hathaway:
We interact with them like anyone else. But we pledge never to treat others condescendingly because of their race.

We want those of every race to do well and prosper without the slightest trace of oppression or tyranny.

Now, let's say that a person has an aversion to someone of another ethnicity. Is it best to pretend that reluctance—that shadowy feeling does not exist?

According to Jungian analytical psychology, that shadow is an unconscious aspect of the personality that does not correspond with the ego ideal, our self-concept of being kind and loving everyone, for example.

However, denial and suppression of that antagonism lead the ego to project those shadow animosities onto others, blaming them for our faults, especially those inconsistent with our self-image.

One might continue that charade for a while, only to be contradicted by the unconscious animus that one has deliberately buried. Therefore, it is best to reconcile that incongruity.

If not, the shadow will only become more pronounced when it inevitably emerges from the unconscious as hostility or subservient, saccharine politeness. Both are unnatural.

I believe that Jungian concept is a foundational premise for harmony amongst various ethnicities.

Hardcastle:
After reading your book, I feel that it is safe to say that Sylvanism is foursquare against Marxist and Trotskyite communism. Does that mean Sylvanists hate its followers?

Hardcastle:
Not at all.

We denounce hatred of all and any kind. So, while we strongly disagree with and dislike communism, we separate the ideologue from the ideology, and thus, we do not hate them. We merely regard them as enemies.

Hardcastle:
Who are the communists?

Hathaway:
Excellent point.

There are avowed communists, those who are outspoken followers of Marx. Many of these are amateurs.

Then there are the societal communists, most of whom are following Marxist ideologies without knowing what they're doing.

They are often the followers of least resistance and unwitting communist stooges. Many of them are proponents of political correctness and other far-left agendas without a rational basis for their beliefs.

However, the most dangerous are the cryptic Marxists.

They're in churches, and sometimes are high-ranking officials like the late and former Dean of Canterbury Cathedral, Hewlett Johnson [who was discussed on page 67].

What about the president of the United States who deliberately, *egregiously* violated the constitution, stole sovereignty from the states, and acted politically and violently like Stalin later behaved?

Add this to the fact that after centralizing the US government and waging *the war against the states*, as I call it, in which over 600,000 US citizens died and many others were grievously wounded, he received a letter of laudatory praise from none other than Karl Marx.

Would you say that president was a communist?

Hardcastle:
I would say that we must reexamine that president.

Hathaway:
Indeed.

CEOs of big tech companies, prominent news anchors, members of congress, superintendents of public schools, and . . .

Hardcastle:
Forgive me for interrupting, but look at the school board members who add critical race theory to our children's learning curriculum but fail to teach them reading, writing, and arithmetic.

Hathaway:
Yes.

There are people in every walk of life who are purposefully veiled and vague Marxist. Yet, make no mistake about it, they comprise the most well-organized, well-funded, and deep-rooted ideology on Earth.

Let me be quick to add that we do not want to be like our foes, who revel in making knowingly false accusations. We don't want to say that someone is a communist without hard and fast proof.

Perhaps saying that "some people feel" that so and so "seems to behave like a communist" is quite enough.

Hardcastle:
What piqued your interest in communism?

Hathaway:
While serving as a soldier in the army, I wanted to know what we were defending America from. After all, the Department of the Army was part of the Department of Defense.

So, after duty hours, I often went to the post library and read about communism. I read *Alienated Labor* and *The Communist Manifesto* by Karl Marx.

That's when I read *The Gulag Archipelago* by Aleksandr Solzhenitsyn. I read *Nicholas and Alexandra* [by Robert Massie]. I read that one twice.

[I read] *The Persecutor* by Sergi Kourdakov about a military unit whose mission was to break up a church service, kill the pastor, and beat members of the congregation. I devoured biographies of Marx, Lenin, the history of their era, and other expository works about Marxist ideology.

But even these excellent books did not unravel the cryptogram that is the crux of communism.

Later, I took a course about communism while completing my undergraduate degree, and eventually traveled to Russia for a closer look.

Standing in Red Square was breathtaking. St. Basil's Cathedral and the gold-gilded churches of the Kremlin were fascinating.

Of course, the Russian people were not the real communists; they were only occupied by them against their will. It took decades before understanding the essence of that psychological monster and assassin known as communism.

Hardcastle:
Are you obsessed with communism?

Hathaway:
Oh, no. Far from obsession. To be obsessed is to be controlled by a fixation of repetitious thoughts whereas, this is a serious interest, one that is indispensable to our survival.

Hardcastle:
True. You have many interests. I've seen some of your paintings, which are quite good.

Now, is love truly the way to win our liberation from them?

Hathaway:
Yes, undoubtedly.

This is the same idea Fyodor Dostoevsky presented in his book, *The Idiot*. He wrote, "Beauty will save the world."

Yes, Dostoevsky was right. Beauty will, indeed, save the world.

As you recall from reading [chapter one] the biography of King Alfred, it was the love of his people that strengthened him to protect them from the terror of murder, rape, torture, and pillage by the Great Heathen Army, which were, of course, the Vikings.

I am quite certain that if he hated his enemies, he would have failed. But the love of his people gave him a spectacular triumph in the face of seemingly unsurmountable hostility.

Hardcastle:
How do you see communism playing out? That is, ending.

Hathaway:
How did it play out in Eastern Europe?

Hardcastle:
Well, I suppose the answer would be economic implosion.

Hathaway:
Correct.

When there is little or no incentive for exemplary performance, few people are motivated to work. Everyone is
rewarded equally, no matter how excellently or poorly they
produce, or if they don't produce at all.

Another fiscal predictor is the abandonment of the gold
standard for our money's value.

The Austrian theory of economics states that a currency's
worth must be supported by the price of gold. Whereas, the
value of Keynesian money is determined by government
decree.

Now, does what I'm about to say sound like an act of Marxism?

Keynesianism was adopted in the US in 1933, when President Roosevelt ordered everyone to surrender all gold to the
Federal Reserve, a private bank that operates in direct violation of the United States Constitution.

Roosevelt's confiscation of gold was mandated with the
threat of a $10,000 fine, which was a fortune back then, and
ten years in prison. In other words, it was armed robbery of
private property. FDR used the excuse of supporting the war
efforts overseas, which were unnecessary.

All of which leads us back to your comment, economic implosion.

Keynesian currency historically always goes to zero value.
That's why some people liken it to a drug addiction in
which the addict experiences episodes of ecstasy only to

crash in a more miserable state than before.

Consequently, the United States' economic system may implode like the USSR.

Hardcastle:
Do you feel that the champion of our people, the champion of freedom for all people, will be a politician or religious leader?

Hathaway:
Not really.

Some of them are good. But most are two breeds of demagogues—politicians and religious leaders—who are drunk with "filthy lucre." We must not expect them to do anything but protect their "ill-gotten gain."

Hardcastle:
What will our world look like after the demise of communism?

Hathaway:
We'll have the freedom to say what we wish. It's a long forgotten right called freedom of speech.

We won't be enslaved to provide for those who refuse to work. We can live among, employ, and associate with whomever we wish.

One evolution that will result from our emancipation from Marxism is economic reconciliation of the brightest and best. The incompetent will no longer be exalted above the proficient.

Moreover, *natural economics*, as I call it, is based upon the well-being of the individual rather than profits. Of course, a business must break even and make some profit, but that will not be the objective.

By contrast, the industrial target will be the happiness and fulfillment of the citizen and the family.

That may sound innocuous. But consider the elementary simplicity with which Newton's *Principia* begins and spirals to profound complexities. His uncomplicated premises determine far-reaching conclusions, which are beautifully intricate.

Likewise, such an ingenious shift in the premise of an economic theory can present us with a new world of true prosperity instead of the luxuriousness of the Marxist robber barons who oppress all those except themselves.

Hardcastle:
I know from a previous interview and discussions that you believe our ecological quest is a spiritual war. Do you feel that our struggle against communism is also metaphysical?

Hathaway:
Yes. I feel that what we see happening in the material world all about us is representational of the unseen war waging in the spiritual realm.

The good news is that we are destined to win that war if we continue walking in the light.

"The night is far spent. The day is at hand. Let us, therefore, cast off the works of darkness, and let us put on the armor of light."[21]

Hardcastle:
That's from the Bible, isn't it?

Hathaway:
Yes, Romans, I believe.

Hardcastle:
Can Christians be Sylvans?

Hathaway:
Of course.

Sylvanists agree with the teachings of Christ and the Biblical ideas of family values. Christians are our friends, although we tacitly question the notion of loving one's enemies.

Thus, we celebrate a host of the Christian holidays and customs with them, and many Sylvans attend church regularly, as well.

Yet when religion is bereft of "love, joy, peace, patience, kindness, gentleness, and self-control" it becomes dogmatic madness. This is an example:

---

[21] Romans 13:12

In his masterfully researched book, *The Rise and Fall of Alexandria*, Justin Pollard describes the Great Library of Alexandria, founded around 285 BC, which was a repository of all the world's books with similar objectives of today's Library of Congress and the British Library.

According to Pollard, these included approximately 750,000 scrolls about locomotion, physics, geometry, trigonometry, astronomy, art, literature, history, architecture, hydrology, philosophy, social science, musicology, geography, and medical discoveries that, in some cases, would take two thousand years to rediscover. But most were lost forever.

And so, with its library and towering lighthouse, Alexandria was known as the Light of the World.

These were the blossom of a flower that required as much as 40,000 years to germinate and reach toward the light, for that is the time postglacial paleolithic man struggled upward from his primitive debut.

However, that was the culmination of millions of years in the primordial swamp, preceded by an inconceivably colossal supernova spiraling from the Sun that became our planet billions of years ago.

So, those advancements archived in the Great Library over 2,000 years ago—the measurement of the Earth's circumference, the discovery of the circulatory system, the mastery of geometry, and many more invaluable innovations and discoveries—had a prerequisite of eons that make all of history seem but a thing of yesterday.

Yet all who subscribed to those precious discoveries that elevated humanity at costs beyond measure were persecuted, their ideas debased, and their books burned by Christians, the lion's share of the library's volumes later set ablaze by the invading Muslins in AD 642.

And though Pollard states that Alexandria "dwarfed" Athens and Rome in wealth, population, and especially scientific and mathematical achievement, barely a vestige remains of that former Light of the World.

Its destruction was the most reprehensible assault on progress in human history, all due to manic religiosity.

Hardcastle:
It is mind-boggling to think of what was stolen from all of mankind by these religious vandals—the world's generations for the next 2,000 years robbed.

Hathaway:
Not just the next 2,000 years, but forever, permanently. We'll never know the scope and scale of that loss.

How many books that were as critical as *The Odyssey*, *Politics* by Aristotle, or *Elements* by Euclid were lost, with all their precious wisdom perhaps never relearned, and fantastic discoveries lost and never rediscovered.

Hardcastle:
'Tis a heavy thing to bear.

Hathaway:
Over 1,500 years later, the same thing happened to Galileo

when the Catholic Church threatened him with torture and sentenced him to house arrest for the remainder of his life— all for discovering that Earth orbits the Sun.

Hardcastle:
It's the endless struggle of the incompetent against the competent.

Well, now on another subject. Undoubtedly, foes of Sylvanism will attempt infiltration and subversion. Some of our listeners may belittle that notion as paranoid thinking.

What do you say to that?

Hathaway:
Infiltration is how ideological contests are played by communists. They infiltrate many organizations.

But we don't do such things.

Hardcastle:
So, how do you plan to avoid communist plants in Sylvanism?

Hathaway:
Another superb question.
Let me explain it this way. Whenever one builds a sandcastle on the beach, some will praise your work, others will barely see it.

However, and this is simply bewildering to me, but others will be intimidated by it! Intimidated by a sandcastle! It's a psychological phenomenon.

And some of those terribly frighten, lost souls will kick it down, which is a metaphor of Marxist behavior.

Build a sand castle on any beach in the world, then sit several feet away from it and watch. You might see a pitiful commentary on human nature. I'm not proposing that you will attract a communist in that way, but possibly those who think like them.

It's the same with any business, even those that are charitable. Many people will seek to destroy your organization. Build an organization and see for yourself. And, it's the case with a virtuous philosophy like Sylvanism.

Therefore, it is necessary to avoid anyone who suggests violating any portion of the Sylvan Pledge. This is a well-known communist tactic of subterfuge.

Remember, Marxist communism defined in a single word is *sabotage!*

Let's look at the Sylvan Pledge. A communist plant will do one or all of the following to undermine our Sylvan Pledge:

1.  They will talk about another race or religion hatefully or propose hateful behavior.

2.  They will suggest unlawfulness or criminal behavior.

3.  They will, even in the slightest way, suggest violence.

4.  They will treat others condescendingly because of

their race, creed, or religion.

5.  They will mock the notion that love is the highest power.

6.  They will belittle King Alfred the Great.

7.  They will trivialize the twelve Sylvan tenets.

8.  They will scoff at the importance of the flora and fauna.

9.  They will scorn the idea of working and loving with all one's heart.

In addition to shunning those because they are possibly a Marxist spy, get away from them because they are not a Sylvan. Accordingly, we have nothing to gain and everything to lose by association with them.

Dear friends, communists infiltrate the organizations of their enemies.

Should you still look upon that idea with a smug supercili-ousness, then you might be surprised. Marxist communism has cast an almost seamless network across the United States, Western Europe, and the four corners of the world.

They are the most well-organized, well-funded, and covert organization in world history.  Be certain of that fact.

Hardcastle:
Suppose someone who has a criminal background wishes to be a Sylvan. Imagine that someone is a former convict, is a

convicted felon, or has a DUI (Driving Under the Influence). What would you tell him or her?

Hathaway:
We believe the redeemed individual is of vital worth to society for it demonstrates that we may also find redemption.

And, remember, Sylvanism is not a club or sect or cult nor a religion that one joins. One cannot join Sylvanism any more than someone can join Epicureanism or Nietzscheism.

Sylvanism is something one does, which implies the present and future tense. Therefore, when someone says, "I am a Sylvan," it indicates who he is and what he shall be and do.

So, besides a path to nature and spiritual growth, Sylvanism is a way of repentance. A fresh passage for a man or woman to start their lives anew. Please never confuse that with religion.

Now, after taking the Sylvan Pledge, a man or woman should honor those solemn words with their actions.

Of course, we all are imperfect and will often fail. The key is to get up one more time than we fall.

It is particularly bitter to me when people don't stand to their feet after a fall, because such people are not altogether to blame for their unhappy plight.

Which leads me to ask, did you read "The Warmth of the Sun?" [the essay in Part IV]

Hardcastle:
Yes, I did.

Perfect segue from Shakespeare's *Sonnets* about the wisdom and beauty of having children to your essay about parenting.

That is one of my favorite parts of your book. It's an excellent commentary about the astonishing impact of parenthood. [It's] how good parenting virtually eliminates antisocial conduct, especially criminality.

Hathaway:
Yes.

I feel that, all being said and done, it [the essay, "The Warmth of the Sun"] is one of the most meaningful ideas within *The Tribe of Sylvan.*

Hardcastle:
Work and love is the maxim of *The Tribe of Sylvan.* Why did you choose work and love?

Hathaway:
I may have answered that question in the chapter, "Our Maxim: Work and Love." Perhaps, I can add to that. But it's easier to collect and assemble my thoughts when writing.

I'll try to put those [ideas] into words, to verbalize them rather than writing them. First, working and loving are the hallmarks of normality.

A reporter once asked Sigmund Freud, "What is a normal person?" Freud replied succinctly, "Anyone who works and loves." While I disagree with several of Freud's theories, he was correct on that point.

Those well-adjusted individuals, in turn, comprise an orderly culture. Indeed, unified as one dynamic, work and love is both infrastructure and equilibrium of an urbane society.

Therein, incalculable innovations exalt us above primevalness, the most theoretical of which is our language. Many people don't think of our vocabulary as a modernization, but its scope and scale are positively constitutional to civilization.

Indeed, our language, rich in subtleties and nuances, correlates to the depth of our work and love, which is societal oxygen, water, and food.

How long can one live without oxygen, water, and food? How long can a society live without a singular and developed language?

The collective work and love of our commonwealth is an all-consuming, vast super-engine. So colossal a thing that it is diaphanous, almost invisible, like the imperceptibility of a brontosaurus to the tiniest ant.

Yet, it is there. Too big to be seen.

In other words, you may watch one thousand workers in a huge plant, each busy with their specialized responsibilities, but one can never see the tremendous culminations of one day's work of a country.

The mothers at home cleaning house, taking care of four

children, washing and folding the laundry, dressing the children, taking them to school and picking them up on time, and cooking for six people.

The father planning the year's activities and goals in order to generate enough revenue to keep the company profitable.

His meetings with customers to resolve complaints. The pressure to make payroll, to attract and retain quality employees, to go up against the competition who is planning to take his customer base from him. The never-ending politics.

And, fraught with the challenge of paying for a mortgage, car payments. Clothes, medicine, and food for a family of six.

Multiply that millions of times across a nation. That's not just work. It is work inspired by love.

We are distinguished among all people because of work and love's dual dynamical bounty that we richly enjoy.

For trust and cooperation are derivatives of that two-fold influence upon which industry rests. Even so, consider all the ages that rolled away before the industrious invention of something that is seemingly innocuous as the matchstick.

I own a history book that was published in the nineteenth century that provides an account of the first practical and widely produced matchstick, an innovation that changed the world around 1820.

I use the illustration of the match because most of us feel

that it was rather uneventful. But its impact was profound. Imagine that you are lost in the remote wilderness, so far from cities and towns that you have no means of communication. You have only the clothes you wear.

How would you start a fire for protection from freezing to death? Striking flint stones together? First you must find the stones. Perhaps you would try the friction of small sticks.

Suppose it was raining and all the stones and sticks were soaked. How long would it take to build a shelter and dry the stones or sticks to kindle a tiny fire?

Even experienced campers may take an hour or more to spark a tiny fire in such conditions.

What would you pay for a match in sub-zero temperatures while trembling uncontrollably as your life ebbed away?

Please bear in mind that few societies enjoy the consequences of work and love. Those that have the least, are most primitive; those with the most are civilizational pinnacles, wherein technological breakthroughs such as the match-stick supersede mundane humanity.

We typically don't think of the match changing the world. But it did. Before then, city dwellers borrowed fire from a neighbor if they weren't too far away.

However, most people were somewhat isolated country folk who rubbed sticks together or struck flint stones for a spark, which were cumbersome, time-consuming tasks during freezing temperatures.

Thus, the invention of a workable, mass-produced match was one, only one, of the measureless benefits of dynamic work and love.

But it was only a dream for many years as numerous attempts to create a mass production match failed. Therefore, ponder how long it took to create the matchstick that was mass produced and therefore available to wider society.

Consider the similar limitless ingenuities that we seamlessly enjoy.

Like the match, they are by-products of a society luxurious with work and love.

For work is indefatigable upward striving.

Love engenders trust and cooperation.

Of course, our highest benefit is that families flourish in societies where work and love are, at least, somewhat pervasive.

Hardcastle:
And with all that upward struggle, our 400 centuries of striving, others are clinging to us and dragging us down. I wonder how many years the Marxist have stolen.

For example, let's say Marxism slowed human advancement since 1865. Now let's assume that Marxism also reversed it.

Where does that put us?

Hathaway:
Right. We might feel that we are advanced with all of our technologies. Yet human progress is not measured in technologies but in peace and freedom and art.

But I look around and see less of these virtues than existed fifty years ago. So, I ask you, have we evolved, or devolved?

We look back 500 years for our finest literature, Shakespeare. 2000 years for the finest architecture and philosophy.

Hardcastle:
I agree.

I remember reading in your book, it was a quote by Plato and I have it marked here. "Utopia must begin in the body of man." Do you feel that is the way out of this mess?

Hathaway:
Yes, because, ultimately, we are alienated from nature. And perhaps none are more unnatural than Marxists.

So, as we reconnect our bodies, our minds, our souls with nature, we will emancipate ourselves from communist rule.

Hardcastle:
And that is why you devote over one hundred pages to health remedies [in *The Tribe of Sylvan*]. Am I correct?

Hathaway:
Yes, you are right. For individual freedom, for human free-

dom.

Hardcastle:
As you know, the ones I tried worked for me.

I know from earlier conversations that you eat a plant-based diet. Do you recommend it to everyone?

Hathaway:
I suggest that everyone eats more organic fruit, vegetables, nuts, and seeds in their raw, natural state. I feel that most doctors would agree with that.

Most people eat raw food. A smoothie is raw. A salad can easily be raw. An apple, orange, avocado, strawberry, blueberry, pineapple, and tomato are all raw.

But, eating plant-based is not prerequisite to the Sylvan lifestyle. I took two friends to dinner not long ago and they both ordered hamburgers, which was perfectly fine with me because they were my guests and I wanted them to order anything they wanted. I wanted them to enjoy their dinner.

But if you can eat all plant-based that's great because it's exceptionally good for our bodies and, in turn, for the environment. Nothing is better for the ecosystem than for humans to be plant-based.

Yet it probably does not help to be evangelistic about it, wanting to proselytize all around us. Such provinciality must seem small-minded to others—impolite and even condescending.

Speaking of which, may we talk a little about good manners in general?

Hardcastle:
By all means. I think it's a needed topic.

Hathaway:
Good manners are the Sylvan way.

They are an expression of love, a subset of our maxim's equation, which, one by one, geometricizes into a suave, polished society.

Their use elevates our written and spoken words and, thus, our interpersonal relationships. For they are buffers in cities that may sometimes feel like a savage jungle.

Basic examples are: Please. Thank you. May I. You're welcome (rather than "no problem").

When writing an important letter or email, it's always a good idea to begin by thanking the recipient for his time, and end with the same courtesy.

When [you are] a guest in someone's home and it's time to leave, rather than just standing up and leaving with barely saying goodbye, say something like, "Thank you for having me over. I enjoyed it."

Even if you didn't enjoy it, politely say, "Thank you for having me over."

Such politeness is not to be confused with haughtiness and snobbery, which is another thing altogether that we want to avoid.

On the other hand, exercising good comportment and etiquette will improve our relationships; and, eventually they will become second nature.

Of course, we cannot review all the examples of well-mannered behavior here. So, you may wish to buy a book about them and study it. Your life may become easier.

Hardcastle:
You discuss the research conducted by Dr. Robert D. Putnam at Harvard University, in which he concluded that racially heterogeneous societies are comparatively weak to those that are homogeneous.

Do those findings suggest that some xenophobia has its virtues?

Hathaway:
Thank you for that good question. But such muddled thinking of others—not yours, of course—is never helpful and blocks mind expansion. We do not want to hate or fear foreigners or cultures and customs differing from ours.

I must be the very opposite of xenophobic since I revel in the kaleidoscopic wonders of countries that are Oriental and non-Western, thrilled by their uniqueness.

That's what drove my wanderlust for almost three years as I circled the globe one and a half times.

How pathetically nonplused would be our world if we were all the same! Yet how dreadfully hopeless if our villages were nebulous, undefinable!

I recall that Carl Jung spent time with the Pueblo Indians of New Mexico and observed in his book *Memories, Dreams, Reflections* that they had no individual or societal problems.

Jung suggested this was due to arising each morn to help the Sun travel across the sky and that purposeful life gave them meaning, the naivety of which is somewhat perplexing.

Now, let us suppose that a Buddhist family from Thailand, a Hindu couple from Nepal, a Shinto family from Japan, and a Voodoo priest, his wife, and children from Haiti came to live with them, each religious and ethnic group adhering to their culture, customs, and language rather than assimilating.

Let us suppose that those families multiplied and invited their foreign relatives to migrate to these villages in New Mexico. Soon, the individual and societal serenity that Jung noted among the Pueblos would diminish and all but vanish.

Perhaps, that truism was lost upon Jung since he came from a homogeneous culture, whereas we live in a heterogeneous society, which makes the contrast brighter.

I hasten to underscore that those variegated ethnicities and their accompanying customs, cultures, and religions are not necessarily bad, except for Voodoo, of course.

Yet when they are present in the same neighborhoods and

communities, according to Putnam, that society becomes anemic, just as many ingredients cooked in the same pot will lose their flavor. The robust taste of the individual spices and vegetables becomes bland.

Likewise, the tribal qualities that provided the individual and communal tranquility of the Pueblos would be sacrificed for perpetual paranoia and loss of identity, and the Pueblos would be a lost tribe.

Now, if we examine Putnam's work on this subject [page 148], I feel we will find he proposes that it is less fear and hatred of another's race, culture, and custom and more of an aversion to losing our sense of homeostasis when out of our norm.

We merely feel more comfortable in the familiar.

And that affinity for the domestic commonplace allows an easy trust, which "is the lubrication of industry." All people, Putnam proved statistically, function with higher efficiency in that environment.

Despite the unambiguous results of Putnam's study, the most exhaustive of its kind ever conducted, the Marxists create a Niagara of propaganda stating the precise opposite, that "racial diversity is our strength."

The profundity of its Orwellian nature is positively stunning and a crystalline example of "doublespeak" disinformation directly from the pages of *Nineteen Eighty-Four: A Novel*. Of course, that fictional work is George Orwell's exposé of real-world communist tyranny.

So, I admire those of other races and countries and am thrilled by our world's variegated customs and culture. Yet, like most foreigners, I prefer my kith and kin, which is purely normal.

Of course, the Marxists despise our natural affinities and continuously seek their subversion.

Thus, while birds of a feather flock together, which is normal, it is the Trotskyites and Marxists that we should fear, not those of other races and cultures.

The Marxists imprisoned Emperor Nicholas and Emperess Alexandra of Russia, and their five children without a trial, where they were humiliated, abused, and murdered in cold blood. They were savagely shot, stabbed, and beaten to death.

Handsome little Tsarevich Alexis, heir apparent to the throne of Russia, was kicked in the head until he died.

However, the Rightful Czar and Czarina of Russia were virtuous people who never committed a crime, and their five little children, who were the great grandchildren of Queen Victoria, were angelically innocent.

But that grisly murder was not enough to satisfy the unquenchable hatred for our people by the Marxists. They dismembered the bodies of Russia's Royal Family and burned their remains for three days.

In his meticulously researched book *Nicholas and Alexandra,* Robert Massie writes that one of those who committed those macabre atrocities was, soon afterward, rewarded by being appointed the Russian Ambassador to Poland. [22]

And as we speak, there is an aggressive Marxist plan to destroy the British Monarchy.

Behind the marionette faces you see attacking the throne are Marxist puppeteers pulling their strings and speaking their words. After studying Marxism for several decades, it is positively unmistakable.

Hardcastle:
Doesn't that accentuate the need of our homeland? What do you say to those who want an ethnic homeland?

Hathaway:
Saudi Arabia, Japan, Israel, Nigeria, Thailand, China, Singapore and several others are ethnocentric. There's nothing wrong with that. I feel it's their humanitarian right.

But it would be a gross misfocus for us to think about such things when the task at hand is emancipation from communist rule.

The same applies to abortion, the atomization of the family, critical race theory, and many other acts of subversion.

---

[22] "So satisfied were the murderers that they had obliterated all traces [of the royal family] that Viokov, the member of the Ural Soviet who purchased the gasoline and acid, proudly declared, 'The world will never know what we did with them.' Later Voikov became Soviet Ambassador to Poland."

It is the Marxist, Trotskyite communists who are instigating these anti-social ideas. So, it is they that we must isolate and expose in accordance with the law.

We must not take our eye off the ball. We cannot yet join

> "The shout of them who triumph,
> the song of them that feast."

First, we have much work to do.

A philosopher once said, I forgot who it was, but he once compared three types of people who attended the Olympic games.

The lowest of these being the hawkers, who went to the games only to sell trinkets and souvenirs. The Olympians, those who competed in the games, were of a higher character.

Yet, he said, those who merely watch the spectacle have attained the highest order, who through their disinterested observation, have emancipated themselves from the wheel of birth.[23]

I respectfully disagree.

I believe we are here to work until we have liberated our people and, as a result, to help those of every race, creed,

---

[23] John Burnet in *Early Greek Philosophy*.

and religion.

Hardcastle:
Very good. Do you feel that we have a special calling?

Hathaway:
I believe that every member of the flora and fauna, includ-ing the, quote, "civilized" genre, is called for a particular reason. And, it is not to lay down and surrender.

Yes, we are all chosen and I try in my own feeble way to answer that divine beckoning as all of us should.

Thus, I am only a constituent particle in "a great cloud of witnesses" of those who have gone before me and who are yet to come.

My calling is indistinguishable from the woman who wash-es clothes in a river in Bangladesh, a village farmer in Peru, or an artisan who sells his handiwork in the market place in Algiers.

Hardcastle:
We are members of the Tribe of Sylvan, and also members of the family of humankind.

Hathaway:
Exactly.

Now, going back to the notion of what might be called uni-versal selection, or the idea that all living things, including people, are invisibly christened. I'm speaking metaphorically.

In other words, all of us are given a mission to fulfill. Even the apparent mundane life lived in solitude can be archetypically heroic. Heroism has nothing to do with fame and notoriety.

All have a calling. That is not to be confused with the *messiah complex*. And, I wish to put a fine point on that topic.

I'm not an authority on the messiah complex, but in this mental disorder, delusions of grandeur and the imagined powers to save others becomes a fantastic, warped reality within the mind of the afflicted person. I understand that it sometimes accompanies paranoid schizophrenia.

So, a person suffering from a messiah complex believes he is, or is destined to become, a savior, which is a profoundly disturbing idea. The notion is simultaneously absurd and, if it weren't so sad, humorous.

But I suppose we shouldn't laugh, for it seems such people have no compunction about harming others to fulfill their grandiose illusion.

Napolean trampled over as many as six million corpses seeking his fantasy, and in his book about Napoleon [*Napoleon; Soldier of Destiny*], Professor Michael Broers of Oxford University said that one of Napoleon's foremost sayings was, "Burn a village."

Now, from my research, there seems to be a second definition [of the messiah complex]; the term can also refer to an individual who believes he is responsible for saving or assisting others.

Hardcastle:
Nothing wrong with that.

Hathaway:
Well, yes. But the glaring contradiction comes when the desire to help others is obsessional.

I was a Water Safety Instructor with the Red Cross, taught advanced lifesaving courses, and once saved someone's life who was drowning.

But if I was fixated, if overpowered with the idea of saving people from drowning, I might have done more harm than good.

Hardcastle:
If I hear you right, there is a fine line between feeling *responsible* for helping everyone, and being the kind of person who is there to help if needed.

Hathaway:
That's right. And, feeling responsible for saving everyone is an unnatural emotion, an outlandish burden to carry. And I imagine it would become irksome after a while, and that angst might be directed to those who he envisions saving.

That is the glaring difference between the false virtue of pretending to save and help others, and the willingness to do so if the urgent need occurs.

Hardcastle:
You are concerned with animal welfare, animal rights, and helping humanity, but you don't feel an irrational compulsion to do so. Have I got that right?

Hathaway:
Right. But I've often gone to the rescue of animals or people in distress while others stand around and watch or walk away.

Hardcastle:
Tell us . . .

Hathaway:
These were . . . I'm sorry. Go ahead.

Hardcastle:
Sure. Tell us about that.

Hathaway:
Three cases come to mind in which people were in deadly peril.

One was a man who had fallen, hit his head, and was semi-conscious and bleeding. Another was a man has passed out in heavily congested traffic. On another occasion, a woman was drowning.

Many people were present, except in the drowning incident in which my father and uncle were there watching but froze. I was the only one who helped.

Then there was a fourth case—the moment I first saw my little dog, Blackjack. He was sitting by the door of a gas station, which was bustling with customers walking right by him, almost stepping over him.

The station manager said he had sat there for two days and

of all the thousands of people going in and out of that hectic place, not one stopped to help him.

He was only three months old and was so beautiful that he didn't look real. He looked like a perfect little stuffed doll. And no one was caring enough to help that little baby.

But it was meant to be because after pulling up to the pump, I opened my car door and there he was, looking up at me, wiggling with excited love. He knew I was the one.

From his spot by the door, he had run across that gas station parking lot, scrambled through cars coming and going and chose to be my best friend.

Hardcastle:
What breed is Blackjack?

Hathaway:
He was a flat-coated retriever mix. Luxurious jet-black coat like rabbit fur with a rich mane around his neck. He had a nobly shaped head and matching demeanor. Oh, what a high breed of character! A finer person than I.

Hardcastle:
He sounds beautiful.

So, we want to be the type of people who help others in need without feeling that overburdensome notion that rescuing them is our unique mission.

Hathaway:
Exactly.

But there is a healthy balance. For example, wouldn't you agree that all lifeguards have that composure? Coast Guard members, firemen, emergency room doctors, and every true soldier who defends his homeland?

And what about King Alfred? Did he have such a messiah complex? No, I don't think so at all.

Read what Charles Dickens said about where we would be without the intervention of Alfred. That's in my chapter about Alfred.

What about Joan of Arc? She alone bears the title *Deliverer of France,* an honor given to her when she was seventeen.

What about El Cid, Charlemagne, or Lord Nelson? But how could they, or anyone else, compare themselves to the Messiah? Christ is perfection.

Without being disrespectful at all, I feel more comfortable with the adventures of Zeus and Hera.

I'm likening them to the old television show, *The Adventures of Ozzie and Harriot,* because possibly Zeus was more like Ozzie—in charge but also laughably human.

But your question about this complex opens up other aspects that I wish to pursue.

When writing *The Tribe of Sylvan*, I wrote two pages that I felt could be helpful to the future of all people of every race, religion, and creed.

It was not the alpha and omega. It was not about saving the whole world, but influencing a small portion of people who would, in turn, persuade and lead others.

I decided to make those two pages into a book.

That's how *The Hathaway Equation; the Plan to Halt and Reverse Ecological Collapse* came to be, which is the prelude and premise to *The Tribe of Sylvan*.

I feel that to truly understand *The Tribe of Sylvan*, one should first understand *The Hathaway Equation*.

Both works are compasses that I created.

And what does a compass do?

Hardcastle:
It points the way to true north.

Hathaway:
Yes. Now, please humor me by answering this curious question. Am I a compass?

Hardcastle:
[Laughter.] Not at all.

Hathaway:
Precisely.

If I thought I was the compass, if I thought I always could point in the true direction, then I might have what is defined as a messiah complex.

I'm just another person, however, who has created two compasses.

I'm only another beggar searching for bread, but it just so happens that I know where the bakery is.

I'm not the bread. I'm not the bakery nor the baker.

But I know where they are.

So, it's the message that is essential. That is the thing.

There are so many others who are better than I. Countless numbers of people who possess a finer character. It's comedic to think of me saving them or anyone else.

I'll help others in trouble but I need to focus on saving myself. It reminds me of the missionary who woefully lamented, ". . . oh! who shall convert me?"[24]

Something else about helping others, I don't want to belabor the point, but I want to ensure that our listeners are thinking clearly about assisting others.

Hardcastle:
Sure, go right ahead.

Hathaway:
First and foremost, we must help ourselves before aiding

---

[24] "I went to America, to convert the Indians; but, oh! Who shall convert me?" From *The Journals of John Wesley*, "The Voyage to England."

others.

The airlines instruct us to secure our oxygen masks on a
flight before fastening one on someone else.

So, we must ask: Are we psychologically well? Do we have
friends who support us, and do we reciprocate by uplifting
them? Are we part of our community?

Do we sleep well and deeply? Are we eating life-giving
food? Are we the proper weight for our height? Are we controlling our temper? Do we live in an aura of secrets, or
open honesty?

We all have our challenges, but unless we have our life under control, helping others can be a substitute for our
"personal work."

In such cases, going to the aid of others can be compulsive
since we are, perhaps, pouring energy into our altruistic
mission to avoid self-confrontation. Above all, that applies
to our safety. Our safety is our responsibility. "Safety first"
is part of leadership, by the way.

Secondly, we cannot help everyone, and we should not have
illusions that we can.

Most of us have a small sphere of influence that is typically
quite limited. Even if we have far-reaching persuasion, it is
insignificant to the vast population of our respective countries and microscopic to the world.

Jane Goodall offers sage advice about that. Influence those

around you.

Third, it is best to offer help only when asked.

Even then, it should be given with measured wisdom.

Fourth, although someone is endangered, we must avoid risking our lives to help.

At the same time, firemen and lifeguards risk their lives to save others, but with a calculated risk offset by intense training, equipment, and support.

So, we mustn't be overzealous but take one step at a time.

Hardcastle:
You know, I had the thought about Karl Marx, as you were talking. I wonder if we will ever hear someone accusing him of having a messiah complex. I wonder if Lenin, Trotsky, or Stalin will be labeled with the allegation of messianic?

Hathaway:
Which says something about who makes these recriminations. Moreover, we benefit from the lofty heights to which they set the standards. It's like children saying, "You can't jump over this!"

And then we acquire the athleticism to hurdle it and they are livid.

Hardcastle:
Good illustration. It's also Buddhistic in that we learn from those who dislike us.

Hardcastle:
Are you a utopian?

Hathaway:
The human predicament still reigns supreme. This is what I mean.

The prolific historian William Durant suggests that the sumptuous wealth and splendid lifestyle of India caused their susceptibility to invasion by the Moors, who stole all of India's wealth and killed 80 million Hindus.

Yet he also lays blame on the Hindu ascetics, who through their esoteric elevations influenced society to become listless and lay down their arms.

But throughout history that has never worked.

For we have blessed peace within the context of war.

Tragically, war is a natural state. And so, we "see through a glass darkly" compared to the way we could live.

That is one reason *The Hathaway Equation* is important. I believe it has the potential to lessen warmongering.

In the meantime, we live in such darkness that when we glimpse the tiniest flicker, the faintest glimmer of light that it can transform a hopeless curmudgeon to a saint.

Ebenezer Scrooge was born within the sublime intelligence of Charles Dickens to show us that we, too, might find redemption in the spirit of Christmas.

Jean Valjean was sent to us through the exalted heart of Victor Hugo. Jean Valjean, the apparent reprobate, became a glorified soul to teach us redemption.

So, there is hope.

As long as there exists one soul upon the Earth, there is hope of restoration.

We were given infinitesimal miracles all about us, and we must do all we can to be good stewards of them.

Hardcastle:
I and many others share your vision. We must be reminded of it again and again.

We're running out of time, but there are still so many things on my list to discuss.

I know the answer to this question. But for the sake of our listeners—we know that Sylvanists pledge to not treat other disrespectfully because of their race.

Yet can they be anti-Arab, anti-Black, or any other anti-race, which differs slightly from treating them respectfully?

Hathaway:
Anti-Arab, anti-Black, or anti-Semitism is irreconcilable and antithetical to the heart and soul of Sylvanist thought.

To be against someone because of their ethnic descent or to blame them for the world's problems is as foolish as critical race theory, which falsely implicates those of European descent for the woes of mankind.

Sylvanism is not against people. It is for them.

Yet Sylvanism is in foursquare opposition to the ideology of Marxist communism, for example. So, we tacitly differentiate between the ideologue and ideology.

Therefore, we do not hate Marxists, although they should be brought to justice for their crimes.

We choose to not hate anyone or anything—even communism, although Sylvanism is staunchly against it.

Hardcastle:
If I may touch on critical race theory again:

Your foreword [of *The Tribe of Sylvan*] is a superb rebuttal to critical race theory. Perhaps reading part of it in a school board meeting might be a good idea.

Another counterargument is to pose these questions in such a meeting: How did everyone arrive here? Did you drive a car? Did you start your car with a battery?

Did you listen to a radio in the car? Were [you] cooled by an air conditioner?

How did the lighting in this room come to be? Are you using a cell phone? Those are all inventions of people of European descent whom you claim in critical race theory cause all the troubles of the world.

Hathaway:
Excellent point.

Hardcastle:
Now, if I put the message [of *The Tribe of Sylvan*] in a nut-shell, I suppose it would be that the people of European descent must think and act and live as one family.

Doing so inadvertently causes the ideology of Marxism to be irrelevant.

Is that a fair summation?

Hathaway:
I think so. In addition, those of European descent need a track to run on—values and beliefs to embrace.

And remember, if only three percent of the population identifies with this way of life, they can influence and change a significant percentage of society.

Hardcastle:
I suppose that just about wraps it up. Thank you, Phillip, for our time together.

One final question. If you could tell all the people of European descent just a few things, what would they be?

Hathaway:
Our people are presently a lost tribe.

That is why critical race theory is central to our children's learning curriculum.

That is why political correctness looms over our every word like a "Big Brother" monitor.

That is why our society is turned topsy turvy by saboteurs.

It is because we are a lost tribe.

What is more, our lostness is triple, for we are unaware we are lost, that we are one group, and that we possess inherent ethnological needs, especially a sense of belonging.

To find our way home, we must first come to grips with the fact that we are lost.

To cease that desultory wandering, we must coalesce as one tribe.

To form a single tribe, we must acknowledge our anthropological identity. We are a family.

At last, there is a way home via the philosophical lifestyle and ideology of Sylvanism.

What shall we do with this ideological philosophy? How do we breathe life into this lump of clay? I suggest four things.

First and foremost, read *The Tribe of Sylvan* and take the Sylvan Pledge.

Discuss the book with other Sylvanists. Thus, you may be savvier than your contemporaries in a culture where even the word prudence is a mockery.

Moreover, reading the book gives us a track to run on.

A mammoth locomotive can pull one hundred train cars three thousand miles at seventy miles per hour.

But it is utterly useless without rails. And so, it sits and rusts, all its enormous potential wasting away.

Likewise, when unfocused, we are as a train engine with nothing to direct its power. Yet when unified, we can produce mighty works with mercurial speed.

That's what reading the book does for us.

And remember the solemnity that King Alfred expected of his people who took a pledge.

Take the Sylvan Pledge with the same gravity.

After taking our vow, you might wish to repeat it aloud to yourself occasionally.

Second, tell others about *The Tribe of Sylvan.*

The most powerful means of reaching our people is through word of mouth, one person telling another in an organic, grassroots awakening.

So, politely suggest the book to others, but never in a pushy way. Plant the idea courteously and let it grow. Perhaps you could write an honest review and post it online.

Third, is our maxim of work and love, which are the hallmarks of a healthy, well-adjusted individual, and, as a tribe, an expression of peace and goodwill to greater society.

Beyond that, to every race and creed throughout the world.

As King Alfred exceeded his regal station, let us work and love— *plus royalement qu'un roi* —more royally than a king.

Fourth, smile and laugh, which are symptoms of winning. Keep a healthy sense of humor. Enjoy life.

So, read the book and take the pledge, tell others, work and love, and be lighthearted.

The vital key to it all is this:

From primordial stages, all life wishes itself unto fullest flower—a baby, a tree, the fauna, a star, an ideology. All are the dynamic excitement of a wish, directed and controlled.

That is why Lord Montaigne[25] said, "Men are nothing until they are excited."

The excitation—the brilliant animation of the upward triumphs that lie before us are matchless.

We must dearly wish for it with all the heartiness that be-

---

[25] Michel Eyquem, Sieur de Montaigne (1533-1592) was a renowned French philosopher.

come deeds. Then it shall manifest before us.

Thus, we challenge Marxist internationalism with superior internationalism.

We confront Marxist tribalism with superior tribalism.

We meet Marxist ideology with superior ideology.

The Overton window is opening each day and might slam wide upon its hinges one morning when we awake to a world drenched with pure sunlight.

That will happen organically, one person telling another, and so on.

Remember, The Great Heathen Army crushed six kings.

Yet the seventh king stood alone.

After enduring betrayal by the selfsame people he sought to save—after being a homeless and woebegone king, many thought that they would never see Alfred again.

But word began to spread slowly from yeoman to yeoman that Alfred yet sought to liberate them from their oppression.

As Alfred walked through the winding path in the deep, cold, and darkened forest, he asked himself . . .

. . . *would the yeomanry awaken?* Would they fight for their people?

Onward he made his way, hoping yet not knowing the answer.

Then he stepped into an open field, made bright with warm sunlight.

And he beheld an army of men, each of whom stood to his feet with the light of hope in his eyes when seeing Alfred's face.

And the forest echoed with peals of roaring triumph!

For "when they saw the king, receiving him (not surprisingly) as if one restored to life after suffering such great tribulations, they were filled with an immense joy," wrote Asser. [26]

Now, dear friends,

> "Think of all the times we have boasted
> at the meade-bench, heroes in the hall
> predicting our own bravery in battle.
> Now we shall see who meant what he said."

>                    *The Battle of Maldon*

And so, you have a choice of slavery or freedom.

---

[26] Story and quote from *Alfred the Great, The Man Who Made England*, by Justin Pollard.

As Pericles [27] so eloquently said at his famous funeral oration, as recorded by Thucydides [28], ". . . happiness depends on being free, and freedom depends on being courageous."

Therefore, be courageous.

---

[27] Pericles (c. 495-425 BC) was an Athenian statesman, orator, and general whom many consider the foremost leader of Athens.
[28] Thucydides (c. 460-c. 400 BC) was an Athenian historian and general. His *History of the Peloponnesian War* has been described as "exhaustingly factual" and is one of the most important history books regarding the ancient world.

# About the Author

AFTER a three-year tour of duty with the army, Hathaway studied the social sciences in North America and Europe, earning a bachelor's and a master's degree. He traveled the world for the next two years, visiting twenty-five countries on five continents.

Then settling into his writing, he authored several books, including works of philosophy, psychology, ecology, novels, short stories, screenplays, poems, epic verse, and the retelling of *The Odyssey* in heroic couplet. He has also written scholarly papers, articles, an Elizabethan stage play, and even the original libretto, lyrics, and melodies of a full-length classical, operatic musical featuring twenty-seven new songs.

In his free time, he sometimes paints and draws. Some people feel that his graphite portrait of Lord Nelson may be one of the better likenesses of Nelson.

Hathaway has been an active wildlife conservationist for several years, focusing on protecting elephant herds in Sub-Sahara Africa. He has a small yet busy wild bird sanctuary at his home in the United States, hosting over twenty-eight species of wild birds.

# Bibliography

*regarding King Alfred*

*Alfred the Great, Asser's Life and Other Contemporary Sources,* trans. Simon Keynes and Michael Lapidge, Penguin, London, 1983.

*Alfred the Great, The Man Who Made England*, Justin Pollard, Murray, London, 2005.

*Anglo-Saxon Chronicle,* trans. Michael Swanton, Routledge: New York, 1998.

*The Golden Dragon, Alfred the Great and His Times*, Alf J. Mapps, Jr., Madison, London, 1985.

*The White Horse King, The Life of Alfred the Great*, Benjamin Merkle, Thomas Nelson, Nashville, 2009.

*The Year 1000: What Life Was Like at the Turn of the First Millennium, An Englishman's World,* Robert Lacey, Little, Brown, and Company, London, 1999.

*History of the Kings and Queens of England,* David Williamson, Konecky& Konecky, Old Saybrook, 2003.

# *Endnotes*

*for PART II, Chapter One, Civic Realism*

1.  C. E. Robinson, *Everyday Life in Ancient Greece*, (Oxford, England: Clarendon Press, 1933).

2.  Edith Hamilton, *The Greek Way*, (New York City: W.W. Norton and Company, Inc., 1930).

3.  Thucydides, *The History of the Peloponnesian War*, (New York City: Penguin Classics, 1954).

4.  Aristotle, *Politics*, (New York City: The Modern Library, Random House, 1942).

5.  Aristotle, *Politics,* (New York City: The Modern Library, Random House, 1942). bk. 4, 1296 a 1-3.

6.  Victor Hugo, *The Hunchback of Notre Dame,* (New York City: Signet Classics, 2005).

7.  George Bernard Shaw, *Man and Superman,* (Glacier Park, Montana: Kessinger Publishing, LLC, 2005).

8.  John W. McFarland, *Lives from Plutarch: The Modern Edition of Twelve Lives,* (New York City: Random House, 1966).

9. President George W. Bush, *President Bush Discusses Progress in the Global War on Terror*, (Atlanta, Georgia: Office of the Press Secretary, The White House, September 7, 2006).

10. Patrick J. Buchanan, *The Democracy Worshiper*, (www.buchanan.org, June 19, 2007).

11. Stephen Kinzer, *Overthrow, America's Century of Regime Change from Hawaii to Iraq,* (New York City: Times Books, 2007).

12. Judge Andrew Napolitano, *The Constitution in Exile*, (Nashville, Tennessee: Thomas Nelson, 2006).

13. Judge Andrew Napolitano, *The Constitution in Exile*, (Nashville, Tennessee: Thomas Nelson, 2006).

14. Douglas Southall Freeman, *Robert E. Lee; A Biography*, (New York City and London: Charles Scribner & Sons, 1934).

15. Thomas DiLorenzo, *The Real Lincoln; A New Look at Abraham Lincoln, His Agenda, and an Unnecessary War,* (New York City: Prima Lifestyles, 2002).

16. The Illinois Historic Preservation Agency, (Springfield, Illinois: The Illinois Historic Preservation Agency, 1999).

17. Harold Holzer, *The Lincoln-Douglas Debates, The First Compete Unexpurgated Text*, (Bronx, New York: Fordham University Press, 2004).

18. Kirsten Scharnberg, "Governors Say War Has Gutted

Guard," (Chicago: The Chicago Tribune, May 13, 2007).

19. Judy Woodruff, "National Guard Underfunded, Not Prepared for Crises," (Arlington, Virginia: Public Broadcasting Service, March 1, 2007).
20. Bob Bauman, *The Sovereign Society Newsletter*, (Waterford, Ireland: The Sovereign Society, Volume 9, Number 67, March 19, 2007).

21. Judge Andrew Napolitano, *The Constitution in Exile*, (Nashville, Tennessee: Thomas Nelson, 2006).

22. Lou Dobbs, Dobbs: "Big Media Hide Truth About Immigration," (New York City: CNN, www.cnn.com, June 20, 2006.

23. "More Americans Killed by Illegal Aliens Than Iraq War, Study Says," (Warrenton, Virginia: National Border Patrol Council, www.nbpc.net, February 22, 2007).

24. "Illegal Aliens Kill More Americans Than Iraq War," (Arlington, Virginia: Family Security Matters, www.family securitymatters.org, February 16, 2007).

25. President Theodore Roosevelt, *The Oxford Dictionary of Quotations,* (Oxford, England: The Oxford University Press, 1999).

26. "France Says No to Mass Legalization of Undocumented Immigrants," (London: The Daily Mail, May 21, 2007).

27. North American Free Trade Agreement, (Washington, D.C.: Public Citizen, www.citizen.org).

28. Ross Perot, *Save Your Job, Save Our Country; Why NAFTA Must be Stopped Now*, (New York City: Hyperion Books, 1993).

29. Roger Boyes, "Backlash at Jailing of Historian Who Denied Holocaust," (London: The London Times, www.timesonline.co.uk/tol/sport/football/european_foot ball/article733099.ece, February 21, 2006).

30. Tobias Buck, "EU Aims To Criminalize Holocaust Denial," (London: The Financial Times, April 17, 2007).

31. Euripides, *The Phoenissae*, (Oxford, England: The Oxford University Press, August 11, 1994).

32. John Stuart Mill, *On Liberty*, (Amherst, New York: Prometheus Books,1986). 23, 24.

33. Euripides, *Fragments of the Oxyrhynchus Papyri*, (Oxford, England: The Oxford University Press, 2005)

34. The Association of Psychological Science, (Washington, D.C., The Association of Psychological Science,  2007).

35. Greg Mitchell, "'Devastating' Bill Moyers Probe of Press and Iraq Coming This Week," (St. Petersburg, Florida: St. Petersburg Times, April 21, 2007).

36. George Orwell, 1984, (London: Secker and Warburg, January, 2003).

37. Greg Mitchell, "'Devastating' Bill Moyers Probe of Press and Iraq Coming This Week," (St. Peterburg, Flor-

ida: St. Petersburg Times, April 21, 2007).

38. Al Gore, *Assault on Reason*, (BocaRaton, Florida: Penguin Press H. C., May 22, 2007).
39. Georgie Anne Geyer, "Who Will Report the Future?" (Tulsa, Oklahoma: The Tulsa World, May 26, 2007).

40. J. C. Holt, *Magna Carta*, (Cambridge, England: Cambridge University Press, January 31, 2006).

41. Edward Vallance, *Glorious Revolution, 1688: Britain's Fight for Liberty,* (London: Pegasus Books, May 15, 2007).

42. Prometheus Radio Project v. F. C. C., Case No. 033388, (Philadelphia, Pennsylvania: United States Court of Appeals Third Circuit, June 2004).

43. "Israel Breached NZ's Sovereignty and International Law, Says PM," (Auckland, New Zealand: The New Zealand Herald, July 15, 2004).

44. David R. Francis, "Economist Tallies Swelling Cost of Israel To U.S.," (Boston: The Christian Science Monitor, www.csmonitor.com/2002/1209/p16s01-wmgn.html, December 9, 2002).

45. The Wichita Massacre, (London: wikipedia, wikipedia. org/wiki/The_Wichita_Massacre).

46. "Channon Christian and Christopher Newsom Murders," (London: Wikipedia, wikipedia.org/wiki/ Channo_Christian_ and_Christoher_Nesom_murder).

47. Amy Westfeldt, "Ex-NFL Player Charged In NJ Murder," (London: The Associated Press, March 23, 1999).

48. "Duke Lacrosse Players: Case Closed," (Raleigh, North Carolina: CNN, www.cnn.com/2007/LAW/04/11/duke.lacrosse/index.html,April 12, 2007).

49. United States Congressman, Dennis Kucinich, (the details of Congressman's Kuncinich's remarks are forthcoming).

50. United States Senator Ernest F. Hollings, "The United States Has Lost Its Moral Authority," (Washington, D.C.: Congressional Record, www.gpoacess.gov/crecord/index.html, June the 23rd, 2004).

51. Matthew Mosk, "Disclosure Forms Show Wealthy Lot of Hopefuls," (Washington, D.C.: The Washington Post, May 17, 2007).

52. Frank Phillips and Brian Mooney, "Govenor's Race May Set A Record," (Boston: The Boston Globe, June 10, 2006).

53. Ronald Kessler, *Sins of the Father, Joseph P. Kennedy and the Dynasty He Founded*, (New York City: Warner Books, March 1, 1997).

54. Nellie Bly, *The Kennedy Men; Three Generations of Sex, Scandal and Secrets*, (New York City: Kensington, November 1, 1996).

55. 1960 Presidential Election Results, (Cambridge, Massa-

chusetts: David Leip's Atlas Of Presidential Elections, www.uselectionatlas.org/RESULTS/national.php?year=1 960 &f=0, May 31, 2007).

56. President Richard Nixon, (Yorba Linda, California:  The Richard Nixon Library Archives).

57. President Dwight Eisenhower, *Public Papers of the Presidents of the United States; Dwight D. Eisenhower*, (Washington, D.C.: Office of the Federal Registrar, 1960).

58. Edward Gibbon, *Decline and Fall of the Roman Empire*, (New York City: Random House, 1954).

59. Ralph Z. Hallow, "Bloomberg Poised for Third-Party Campaign," (Washington, D.C.: The Washington Times, http//washingtontimes.com/national/20070515-1231423314r.htm, May 15, 2007).

60. Edith Hamilton, *The Roman Way*, (New York City and London: W. W. Norton and Company, Inc., 1932).

61. Bertrand Russell, *A History of Western Philosophy*, (New York City, Touchstone, published by Simon and Schuster, 1945).

62. Aristotle, *Nicomachean Ethics*, (Cambridge, Massachu-setts, and London: Harvard University Press, 1926).

# *Index*